THE LONGMAN REGISTER OF NEW WORDS

THE LONGMAN REGISTER OF NEW WORDS

John Ayto

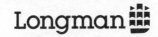

Longman Group UK Limited,
Longman House, Burnt Mill, Harlow,
Essex CM20 2JE, England
and Associated Companies throughout the world

First published 1989

British Library Cataloguing in Publication Data

Ayto, John
    The Longman register of new words.
    1. English Language. — Dictionaries
    I. Title
    423

Cased edition:
ISBN 0 582 03772 7
Paperback Edition:
ISBN 0 582 03771 9

Set in 10/13pt. Nimrod

Printed in Great Britain
by The Bath Press Ltd., Avon

INTRODUCTION

Less than three years ago there probably was not an English speaker anywhere in the world to whom expressions such as 'a woopie receiving a golden goodbye' and 'infection with an electronic virus' would have been anything other than gobbledegook. Yet today there are some, at least, for whom they present no more difficulty in understanding than 'the cat sat on the mat.' The frontiers of language advance more precipitously in vocabulary than in any other area, and the aim of the *Longman Register of New Words* is to chart their latest course and build up a rounded picture of the ways in which English has grown and developed over the years 1986 to 1988.

It keeps the leading edge of innovation firmly in the centre of its sights: some of the words it records for the first time will no doubt turn out to have been ephemeral, fashions of the moment, yet equally certainly many will have a long and distinguished career. But the process of lexical growth and establishment does not happen in a uniform way; not every new item leaps to immediate currency. So this survey of recent developments in English vocabulary does not concentrate exclusively on brand-new words. Several of the items in the following pages slipped unobtrusively onto the stage in the 1970s, the 1960s, or even earlier, but have only in the last two or three years had the spotlight turned full on them, becoming in some cases buzz words of the late 1980s (*airmiss*, for example, *synergy*, and *value-added*). Often, significant changes in meaning or application or even in legal status will have brought an established word to wider attention (*agony aunt*, *Amerasian*, *compliance*, *enterprise*, *McGuffin*, and *refusenik*). And in a few instances real veterans, which had seemed to be put firmly out to grass decades or centuries ago, have made an unexpected comeback (*memorious, velocious*).

By definition, the introduction of new words – and of new meanings for old ones – reflects developments and innovations in the world at large and in society. So the vocabulary items in this collection present in microcosm the concerns that have impinged on speakers of English worldwide, but particularly British English, in the late 1980s.

Do any particular trends emerge? A major new strand consists of words reflecting the Thatcher government's increasing penetration into the social fabric of Britain. In the early 1980s talk was of technical aspects of economic management, *monetarism* and *PSBRs*. But by the middle of the decade the scope had widened, encompassing an attempt to remould society fundamentally: the *learned helplessness* of yesterday's *dependency culture* is to be swept away, and replaced with an *enterprise* culture, in which *can-do shareowners* with *gold cards* make *loadsamoney*, thereby revitalizing the nation at large. *Heritage* takes the place of history, and *lifestyle* threatens to oust life. And on the subject of lifestyles, the flood of *yuppie*-lookalike terms, already evident in the pages of *Longman Guardian New Words* (Longman, 1986), shows no sign of being stemmed: *buppies* and *Juppies*, *dockneys* and *Mockneys*, *pippies* and *yeepies*, *crinklies*, *crumblies*, and *wrinklies* continue to be spawned with remarkable fertility – often enough, one suspects, by news editors desperate to out-yuppie *yuppie*.

The Conservatives have not had it all their own way, of course (*wobbly Thursday*), and the other British political parties have made their contribution to the expanding lexicon. There have been the new *Social and Liberal Democrats*, who, apart from their name (arrived at after extensive agonizing), have contributed *dead parrot*, *mergerite*, and, from their premerged incarnation, *fudge and mudge*. Further to the left, the spotlight has been on the bourgeoisification of the Labour party, with talk of *Ramada socialism* and accusations of *electoralism*. Transatlantic additions to the vocabulary of politics, several of them gaining wide currency during the US presidential election in 1988, have included *parachute candidate* and *retail/wholesale politics*.

On the wider international scene it has been the era of perestroika. Mikhail Gorbachev's reforms have so swiftly captured the Western imagination that the two key Russian terms in this area have already developed wider metaphorical meanings in English and grown English adjectival endings (*glasnostian* and *perestroikan*), and other Russian borrowings are following in their wake (*khozraschot* and *pryzhok*). The Chinese, meanwhile, have their own version (*gai-ge*). High on the glasnostian agenda has been nuclear arms reduction, with its own particular jargon of *zero options*, *zero-zero*, *twin-tracking*, *linkage*, and *targetry*.

Reflecting its continuing vigour, the financial sector remains a prodigal coiner of neologisms, both sober and fanciful. The lay person trying to navigate the City's treacherous waters has had a Sargasso sea of new jargon to cope with: *circuit breaking*, *dead-cat bounces*, *dysergy*, *fan clubs*, *foothold buying*, *grey markets*, *rocket scientists*, *swaptions*, *tin parachutes*, and *white squires* pepper the financial pages, scaring off outsiders. There has been a modest market, too, in new slang terms for amounts of money: *Archer* has been best publicized, but we have also had *Hawaii*, *Placido*, *Jack*, and *Seymour*.

Not far behind wealth as a word-creator comes computing. A particular linguistic growth area here has been the deliberate damaging of software by introducing destructive rogue programs; this rather sick practice has produced *bogusware*, *electronic virus*, *phantom bug*,

Trojan horse, and *vaccine*. Other innovations have included the charmingly named *earcon*, as well as *lans* and *wans*, *keprom*, *connectionism*, *exput*, and *vapourware*. In the wider scientific sphere, the search for a theory of *everything* has given us concepts easier to name than to grasp, such as *superstrings* and *supermembranes*, *graviphotons* and *cosmic strings*, while the notion of *chaos* threatens to undermine the whole basis of classical physics.

AIDS continues to have a strong impact, lexically as well as socially. The explosion in condom-awareness has produced a linguistic mini-saga. Apart from interesting changes in its pronunciation, the word *condom* has been developing new metaphorical meanings, and entering into a distinctly promiscuous range of compounds (*condomania*, for example). AIDS has also contributed *ARC*, *buddy*, *immunocompromised*, *PWA*, and, unfortunately, *homophobia*. The medical world at large has introduced us over the last two or three years not so much to new illnesses as to ones we have at best been only dimly aware of before: *Anderson-Fabry disease*, *cerebellar syndrome*, *Lyme disease*, and *myalgic encephalomyelitis* (with its many synonyms, such as *Royal Free disease* and *yuppie flu*).

The verbal turnover in the pop scene is as frenetic as ever, with *acid house*, *beach music*, *Bhangra*, *goth*, *House*, *psychobilly*, *shag*, *speed-metal*, and *thrash* putting in appearances of unpredictable duration. Acid house harks back to the LSD-induced psychedelia of the 1960s, but today's drugs are sterner stuff. Crack enlarges its vocabulary (*hubba*, *lick*, *pipe*, *ready-wash*), but the new flavour of the month is *ecstasy* (variously known as *Adam* and *MDMA*).

But what of people's everyday lives in late 1980s Britain? It may seem to the jaundiced eye that we have become a nation obsessed with appearances, hanging on the lips of *style counsellors* and *tastemakers* for the words that will determine our *lifestyle*, while market-slot has overtaken quality as a criterion of approval (*middlemarket* has now joined *up-* and *downmarket*), and every aspect of human endeavour seems on the verge of becoming *themed*. But while the *Dinkies*, *Deccies*, and *Whannies* get on with their *rag-rolling* and *liming*, for most of us the world turns much as before. The spending of money (for those who have it – and even for those who do not) becomes insidiously easier in the *cashless* society, with its *ATMs*, *cardswipes*, *eft/pos*, *home banking*, and *smart cards*, but, whether through altruism or guilty conscience, charity is doing fairly well. *Compassion fatigue* may have set in in some quarters, but *conscience investment*, *corporate welfare*, and *volunteerism* help to alleviate hardship. Crime is as innovative as ever, with gangs of *steamers* terrorizing public places and the whole horrifying panoply of street weapons, such as *death stars*, wielded by *survivalists* and others, making inner-city life more fragile. Among law-enforcers, alternatives to prison have been an area to explore, and we have become familiar with *home parole*, *receiver-diallers*, and *trackers*. Youth cults to attract the headlines have included *tagging* and *train surfing*. The world of industrial relations has given us *single-union agreements*; from education has come *hot-housing*, from the old-people's-home industry, the shady *granny farm*, and from the investigation of child sexual abuse, *reflex anal dilatation*.

The perennial urge to euphemism is as marked as ever. Weapons of unparalleled destructive capacity have become *assets*, spying on one's business rivals is *competitor analysis*, and if something gets worse it *disimproves*. *Downsizing* and *deaccessioning*, *ticket-brokers* and *encounter parlours*, the *immunocompromised*, the *physically different*, and the *print-handicapped* are all part of the same syndrome, but undoubtedly the most notorious circumlocution of the mid 1980s was *economical with the truth*, Sir Robert Armstrong's elegant redefinition of lying at the Australian *Spycatcher* trial in 1986.

The bread-and-butter routes to the formation of new words in English are compounding and the addition of prefixes and suffixes, but among the more eye-catching methods the most productive over the past two or three years seems to have been blending, in which parts of two distinct words are joined together to form a third. So *affluence* and *influenza* have given us *affluenza*; *fertilize* and *irrigation* produce *fertigation*; and *magazine* and *catalogue* combine to form *magalog*. With boundless ingenuity, speakers of English have come up with *dockominiums*, *gazwelchers*, *geeps*, *gennakers*, *squaerials*, *swaptions*, and *zootiques*. An area particularly rich in blends, though, has been the crossover genre in television and other media. This phenomenon seems to have begun with the *docudramas* and *faction* of the early 1980s, but the trickle has now become a flood of *docufantasies*, *dramacoms*, *dramedies*, *gastrodramas*, *infomercials*, *plugumentaries*, *rockumentaries*, *sit-tragedies*, *telebooks*, and *toytoons*.

Next in popularity to blends is the omnipresent acronym. The successors to the *yuppie* – the *dinky*, the *glam*, the *lombard*, and so on – continue to proliferate, but few areas of activity are acronym-free in the late 1980s. So *Erops*, *Footsie*, *Gerbil*, *Hero*, *Joshua*, *NIC*, *PINC*, *ploms*, *scaf*, *vad*, *wan*, and *Zift* make their claim for a place in the language.

Conversion – the reallocation of a word to a different part of speech – continues vigorously, producing mainly verbs, from nouns and adjectives (*feeder*, *flan*, *gender*, *office*, *rear-end*, *silicone*, *source*, *stiff*, *Velcro*, *wide*) but also transforming verbs into nouns (*spend*). A related phenomenon, typically originating in American English, is the reversal of a verb from transitivity to intransitivity and vice versa (*air*, *appeal*, *commit*, *lag*).

Currently thriving prefixes and suffixes include *-aholic* (*clothesaholic, milkaholic*), *-ati* (*jazzerati, numerati*), *cross-* (*cross-marketing, cross-selling, cross training*), *-cred* (*force-cred*), *-eur* (*arbitrageur, conglomerateur*), *-ie*, 'an obsessive enthusiast' (*Cuppie, deccie, Stealthie, winie, yottie*), *-ism/-ist* (*alphabetism, fattyism, genderist, heightism*), *loadsa-* (as in *loadsamoney*), *must-* (*must-buy, must-see*), and *-nomics* (*Reaganomics, Rogernomics*); while *mega* and *retro* have started out on careers of their own as fully-fledged adjectives. Words coined by removing an affix or similar element from an existing word (back-formation) include *accreditate, bezzle, cathart, explete, flake, go-get, gram, stand-off*, and *tack*.

English continues to suck in words from other languages like a black hole. The spirit of glasnost has ensured Russian a high profile as a lender (*perestroika, khozraschot, pryzhok*), but French remains a major source, notably in the field of gastronomy (*frisée, fromage frais, pêcher*) but not exclusively so (*tranche, unijambist, visagiste*). Other borrowings have come from Chinese (*gai-ge, qinghaosu*), Japanese (*nashi, waribashi, zaitech*), German (*kletten prinzip*), Polish (*Nizinny*), Arabic (*intifada*), and Hindi (*paneer*).

Such word-trading does not, though, happen only between different languages, but also between varieties of the same language. The best-known (and most often criticized) instance of this is the borrowing of American English words and meanings into British English, and this dictionary contains several examples that have been current on the other side of the Atlantic for years, or in some cases decades, but are now becoming established in Britain (*advance man, gofer, honcho, off-limits, patsy, pork-barrelling, preschooler*). And on a still more domestic level, dialectal expressions can, by a twist of history, infiltrate more cosmopolitan linguistic strata: *haar* has come by this route, but the most illustrious recent example is Margaret Thatcher's *frit*.

So here are gathered together 1200 new pieces in the never-finished jigsaw of the English language. In terms of sheer numbers, of course, this is but a sample – the *Longman Register of New Words* does not set out to be a record of every last coinage over the past three years – but it is a representative sample plotting the peaks in the graph of lexical change. Virtually every medium of human communication has made its contribution – conversation, books, radio and television broadcasts, films – but newspapers and magazines naturally assume a leading role, capturing innovation as they do and enshrining it in print. Over 130 were used as sources of evidence in compiling this collection (all published in the UK unless otherwise indicated):

Asian Times

Best
Blitz
Bookseller
Bridgwater Mercury
Business
Business Times [Malaysia]

Cambridge Pride
Cambridge Weekly News
Camden Magazine
Campaign
Caribbean Times
Chicago Tribune [USA]
Christian Science Monitor [USA]
City Limits
Company
Computer Weekly
Cosmopolitan
Cricketer

Daily Express
Daily Mail
Daily Maine Campus [USA]

Daily Mirror
Daily Telegraph
Daily Telegraph (Sydney)
  [Australia]
Dateline [Turkey]
Decanter

Eastern Daily Press
Economist
Elle
English Today
Environment Now
Esquire [USA]
Essentials
Essex Countryside Magazine
Excel

The Face
Family Circle
Financial Times

The Gazette (Montreal) [Canada]
Gleaner [Jamaica]
Globe and Mail (Toronto)
  [Canada]

Good Housekeeping
Green Line
Guardian

Hackney Gazette
Hackney Herald
Here's Health
Herts & Essex Observer
Homes and Gardens

Ideal Home
Independent
International Herald Tribune
  [France]

Jackie

Kerrang

Language Technology [Holland]
Law Society's Gazette
Listener
London Evening Standard

Melody Maker
Mini-Micro News
Money Management
Montreal Daily News [Canada]
Ms. London

National Geographic [USA]
Nature [USA]
New Musical Express
New Scientist
New Society
New Statesman
New Statesman & Society
News of the World
News on Sunday
Newsweek [USA]
New York Times [USA]

Observer
Options
Oxford Star

Patches
Port Alexandria Gazette Packet
  [USA]
Private Eye
Publishing News
Punch

Radio Times
Roanoke Times and World-
  News [USA]

Saffron Walden and Stansted
  Reporter
Saffron Walden Weekly News
San Francisco Sunday Examiner
  and Chronicle [USA]
Sassy [USA]
Scientific American [USA]
Scottish Field
She
Somerset County Gazette
Somerset Evening Post
Sounds
South China Morning Post
  [Hongkong]
South London Press
Spectator
The Sport
Star
Star [Malaysia]
Sun
Sunday Express
Sunday Telegraph
Sunday Times
Sunday Today

Sydney Morning Herald
[Australia]

Tablet
Time [USA]
Time Out
The Times
Times Educational Supplement
*Times Higher Education
Supplement*
Times Literary Supplement
Today
Top
Turkish Daily News [Turkey]
TV Times

UK Press Gazette

Underground
The Universe
USA Today [USA]

The Vine

Wall Street Journal [USA]
Weekly World News [USA]
Western Mail
What Video
Where: Chicago [USA]
Which?
Which Computer?
Wine
Working Woman

Yachts and Yachting

To monitor such a newsagent's warehouse-ful of printed material would have been a task beyond one person, even the most devoted journomaniac, and I am grateful to readers Suzy Allen, Wendy Crowdy, Sarah Dickens, Sue Engineer, Jessica Feinstein, Betty Kirkpatrick, Kate Lovell, and Deborah Tricker for the cornucopia of contributions they have made to the Longman Citation Bank, which provided the basis for this book. I am in the debt of many patient people whom I have rung up at odd hours for verification of what to me was an obscure point, among them Michael Banks, John Cole, Carla Garapedian, and *Observer* chief librarian Jeffrey Care. My particular thanks go to three members of the Longman Dictionaries and Reference Division: to Brian O'Kill for his invaluable and wide-ranging expertise, notably in matters etymological; to Heather Gay, for her watchful eye on scientific entries; and to Elizabeth Walter for organizing the gathering of citations. And finally, my thanks to Jean Aitchison, without whom . . .

John Ayto

ableism *noun* unfair discrimination in favour of able-bodied people

The Labour party in Haringey has come up with the 'ism' to cap the lot. The latest term, referred to in a recent press release, is 'ableism,' presumably coined to describe those sinners who discriminate in favour of able-bodied persons for jobs on building sites.

Daily Telegraph 8 Nov 1986

The Labour controlled [Camden] council's homosexual unit ... says in a report ... 'In the same way that racism, sexism, ableism, ageism and classism are institutionalised forms of oppression, so is heterosexism.'

Daily Telegraph 26 June 1987

abzyme *noun* an antibody which can transform the target (e g a protein molecule) to which it binds by catalysing chemical reactions

This year's buzz word for biotechnologists will probably be 'abzyme.' This is a new name for an enzyme that started life as an antibody. An enzyme is a machine tool in the body's factory; an antibody is a rifle in the body's army. Abzymes are machine tools that were made in the rifle factory.

Economist 7 Feb 1987

▶ As the above extract suggests, abzymes combine features of antibodies (immune-system proteins that identify and search out specific antigens) and enzymes (proteins that bind to targets and catalyse them). They promise to be powerful tools in the chemical industry. Their name, a blend of '*anti*body' and 'en*zyme*,' was suggested by scientists at the Research Institute of Scripps Clinic in the USA who, along with researchers at the University of California at Berkeley, were the first to describe these hybrid proteins.

1

account card *noun* STORE CARD

She has ... an encyclopaedic knowledge of Laura Ashley's new catalogue, a Marks and Spencer's account card and a couple of soft velvet track suits in zingy colours.

Daily Mail 29 June 1987

accreditate *verb* to give official authorization to; accredit

Such a new system would require the Royal Institute of British Architects and Architects Registration Council to stop accreditating the first architecture degree and retain only an advisory role.

Times Higher Education Supplement 8 Jan 1988

▶ This verb is produced by back-formation from *accreditation*, ousting the expected *accredit*; the same process gives, for instance, *administrate* (instead of *administer*) from *administration* or *administrator*.

acid cloud *noun* an area of mist or low cloud containing high concentrations of sulphuric and nitric acid

On the top of Great Dun Fell in Cumbria, the acid 'cloud' deposits up to 60 parts per million by volume of acidity, four times the concentration [of acidic pollutants] found at the base of the fell.

New Scientist 17 Mar 1988

▶ Such clouds leave a film of acidic water on vegetation in upland areas, which has been shown to be up to eight times more damaging than acid rain.

acid house *noun* a youth cult featuring HOUSE pop music and the taking of psychedelic drugs

As Ecstasy tablets cost £20 and £25 they are too expensive for many of the young 'acid house' adherents who have been using LSD instead.

Observer 7 Aug 1988

The videos range from loud, lurex pop nonsense ... through acid house psychedelia (permanent brain damage anticipated after two minutes) to experimental, Eastern European grumpiness.

Time Out 10 Aug 1988

▶ In many ways acid house is a return to the psychedelic sixties, with the new drug ECSTASY often taking the place of LSD (whose slang synonym, *acid*, gives the cult its name). It appears to have begun in four London clubs, the Trip, Spectrum, the Future, and Shoom, and spread like wildfire through Britain during the summer of 1988. Its music is largely computerized compilation (see HOUSE), but its main feature is the taking of drugs, under whose influence devotees (called ECSTATICS or *Shoomers*) dance the night away.

active suspension *noun* a computerized suspension system for motor vehicles

> Before the start of this Grand Prix season Frank Williams said that his team would race active suspension cars when they felt it necessary to keep pace with the opposition and their own system had been race proved.
>
> *Daily Telegraph* 8 Sept 1987

> Britain's Lotus ... is developing what is called an active suspension. It allows an auto to bash over rough pavement without upsetting the occupants, yet take corners flat like a Formula 1 racer.
>
> *USA Today* 8 Feb 1988

▶ An active suspension system operates by means of sensors at each corner of a vehicle, which constantly monitor the vehicle's attitude and relay this information to a central computer processor which analyses it and automatically adjusts the suspension to give a smooth ride.

It was pioneered by motor-racing manufacturers, and was first seen in 1983 when JPS Lotus experimented with it. Teething troubles led to a temporary withdrawal, but a revamped version was used in races in 1987 by both Lotus and Williams, with some success. However, the potential advantage active-suspension cars hold over ordinary cars (e g in maintaining an optimal drive-height throughout a race despite fuel loss) proved controversial, and at the end of 1987 it was announced that active suspension would be banned in Grand Prix races in 1988.

The system used in racing cars is relatively complex and expensive, because it uses special parts and the vehicle is supported on continuously powered hydraulic rams. However, a much simpler system is being developed by motor-suspension consultant Michael Mumford, in which the car rides on ordinary springs, and computer-controlled rams come into operation only when the car corners, etc; this is expected to be usable for ordinary road vehicles.

actressocracy *noun* actresses ennobled by virtue of marriage, considered collectively

The vision of the Countess of Dudley crying in court over Mr Alastair Forbes's uncomfortable revelations, published a mere three years ago, in the Literary Review could well provoke polemics on the gross absurdity of the libel laws or the sickening hypocrisy of the upper classes, but it also affords a striking example of the apotheosis of the 'actressocracy.' For, in an earlier incarnation, Lady Dudley ... was of course Maureen Swanson, the 1950s starlet – oops! – actress.

Daily Telegraph 1 Apr 1987

Adam *noun,* *slang* the drug methylene dioxymet-amphetamine (see ECSTASY)

One close relative of MDMA, known as Eve – MDMA is sometimes called Adam – has already been shown to be less toxic to rats than MDMA.

Economist 19 Mar 1988

A-day *noun* 29 April 1988, the day on which the provisions of the Financial Services Act 1986 came into force making it an offence to conduct investment business without authorization or exemption

Mr Francis Maude, Minister for Corporate Affairs, announcing the timing of 'A-day' in a Commons written reply, said the Government would bring into force the remaining investor protection provisions of the Financial Services Act on that day.

The Times 25 Mar 1988

▶ See also COMPLIANCE.

adipsin *noun* an enzyme present in fatty tissue which appears to have a role in preventing obesity

Research on mice and rats has revealed an enzyme known as adipsin, a shortage of which could cause obesity. Adipsin, which carves up proteins, should provide many clues to the way fat cells function.

Daily Telegraph 12 Aug 1987

▶ Adipsin is a recent discovery of researchers at the Dana Farber Cancer Institute and Harvard Medical School. The name is based on the term *adipose tissue*.

adoptive immunotherapy *noun*   a cancer treatment in which the patient's own white blood cells are used to attack cancer cells; see LAK CELL

During the past decade, cancer specialists have experimented with increasing enthusiasm on a form of treatment known as adoptive immunotherapy.

New Scientist 25 Sept 1986

adultify *verb*   to cause (a child) to take on adult behavioural features prematurely

If there is one feature of our society more troubling than the adultifying of children, it is perhaps the infantilising of adults.

Guardian 24 Aug 1987

▶ As the age of physiological puberty inexorably falls, growing concern has been voiced in recent years that in other respects too, children are being robbed of their childhood. The traditional Western (bourgeois) pattern of twelve or more years' protection within the family nest is being steadily eroded, as preteens exhibit a worldliness which bemuses many of their elders.

advance man *noun*   someone who makes arrangements for visits and appearances by an eminent person, and goes in advance to ensure that they proceed smoothly

Officially Mr Thomas is director of presentations for the Conservative party: unofficially he is the Prime Minister's personal advance man, as the current phrase goes. This is the year of the advance man. And when people say advance man, they usually mean Harvey Thomas.

Daily Telegraph 4 June 1987

▶ A word of US origin.

aestheticienne *noun* a female beautician

Aestheticienne Eve Lom developed her unique skin cleansing method from years of experience with problem skins. Her aromatic oil Cleansing Treatment is massaged into the face, then wiped away with a muslin cloth and hot water, followed with cold water pressed to the skin.

Cosmopolitan Mar 1987

▶ A fairly direct borrowing of French *esthéticienne*, 'female beautician.'

affluenza *noun* psychological disturbance arising from an excess of wealth

Psychologists in America believe they have discovered a new disease that is afflicting the wealthy: affluenza. New York psychologist Arweh Maidenbaum explains that affluenza can stretch back to childhood: 'Rich kids grow up in a golden ghetto without the walls.'

Daily Telegraph 4 Mar 1988

▶ A somewhat jocular blend of *affluence* and *influenza*.

agitpop *noun* the use of pop music to put across a political message

TPE ... try anything once, even if it means falling flat on their ideologically sound faces. But poverty-line agitpop is not for Sharkey. 'I admire That Petrol Emotion for what they are doing but it must get pretty depressing living on £50 a week.'

New Musical Express 16 Jan 1988

▶ The inspiration for this formation is *agitprop*, a term of Russian origin denoting the use of literature, music, art, etc for propaganda purposes.

agony aunt *noun, British* a woman who gives counselling on personal problems

Fifty new 'agony aunts' will be recruited by the Women's Royal Voluntary Service as a first stage in the crack-down on Army bullying. ... The network of Service Welfare ladies ... will listen to the problems of young soldiers.

Daily Telegraph 28 Jan 1988

▶ The term *agony aunt* has traditionally been restricted to someone who hands out her advice, somewhat remotely, in the media, typically in the agony column of a newspaper. It may be the slight air of impersonality in the arrangements proposed by the Army that suggested the term for the squad of WRVS volunteers.

agony uncle *noun, British* a man who advises readers or listeners on personal problems in a newspaper column, on radio, etc; a male agony aunt

Since working together on Forum magazine in the early seventies, their paths have continued to cross and cross. They [Anna Raeburn and Phillip Hodson] have ... become identified ... as the agony aunt and uncle of our media.

Guardian 20 June 1985

▶ Agony aunts have been with us some time (although the term has extended its meaning recently; see previous entry), but the male of the species is a comparatively new phenomenon, and the term *agony uncle* is as yet finding its feet in the language.

agroforestry *noun* the simultaneous use of (partially) wooded areas for the commercial growing of timber and the grazing of animals

Agroforestry, or pasture woodland, means at its best an Arcadia of deer, cattle and sheep grazing under oaks, interspersed with banks of tall standing timber and coppices regularly cropped for fuel wood and small timber products.

Guardian 11 Feb 1987

-aholic *or* **-oholic** *suffix, informal* a person obsessed with or addicted to

▶ The earliest formation based on this suffix was probably *workaholic*, which seems to have been coined around 1968 (see WORKAHOLICISM). So right from the outset the medial vowel of its model, *alcoholic*, was rather arbitrarily changed from *o* to *a*, and to this day *a* remains rather commoner. A

fairly high proportion of these formations refer to particular sorts of food or drink obsessions (the most widespread is probably CHOCOHOLIC), but compulsive collectors
or buyers feature prominently too:

clothesaholic The raspy American drawl [of Elaine Stritch] may
be a little grittier ... but Lady Long Legs, as London cabbies still call
her, is in rumbustuous [sic] form, looking great and as much of a
clothesaholic as ever. 'I'm a clothes horse. I love clothes. I adore
them,' she enthuses with all the fervour of an 18-year-old.

Daily Telegraph 12 Jan 1987

creamaholic See MILKAHOLIC

jadeaholic A few Westerners have become what Hilary Carmody
calls 'jadeaholics.' I met, in addition to Russell Beck, three other
fine contemporary New Zealand nephrite carvers in their studios.

National Geographic Sept 1987

milkaholic The Marsh'uns Tony Hall Bluey's in a right rough
O'state terday. D'yew reckon he's a milkaholic? No – wuss than
that. D'yew mean he's a CREAMAHOLIC? No – even wuss than
that. His condition's reached a new and terrifyin' stage. ... He's a
TINFOILAHOLIC!

Eastern Daily Press 13 Jan 1986

tinfoilaholic See MILKAHOLIC

aiki-jutsu *noun* a form of martial art similar to judo but
involving locks and kicks

Martial arts students from all over the country came to study three
very different fighting disciplines at BishopSport sports hall,
Bishop's Stortford. ... They were instructed in escrima, aiki-jutsu
and ninjutsu, and shown how each provides different forms of
defence against unarmed attackers or assailants using swords,
knives, sticks and firearms.

Herts and Essex Observer 10 Mar 1988

▶ From Japanese *ai* 'mutual' + *ki* 'spirit' + *jutsu* 'skill'.

air *verb, American* to be broadcast

'He has the appeal of Robin Hood and of Macheath in "The Beggar's
Opera",' Alistair Cooke says of Humphrey DeForest Bogart at the
outset of 'Bacall on Bogart', which airs at 8:30 p.m. Friday on
WTTW-Ch. 11.

Chicago Tribune 11 Mar 1988

▶ This verb, derived from the phrase 'on the air,' is fairly well established transitively in British as well as American English, but this intransitive use is a new departure.

airhead *noun, slang* an idiot

> The subject of this sly masterpiece was one Colette Sinclair, gold-digging airhead extraordinaire.
>
> *Listener* 21 Apr 1988

▶ Compare DICKHEAD, MEATHEAD, RUBBLEHEAD.

airmiss *noun* a near-collision of two aircraft in flight

> A Brymon Airways pilot flying 40 passengers to Paris from London City airport missed colliding with a light aircraft over Kent by only 50 feet.... The airmiss was one of two in three days which led to the suspension of the services by the Civil Aviation Authority at the end of last week.
>
> *Daily Telegraph* 24 Dec 1987

> The CAA spokesman said that the details of the incident were now an issue for the joint air miss working group, which would study reports from the pilot and air-traffic control.
>
> *Guardian* 15 Apr 1988

▶ With the ever-increasing volume of air traffic, and the mounting pressure under which air-traffic controllers work, the phenomenon of the airmiss has come more and more to public attention in recent years. Incidents in particular from mid-1987 onwards have been heavily reported. Airmisses are officially categorized into three grades (definite risk, possible risk, and no risk), adjudicated by a committee chaired by an ex-Group Captain.

It has been conjectured that *airmiss* (first recorded around 1970) is a misanalysis of *near miss* (presumably in much the same way as Middle English *a nadder* became modern English *an adder*), but as the second extract above suggests, it is now established as the official term used by the Civil Aviation Authority.

9

Albanianization *or* **Albanianisation** *noun* the voluntary political isolation of a country, and consequent economic impoverishment

Nowadays its Balkan neighbours mischievously speak of Romania's 'Albanianization.'

Economist 12 Dec 1987

▶ For decades Albania has been notorious as the 'forbidden country' of Europe. Resolutely turning its back on the other members of the Communist bloc within Moscow's sphere of influence, which it has viewed as unpardonably lax ideologically, it ploughed its own furrow for a long time, even falling out with its one supporter, China, in the early 1970s. Skulking behind its borders, eschewing virtually all contact with the West, its siege economy has brought little prosperity to its people. Under the rigid régime of Ceausescu, Rumania has in recent years shown similar tendencies, and its living standards have not kept pace with those of comparable Communist countries. Discontent over food shortages led to labour unrest in 1987.

The coining of the term no doubt owes something to *Balkanization*, a process which operated in very much the same area.

aliterate *adjective, noun* (being) a person who is disinclined to read or does not have the habit of reading

Aliterates, a recent report said, are people who know how to read but don't, and the Library of Congress has launched a campaign to persuade them to.

Bookseller 20 Nov 1987

▶ Although from an etymological viewpoint this means the same as *illiterate* (the prefix *a-* meaning 'not'), it has presumably been coined to make a contrast between those who cannot read and those who do not. Compare ILLITERATURE.

all-terrain vehicle *noun* (*abbreviation* **ATV**) a vehicle with large low-pressure tyres and a low-powered engine, intended for use on a variety of rough terrain

[The US Consumer Product Safety Commission] focused on all-terrain vehicles (ATV's), the off-road bikes that have been involved in 900 deaths and 330,000 serious injuries, half of them to children.
Newsweek 18 Apr 1988

▶ All-terrain vehicles are a sort of cross between cars and motorbikes, with three or four large bouncy wheels which enable them to traverse the roughest ground. Intended essentially for use away from roads, their freedom from the restrictions placed on the use of ordinary road vehicles has made them popular with children, whose inexperience as drivers, allied to the vehicles' inherent instability, has led to the sort of accident rates in the USA referred to in the above extract, and to calls for much more stringent regulation of ATVs.

alphabetism *noun, humorous* discrimination on the grounds of the alphabetical place of the first letter of one's surname

I am referring, you will have gathered, to the rampant alphabetism ... that afflicts our society. People are always organised in alphabetical order.
New Scientist 22 Oct 1987

Alan Whelan, a teacher from Ealing, is fed up with coming last ... just because his surname begins with a W. ... Whelan is now convinced he is subject to an insidious type of discrimination – 'alphabetism'.
Daily Telegraph 16 May 1988

▶ This coinage was produced by Ian Stewart (in the first extract above) as a parody of the current proliferation of complaints against alleged discrimination on any grounds, and of statisticians' jargon (see EXTREMILEXIC, FUNDILEXIC, MEDILEXIC, SUMMILEXIC). But facetious as the formation is, it will no doubt evoke a sympathetic response amongst those with names beginning with W who have spent much of their lives waiting while the Andersons, Browns, and Campbells of this world get dealt with first.

alternative *noun* **1** an alternative lifestyle based on environmental awareness and the rejection of traditional or orthodox Western technology, medicine, mechanized agriculture, etc

In its [Network for Alternative Technology and Technology Assessment] *Newsletter* ... we learn that 'Of all the books on "alternatives" published in recent years for the "general public" the ones which have led to the greatest number of enquiries to NATTA ... have been the book *Alternatives* linked to the TV series and George McRobie's *Small is Possible.*'

Environment Now Dec 1987

2 a person who adopts or advocates such a lifestyle

The *Rural Resettlement Handbook* is not for weekend cottagers. Its reputation as a classic amongst the 'alternatives' is well deserved.

Environment Now Dec 1987

ambulance chaser *noun* a person who seeks to profit from others' misfortunes or disasters

Clark Clifford, the Washington operator, is 81, and is considered a Democratic 'wise man.' He recently emerged from breakfast with Jesse Jackson, the populist and foreign-policy ambulance chaser, to say of him, 'What he is doing is bringing a new maturity to the American political scene.'

Roanoke Times and World-News 11 Apr 1988

▶ The notion of the ambulance chaser started life – as long ago as the end of the 19th century – as a contemptuous term for a lawyer who sought out accident victims and tried to persuade them to retain him to act on their behalf in obtaining compensation. This more general metaphorical application is a new development.

ambush marketing *or* **ambushing** *noun* the practice of advertising one's products via an implied connection with an event for which another company has the official marketing rights

McDonald's Corp. paid millions of dollars to be the exclusive fast-food sponsor of the U.S. Olympic committee for the 1988 Winter and Summer Games. So why are the restaurants of rival Wendy's International Inc. plastered with Olympic-like symbols? ... The apparent rip-off is actually an example of 'ambush marketing,' an increasingly popular tactic in special-events advertising ... With the growth of ambushing, some observers wonder if official status is still worthwhile.

Wall Street Journal 8 Feb 1988

▶ Jerry Welsh, former vice-president for marketing at E F Hutton Group Inc, claims to have invented this term. It seems as though the metaphorical possibilities of the word *ambush* are catching on in several areas of activity in the USA, making it the lexical flavour-of-the-month in American English:

And ABC News and the *Washington Post* did what is called an 'ambush interview' on me – that's how we are in the States, it's still cowboys and cowgirls – challenging me with results of their phone poll.

New Statesman 26 Feb 1988

Amerasian *noun* a person of mixed US and Asian parentage; *specifically* one fathered by an American serviceman during the Vietnam war

About 65 Amerasians ... arrived in Thailand yesterday with their relatives on their way to new homes in the United States.

The Times 1 Jan 1988

▶ Although presumably fairly numerous, the Amerasians in Southeast Asia seem only recently to have swum into the USA's consciousness as a problem to be addressed. A resettlement programme began in 1982, since when 4000 Amerasians have gone to live in the USA. Following new legislation introduced in 1988, Amerasians are now legally regarded in the USA as immigrants rather than refugees. (The term itself was coined as long ago as the mid 1960s.)

Amerenglish *noun* American English

Many teach-yourself enterprise books are decked out with charts and diagrams and written in Amerenglish. They talk of 'profit-enhancement' and are clearly targeted at the sort of Americanised

Briton who speaks unselfconsciously about 'shooting matches,' 'whole new ball games' and 'getting off your butt.'

Guardian 22 July 1988

American sock *noun, East African* a condom

In the rural, backwater villages of Rakai [in Uganda] most people do not believe Aids ... is sexually transmitted. ... Roman Catholic teaching and the belief in producing as many children as possible have made condoms – which are given names such as 'American socks' or 'gumboots' – all but taboo.

Daily Telegraph 5 June 1987

▶ With AIDS epidemic in East Africa, prevalent in Central Africa, and seemingly spreading to West Africa, considerable attention is being given to the problem of educating people about the disease. In Sierra Leone, for example, schools hold AIDS workshops in which children are taught songs about the dangers of 'plenti waka-waka' (i e promiscuity) and gain experience in using condoms by rolling them onto bananas; in Uganda, the government is running a campaign against promiscuity with the slogan 'Zero Grazing'.

amicus brief *noun, American* a legal submission by someone who is not party to a case but has an interest in its outcome

Hustler requested an appeal, and the Supreme Court is now collecting evidence from anyone whose interests might be affected by the final judgement. Among those who have submitted 'amicus briefs,' as they are known, is Volunteer Lawyers for the Arts, a pro-bono legal organisation in New York. Volunteer Lawyers says that the Federal Court's decision represents a real threat to any artist or writer wanting free expression under the First amendment.

Independent 23 July 1987

▶ *Amicus* is Latin for 'friend.'

14

anchorette *noun,*   *American* an anchorwoman

> The young fella in the exquisite lapis lazuli silk suit ... half-watching on his cute hand-sized computer the pretty blonde Channel Eleven anchorette introducing the *Early Bird News* programme.
> *Blitz* Mar 1988

▶ The use of the suffix *-ette* to make rather winsome (and to many women offensive) feminine forms is far from new: H L Mencken in 1921 noted *conductorette* and *farmerette,* and a 1939 issue of the *New Yorker* refers to 'welcomettes' employed to 'annoy' visitors to a convention. It did, however, enjoy quite a voguish explosion of use in the 1970s, and this application to *anchor* (a common American abbreviation of *anchorman* which has not really caught on in British English as a noun) suggests there is still life in it. The accidental similarity of this formation to *anchoret,* 'a hermit or recluse,' could scarcely be less appropriate.

Anderson-Fabry disease *noun*   a hereditary disease caused by a lack of the enzyme alpha-galactosidase in the blood, whose symptoms during childhood include skin rashes, the inability to sweat, and shooting pains in the arms and legs, and which leads to premature death

> A local man who is dying of a rare blood disease for which there is no cure, has launched an appeal to fund research into the illness. Only 50 people in England have Anderson-Fabry disease, a condition caused by a lack of a vital blood enzyme.
> *Saffron Walden and Stansted Reporter* 10 Mar 1988

▶ This condition was first described as long ago as 1898, by the British surgeon W Anderson (1842-1900) and the German dermatologist J Fabry (1860-1930), but has only recently come to wider public attention. It affects only men, but is genetically transmitted via the mother. The first symptoms are noticed during childhood, but in the sufferer's 30s and 40s it takes a more serious turn, affecting the kidneys and heart and often producing strokes.

angel *noun, British journalese* a nurse

> TV ad campaign wins a host of new angels [headline] Thousands of people have answered a £2½ million plea for new nurses despite the bitter pay battle on the wards.
>
> *Today* 26 Aug 1988

▶ *Angels* was the title of a popular BBC television soap opera about nurses (first screened in 1976). The term (based no doubt on a sentimentalized perception of nurses as Florence Nightingale-like angels of mercy) was eagerly seized on by the TV-fixated tabloid press as a rather unctuous synonym for 'nurse,' and interestingly has now long survived the demise of the series.

anonymize *or* **anonymise** *verb* to render anonymous

> All pregnant women at the hospital are routinely offered an Aids test. ... 'Very few take up a test,' Professor Heath said, 'and none of the women who proved to be positive in the anonymised tests had done so.' The anonymised screening, he said, went ahead only after careful consideration by the hospital's ethical committee.
>
> *Independent* 27 May 1988

antenuptial *adjective* preceding marriage

> That is why she insisted on an antenuptial agreement which would rule out the possibility of payments to him after the marriage, which she now wants annulled, had ended.
>
> *Independent* 23 July 1987

▶ As the above extract suggests, the recent appearance of this term owed much more to the legal than to the romantic side of marriage. Rancorous divorce proceedings and squabbles over who owns what have led prospective spouses to enshrine the division of property in a legal document well in advance.

antivirus *noun* VACCINE

> The antivirus temporarily write-protects the hard disc whenever the computer user tries out a new program on a floppy disc. If the new program attempts an unexpected write to the hard disc, it fails. At the same time, the user is alerted to the risk.
>
> *New Scientist* 14 April 1988

appeal *noun*   an act of appealing against something

> The U.S. Ski Association board Sunday rejected Mike Brown's
> appeal of his exclusion from the U.S. Ski Team.
> *USA Today* 8 Feb 1988

▶ The transitive use of the verb *appeal*, with a direct object
rather than *against*, is very well established in American
English (indeed an example occurs in the same source as
the above extract: 'Duquesne University basketball player
Pete Freeman will not appeal a seven-game NCAA suspension'). Not so widely recorded, however, is the consequence
of this for the noun derived from the verb: it has become
assimilated to the standard grammatical pattern in such
cases, with the verb's object being related to the noun with
the preposition *of* (as in 'They reduced the amount'; 'the
reduction of the amount'), where in British English one
would expect *against*.

ARC *noun*   AIDS-related condition *or* AIDS-related complex: a condition (e g loss of weight, fever, thrush, herpes
zoster) suffered by someone infected with human immunodeficiency virus, which may precede the cancers
and other diseases affecting those who develop AIDS

> A study of 288 gay men in San Francisco in the US has led
> researchers to predict that half of those infected with the human
> immunodeficiency virus (HIV) will develop AIDS within six years.
> Another quarter will develop AIDS-related conditions (ARC).
> *New Scientist* 31 Mar 1988

Archer *noun,   British slang*   the sum of £2000

> The would-be Prime Minister, Nobel Prize hopeful may have to be
> reconciled to a smaller place in history as a contribution to the
> variety of the nation and a bit of street slang. In the East End £2000
> is still known as an Archer.
> *Guardian* 22 July 1988

▶ When allegations appeared in certain newspapers that he
had paid a prostitute £2000, Jeffrey Archer, then deputy
chairman of the Conservative Party, was forced to resign.

He won a subsequent libel action in July 1987, but wits were not slow to enshrine his supposed indiscretion in the English language.

aristo-pop *noun* pop music dominated by high-earning, capitalist-inclined groups and individuals

But to reduce the pop aristocracy to a question of wealth would be to misunderstand it. The real measure is not money itself but how it's invested. The recent conifer scam, in which rich pop stars took advantage of tax benefits and government grants to ruin huge areas of land, has highlighted the growth of aristo-pop.

New Statesman & Society 17 June 1988

arm-twist *verb* to pressurize someone into doing something

For years the Scots, with five ministers to speak for them, have arm-twisted governments.

Economist 23 Jan 1988

▶ Verbs of this sort, created by back-formation (in this case from the noun *arm-twisting*) seem to be relatively rare, perhaps because the idiomatic phrase on which they are ultimately based (here, 'twist someone's arm') is still available in common use. Other examples do occur, though: in *What can a young Lassie do?*, Robert Burns used '*heart-break* someone' rather than 'break someone's heart':

I'll cross him, and wrack him, until I heart-break him.

arrestee *noun, American* a person who has been arrested

Between Saturday evening and 1:30 a.m. Sunday, police reported 481 arrests, about half of them on the gang-infested south side. About 190 of the arrestees were suspected gang members, Officer Joe Mariani said.

Roanoke Times and World-News 11 Apr 1988

arteether *noun* a drug developed for the treatment of malaria

A Chinese weed may provide doctors with a new, potent drug to treat malaria. The drug, called arteether, has proved effective against the malaria parasite, *Plasmodium falciparum*, both *in vitro* and in animal experiments.

New Scientist 31 Mar 1988

▶ The plant *Artemisia annua* is a traditional Chinese folk remedy for malaria. Chinese scientists isolated from it the active antimalarial constituent – a molecule they called qinghaosu – and American chemists further refined this by replacing an oxygen atom with an ethyl ether group (hence the name *arteether*) to make it more easily assimilable by the body.

arthroscopic *adjective* involving examination of a joint by the insertion of an instrument into the cavity between bones

> Arthroscopic surgery revealed torn cartilage in his right knee.
> *The Gazette* (Montreal) 17 May 1988

artocrat *noun,* *informal* a high-ranking arts administrator

> 'Could this be a plot?' muttered one artocrat cynically, as she and 230 other top arts administrators filed on board the little *Shieldsman*. A handy leak and Richard Luce's problems would be solved in one fell swoop.
> *New Statesman* 17 July 1987

assertion *noun* assertiveness; self-assertion

> Assertion training ... Women-only course in Camden Town. Fee £25 including light refreshment.
> *Time Out* 4 May 1988

▶ Training people to be more self-confident, even aggressively so, is a growth industry of the 1980s, and somewhere along the line the traditional distinction in usage between *assertion* and *assertiveness* sometimes gets blurred.

asset *noun,* *euphemistic* a Star Wars weapon

> The Base Surveillance and Tracking System ... will pick up the plumes of Soviet boosters as they leave their silos and pass this 'target set' to the Space Surveillance and Tracking System (SSTS), which in turn informs an 'asset,' the Star Warrior's jargon for a weapon. ... Dr Richard Burick, director of the Neutral Particle Beam programme at Los Alamos, says: 'You need a very complex supercomputer to communicate with all the assets in an SDI architecture,

> to spot a launch, tell assets where the threat is, and so on.'
>> *Daily Telegraph* 23 May 1988

ATB *noun* advanced technology bomber: a US bomber aircraft built using 'stealth' technology

Subject to satisfactory flight testing, the USAF plans to acquire 132 ATBs in a $36,600 million programme, with first deliveries ... in the early 1990s.
>> *Jane's All the World's Aircraft* 1987-88

▶ The ATB is being developed by Northrop; in conformation it is of a flying-wing shape. The material it is built of and the electronic countermeasures it contains mean that it will not easily be detectable by enemy radar. See also xst.

athetoid *adjective* characterized by athetosis, a form of cerebral palsy which produces uncontrollable writhing movements

The story of Alison, a 24-year-old athetoid spastic, is one of immense courage and determination.
>> *Radio Times* 5 Mar 1988

Alison John is an athetoid spastic, which means that her body moves ceaselessly and uncontrollably. She speaks indistinctly and apparently with difficulty. She walks, but not very steadily. She is unmistakably disabled and equally unmistakably an intelligent and exceptional person.
>> *Daily Telegraph* 11 Mar 1988

Geoff Busby is another who does a highly skilled job 'with a little help from the chip.' He is an athetoid spastic, which means he has little control over his muscles and cannot walk or use his hands effectively.
>> *Observer* 10 Apr 1988

▶ Although by no means a newly recognized condition – W A Hammond coined the term *athetosis* (derived from Greek *athetos* 'not fixed in position') as long ago as 1871 – the plight of athetoid spastics has only recently become highlighted.

ATM *noun* AUTOMATED TELLER MACHINE

As an incentive to encourage customer use of ATMs most banks pass on at least part of the cost saving to the customer in the form of reduced service charges.
>> *The Times* 14 Apr 1986

ATV *noun*   ALL-TERRAIN VEHICLE

audio *noun*   a sound recording featuring a storyline built round the lyrics of a pop song

> Radio 1's latest attempt to dip a toe into dramatic waters consists of taking familiar records and weaving stories into them.... The form is called the 'audio' and is meant to be the aural equivalent of the video. ... These first audios are so excruciatingly badly written, acted and directed they actually ruin the impact of the songs.
>
> *Daily Telegraph* 16 Aug 1988

auteurist   *adjective*   (in film criticism)   advocating the auteur theory, which views the director, rather than the actors, scriptwriter, etc, as the central creative force in the making of a film

> Hawks's last film is a lazy reworking of 'Rio Bravo' in which the director and his scriptwriters ... seem to have started believing too many of the things auteurist critics have said about him.
>
> *Time Out* 4 May 1988

▶ The concept of the 'auteur' now seems to be spreading to other fields in which people think that the credit for what they have produced has in the past been hijacked by others. In Italy, for example, it is the winegrowers who want to make all the middlemen take a back seat:

> I was asked to judge 70 entrants for the title Vini d'Autore (wines of authors – not us [wine writers] but those who estate-bottled them).
>
> *London Evening Standard* 17 May 1988

autochondriac *noun*   a person who constantly worries about the condition of his or her car

> The plague [of showers of Saharan sand] seems to have hit taxis and chauffeurs particularly badly and I heard the sad tale of one poor car telephone salesman spending a fortune over the last few days on trying to regain the sheen of Mayfair from the look of El Alamein. Autochondriacs, however, can sleep easily. 'It was a freak event,' said the Met Office.
>
> *Daily Telegraph* 20 Aug 1987

▶ This is the sort of coinage, cobbled together with a healthy disregard for the derivation of its model, which gives the linguistic purist apoplexy. In Greek, *hypochondria* literally meant 'below the cartilage of the breastbone' (since this area, the abdomen, was supposed to be the seat of melancholy). So the reductio ad absurdum of *autochondriac* (*autos* being Greek for 'self' or 'same') would be 'one's own cartilage.' But in fact this sort of phenomenon – of analysing a compound term for a complex concept as if each distinct element of meaning was represented by a particular, and detachable, part of the word – is not an uncommon factor in English word formation. The words *autocade, motorcade, camelcade*, etc, for example, have been coined from *cavalcade* on the unspoken assumption that the element *-cade* means 'procession,' although in fact it developed from a relatively meaning-free Latin verbal suffix. And of course *Hamburger*, from the city of Hamburg, has spawned a whole menu-ful of *beefburgers, cheeseburgers, baconburgers*, etc, as well as just plain *burgers*. Morphosemantically, *hypochondriac* is a single, indivisible unit in English from a strictly historical point of view, but the fact that it can evidently be analysed as *hypo-* 'oneself' + *-chondria* 'agitated concern about health or condition,' and then used to make new compounds, sheds an interesting sidelight on English word formation.

autocondimentation *noun*   seasoning one's own food with pepper and salt at table

I admire most of all the American who used 'autocondimentation' with the self-confident scientific air all Americans appear to exude. It appears that a prominent American fast-food chain ... decided to test how much salt and pepper the British liked on their hamburgers. ... The cooks ... put yet more salt and pepper in the burgers, but whatever they did the great British gastronome decided to put on more. This highly puzzling behaviour led the American empiricist to conclude that 'the British were obsessed by autocondimentation.'

New Scientist 30 July 1987

autohagiography *noun* self-aggrandizing autobiography

Manuals on how to make it, together with hagiographies and auto-hagiographies of tycoons and plutocrats, have been pouring from the presses this year.

Guardian 22 July 1988

▶ Compare TYCOONOGRAPHY.

automaker *noun, American* a car manufacturer

Nissan, Japan's second largest automaker, saved $657 million last year by slicing costs and streamlining manufacturing methods.

Time 18 Jan 1988

United Auto Workers Vice President Marc Stepp, who took charge of the union's Chrysler department in 1977, first led national nego-tiations with the automaker in 1979.

Roanoke Times and World-News 11 Apr 1988

automated teller machine *noun* (*abbreviation* ATM) a machine which performs various bank-desk functions (such as paying out or receiving cash) when activated by a customer's bank card; a cash machine

The mainstay of the electronic building society is the automated teller machine (ATM).

The Times 14 Apr 1986

The bank also seems likely at last to join a big network of auto-mated teller machines, which it has avoided before.

Economist 5 Sept 1987

The banks continue to pump money into new branch accounting systems, developing on-line networks between branches and their head offices and extending their automated teller machine (ATM or cash machine) networks.

Observer 10 Apr 1988

awfulize *verb, American* to imagine that things are much worse than they really are

When it comes to dealing with daily obstacles, he says, 'we have a tendency toward catastrophizing and awfulizing.' ... We can learn when to fight back, when to walk away from office problems.

Newsweek 25 Apr 1988

babushkaphobia *noun*   dislike of or aversion to grand-children

A few ... biological grandmas go to great lengths to reject all tradi-tional grandmotherly duties. Actress Lauren Bacall is firm about her babushkaphobia: 'I don't baby-sit or anything, that's not my function in life. I say, "I've had my three children, thank you very much; you'll have to deal with your own problems".'
Good Housekeeping Aug 1988

► This no doubt useful coinage is rather curiously formed, since it literally means 'fear of grandmothers' (*babushka* is Russian for 'grandmother').

baby-boomer *noun*   a person born during a period of high birth-rate, specifically (in Britain and the US) 1945-52

To be a baby-boomer is to belong to that generation born when Johnny came marching home at the end of the Second World War.
The Times 11 Aug 1986

The post-war babies who metamorphosed from brats into beatniks and passed from hippiehood through yuppiedom are ... now known collectively as the baby boomers.
Financial Times 14 Dec 1987

► Following the depressed birth rates of World War II, population growth exploded. Between 1946 and 1952 over 5 million children were born in England and Wales. In 1947 the birth-rate was 20.5 per thousand of population, an ex-tremely high figure, falling to 15.3 in 1952.

As this generation grew up, its members took on, or appeared to take on, certain definable characteristics. As teenagers they pioneered the self-indulgence of the swing-ing sixties, embraced revolutionary, or at least liberal politics, and became hippies. As middle age approached, their hair became shorter, but they carried with them quali-ties of open-mindedness and unstuffiness which were a transforming element in society. In the 1980s it was the trendier of the now 30- to 40-year-olds who attracted the epithet:

> Cadbury Schweppes identified two distinct consumer categories for the sauce. First, the 'baby-boomer', or 'yuppie', a fitness conscious group who 'graze' while working, rather than eat formal meals.
>
> *Economist* 15 Nov 1986

baby break *noun* a period during which a woman suspends her career in order to have a baby or babies

> The logic, that helping their female employees to have a short baby break and smooth re-entry to the workforce would minimise the problems, seems to have escaped most of them.
>
> *Guardian* 25 June 1986

▶ The baby break is a distinct career break, as opposed to the brief statutorily enforceable maternity leave. It may extend over several pregnancies, although the trend nowadays is increasingly for women to return to work between babies. The average length of a baby break in Britain is five years.

The application of the term to a man, in the following citation, is relatively unusual:

> With the possibility of more far-flung travel, why would Fleming jump at the chance to photograph home turf? 'I volunteered so I could take a baby break,' the new father says, referring to the birth of his son ... in May 1987.
>
> *National Geographic* Aug 1988

baby bust *noun* a drastic fall in the birthrate; *specifically* that which occurred in Western countries in the mid 1960s

> After the boom comes the bust – not in stocks but in population. The leading edge of the baby bust, that smaller generation born since 1965, is now 22 and starting its long march through maturity.
>
> *Newsweek* 23 Dec 1987

▶ The baby bust switches on warning lights for economies which have been geared to the large populations engendered by the post-World War II baby boom (see BABY-BOOMER). In America, for example, the rate of population growth is slowing down, which means a potential shrinkage in the market for manufactured goods, for services, and for just about everything which keeps the US domestic economy going.

babynap *verb* to kidnap (a baby)

> Raising Arizona (15): Original, inventive comedy from the Coen Brothers. Nicholas Cage is the beguiling recidivist bandit who babynaps one of a furniture magnate's quins to satiate his wife's maternal longings.
> *Daily Telegraph* 5 Sept 1987

babywipe *noun* a disposable moisturized medicated paper towel for cleaning babies (e g when changing nappies, or for sticky fingers)

> The nation could soon be facing a shortage of babywipes. Scott, the world's biggest manufacturer of disposable tissues and towels, has just issued a report warning that British retailers are not stocking up fast enough with babywipes for the summer peak.
> *Daily Telegraph* 28 July 1988

▶ Babywipes were introduced in Britain in 1980.

Bach flower *noun* a flower with therapeutic qualities, used in a variety of remedies

> Dr Lewith comments: 'There has been a great deal of scepticism about Bach Flowers, but all I can say is that I am a clinician, I have used them frequently for patients, and they very often work excellently, sometimes quite rapidly. Yes, it does sound loony, but there it is.'
> *Daily Telegraph* 3 Mar 1987

▶ The notion that flowers have healing properties was put forward by an eccentric Oxfordshire physician, Dr Edward Bach, over 50 years ago. The technique for extracting these properties, which apparently come in the form of beneficial vibrations that can cure negative states of mind, is to float the flowers in pure spring water in the sunshine; this water is then preserved in brandy, and given to the patient in small quantities over several weeks.

back calculate *verb* to perfom BACK CALCULATION

> A high court judge said yesterday that the law which permits police to 'back calculate,' to see how much a motorist under the alcohol limit has been drinking was 'mischievous.'
> *Daily Telegraph* 9 Sept 1987

back calculation *noun* a calculation carried out to determine whether a person below the legal limit of blood alcohol at the time of testing is likely to have been above the limit at some immediately previous time when he or she was driving a vehicle

> In a unanimous test case ruling with wide implications for the drink-driving laws, Lord Justice Watkins and Mr Justice Mann upheld the right of the police to bring prosecutions based on the back calculation of the level of alcohol in motorists at the time they were driving.
> *Daily Telegraph* 29 Sept 1987

back up *verb* to copy (computer data) from a disk to a storage device (e g a tape) as a security measure

> The value of buying a new PC is easily understood but the cost of a tape streamer to back up the data is hard to justify.
> *Guardian* 12 Nov 1987

bagstuffer *noun* a small promotional item, typically a leaflet, that is given away in large numbers

> *The Fifth Child* by Doris Lessing Cape/April 7 Full colour PoS and extract bagstuffers. Lessing will be interviewed on *The South Bank Show* and in *The Sunday Times* and *Cosmopolitan*.
> *Publishing News* 12 Feb 1988

ballistician *noun* a ballistics expert

'Have you heard from our ballistician yet?'
A Case of Deadly Force (US TV movie) 1986

▶ By no means a new term in the world of academic physics, there are signs that *ballistician* may be infiltrating the general language, via crime fiction: when the detective wants to know whether the gun he has found fired the bullet that killed the victim, he no longer sends for the plain ballistics expert, but for the ballistician.

ballizing *noun* a method of boring holes of precise diameter and smooth finish in metal by pushing a metal ball of extreme hardness and smoothness through a previously made, slightly undersized hole

Today, ballizing is rapidly replacing reaming processes as the modern way of hole sizing and bore burnishing.
Advertising leaflet, Spheric Engineering Ltd, 1987

balloon financing *noun* a method of financing purchases in which the vendor lends the purchaser (part of) the price, part of which is repayable in monthly instalments but leaving a large final payment to be made to discharge the debt

A newspaper advertisement by Fiat for a credit scheme to buy the company's Uno car is being investigated by the ASA and there have also been complaints about some advertisements offering interest-free finance. The Fiat scheme is typical of a number now offered by car companies involving a system known as balloon financing. ... Balloon financing is one of a number of schemes developed by the motor trade and finance companies to encourage sales in the fiercely competitive new car market.
Daily Telegraph 23 May 1987

ballpark *noun,   slang* a state of affairs; situation

'It was a new ballpark for me,' Hunter said.
City Limits 24 Mar 1988

▶ A neologism perhaps not likely to establish itself permanently in the language, but nevertheless serving as an interesting illustration of the muddle likely to arise from the use of imperfectly understood idioms from other varieties of English. 'A (whole) new ball game' (which is presumably what the speaker intended) has been around for some time, but in recent years has been joined by *ballpark*, another metaphor drawn from baseball: 'not in the same ballpark' means 'completely dissimilar or divergent,' and from this have developed such expressions as 'a ballpark figure,' that is, an approximately accurate one.

bang on *verb, British informal* to make repeated insistent references to something, often at tedious length

> You can go down to the housing office and bang on till the cows come home about damp and shoddy repairs. Make a video about them, though, and things change.
> *New Statesman* 24 Mar 1985

> 'I've seen her [Mrs Thatcher] banging on and on and on in front of Reagan,' says a former Cabinet Minister, 'and the poor man couldn't get a word in edgeways. The whole thing just washed over him.'
> *Economist* 11 June 1988

bankroll *verb* to pay large sums of money

> There were designers, photographers, models, film-makers, fabric-creators, artists, some of the biggest in the business, some especially flown across Europe for the evening, and some who had simply bankrolled their way in.
> *Blitz* May 1988

▶ To *bankroll* was originally American slang for 'to provide financial backing for an enterprise' (derived from *bankroll*, a wad of banknotes).

Barbour *trademark* a weatherproof jacket or coat of waxed cotton, typically green, as made by J Barbour and Sons of South Shields

The Barbour jacket, traditional attire for the hunting upper classes, has more recently been taken up as the yuppies' weekend favourite.

Guardian 28 Sept 1987

The cult of the Barbour seems to know no bounds.

Daily Telegraph 8 Oct 1987

Young Cheltenham ladies and gentlemen in striped shirts and Barbours quaffed their drinks and guffawed loudly.

Sunday Times 26 June 1988

barristering *noun* practising as a barrister

Mortimer splits his time between the palatial family mansion in Buckinghamshire (his second wife, also a Penelope to his Ulysses, has given up barristering for ministering to his needs) and a flat in Maida Vale.

Time Out 4 May 1988

basket *noun* a group or collection (of currencies)

Sterling has fallen by 13 per cent against the European basket of currencies over the past five months. Against the dollar, the see-saw of the first half of the 1980s has evened out to relative stability.

Financial Times 11 Mar 1986

In London the pound closed just over half a cent ahead at $1.5182 but its trade-weighted index, which tracks sterling's performance against a basket of major currencies, slipped 0.1 to 68.4.

Guardian 3 Feb 1987

▶ The metaphorical use of *basket* for an assemblage or range of things is far from new (a writer in the *Economist* 26 May 1962, for example, asks whether various categories of export might not 'be grouped in comparable "baskets"), but its specific application to a range of currencies whose average value is being compared with that of one other, for example the pound or dollar, seems to be a comparatively recent development. The usage may be based on the notion of gathering disparate things, particularly 'all one's eggs,' into one basket.

basuco *noun* the residue that remains after refining co-caine, used as a drug

> Colombians don't use drugs, at least not in the purer forms which are found on any street corner of any major city in the United States. We simply can't afford them. For local consumption, the drug lords of Medellín developed basuco. ... What previously was thrown away as trash is now being packaged and sold as cigarettes.
> *Newsweek* 14 Mar 1988

batter *noun* a batsman

> As a consequence of anticipating the worst, batters, even top bat-ters, have got it firmly lodged into their heads that they would inevitably receive the unplayable ball at some stage.
> Frances Edmonds, *Cricket XXXX Cricket* 1987

▶ *Batter* coexisted with *batsman* in the late 18th and early 19th centuries ('Such mutual compliments from man to man – bowler to batter, batter to bowler,' Mary Russell Mitford, *Our Village* 1824), but the gradual establishment of *batter* as the term for a baseball hitter (for which *batsman* was occasionally used in the 19th century) meant that *batsman* became the preferred term for cricket. However, recent years have seen a resurgence of *batter*; it is prevalent in the argot of professional players, and via such channels as Tom Graveney's television cricket commentary shows signs of becoming more widely current (much to the disgust of linguistic conservatives).

One practical advantage to the term is that it does not implicitly exclude female players; information material re-lating to KWIK CRICKET, for example, which is consciously aimed at encouraging young girls as well as boys to take up the game, uses *batter*:

> At the end of every over the fielding team move round one place in a clockwise direction and the batters change ends.
> *Kwik Cricket: How to Play the Game* 1988

beach music *noun* a style of American pop music based on black soul music and rhythm and blues and originating on the coast of South Carolina

A latter-day generation of black musicians including The Drifters, Chairmen Of The Board, The Tams, Clifford Curry and Major Lance have preserved and perpetuated a ramshackle genre called beach music.

New Musical Express 5 Sept 1987

▶ Long established locally in the black culture of America's southeastern seaboard, beach music and its associated dance, the SHAG, show signs of becoming an international pop craze.

beat box *noun, informal* a portable stereo cassette player; a ghetto blaster

The concept of singing along to a record is in the New York tradition of doing very private things in very public places; walking down the street with your beat box or (for wimps) walkman, and singing along in a tuneless abandon.

New Musical Express 13 Dec 1986

▶ Other current colloquialisms for this highly interventionist form of entertainment include *jambox* and *boom box*.

bells and whistles *noun, informal* additional features, typically superfluous but superficially attractive

It is not surprising, either, that the recruits have scaled down their ambitions: 'A year ago they'd tell us what sort of salary they expected, and what kind of car they wanted, and what kind of bells and whistles they wanted on the car. Not now.'

Daily Telegraph 1 Sept 1987

Congressmen, being congressmen, could not resist trying to attach all their favourite bells and whistles to the legislation.

Economist 26 Dec 1987

belly bomber *noun, American slang* a small highly-spiced burger

Inside, the red-necked, blue-collar clientele pop tiny, bitesize burgers by the pungent half-dozen. Known with good reason as 'belly bombers' to the fast food gourmets who consume them, these culinary depth charges cost 39 cents each and give your digestive system an experience it will never forget, no matter how hard it tries.

Elle Mar 1988

benchmarking *noun, American* the examination of a rival company's product in order to establish a standard which one seeks to exceed

Many companies literally tear the opposition apart. In a process called 'benchmarking,' General Motors takes competitors's cars apart in a 90,000-square-foot shop toured by more than 19,000 employees last year; Xerox engineers disassemble rival products. Benchmarking also means studying service: Xerox's employees improve their own order processing by watching mail-order maven L. L. Bean.

Newsweek 2 May 1988

Benidormification *or* **Benidorming** *noun, derogatory* the down-market commercialization of a holiday resort

That most chic of resorts, St Moritz, has joined forces with Reuters news agency and installed a facility to keep holidaying financiers in touch. ... Traditionalists, meanwhile, see the scheme as a further example of the Benidormification of the slopes.

Daily Telegraph 8 Mar 1988

Its presenter, Robert Chesshyre of *The Observer*, was concerned with the means by which tourism is 'spoiling the world', and specifically with the Benidorming of Turkey.

Independent 27 July 1988

▶ These coinages are based on Benidorm, the Spanish resort on the Costa Blanca which with its high-rise hotel blocks, fish and chip shops, and 'British pubs,' has become a byword for kiss-me-quick garishness.

benny *noun, British slang* a gormless or slow-witted person; *specifically, derogatory* a Falkland islander

Labour's shadow minister for Foreign Affairs, George Foulkes, should perhaps think twice before venturing near the Falklands again. ... Locals in Port Stanley, who were seriously miffed by his uncomplimentary reference to them as 'Bennies'... on his visit, plan to lob him into the bay.

Daily Telegraph 19 June 1986

'Crossroads' may have ended ... but it has left at least one mark on our literary heritage – the word 'benny,' after one of the series' leading (though dim-witted) characters, which is now routinely used by UK troops in the Falklands to describe the native islanders.

New Society 8 Apr 1988

▶ The character in the British television soap opera *Crossroads* mentioned in the above extract was Benny, a lovable halfwit who first appeared in 1977. The part was played by Paul Henry.

beta-test *verb* (of an organization other than the manufacturer) to test (a new product) before it becomes generally available

Ideal-Escort is aimed initially at ADR's 1,700 users of Datacom/DB worldwide who are also big PC users. In the UK the installed base is 50 companies including confectionery company Mars which has beta-tested Ideal-Escort.

Computer Weekly 25 June 1987

bezzle *noun* the overall (temporary) benefit conferred by undetected embezzlement

Insider trading is, Sir Martin Jacomb of the Securities and Investment board has said, a victimless crime. But Sir Martin cannot be right. If there is no victim, there is no crime. ... The American economist J. K. Galbraith invented the concept of the bezzle. When an embezzler has stolen the money he is better off: when his employer has not yet discovered its loss, he is no worse off, and the bezzle is the social gain from embezzlement. But when the default is discovered, both parties suffer and the bezzle evaporates.

Daily Telegraph 19 Jan 1987

Bhangra *noun* a variety of pop music originating in the Indian community in Britain, based on Punjabi folk music but with various elements of Western rock incorporated into it

'Bhangra has always been dance music,' explains Manjeet Kondal of popular new group Holle Holle. 'People used it for weddings and parties here, because not everyone understands the words to English disco. Then they started booking it for shows, and suddenly Bhangra fever took over.'

News on Sunday 17 May 1987

Apna Sangeet, winners of Network East's Asian pop awards will be
featured with high energy bhangra band Cobra.

Asian Times 27 May 1988

▶ Bhangra was originally a Punjabi folk dance celebrating
a successful harvest, and was introduced into Britain about
ten years ago in response to the Indian community's need
for pop music of its own with words it could understand. At
first it was played in traditional style, but gradually
Western elements such as electronic drums, guitars, and
synthesizers came to be added to it. Today it has tremen-
dous mass appeal, with groups such as Heera, Holle Holle,
and Alaap drawing crowds of thousands to Asian discos and
achieving gold discs.

bicoastal *adjective* involving both the east and west coasts
of the USA

That is the view of the Democratic staff of the Economic Committee
of Congress, whose report, 'The Bicoastal Economy,' makes the
claim that economic growth during the Reagan years has taken
place disproportionately in California and on the east coast.

Economist 19 July 1986

[Isabella Rossellini's] current romance with Lynch is bicoastal.
'It's difficult but David wants to live in Hollywood,' she says. 'I have
my daughter in New York.'

Newsweek 2 May 1988

bid-proof *adjective* not susceptible to being taken over by
another company

A CBI spokesman retorted: 'The CBI is not intervening in a takeover battle between two member companies but pointing out that
the Swiss legal system allows Swiss companies to be virtually bid-
proof while the UK ... is probably the most open market in the
world.'

Observer 8 May 1988

▶ The relative degrees of immunity to takeover bids enjoyed by companies in different countries was highlighted
in early 1988 by the successful attempt on the part of Nestlé
of Switzerland to buy the British chocolate firm Rowntree.

Nationalistic hackles were raised by this threat to the independence of the country's Smarties supply, and talk was of a protectionistic reference to the Monopolies Commission. Swiss commercial law makes it virtually impossible for a company to be taken over unless the company itself wishes to be taken over, a state of affairs very different from that which obtains in the UK, where the market in takeovers is much more open.

big bang *noun* a fundamental and far-reaching set of changes introduced as a single package rather than piecemeal or gradually

The people with the job of collecting the Government's proposed poll tax favour the 'big bang' approach for its introduction. ... At the Rating and Valuation Association conference in Eastbourne ... members said they believed that introducing the new charge at a stroke would make the changeover cheaper and easier than the proposal to phase in the charge over four years.

Daily Telegraph 3 Oct 1987

Far-reaching reforms to modernise the management of the Civil Service are to be announced by Mrs Thatcher in the Commons tomorrow. ... According to Whitehall insiders, Mrs Thatcher has decided against going for a 'big bang' and Ministers will be asked to put forward suggestions for parts of their empires to be used for pilot studies.

Daily Telegraph 17 Feb 1988

▶ This general metaphorical meaning (derived mainly from the term for the cosmological theory) seems to predate the special application to the deregulation of the City of London in 1986 (see *Longman Guardian New Words*), but clearly the financial Big Bang has given considerable impetus to its use in other contexts.

Big Crunch *noun* a theory in cosmology: the universe will eventually stop expanding and then gradually collapse together into a central core

> Some believe that [the universe] will expand forever, while others claim that there is enough matter in the universe for gravity to slow and stop the expansion, eventually forcing it to collapse to a Big Crunch.
>
> *The Times* 19 Jan 1988

▶ The Big Crunch is one of various theories that have been put forward predicting what the future development of the universe will be (the term mirrors, of course, the now generally accepted Big Bang theory, according to which the universe began with a vast explosion). Most cosmologists currently favour a less drastic scenario, in which the expansion of the universe will gradually slow down but never stop completely.

Big Dry *noun*   an extended period of drought

> The Big Dry is not confined to rural areas. From San Francisco to Chicago, severe water restrictions are in effect. In climatic terms, there is no doubting the seriousness of the drought.
>
> *Sunday Times* 3 July 1988

big mo *noun, American slang*   a decisive surge of confidence and popularity deriving from success in an election campaign

> Big mo – decisive momentum – was even used unadorned on the cover headline in *Time* magazine this week now that Mr Bush has finally captured the elusive elixir. You get big mo after exploiting the bounce of early victories.
>
> *The Times* 17 Mar 1988

Big Wet *noun, Australian*   an extended period of rainy weather

> From Dubbo, where they've just experienced their first dry afternoon in a fortnight, reports have come of 1,000 shearers cooling their heels, waiting for the Big Wet to pass so they can get back to fleecing the sheep.
>
> *Sydney Morning Herald* 13 Apr 1988

▶ The term *wet*, often capitalized, has been used in Australian English for a rainy period or season since at least the beginning of this century.

bimbette *noun,   American informal*   an adolescent female pop singer

In the fickle world of pop music teenage girls, and young ones at that, have provided a disproportionate number of the records that have topped Britain's charts so far this year. A similar coup has occurred in the United States, where most of these new stars originate. They have a label, for without a label there is no trend: they are called 'bimbettes.'

Economist 30 Apr 1988

▶ A coinage based, of course, on the currently voguish BIMBO.

bimbo¹ *noun, informal*   **1**   a person of limited intelligence but high sex appeal

Time was when the common perception of the woman golf professional was that of a willowy blonde bimbo in a miniskirt. The male chauvinist hacks of the world were just not interested in the length of the ladies' tee shots. The length of their legs was, apparently, much more important.

Sunday Times 3 July 1988

What a cad, but it's easy to see why Joan [Collins] has fallen for him. Apart from anything else, he is pure beefcake. He has also been labelled a bit of a bimbo – he got his nickname Bungalow Bill because he's not supposed to have much up top ... but a lot down under.

Sunday [News of the World magazine] 24 July 1988

2   a young woman who has an affair with a public figure and then releases details of it to the press

So J. Danforth Quayle has 'bimbo-problems.' On top of being rumbled for vanity, not to mention long-established weaknesses like being inarticulate and none too bright, now he has, according to a gleefully morals-policing press, bimbo-problems. Paula Parkinson kissed and told.

Guardian 1 Sept 1988

▶ This word achieved brief popularity in the summer of 1988 with the so-called 'Battle of the Bimbos.' This cause célèbre involved two young models, Fiona Wright and Jacqui Bell, who shared a flat. Fiona brought a private prosecution against Jacqui, accusing her of stealing her diaries, which contained lurid descriptions of her sexual escapades with an assortment of men, including Sir Ralph Halpern (later extensively exerpted in the *News of the World*). The jury found in Jacqui's favour.

However, the word has been around for at least 70 years, especially in American English (it is Italian in origin, meaning 'little child'). Its earliest use was simply as a contemptuous term for a fellow or chap, but a later sense was a 'whore.'

bimbo² *verb, informal* to release details to the press of one's illicit sexual relations with (a public figure)

> Kissing and telling has laid low many an upstanding pillar of the establishment but it was Gary Hart who first got properly 'bimboed.'
>
> *Guardian* 1 Sept 1988

bin *verb* to throw away by putting into a wastepaper basket

> This is assuming that 95 people out of every 100 people you mail do absolutely nothing with this opportunity and bin this packet.
>
> Chain letter (British) 1987

bioastronomy *noun* the scientific search for extra-terrestrial life forms, or for locations in the universe which might support such life forms

> Scientists prominent in the search for extraterrestrial intelligence (SETI) gathered in Balatonfüred, Hungary, during the last week of June. Under the auspices of the International Astronomical Union Colloquium on 'Bioastronomy,' they discussed both the possibility of other life forms existing in the Universe, and the best ways to find intelligence if it does exist.
>
> *New Scientist* 23 July 1987

biodot *noun* a small temperature-sensitive device that can be stuck to the skin

> Biodot International of Indianapolis has introduced 'biodots,' temperature-sensitive adhesive devices that workers can attach to their hands to determine their stress levels.
>
> *Newsweek* 25 Apr 1988

▶ The biodot works on the principle that it can detect when there is a reduction of blood flow to the extremities, which can be indicative of stress. By monitoring the biodot's message, the individual can use the biofeedback method of reducing his or her level of stress.

bio-ethics *noun* the ethical aspects of various techniques of human intervention in biological processes, such as genetic engineering and birth control

The statement was drafted by a working party of a joint bio-ethics committee of the bishops' conferences of England and Wales, Scotland, and Ireland, and was approved by the bishops' conference of England and Wales last November. ... The bishops' view on the effects of the post-coital pill is supported by the recently published spring issue of the newsletter of the Association of Lawyers for the Defence of the Unborn.

The Universe 21 Mar 1986

biofundamentalist *noun* someone who is opposed on religious or ethical grounds to modern techniques of human intervention in biological processes, such as biotechnology and genetic engineering

Now biotechnology is ready to revitalize agriculture, in a manner that is much faster, indeed, which biofundamentalists say is indecently so.

Daily Telegraph 6 July 1987

biometric *adjective* taking or using measurements of physiological features

The days of the hotel key are numbered, he said. Credit cards and other magnetic cards are already being used in some hotels though eventually 'biometric' systems will be introduced. One type uses an electronic finger-print reader. Another takes an 'eyeprint' by measuring the pattern of veins on the retina.

Daily Telegraph 19 May 1988

▶ This is a new semantic development for *biometric*, which hitherto has been used to mean 'concerned with the statistical study of biological data' (and also, in the 19th century, 'measuring longevity').

biosensor *noun* a sensor consisting of an electronic chip to which is bonded a layer of enzymes or antibodies which detect the presence of a particular substance

Plessey scientists reckon that biosensors should be working properly out of the laboratories in three to five years time. Looking well into the next century, they see the possibility of an interface between man and machine through biosensors.
Sunday Times 24 Apr 1988

▶ The biosensor works on the principle of electronically measuring and analysing the chemical reaction of a protein to a particular substance, such as a gas or a pathogen. Among the uses contemplated for it are the diagnosis of illness and the detection of explosives and illegal drugs.

biting *noun, slang* the practice of buying or copying someone else's TAG

bizzy *noun, British slang* a policeman

During his time as Rod Corkhill, Jason Hope has signed the odd autograph. But now the *Brookside* scriptwriters have cast him as a bizzy, the people on Jason's real-life beat seem to think he's never off-duty.
New Musical Express 2 May 1987

It's the bizzies (*police*) down here that piss me off. I've got pulled nearly every day since I've been here. ... I'll be outside Centrepoint, waiting for it to open, trying to deal with all these perverts and drug pushers, and up comes the bizzy, asks me what I'm doing.
Blitz May 1988

▶ This is probably a new form of *busy*, meaning 'a detective', which dates back at least to the turn of the century.

Black Monday *noun* Monday 19 Oct 1987, the day on which share prices on world stock markets fell dramatically – called also *Meltdown Monday*

The world is about to find out what really happened on Black Monday ... when the Dow Jones industrial average plunged a record 22.6%.
Economist 19 Dec 1987

► Black Monday signalled the end (for the time being, at least) of the stock market boom which followed deregulation and the Big Bang, in which share prices rose dizzyingly to ever new heights. On October 19 the Dow Jones average on the New York Stock Exchange fell 508.32 points to 1738.41, a decline of 22.6% – far worse than the fall of 13.2% on October 29 during the famous crash of 1929. In London, the Financial Times 100 share index was down 249.6 points to 2052.3, a fall of 10.6%, and the 30 share index fell 10.1%, down 183.7 to 1629.2; it was the worst day since the end of World War II. In Tokyo, the stock market fell by 14.9%.

The crash was attributed mainly to the large US trade deficit and to various new money-moving techniques (such as INDEX ARBITRAGE and PORTFOLIO INSURANCE) which destabilized the market.

blackwash *noun, informal* (in cricket) the winning of all the matches in a Test series by a West Indian team playing a white team

> On David Gower's tour to the Caribbean 18 months ago the West Indians completed their second successive 'blackwash,' winning all five Test matches by large margins.
>
> *Daily Telegraph* 31 Oct 1987

> After the 1984 blackwash by West Indies of David Gower's side here, the Palmer Committee was empowered to discover what was wrong with England cricket.
>
> *Daily Telegraph* 9 Aug 1988

► This meaning of *blackwash*, based punningly on *whitewash*, was coined in 1984 when the powerful West Indies side, with its battery of inexorable fast bowlers, beat England 5-0 in England, the margins of victory being an innings and 180 runs; 9 wickets; 8 wickets; an innings and 64 runs; and 172 runs. It was the first time England had lost all the games in a 5-match series in England, and it was only the fifth whitewash in Test-cricket history. One of the many exultant West Indies supporters in the crowd at the Oval during the final Test waved a banner proclaiming BLACK-WASH, and the coinage was enthusiastically picked up by the press.

Then in the tour of the West Indies in 1986 England provided the word with an opportunity to become even better established by sustaining another 5-0 defeat, if possible even more comprehensive than before; margins were 10 wickets; 7 wickets; an innings and 30 runs; 10 wickets; and 240 runs. No England batsman scored a century.

In 1988 England were again overwhelmed, but were saved from a blackwash by drawing one of the five Tests.

Although it has suddenly been invested with this new meaning, *blackwash* is not in fact a neologism. It originally meant a sort of poultice or lotion made from calomel and lime water, and from at least the middle of the 19th century it was used for a literal black version of whitewash, for colouring things black. Its first metaphorical application, referring to the blackening of someone's character, was not long to follow, as both noun and verb:

> A skilful counsel ... using as much whitewash as he can for the accused, and applying plentiful blackwash to the witnesses for the prosecution.
>
> *Chambers's Journal* 28 Apr 1877

blaxploitation *noun*   exploitive treatment of black people in films or publications, by emphasizing stereotypical characteristics calculated to bring commercial success

> His interpretation of hip-hop is unsubtle: placing Hurby at the centre in a blaxploitation shot, with the girls crawling up his legs, and dollars flying through the air.
>
> *City Limits* 18 Feb 1988

▶ A blend of *blacks* and *exploitation*, probably modelled on the popular blend *sexploitation*.

blow out *verb,   slang*   to cancel

> Rather than face further probing inquiries from representatives of the last word in white hot pop press, the Crue have blown out their European tour, which was due to start later this month.
>
> *New Musical Express* 16 Jan 1988

blush wine *noun* rosé wine

> Take Blush wines. Last summer every London wine bar and a
> great many shops and restaurants were doing a roaring trade in
> so-called blush wines. A year before the same places could hardly
> give such wine away, because in 1986 it was still called rosé – and
> rosé had been distinctly démodé since the Seventies.
> *Sunday Times Magazine* 27 Mar 1988

▶ The marketing ploy of renaming rosé wine 'blush' originated in California. Wine growers with a glut of red grapes
on their hands in a market moving towards white wine real-
ized that provided they could adjust its image, making them
into rosé wine would be an excellent way of shifting them.
The success of this move was not lost on growers in other
parts of the world, and soon blushes began appearing from
Australia, Germany, Italy, and France; but the quality of
many of them suggested that their name came not from
their colour but from the shamefacedness of their
producers.

bobbing and peering *noun* bending down and looking at
  the drivers of cars by prostitutes soliciting for business
  in the street

> They bob and peer and wiggle at the cars passing – 'bobbing and
> peering' has become police jargon for courtroom evidence of soli-
> citing.
> *Guardian* 13 Apr 1987

boffo *adjective,* *chiefly American informal* wonderful;
stupendous

> Governor Mecham is in a position to become rich and famous and,
> if he is only a little forbearing and plays his hand right, also per-
> haps a widely beloved figure in the land, a boffo regular on all the
> talk shows.
> *Newsweek* 8 Feb 1988

> Outside the wind is flinging wet clouds and snow across the scen-
> ery in an unseasonable April tantrum. It's a boffo show, but no one
> inside Virginia Tech's arts center pays any attention.
> *Roanoke Times and World-News* 11 Apr 1988

'Beetlejuice' opens next week trailing a bucketload of US critical praise and boffo box office.

Time Out 10 Aug 1988

▶ As the above extracts suggest, this word is usually used in show business contexts. Merriam-Webster's *12,000 Words* derives it from *boffola*, a 'belly-laugh,' which in turn comes from *boff*, a 'belly laugh,' 'gag,' 'hit,' perhaps based on '*box office*.'

bogusware *noun* computer software intended to damage the computer it is used with

> In a more humorous vein, computer folk also speak of 'liveware' when they mean the staff who keep computers running and of 'vapourware,' products announced at exhibitions but not yet ready for sale. What is definitely not so comic is something known as 'bogusware,' a transatlantic peril which is threatening to hit Britain.
>
> *New Scientist* 28 Jan 1988

▶ Bogusware is the general term for a whole range of usually malicious programs which have started to plague the computer world in recent years. Often disguised by their creators with legitimate software names, they commonly sell through electronic bulletin boards and mail systems. When inserted they create all kinds of havoc, typically by deleting essential data. See ELECTRONIC VIRUS, PHANTOM BUG, TROJAN HORSE; see also *logic bomb* (*Longman Guardian New Words*).

bolt-on *adjective* additional

> Getting a nasty shock when the invoice arrives because of bolt-on charges to the basic price is another source of misery. But help is at hand in the form of the new Consumer Protection Act, which comes into force in September and makes it illegal for any business to give a misleading indication about the price of the goods or services it sells.
>
> *Sunday Times* 3 July 1988

▶ The usage derives from additional mechanical parts which are bolted on to a basic mechanism.

bong *noun* a pipe for smoking marijuana

> During the raid ... 89 cells were investigated and 56 prisoners strip-searched. The team found four bongs ..., five pairs of scissors, a jailmade tattoo gun and a brewing kit.
>
> *Sydney Morning Herald* 13 Apr 1988

bonk¹ *verb, British informal* to copulate (with)

> Fiona, wife of the stuck-up toff Charles Seymour (Con.) has become so frustrated that she has been bonking the chairman of the neighbouring constituency's Conservative association. This goes down with Charles like a Labour landslide.
>
> *Daily Telegraph* 29 Oct 1986

> Thirty per cent of Alliance supporters have had no sexual partner in 12 months compared to 26 per cent of Labour, and the Tories are doing a lot better on 19 per cent. The Celtic fringe, Welsh Nationalists and chaps like that – ... twenty per cent of them have had two or more partners. ... They must be bonking away like mad.
>
> *Daily Telegraph* 21 May 1987

▶ The verb *bonk* seems to have been current for a few years now, but it leapt to notoriety in the summer of 1987, when the tabloid press used it prominently in its reports on the doings of the German tennis player Boris Becker:

> Much of the space in the Sun which hasn't been occupied recently by stories about 'Bonking' Boris's sex life has been devoted to attacking Everest Double Glazing, and the reason is simple enough.
>
> *Guardian* 1 July 1987

A number of bizarre theories have been advanced for its derivation, ranging from internal spasms experienced by cyclists to a northern and Scottish term for holding a glass of beer backhanded, but it seems most likely that it is merely a metaphorical extension of the word *bonk* meaning 'hit, tap' (as in 'bonk someone on the head'), probably on analogy with *bang*.

bonk² *noun, British informal* an act of copulating

> Our International No 1 Superseller of the year was about to be banned from one of the biggest export markets – all because of one

piffling sex scene. The problem was that the erotic event in question lasted for eight searing, startling, sizzling pages and cut that
bonk and confusion would follow.

Publishing News 13 Mar 1987

bonk journalism *noun, derogatory* journalism concerned
with obtaining and printing accounts of the supposed
sexual activities of well-known people

Bonk journalism is a cross between private investigation and porn.
The investigation needs to be, and usually is, thorough. Sur-
veillance equipment and hidden tape recorders are vital props of
the trade. The porn can either come through words or pictures.
The first six months of the year saw the X-rated versions of
Golding, Frank Bough, Mike Gatting, Major Ron Ferguson and
Mark Phillips.

Guardian 1 Aug 1988

boomflation *noun* inflation fuelled by a high level of consumer spending in an expanding economy

The problem, they say, is that the economy is growing faster than
even they predicted. Sir William Clark, chairman of the Tory
finance committee at Westminster, has coined a phrase for what
the Treasury believes is happening – he calls it 'boomflation.'

Sunday Times 28 Aug 1988

▶ *Boomflation* contrasts with *slumpflation* (a coinage of the
early 1970s), but the first of the *-flation* compounds seems to
have been *stagflation*, originally used by Iain Macleod in a
House of Commons speech in 1965.

booster buster *noun, informal* SBKKV (space-based kinetic
kill vehicle)

The sudden enthusiasm for the 'Booster Buster' springs from a test
last September in which two small rocket-powered satellites col-
lided in space.

Daily Telegraph 19 Jan 1987

boosterism *noun* commercially-minded hype

Self-deprecation and comic pessimism are as basic to the British as
'boosterism' is to the Americans or chauvinism to the French.

Daily Telegraph 17 Nov 1986

The Navajo, the largest Indian tribe in the United States, hope that a dose of free enterprise will restore their fortunes.... So far, most businessmen remain somewhat suspicious of the Navajos' sudden conversion to boosterism.

Economist 8 Aug 1987

boot sale *noun, British* a sale to which people bring unwanted items for sale; jumble sale

No doubt the proper modern artists who exhibit at the Academy look bad because they don't bother to put their best work into this boot sale of an exhibition.

Guardian 14 May 1988

▶ The full form, *car boot sale*, seems to have been in the language for some time, although there is no record of it in the *Supplement to the OED* 1972, but this abbreviation is more of a novelty. The institution itself is simply an adaptation of the traditional jumble sale to the age of the two-car family: any junk one wishes to get rid of is loaded into the boot of the car and driven down to the sale site to see if it will attract any takers.

bottom *noun, British* political solidity and dependability

Mrs Thatcher is said to be genuinely reluctant to see him leave her government. A former PPS to Mr Prior, Mr Fred Sylvester, the Conservative MP for Withington, said he would be a great loss. 'He is unique in the party. He has a certain amount of bottom which a lot don't have.'

Guardian 16 Aug 1984

Mr Beith is favoured by a majority of the Democrats' 19 MPs. He is considered to have more 'bottom' than Mr Ashdown: a word which loosely represents the traits of solidity, sober judgment and weightiness.

Economist 21 May 1988

▶ A word much in vogue amongst Conservative politicians in the mid-1980s as a term of approval. It implies a certain indefinable political gravitas and determination; someone with bottom can always be relied upon, although he or she may not (as in the case of James Prior) be entirely 'sound' ideologically.

bottom-line *verb* to state definitively what the final cost of (something) will be

For people to whom financial plainspeaking is the language of their labours, accountants can be remarkably reticent about their own charges. ... Accountants indulging in legerdemain? Not at all, says John Warne, secretary of the Institute of Chartered Accountants in England and Wales. 'You cannot bottom-line a job until it is time-costed.'

Daily Telegraph 3 Jan 1987

▶ The literal 'bottom line' is of course the final set of figures in a balance sheet or other financial statement, showing the net profit, cost, etc after all deductions or adjustments have been made. Its metaphorical possibilities have been thoroughly exploited in recent years, particularly in the sense of a 'sticking point, below which one will not go':

Our 'bottom-line' has always been to protect jobs and services in our boroughs. In London, with a good deal of help from the GLC, we should survive.

Guardian 21 June 1985

boutique¹ *adjective* involving small-scale specialization in business, aimed at excellence

Even so, larger houses, such as Barclays de Zoete Wedd Investment Management and Mercury Asset Management, aim to provide a comprehensive service under one roof. ... Stephen Zimmerman of Mercury aims to provide a boutique operation within the parameters of a larger business managing a total of nearly £22 million.

The Times 9 Sept 1987

Heitz's major competitor as a 'boutique' Cabernet [Sauvignon] producer is Ridge Winery, way down to the south of San Francisco.

Wine May 1987

boutique² *noun* a winemaking establishment, especially in the USA or Australia, which aims at producing small quantities of high-quality wine

Then there is the unusual ... Australian habit of cross blending wine from different areas ... While the smallest boutique winery will only make wine from its own grapes, the bigger boutiques, medium and large wineries will commonly truck grapes or wine hundreds ... of miles. ... Most leading Australian winemakers believe this practice is important to the overall finish of the wine, but there are many boutiques making excellent wines in their own right from just their own grapes.

Decanter Mar 1988

box *verb, informal* to present on television

Royalties from Evelyn Waugh's works in the couple of years after Brideshead was boxed brought about £20,000 to each of his six children.

Guardian 16 Mar 1985

brain-derived neurotrophic factor *noun* a protein essential to the formation of connections between nerve cells in the brain

A protein enabling cells in the brain to 'wire up' has been discovered which may explain the cause of dementia. The protein, dubbed brain-derived neurotrophic factor, was taken from the brain of pigs by Dr Yves Barde and Magdalene Hufer of the Max Planck Institute for Psychiatry in Munich, West Germany.

Daily Telegraph 11 Apr 1988

▶ If connections between certain sorts of brain cell are not maintained, they die. This seems to be the basis of degenerative diseases such as Alzheimer's and Parkinson's, so the isolation of brain-derived neurotrophic factor may be a crucial development in their treatment.

bratpack *noun* **1** a coterie of precociously successful and fashionable young performers, writers, etc

Bloomsbury's and London's current literary wonder is Candia McWilliam, whose first novel, 'A Case of Knives,' has made her both leader and sole member of the new British brat pack.

Observer Magazine 27 Mar 1988

At the moment there are two young American novelists. They are called the literary bratpack, or as we say in England, the pratpack, much like a six-pack only smaller.

Private Eye 19 Aug 1988

2 a group of annoyingly ill-disciplined (young) people

Funny that the back bench bratpack hasn't been sounding off about the reshowing of this, one of the most political British films of the decade, especially as it brings in the Falklands and was directed by that Tumbledown chappie Richard Eyre.

Guardian 25 June 1988

▶ The notion of the *bratpack* originated in Francis Ford Coppola's 1983 film *The Outsiders*, for which he hired a cast of unknown young actors to play the Oklahoma teenagers around whose troubled lives the story was based. All of them (they included Emilio Estevez, Rob Lowe, C Thomas Howell, Matt Dillon, Ralph Macchio, Patrick Swayze, and Tom Cruise) have since become stars. It was not long before the term spread more widely in the world of entertainment (see the quotation at BRAT-PACKER), but a split in usage seems to have occurred: alongside the original sense, which, while having disparaging connotations of uppishness, conceded an early-flowering talent, has come a reversion to the simply rowdy, ill-mannered brat of the type the tabloids loved to epitomize as John McEnroe.

brat-packer *noun* a member of the BRATPACK

Bratpacker Andrew McCarthy is the star of Mannequin.

Bridgwater Journal 7 Dec 1987

Temperamental brat-packers such as the Poison Penns – Madonna and her husband Sean Penn – John McEnroe and Tatum O'Neil should take note.

Daily Express 18 Mar 1988

brilliant *adjective* (of a weapons system) capable of extremely precise self-guidance to target individual enemy sites

Where the alliance may have some leverage ... is in seeking deep Soviet cuts in return for a Western agreement not to deploy the coming generation of 'brilliant' self-guided weapons capable of seeking out individual targets deep behind enemy lines.

Newsweek 14 Mar 1988

▶ The notion behind this choice of terminology is that these weapons' electronic guidance systems make them not merely 'smart,' like the previous generation of missiles, but positively 'brilliant.'

Britannia *noun*   a British gold coin, issued in four denominations: £100 (1oz); £50 (½oz); £25 (¼oz); and £10 (¹⁄₁₀oz)

▶ The Britannia was first issued in 1987. Minted in 22-carat gold, it is legal tender, but essentially it is a bullion coin, for investment rather than day-to-day financial transactions. As in the case of the Canadian 'Maple Leaf,' the American 'Eagle,' and the Australian 'Nugget,' its introduction was prompted by the banning of imports of the South African Krugerrand in May 1986.

The connection of Britannia with British coinage goes back as far as 1672, when she appeared on a copper halfpenny; but on the debit side, the reminder of 'Britannia metal,' a cheap alloy of tin, antimony, and copper, is perhaps unfortunate.

brown goods *noun*   *plural* electrical goods of a type traditionally housed in wooden cabinets, for example televisions, radios, and hi-fis

> Whoever bought Comet would need experience of selling white and brown goods and be prepared to take on a rival, Dixons.
> *Today* 23 Apr 1986

> Last weekend Amstrad showed its Spectrum Plus 3 micro with built-in 3in 173k disk drive ... at a 'brown goods' exhibition.
> *Guardian* 21 May 1987

▶ This is a trade term coined on the model of 'white goods,' items such as fridges and washing machines which are usually made in white. It recalls a time when televisions and radiograms came in resplendent mahogany cabinets, although many present-day members of the category, such as video-recorders, have never seen a whiff of veneer. Although basically a term for audio and video equipment, *brown goods* apparently also includes microwave ovens.

brown land *noun* disturbed land that has been used in the past for industrial or commercial purposes, especially as contrasted with green-field sites

> ... building on brown land such as disused gravel pits, former industrial sites, and railway embankments.
> *Thames News*, Thames TV, 9 June 1988

bubble *noun* a new television serial developed from an already existing one (typically a soap opera) and incorporating some of its characters

> *South* was the first spin-off [from *Brookside*] (did you know they call it a bubble now?).
> *Open Air*, BBC1, 21 Mar 1988

▶ The underlying thought behind the coinage is of a 'soap bubble'.

bubblegum *noun* something (a film, piece of pop music, etc) that appeals mainly to adolescents

> *Pretty in Pink* (Cannon) with wonderful soundtrack by Psychedelic Furs, stars Molly Ringwald and Jon Cryer who plays Duckie, the besotted childhood friend. It catalogues the life of Andie, a scholarship student at a rich kids' school. It's bubblegum but a lot of fun.
> *Cosmopolitan* May 1987

▶ The usage is of American origin, based apparently on children's predilection for bubblegum. It had its beginnings in the term *bubblegum music*, coined in the late 1960s.

bubble skirt *or* **bubble** *noun* a short skirt with a puffy, rounded outline

> It is also quite easy to make your own version of this winter's most popular party stunner, the bubble skirt, without being the most proficient of needle women.
> *Daily Telegraph* 1 Dec 1986

> DIY with Cosmo style! Be bright and bouncy in a bubble skirt. Change your watch strap to fit your mood. Focus on feet with a splash of colourful individuality.
> *Cosmopolitan* Mar 1987

The Bubble [is] usually achieved by doubling the fabric, sewing both edges into the waist band while giving the under layer a twist to bring fullness to the hem.

Daily Telegraph 16 Feb 1987

▶ The bubble skirt's globular effect is achieved either as described in the final extract above, or by having a tight elasticated hem which can be pushed up.

buddy¹ *noun* a volunteer who acts as a companion and helper to someone with AIDS, specifically one working under the auspices of the Terrence Higgins Trust

The Trust now has 350 volunteer workers, 150 of them 'buddies.' ... It assigns buddies – volunteers – to visit sick people on an individual basis.

Cosmopolitan Feb 1987

The Terrence Higgins Trust is in need of volunteers to work as 'buddies' for people with Aids, particularly in the West London area.

Observer 1 May 1988

buddy² *verb* to act as a buddy to

One controversial issue within the Trust is the buddying of PWAs [people with AIDS] whose contact with the illness has come from sharing the needles used for drug-taking.

Cosmopolitan May 1987

bufferism *noun* scornful intolerance of modern ways, typical of a reactionary old buffer

The pavilion at Lord's remains one of the strongholds of what one might term 'bufferism.' It is reflected in the judgements of today's cricketers: '... magnificent player, of course, but personally I wouldn't have him in the team, the man's a complete... .'

Daily Telegraph 28 Mar 1987

bull ring *noun, American* a circular stadium or arena

'I guess now I don't have to keep hearing from fans why I can't win on a short track,' a grinning Elliott said after scoring his first victory in 52 career starts on NASCAR's [stock car racing] bull rings.

Roanoke Times and World-News 11 Apr 1988

bummed out *adjective, American informal* disappointed, gloomy

> Guitarist Ray rises to defensive animation. 'You're talking about gloom, but that's not what we're about. Maybe it's easier to focus on sad things in the lyrics, but I don't want it to appear that we're all bummed out.'
> *New Musical Express* 15 Aug 1987

> 'I'm a little bummed out at the present time,' Calcavecchia said. 'I didn't expect him to make birdie. Under the circumstances he was closer to making bogey.'
> *Roanoke Times and World-News* 11 Apr 1988

▶ The adjective probably derives from the noun *bummer*, 'something disappointing.'

bump *verb* (of an airline) to exclude (a passenger with a booking) from an overbooked flight

> One such operator is Cyprus Turkish Airlines ... which, with its virtual monopoly of flights to and from the north of the island, regularly 'bumps' dozens of pre-booked passengers, simply telling them 'Come back tomorrow.' ... Last Tuesday, passengers who had bought their tickets months ago were 'bumped' after they had queued for three hours to check in.
> *Observer* 7 Aug 1988

buncing *noun, British* (in the retail trade) the practice of increasing prices to cover losses incurred through shop-lifting

> 'Buncing' ... was more deeply ingrained at Fine Fare than Dee realised, and has delayed the introduction of Gateway-style prices.
> *Daily Telegraph* 24 July 1987

▶ The word is presumably based on *bunce*, a slang term of some antiquity for 'a bit of extra profit gained on the side.'

buppie *noun* a black yuppie

> Things were better now, said a black Chicago yuppie ('buppie,' we were told, was the right word), but slow.
> *The Tablet* 26 Mar 1988

> It was Friday night at V's On Peachtree [in Atlanta, Georgia], one of the most popular bars for 'buppies.'
> *National Geographic* July 1988

buy-in *noun*   the purchase of a majority holding in a company by or on behalf of a group of outside executives who thereby take over the running of the company

Almost invariably management buy-ins originate out of the failure of an attempted management buy-out by a discontented group of executives – fed up because they had been given little or no share stake in their company and who passionately believe they could run it much more efficiently than the existing owners. Thus unemployed, the frustrated whizzkids must move fast and identify a similar sort of situation where they can apply their specialized business skills.

Daily Telegraph 30 Nov 1987

The principles behind buy-outs and buy-ins are identical.

Economist 11 June 1988

▶ The management buy-out, in which a consortium of executives buys control of its own company, typically in the face of a threatened takeover bid, is now fairly familiar (see *Longman Guardian New Words*). The buy-in, on the other hand, is a comparatively new phenomenon. Here, the executives move in on a new company, either financed by themselves or in many cases put in place by a merchant bank or other institution which has identified the company as being poorly managed.

buy into *verb,*   *Australian*   to become involved in

But I'm not going to buy into the consumption tax argument. I'm going to let Mr Howard and his colleagues sort it out, and I'm hopeful they will sort it out very quickly.

Sydney Morning Herald 13 Apr 1988

cable up *verb* to (cause to) become connected to a cable television system

In the States there are 44 million homes cabled up, which is why MTV, in spite of recent hiccups, is the number one advertising earner in cable.

Guardian 22 June 1987

call-and-recall *noun* a system of issuing reminders to ensure that people receive regular necessary medical check-ups, specifically smear tests for cervical cancer

And unless inadequate facilities to treat women are improved, this new attempt at an efficient call-and-recall system will do little to reduce the increasing number of sufferers: call-and-recall can only prevent cervical cancer if treatment is provided for those women who need it.

Sunday Times 20 Mar 1988

▶ The need for an effective system of regular monitoring for cervical cancer became highlighted in the 1980s, as an increasing number of cases were reported of women falling through the net. Screening was begun in Britain in 1964, but the system always suffered from lack of national coordination and inadequate follow-up, so that in a few cases women with abnormal smears were not treated. In 1988 a new nationwide computerized system was set up by which every woman between the ages of 20 and 64 is automatically sent a reminder every five years that it is time to go back for a fresh smear test.

can-do *adjective* willing to accept challenges and confident of meeting them; positive

Bud McFarlane picked up where his predecessor had left off, treating North like a son. McFarlane took him under his wing, bypassing a complicated chain of command. 'Bud is careful, circumspect,

and along comes can-do Ollie to fulfil his Walter Mitty fantasies,'
says one Capitol Hill insider.

Observer Magazine 26 July 1987

Slowly, and unevenly, a 'can-do' attitude is beginning to replace
the inertia bred of vested interests in local school districts and in
teacher unions.

Economist 31 Oct 1987

Neither man fits either the Olympian mould of the civil service
supposed to pre-date Mrs Thatcher, or the unthinking 'can-do'
mentality with which she is said to surround herself.

Economist 9 Apr 1988

▶ *Can-do* has been a key approval-word of the go-getting,
survival-of-the-fittest 1980s. People with can-do attitudes
are essential to the ENTERPRISE culture.

The word derives from the expression 'Can do!', an affirm-
ative reply to a request or order which has been in existence
since at least the beginning of this century.

canned hunt *noun, American* a big-game hunt within a
fenced area in which quarry is provided by the
organizers

Another operator, Jay Taylor, who runs Turkey Spring Exotics,
near Mason, central Texas, promises 'No kill, no pay' ... 'I'm not
ashamed of canned hunts,' says Taylor. 'They do the same thing in
Africa.'

Sunday Times 12 June 1988

capital flight *noun* the export of capital from a country to
which it has been lent for the purpose of developing that
country's economy

Foreign creditors are understandably loth to give fresh loans to
developing countries when so much then leaves in a false-
bottomed suitcase on the next flight to Zurich. But nobody is sure
how much does, because capital flight is an elusive concept disguised in unreliable balance-of-payments statistics.

Economist 3 Oct 1987

▶ A not insignificant contribution to the world debt crisis (see under RESCHEDULE) was made by capital flight. Instead of putting international loans to the use they were intended for, Third World politicians, businessmen, bankers, etc to whom they were entrusted salted them away in numbered accounts in Switzerland, Liechtenstein, and Florida. A notable and notorious culprit was Ferdinand Marcos of the Philippines. The problem was at its worst in 1982, when Nigeria, the Philippines, and eight Latin American debtor nations between them 'lost' $26 billion. Things have improved since then (in 1986 only Brazil, Ecuador, and the Philippines were still losing money in this way), but capital flight continues to be a problem.

carbuncle *noun, British* a building or other structure offensive to the sight; an architectural eyesore

> Local councillors and conservationists claim the projected design [for a golf museum] is a 'carbuncle,' an eyesore and more suited to a Third World airport.
>
> *Sunday Times* 28 Aug 1988

▶ This extended meaning of *carbuncle*, 'a large unsightly boil,' was popularized by the Prince of Wales's celebrated comment on the proposed new extension to the National Gallery, London, designed by Ahrends, Burton and Koralek. In a speech to the Royal Institute of British Architects on 30 May 1984, he called it 'a monstrous carbuncle on the face of a much-loved and elegant friend' (and also likened it to 'a vast municipal fire station'). Ironically, an earlier metaphorical application of the word, in its original sense of 'a large red precious stone,' was to something of great splendour: the medieval Scots poet Gavin Douglas, in his translation of the *Aeneid*, wrote of 'Thou peerless pearl, chosen carbuncle, chief flower.'

carcass trade *noun, British slang* the practice of cannibalizing the framework of old but dilapidated pieces of furniture so that they can be reconstructed with new veneer and passed off as genuine antiques

'What about the carcass trade ...?' he asked me enigmatically. 'That would surprise a lot of your readers. You see, anybody can fake a Queen Anne lowboy or a George I kneehole desk – and plenty of them do. Anybody can hide anything under a nice piece of veneer. What you can't fake are the insides or the back panels where there is no veneer.'

Guardian 16 Mar 1987

▶ *Carcass* is a cabinetmaker's term for the internal framework of a piece of furniture.

cardmember *noun* a holder of a credit card

The new American Express Optima card will complement, rather than replace, the existing green, gold and platinum cards. Green and gold 'cardmembers,' as American Express likes to call them, will pay $15 a year for it, but it will be free to those holding the top-of-the-line platinum card.

Globe and Mail (Toronto) 17 May 1988

▶ Compare GOLD CARD.

card swipe *noun* a machine which decodes the information contained in the magnetic strip on a credit or debit card passed through it

Each user has a terminal with digital display, keyboard and a 'card swipe' which takes Lloyds Cashpoint card and personal identity number (Pin).

Observer 10 Apr 1988

carer *noun* a person who looks after someone who is ill, elderly, or disabled, especially in the home

The main cost borne by most carers is that of lost earnings. Most women who find themselves looking after elderly relatives are in the second half of their working lives.

Economist 23 May 1986

'Who else would do a job 24 hours of the day? Doctors and nurses go home, but a carer doesn't, she stays put'.... We take a look at the importance of support groups for carers.

New Society 25 Mar 1988

Many carers feel guilty that they think of taking a break, even for a brief time. It is really important for the carer to relax for a few days, or even a few hours, away from the routine.

TV Times 23 Apr 1988

▶ The word *carer* goes back at least to the late 17th century, but this specialized sense has emerged only in the last decade. Partly, no doubt, the reason is that the number of such people – a grown-up daughter or son, say, looking after an aged and infirm parent – has increased, with the rising proportion of elderly people in the population (various estimates put the number of carers in Britain in the late 1980s at one to three million), but also public awareness of their existence and of the problems they face has become much sharper, sufficiently so to recognize them as a group within society meriting a term of their own to define them.

car toppable *adjective* capable of being carried on a car's roof rack

> Car toppable 10′ or 12′; easy to sail for fun or race 14′ or 15′; sheer exhilaration 18′ or 19′. [advertisement]
> **Yachts and Yachting** July 1988

▶ Compare OVENABLE.

cashless *adjective* involving financial transactions using credit or debit cards rather than cash

> Mercury hoped to have several boxes by the end of next year offering coin and credit card facilities. Eventually Mercury wants 'cashless boxes' to reduce vandalism.
> **Daily Telegraph** 1 Dec 1987

▶ Compare EFT/POS.

cash-limit *verb* to impose a cash limit on

> 'As with all our budgets, the fund from which we pay consultants for socially necessary operations is cash-limited,' the authority's general manager ... said yesterday.
> **Western Mail** 26 Jan 1988

cassette *noun* a package of genes from one species injected into a fertilized egg of another species – called also *construct*

The package of foreign DNA, called a cassette or construct, was composed of two parts: the rat-hormone gene, and a promoter to switch on the foreign gene.

Economist 30 Apr 1988

catastrophize *verb, American* to treat a trivial problem as if it were a major catastrophe

When it comes to dealing with daily obstacles, he says, 'we have a tendency toward catastrophizing and awfulizing.'

Newsweek 25 Apr 1988

cathart *verb* to relieve (feelings of anxiety or tension) by expressing them

It's hard to find a precedent for Hurt's quietly astonishing style, so natural and knowing. He hates the Method: 'We're not schizophrenics. You are not there to cathart personal angst in front of somebody.' He doesn't sell his personality, and he hasn't created an unmistakeable screen persona like a Jimmy Stewart or a Humphrey Bogart.

Company Mar 1987

▶ This curiously curt coinage, based on *cathartic*, at least has the merit of getting out of the usual humdrum *-ize* rut. *Catharsis* is a term in dramatic theory, relating to the expurgation of strong emotions by seeing them enacted on stage.

cathiodermie *noun* a facial cosmetic treatment in which a specially formulated gel is applied to the skin and an electric current is passed through it by means of roller electrodes

Basically, a cathiodermie deep cleanses and oxygenates the skin, boosting the circulation, banishing bacteria and encouraging new cell growth.

Cambridge Weekly News 11 June 1987

▶ The principle on which this treatment supposedly works is that the electric current reacts with the gel to form ozone, which cleans the skin. It was invented by the French cosmetologist René Guinot, who coined the term: hence the *-ie* termination, where in an English word one would have expected to find *-y*.

CDV *noun* COMPACT VIDEO DISC

ceramophobiac *noun*　a person who is afraid of crockery and other earthenware

> [The Portland vase] has never quite recovered from being 'dashed into atoms' by escaped lunatic William Lloyd in 1845, who had a fear of ceramics. ... When back on display the vase, bought from the Portland family in 1945, will be protected from any other 'ceramophobiacs' by a bullet-proof screen and a constant guard.
>
> *Daily Telegraph* 19 Mar 1988

▶ The re-formation of the combining form *-phobic* as *-phobiac* is not uncommon, especially in noun forms, although the OED does not record it. It mainly arises, of course, from association with the noun combining form *-phobia*, but it is probably influenced too by compounds ending in *-maniac*, such as *kleptomaniac*.

cerebellar syndrome *noun*　a set of symptoms (e g loss of muscle tone and muscular coordination, impaired speech, and involuntary spasmodic movement of the eyeball) indicating disease of the cerebellar hemisphere

> Glyn Worsnip received more than 1000 letters from well-wishers after sharing his feelings on radio about contracting cerebellar syndrome, a rare brain disease that affects both speech and movement.
>
> *Radio Times* 21 May 1988

▶ Cerebellar syndrome is a well-documented medical condition, but had not really impinged on public awareness until 1987, when television presenter Glyn Worsnip revealed that he was suffering from it. It is alternatively called Nonne's syndrome, after Max Nonne, a 19th-century German neurologist.

cervicography *noun*　the photographing of the cervix (neck of the womb) for diagnostic purposes

A more accurate method of screening for cervical cancer was launched at the Marie Stopes clinic in London yesterday. Cervicography can detect very early abnormalities which may be missed by existing screening methods.

Daily Telegraph 17 Feb 1988

The consultant in charge of the unit [at the Royal Northern Hospital, London] ... explains that the delays have been reduced by a new screening test at the hospital, cervicography, which uses a special camera to take a photograph of the cervix.

Sunday Times 20 Mar 1988

▶ Cervicography is used in conjunction with colposcopy for early identification of cervical cancer.

chain-chew *verb,* *American* to chew (gum) continuously, starting a new piece once the old piece is finished

In contrast to his brothers and many of his friends, he doesn't use drugs, drink or smoke – instead, he chain-chews peppermint gum – and has stayed out of trouble with the law.

New York Times Magazine 12 June 1988

chalkface *noun* the classroom as the teacher's place of work and as the place of interaction between teacher and pupils

School inspectors are set to return to the troubled London borough of Brent this week to see how the council's 'racial equality development' programme is actually working out at the chalkface.

Daily Telegraph 18 Jan 1988

▶ The term is modelled, with obvious reference, on *coalface*, which is used metaphorically for the place where the actual work in an industry or business is done.

champagne socialist *noun,* *derogatory* a person with an extravagant lifestyle at odds with his or her professed socialism

Mind you, I'm not complaining. Like a good champagne socialist, I've embraced the lexicon of capitalism with gusto. I can talk confidently about amortisation and discounted future cash flows without having a blind idea what they mean.

Listener 19 Nov 1987

▶ Compare RAMADA SOCIALISM.

champenize *or* **champenise** *verb* to make (still wine) into sparkling wine using the champagne method

The Vouvray AC regulations now allow still wine vinified within the appellation to be champenized elsewhere.

Decanter June 1988

▶ The distinctive feature of the champagne method is that the bubbles are created by a fermentation within the bottle (as opposed to the inferior *cuve close* method, in which fermentation takes place within the vat). This gives a finer, longer-lasting mousse.

chancy *adjective* happening by chance; fortuitous

Archaeologists have long known of beer's chancy discovery by the formerly teetotal Sumerians.

Daily Telegraph 25 Mar 1987

▶ *Chancy* standardly means 'risky,' of course, but may now be encroaching on the adjectival use of *chance* ('chance discovery' is a common collocation).

chaologist *noun* an expert in or advocate of CHAOLOGY

Hurricanes, share price crashes, heart attacks, any of the unforeseen catastrophes usually referred to as acts of God are fair game nowadays for a new, mainly American, breed of troubleshooters, the chaologists.

Sunday Times 3 July 1988

chaology *noun* the scientific study of CHAOS theory

'The rare scholars who are nomads by choice are essential to the intellectual welfare of the settled discipline,' one of chaology's pioneers, Benoit Mandelbrot, remarks rather sniffily.

Sunday Times 3 July 1988

chaos *noun* (in physics) the irregular and unpredictable behaviour displayed by dynamic systems

Because this new discipline of chaos is essentially about properties of mathematical equations and algorithms which can apply ... across the entire range of subjects, it has fostered an extremely interdisciplined clientele anxious to trade problems and methods of solution.

New Scientist 26 May 1988

What the theorists of chaos maintain is that three central tenets of scientific faith are, quite simply, wrong. These are the propositions: simple systems behave in simple ways; complex behaviour implies complex causes; and different systems behave differently. Not true, say the chaos boys, who have found that the simplest of dynamical systems are capable of exceedingly complex and unpredictable behaviour.

Observer 29 May 1988

▶ The chaos theory has developed over the last decade, challenging the basic assumption of Newtonian physics that the universe is ordered according to a set of mathematical rules, all of which are in theory discoverable.

chapess *noun, British informàl* a woman

And remember: the most important thing to do when you arrive at the hospital is to turn back for just a few seconds and give those chaps and chapesses a wave.

Observer 7 Aug 1988

▶ This facetious formation has almost certainly been in existence for some time, but it has not hitherto been recorded in the dictionaries of English.

chartist *noun* 1 a person who studies price trends on the stock market and makes forecasts based on them

Share buyers gained in confidence yesterday, with takeover fever fuelling speculative activity. Chartists were heartened by the psychologically important breakthrough of the 1800-level in the FTSE 100 Share Index, which finished the session an impressive 26.8 higher at 1808.7.

Daily Telegraph 3 Mar 1988

In the City, 'chartists' no longer campaign for political reform and attack the oligarchy, but read the entrails of past performance with as much skill as astrologers scry the planets.

Times Literary Supplement 8 Apr 1988

According to one chartist, the ST index is close to breaching the 200-day moving average.

Business Times [Malaysia] 3 June 1988

▶ The name comes from the plotting of share-price move-ments on charts, apparently a favourite technique used by these financial diviners.

2 a person or group whose record gets into the list of best-sellers

The sessions recorded specially for her Sunday night radio show range from soulboys Terry D'Arby and Well Red to independent chartists Jack Rubies and The Brilliant Corners.

New Musical Express 15 Aug 1987

chateau-bottled socialist *noun* CHAMPAGNE SOCIALIST

This last phrase does not suggest scorn at the fact that a socialist might enjoy the odd visit to the theatre, whereas 'chateau-bottled socialist' and other papers' unprompted references to the drinking habits of some of our better known anti-Thatcherites are designed to remind readers that the word of a left-winger cannot be trusted unless ... they have pledged themselves to a life of abstention.

London Evening Standard 16 Aug 1988

chatline *noun* a telephone service offering the facility of joining in a general conversation with other callers

British Telecom has suspended its Talkabout chatline service rather than accept restrictions to curb abuses.

Independent 23 Feb 1988

Curbs on 'soft porn' recorded phone messages and a ban on chat-line services are sought in moves announced yesterday by Prof Bryan Carlsberg, director general of Oftel.

Daily Telegraph 20 July 1988

▶ The British Telecom service mentioned in the first ex-tract, Talkabout, was originally launched in Bristol in 1983, and its benefits were soon available to the whole country. It came in for a large amount of criticism, not least because many youngsters were using it so heavily that they ran up phone bills of thousands of pounds on their parents' acc-ount. A further cause for disquiet was the prospect of the service being used, despite the presence of a moderator with the power to cut off a caller, as an unofficial dating agency which could be abused by undesirables: three 15-year-old girls, for example, were lured into an assignation with a 50-year-old man who forced them to watch pornographic films.

chemical laser *noun* a device that generates a high-energy beam of infrared light by means of a chemical reaction

> The weapon is a chemical laser, one of the best-developed options available for star-wars defence systems.
>
> *New Scientist* 14 Jan 1988

▶ Chemical lasers work by causing a reaction between atoms of fluorine and hydrogen, which produces hydrogen fluoride compounds that give off energy in the form of infrared light. As the above extract suggests, they are being developed in the role of beam weapons as part of SDI.

cherry pick *verb, informal* to cream off the choicest items

> BT chiefs believe that Mercury is 'cherry picking' by going for high volume, high margin business and that it cannot yet compete on all fronts.
>
> *Campaign* 6 May 1988

▶ The metaphor of 'cherries' as the most desirable elements of something may be a reminiscence of the 'bowl of cherries' which life is proverbially not.

Chiantishire *noun, humorous* Tuscany, Italy, as noted in the 1980s for its large number of second homes owned by Britons

> The British are coming, flooding into Pisa airport, known as Pizza to the BA hostesses. They're invading Tuscany, part of Italy which has become part of England, so that it's known as Chiantishire to the natives.
>
> *Mortimer in Tuscany*, BBC 2, 17 May 1988

▶ Tuscany has long been a favourite stamping ground for the Brits, from tourists staring their way around Florence to more literary denizens such as D H Lawrence and E M Forster. In the 1980s, however, there has been a growing vogue among the British moneyed classes for buying up

Tuscan farmhouses either as summer homes to holiday in or rent out, or as more or less permanent residences. The increasing availability of Earl Grey in the local groceries acts as a barometer of the infiltration. The wine Chianti is made in Tuscany.

chicken *noun,* *slang* a young inexperienced male prostitute

> One of these [experienced male prostitutes] is Nick, now 31, who first came on the central London scene 14 years ago. He explains: 'The chickens ... these days are much wiser. They don't hang around Euston Station, they come straight to the places they have read about where they know they can do business.'
>
> *Guardian* 13 May 1988

chicken-dancing *noun* a type of dancing to pop music in which participants raise and lower their arms bent-elbowed, as if flapping wings

> There's none of the macho chicken-dancing and 'Show us your tits' shit at their concerts that even The Shop Assistants had before the departure of Alex Taylor.
>
> *New Musical Express* 15 Aug 1987

▶ Chicken-dancing is a hazardous pastime: devotees often find that they get an elbow in the eye from the dancer next to them.

chiddler *noun* a young child

> If you're going to grab these chiddlers before they switch on the television, you have to give them very strong medicine; they're half-civilised little buggers and they have very strong feelings and they see things in very strong colours. ... What the chiddlers love is when you go overboard.
>
> *Daily Telegraph* 30 Apr 1988

▶ The word is a coinage of Roald Dahl's, who in the above extract summarizes his philosophy of writing for children. It is presumably a blend of *child* and *tiddler*.

Chinese restaurant syndrome *noun* a set of symptoms (e g dizziness, nausea, heart palpitations) associated with excessive intake of monosodium glutamate

But what about Dr Kwok's Chinese restaurant syndrome? He it was who proved that a surfeit of MSG can give rise to symptoms ranging from dizziness and nausea to heart palpitations and pain in the neck.

Listener 24 Apr 1986

▶ The name chosen for the syndrome refers to the high amounts of MSG typically used in Chinese restaurant cooking.

chocoholic *noun, informal* a person with a compulsive desire to eat chocolate

I fell to wondering why chocolate is such compulsive stuff that those who love it have earned the unlovely nickname of 'chocoholics.'

Daily Telegraph 26 Mar 1988

Studley Priory is laying on a Chocoholics Weekend in October – with chocolates of all shapes, colours and sizes for breakfast, dinner and tea.

Oxford Star 28 July 1988

▶ Of all the various humorous *-aholic, -oholic* compounds formed in the past few years (see -AHOLIC), *chocoholic* must be by far the commonest, reflecting the peculiarly addictive nature of chocolate. See also WORKAHOLICISM.

Christmas tree *noun, American* a congressional bill to which various extraneous clauses are added, typically near the end of a session in order to facilitate their passage

If the Republican-controlled Senate were to produce a bill that preserved everyone's loopholes, the Democrats would undoubtedly try to exploit it as an election issue; on the other hand, the Democrats would be similarly vulnerable to charges that the House tax bill was a Christmas tree.

Economist 24 May 1986

▶ When insufficient time for debate looks set to defeat a bill in the US Congress, the practice has grown up of attaching it to another bill, which may well have nothing to do with it but which is certain to go through, in order that the legislation shall not be lost. The resulting hybrid bill may well be said to resemble a Christmas tree, hung with stray clauses like so many candles, glass balls, and presents. The procedure itself is termed *Christmas treeing*:

> Mid-term elections loom and it is still uncertain that a federal repeal bill can be passed by Congress this year. Various plans are being considered. One possibility is 'Christmas treeing.'
>
> *Economist* 2 Aug 1986

chronemics *noun* the linguistic study of the timing of turn-taking and pausing in conversations

> If you want to know more about the arcana of ... chronemics..., then he will point you in the right direction.
>
> *Daily Telegraph* 25 Apr 1988

churn *verb* to engage in excessive buying and selling of (shares, etc) so that large commission fees are payable to agents or brokers

> Consultants are also guilty of drawing attention to short-term performance, as are commission-hungry stockbrokers, driving clients to 'churn' their portfolios.
>
> *The Times* 9 Oct 1987

circuit-breaking *noun* the imposition of artificial limits on the extent to which share prices may rise or fall on a particular day

> The report produced in the US by the presidential commission appointed to investigate the [stock market] crash suggested circuit-breaking.
>
> *Business* Mar 1988

city technology college *noun* *(abbreviation* **CTC***)* (in Britain) a form of secondary school providing a science-based education in inner-city areas

City Technology Colleges represent an attempt – last tried in 1944 – to give technical education a bit of chic.

Economist 18 Oct 1986

City Technology Colleges ... will be free and financed jointly by the Government and private industry.

Daily Telegraph 21 Nov 1987

▶ The city technology college is one of a package of educational reforms put forward by the Conservative government in the late 1980s (see GRANT-MAINTAINED SCHOOL). The first, Kingshurst School, opened in Solihull in September 1988.

civil society *noun* the grassroots pressure groups of Eastern Europe which oppose monopolistic state power

'The question now is how can civil society influence decision making,' says Ferenc Koszeg, the editor of a samizdat journal. Activists have even found support for their demands within the Hungarian Communist Party.

Newsweek 18 Apr 1988

▶ The term *civil society* has a considerable pedigree in political theory, with successive ages adapting it to their own conditions. The Roman writer Cicero used it (*societas civilis*), and the first reference to it in English is by the theologian Richard Hooker in his *Laws of Ecclesiastical Polity* 1594: 'Ciuill Society doth more content the nature of man then any private kind of solitary living.' Here, of course, it simply means living in a community, rather than solitarily. Locke and Rousseau used it, and Hegel (*bürgerliche Gesellschaft*) paved the way for its introduction into Marxian philosophy. The key text for its recent use in Eastern Europe, in the context of Mikhail Gorbachev's PERESTROIKA, is a contribution by the Soviet theorist Fedor Burlatsky to the July 1988 issue of *Marxism Today*. At the heart of this usage is the notion of consciousness raising: the creation of a society that is politically aware rather than just existing passively beneath the state's yoke, and so will press for reforms in areas such as religious freedom, environmental protection, and of course civil rights.

clocker *noun* a person who engages in CLOCKING

> While an official working party has been set up by the Office of Fair Trading to consider fraudulent 'clocking' of car mileage recorders, the RAC is offering its own 'beat the clockers' service to short circuit the cheats.
>
> *Daily Telegraph* 6 Apr 1988

clock gene *noun* a gene responsible for determining the nature of an organism's 'biological clock,' the timing mechanism for various cyclical biological processes

> Researchers at Brandeis University in the United States have identified a 'clock gene,' part of the fruit fly's genetic blueprint responsible for regulating its biological rhythm.
>
> *Daily Telegraph* 17 Nov 1986

clocking *noun* the fraudulent turning back of a vehicle's odometer so that the vehicle appears to have travelled a smaller distance than it really has

> A Bill to stamp out 'clocking' ... is being prepared by the Motor Agents Association.
>
> *Daily Telegraph* 28 Oct 1987

▶ This notorious ploy of second-hand car dealers gets its name from the 'clock,' a term used colloquially for 'mileometer' since at least the mid-1960s.

clogs *noun plural* – **pop one's clogs** *British informal* to die

> It was the breathalyser that brought on the rush of 'pub grub' signs. A national institution was about to pop its clogs if landlords didn't find a solution.
>
> *Wine* June 1988

▶ *Pop* is 'pawn,' as in 'pop goes the weasel': thus, when one expires, and has no further use for one's clogs, they are pawned.

clubbite *noun, chiefly West Indian* a club member

> When the youth club was formed three years ago, the members used to be involved in many activities which included indoor

games and table tennis. Migration took its toll on the club as some clubbites went abroad and some went to Kingston and to other parishes where the grass was greener.

Gleaner (Jamaica) 7 June 1988

▶ Thackeray in the mid 19th century used *clubbist* ('Among the youthful Clubbists is the Lady-killing Snob,' *Book of Snobs*), but *clubbite* seems to be a new coinage.

cluster suicide *noun*   one of a large number of suicides over a short period in the same area, with one triggering off another

In a dramatic suicide on Wednesday morning, four local teenagers locked themselves in a garage, climbed into a car and switched on the engine. ... Although 'cluster suicides' are common in the United States ... a suicide pact such as this one, among four teenagers, is rare.

Guardian 14 Mar 1987

coconut *or* **coconut head** *noun,   derogatory slang*   a black person who adopts white cultural characteristics

There is a real concern among the majority of the black community ... to observe the trend of 'black' individuals, who are known in some circles as the 'coconut heads,' attempts at polarising the black self-help movement in general, in their misguided efforts to bring to bear eurocentric leadership ... to the black community. ... Many of the 'coconut heads' are found among the newly appointed 'black' skin individuals by certain central and local government departments ... among white-managed local and national voluntary organisations.

Asian Times 27 May 1988

Mrs Boateng, former member of Lambeth council's social services committee, has been barred from Brent's Black Section for two years after being branded a 'coconut.' ... She has been 'suspended' for 'gross disrespect for the black community' and for being 'abusive and disruptive' at a section meeting.

Daily Telegraph 25 June 1988

▶ The metaphor is based on the coconut's brown exterior and white interior.

Colbertism *noun* (in France) economic policy characterized by state interventionism and centralized direction

In the [French] economy, Colbertism ..., a busy state hand on the
economy, vigorous support for the nuclear industry and modern
engineering projects, for regional planning and for export subsidies. Weak private industry made a feeble counterweight to
Treasury officials' or planners' powers.

Economist 12 Mar 1988

▶ Jean-Baptiste Colbert (1619-83) was one of the leading
reformers in French economic history. As Louis XIV's
comptroller general of finance he placed much of French
taxation, tariffs, and financial administration on a new footing, strengthening the role of government in the economy.

cold-calling *noun* the practice of making unsolicited phone
calls or home visits to try to sell products or services,
especially financial services or investment packages

The draft rules published yesterday prohibit cold calling for investment purposes – except where the recipient is an investment
professional. However, life assurance and unit trust salesmen will
still be allowed to make unsolicited calls.

Guardian 27 Mar 1986

The contentious issue of cold-calling (uninvited attempts at selling
in your home) has been solved by banning it for all but life
assurance and unit trust sales.

Daily Mail 17 Sept 1986

'Cold-calling' of unit trusts will regrettably be permitted from 1
July, although this new measure is not viewed with much enthusiasm by any but the somewhat insurance-driven unit trust groups.

Observer 8 May 1988

▶ The term is American in origin.

cold surgery *noun* preplanned surgical operations to treat
chronic conditions (as opposed to acute surgery to treat
emergencies)

I think cold surgery ... which accounts for 20 per cent of the market,
should be separated from acute.

Business Mar 1988

▶ The metaphor is presumably derived from such phrases as 'in cold blood,' meaning 'with premeditation,' although paradoxically 'cold' is also used for 'without preparation or rehearsal,' as in 'I had to recite the entire speech cold.'

colour-blind *adjective* making no distinctions on grounds of skin colour or ethnic origin

> Influx control should be replaced by a colour-blind 'strategy for orderly urbanisation' in which a specially created urbanisation board would play a key role. The committee further recommended that all South Africans should carry uniform identity documents.
>
> *Guardian* 13 Sept 1985

> Hutt ceaselessly taught that the best way to raise the economic and social status of minorities was through the competitive market which was 'colour blind'.
>
> *Daily Telegraph* 25 June 1988

comedogenic *adjective* tending to form blackheads

> Myosphere [skin preparation] from RoC: the woman who lives for today; without forgetting tomorrow. Tested non comedogenic. Made in France. [advert]
>
> *Options* Apr 1988

> Its fresh water-based formula is like second nature to your skin. And as always, it's non-comedogenic. [advert]
>
> *Sassy* June 1988

▶ *Comedo* is a medical term for 'blackhead' introduced in the 1860s. Its etymology is not for the squeamish: Latin *comedo* means 'corpse-devouring worm,' which supposedly bears a resemblance to the matter extruded when a pimple is squeezed.

come from *verb, chiefly American* to have as (the background to) one's particular concern, intention, or meaning

> Oliver North is history banging its head against the wall. But understand where he's coming from: he feels like he's a character in a military Horatio Alger story, who goes from athletic mediocrity to naval academy boxing champ, from basic wimp to war hero with a Silver Star and two Purple Hearts.
>
> *Observer Magazine* 26 July 1987

▶ In current American English, to know where someone is coming from has come virtually to mean simply 'know what someone means,' although the above extract retains elements of the expression's origins in an awareness of what lies behind a person's statements or actions. There are signs that it may be gaining some currency in British English.

commit *verb, American* to make a commitment

> Wharton Real Estate, a smaller Old Town Brokerage Firm for over 35 years, is seeking one or two additional sales associates. We will commit to your success.
>
> *Port Alexandria Gazette Packet* 15 Apr 1988

▶ This use of *commit* without an object is a new development. American English permits far more freedom than British English in the conversion of transitive to intransitive verbs, and vice versa.

commodification *noun* the treatment of money as an article to be traded and speculated in

> For the past five years banking talk has been dominated by three ghastly -ations: globalisation, securitisation and commodification. These trends – of a worldwide market, of borrowers shifting from loans to securities, of money becoming more like a commodity – have indeed been strong.
>
> *Economist* 26 Mar 1988

> Nick Rowling's informative and readable essay [*Commodities*] has suffered a bit of commodification itself at the rather exorbitant price of £9.95.
>
> *Listener* 14 Jan 1988

▶ For *securitization*, 'the practice of making debts marketable', see *Longman Guardian New Words*.

comms *noun, informal* communications

> The Metropolitan Police has issued contracts to Datacom Systems and Husky Computers for new comms equipment to support an improved car clamping and vehicle removal scheme.
>
> *Computer Weekly* 10 Mar 1988

community politics *noun* a concept of political activity in which a party focusses attention heavily on local issues within a given area

The sole SDP councillor, Mr Mick Wilkes, who won in Hall Green two years ago, was a newcomer to politics in 1981. He now preaches and practises the Liberal gospel of community politics with its grass-roots organization and local grievances, focus leaflets and mini-newspapers.

Financial Times 6 May 1986

▶ The notion of community politics has played a key role in the Liberal party's electoral strategy over the past 20 years. Squeezed out of the national picture, it has seen local government as an area in which by carefully targeted effort it can begin to rebuild a power base. Liberal activists home in on issues like local bus services and the provision of lollipop ladies and pursue them relentlessly and conspicuously (critics would say overpoliticizing them in the process). This vigorous campaigning brings victory in local elections and also (or so the theory goes) makes people more inclined to vote Liberal nationally. The first part of the equation has yielded undoubted electoral successes (notably in Liverpool), but the second remains unproven.

compactor *noun* a mechanical device which squashes refuse into a solid easily disposable mass

Compactors have a magic way with rubbish, squashing bottles, cans, cartons, and the like into a quarter of their original size.

Taste May 1986

Hard-line free traders say such measures would prompt a damaging trade war. To them, the bill has become the legislative equivalent of a trash compactor: a bunch of garbage was thrown in, and out came a smaller, tightly wrapped package of the same stuff.

Newsweek 2 May 1988

▶ After waste-disposal units come compactors. Traditionally thought of as spectacular crushers of unwanted cars, they have now moved into the home. You can have them installed as a unit under a worktop, and you simply throw your rubbish into a strengthened bin where it is decisively compressed by a plunger with a force of 2.5 tonnes.

compact video disc *noun* *(abbreviation* **CDV**) a compact laser disc which plays both pictures and sound

Compact video discs, or CDVs, are just starting to appear in the shops. Compared with video cassettes, they have better sound, last longer, give easier and faster access to the section you want, and have better freeze-frame. You can't, however, record onto or from them.

Good Housekeeping Mar 1988

▶ The basic technology of the CDV is similar to that of the audio or sound CD (called CDS to distinguish it). They look the same, but CDVs are usually coloured gold, whereas CDSs are silver. Initially they are being made in three sizes, which contain respectively 6, 20, and 60 minutes of audio-visual material on each side.

company doctor *noun* a consultant called in to analyse the management and financial affairs of an ailing company and restore it to success

In the City he is known as the company doctor supreme. (He hates the title 'company doctor,' preferring instead to be known as a 'financial engineer.') Aitken specialises in saving companies, lots of them.

Business Mar 1988

comparative advertising *noun* advertising in which one's competitors' products are explicitly mentioned and overt comparisons made with one's own

The rules on knocking copy – 'comparative advertising' as it is known – are unambiguous. The IBA Code decrees that commercials 'should not unfairly attack or discredit other products, advertisers or advertisements directly or by implication' and that 'points of comparison should be based on facts which can be substantiated.'

Daily Telegraph 26 Apr 1988

compassion fatigue *noun* growing reluctance to continue making donations to (a) charity, as prolonged exposure to the object of the charity leads to indifference

What the refugee workers call 'compassion fatigue' has set in. Back in the 1970s, when the boat people were on the front page, the world was eager to help. But now the boat people are old news.

Listener 29 Oct 1987

competitor analysis *noun*　the finding out of information about the financial and other affairs of competitor companies

Company sleuths have their own secret: almost all the data they are asked to find are public. 'Corporations, by the very nature of doing business, are open books,' says Liam Fahey, who teaches competitor analysis at Boston University. 'It's just a matter of knowing what book to look for.'

Newsweek 2 May 1988

▶ As the above extract suggests, competitor analysts are very anxious to distance themselves from any taint of industrial espionage by pointing out that the information they discover is in the public domain, although perhaps a cynic might suspect that they protest too much.

competitor analyst *noun*　an exponent of COMPETITOR ANALYSIS

They prefer to be called 'competitor analysts.' But whatever the euphemism, a growing number of professionals are taking corporate sleuthing out of the back alley and into the boardroom.

Newsweek 2 May 1988

compliance *noun*　acting in accordance with the terms of the Financial Services Act 1986

An army of law enforcers and corporate compliance officers is forming up. The [Financial Services] Act requires that each investment organisation appoint a member of staff whose sole responsibility is compliance. The Securities Association aims to have 75 people reporting to a sternly-titled Director of Enforcement, and firms are installing compliance teams ranging from two to more than 20 people.

Business Mar 1988

Chapman immediately alerted his senior colleagues in Morgan Grenfell and brought in Nick Tatman, the compliance officer, to investigate. It is the compliance officer who has the responsibility to ensure that staff conduct their private and professional dealings according to house rules.

Sunday Times 21 Aug 1988

▶ The 1986 Financial Services Act introduced a vast book of rules governing the activities of investment companies, under the general oversight of the Securities and Investments Board. It covers such areas as compulsory segregation of client money, the banning of COLD CALLING, and the provision of investor complaints procedures. The essence of these rules (bankers, investment managers, etc being upright citizens) is that they should be self-policing. Hence the talk of 'compliance,' provision for which could well in due course force up the rates charged to customers by firms selling financial services.

computer fiction *noun* INTERACTIVE FICTION

For several years software writers have been producing works of 'interactive fiction,' which are read on computers. ... Critics sniff that these are overgrown computer games, but the genre is now attracting serious attention: the first university course on writing computer fiction started this semester at Carnegie Mellon.

Newsweek 25 Apr 1988

condom *noun* 1 a sheathlike contraceptive device made of thin rubber

A British-made condom for women, claimed to be the only device designed for use by women to protect against pregnancy and sexually-transmitted diseases, was unveiled in London yesterday.

Daily Telegraph 21 Apr 1988

A condom for women shifts the responsibility for birth control back to the girls. ... That's why gynaecologist John Guillebaud describes the female condom as 'a good alternative'.

Herts & Essex Observer 19 Aug 1988

▶ The condom has over the centuries been strictly a male preserve, but in these days of sexual equality women are getting one too. The new female contraceptive, similar in material and in general contour to the penile sheath, will cover the vaginal walls as well as the cervix, thus giving protection against AIDS and other sexually-transmitted diseases.

2 any flexible protective covering

> Ceretech showed a range of replacement keyboards at between £155 and £1,175, but to save the need of getting replacements it sold for £20 a 'keyboard condom,' a soft plastic cover that lets you use the board, but keeps dust and coffee out of its innards.
>
> *Daily Telegraph* 6 July 1987

▶ *Condom* is by no means a new word, of course (it has been around since at least the beginning of the 18th century), but the pronunciation which has recently become attached to it makes it sound like one. Up until the late 1980s it has existed inconspicuously enough, being pronounced /ˈkɒndəm/ whenever the need to utter it arose – that is, to sound rather like *kingdom*, with the reduced vowel in the unstressed syllable which one might reasonably expect in a well-established word. Now, however, the spread of AIDS has brought *condom* to the lips of newsreaders and other media folk, and they have reacted as if it were an outlandish neologism, with each vowel to be gingerly given its full force – /ˈkɒndɒm/.

condomania *noun, informal* excessive and widespread interest in or obsession with condoms

> Condomania did hit the TV screens, but for one week only. Some programmes were good, some were appalling, but at least most of us got the drift.
>
> *New Statesman* 19 Feb 1988

▶ The cause of the mania in the late 1980s was of course AIDS, which produced a range of publicity, more or less explicit, recommending the use of condoms to avoid contracting the disease, and no doubt did a lot of good to the condom manufacturers' sales.

condom fatigue *noun, informal* severe diminution in one's interest in condoms, due to excessive exposure to information or discussion on the subject (e g during official publicity campaigns about AIDS)

What was needed at that point to stop us drifting off into condom fatigue were follow-up programmes and ads, with explicit information about safe sex, targeted at a wide range of specific groups.
New Statesman 19 Feb 1988

▶ The immediate model for this facetious formation was probably COMPASSION FATIGUE, based metaphorically in its turn on items such as *battle fatigue*. It should be noted that the underlying syntactic-semantic structure of the compound *condom fatigue* is not the same as that of *metal fatigue*.

condommed *adjective*　wearing a condom

Maybe I'm limiting my experience. Fine. Sex with Tories, condommed or not, is an experience I can do without.
Cosmopolitan July 1987

conductive education *noun*　a form of therapy for children with gravely impaired motor coordination, in which they are encouraged repeatedly to attempt actions such as walking and dressing until they are able to do them

No one claims miracles for 'conductive education'. ... Crucially, the Hungarian philosophy raises expectations and inspires hope in contrast to the passive and ultimately dispiriting, though often caring, approach in many British centres.
Daily Telegraph 28 Oct 1987

▶ Conductive education was the brainchild of Dr Andreas Peto, and the chief centre of its practice is the Peto Institute for Motor Disordered Children in Budapest. It works on the principle of challenging children to perform tasks which their muscles are unable to do, so that in attempting them their bodies gradually learn the skills of sitting, standing, walking, dressing, self-feeding, etc – 'orthofunction,' as proponents of conductive education call them. It originated over 40 years ago, but has never caught on to any extent in Britain; recently, however, there have been increasing calls for its introduction, with lobbying groups such as Rapid Action for Conductive Education (RACE) being set up.

confrontive *adjective* challengingly direct or frank

> Most of his [Robert Mapplethorpe's] affectionate or confrontive
> portraits of gay men, amongst the most memorable of his pictures,
> have also been left out. The results are impressive but not exciting.
> *Time Out* 4 May 1988

connectionism *noun* a theory of memory which proposes
that memories of a given experience, word, etc are distributed throughout the brain in several 'processing
units,' and that it is by the activation of neural connections between these units that the brain functions

> A philosopher visiting the world of computers is held to be interfer-
> ing in someone else's internal affairs. A solution to this clash of
> cultures may be provided by a new method of computing called
> 'connectionism,' which uses 'neural nets' to mimic the behaviour
> of the brain. These computer complexes are not programmed so
> much as taught.
> *Listener* 25 Feb 1988

▶ Connectionism represents the major development area
of the cognitive sciences in the 1980s, and as the above extract suggests it has been greedily seized on by computer
scientists to provide models for the new generation of computers. Its crucial benefit is that it contains the notion of
learning: standard computer programs simply give a set of
explicit instructions, but a connectionist model can be given
a general set of data from which through use – including the
making of mistakes – it can extrapolate rules for itself. The
way in which it does this is by exploring and refining the
various possible connections between the processing units.
See also NEURAL NETWORK.

connectionist *noun* an advocate of CONNECTIONISM

> Connectionists sometimes claim that their networks are closer to
> the 'hardware' of the brain. Its cells respond slowly, fatigue rapid-
> ly, and often die. Yet mental life continues apparently unaffected,
> with a grace under pressure that is mirrored by parallel networks.
> P N Johnson-Laird, *The Computer and the Mind* 1988

connectivity *noun* the ability to intercommunicate between computers or computer systems of different types

The latest buzzword on the tip of every corporate tongue is 'connectivity'.

Which Computer? Nov 1986

Someday soon, such standard [software communications] protocols will enable a customer to plug almost anybody's computer into a network that will enable it to swap data with anybody else's. Demand for such 'connectivity' is already too strong for computer companies to ignore.

Economist 16 Jan 1988

conscience investment *noun* an approach to stock exchange investment in which shares are bought only in companies which satisfy certain ethical standards (for example in not having discriminatory employment policies, not carrying out research on animals, not trading with countries with repressive regimes, not manufacturing armaments)

For those whose millions are a millstone around the neck comes a new Yuppie buzzphrase to take the guilt out of greed – conscience investment. Advisers who build investment portfolios not on the basis of how much you'll make, but on how you can live with yourself when you get the cheque, are reporting an upsurge of interest and an inflow of money.

Today 26 May 1987

▶ Another term for this phenomenon is *ethical investment* (see *ethical* in *Longman Guardian New Words*).

construct *noun* CASSETTE

cook-chill *noun* a method of mass catering in which meals are pre-cooked, fast-chilled, and later reheated for consumption

Plans which could see the introduction of new catering methods in some schools in Taunton Deane and West Somerset took a further step forward this week. Somerset Education Authority wants to introduce a cook-chill system in some of its primary schools.

Somerset County Gazette 20 Nov 1987

Professor Richard Lacey, of Leeds University, chairman of Wakefield Health District's control of infection committee, called cook-chill 'microbiologically unsound and nutritionally unsafe.'
Guardian 1 Oct 1987

Edwina Currie, Britain's junior health minister, last week dismissed alleged links between cook/chill catering – a method of food preparation that accounts for 1 in 10 hospital meals – and cases of the infectious disease, listeriosis.
New Scientist 4 Aug 1988

▶ The technique of cook-chill has become very popular with catering managers of hospitals, schools, airlines, and the like in the late 1980s, with its promise of considerable cost-saving arising from the concentration of cooking facilities in one centre, from which meals can be distributed to outlying points. It has, however, caused a certain amount of disquiet from a food-safety point of view: careful supervision of temperatures, keeping times, and all aspects of hygiene are essential to avoid any risk of food poisoning.

copycat packaging *noun*　the selling of inferior articles in packaging which makes them appear to be well-known high-quality brands

Many stores deal in copycat packaging: fake SONY cartons printed in Taiwan disguise substandard, sub-Asian stock. Other supposedly 'authorised' dealers turn out to have bogus links – instead of licenses to represent SONY, Panasonic, Technics, or Sharp.
City Limits 24 Mar 1988

corporate welfare *noun, American*　the compulsory funding of public welfare programmes by commercial organizations

Since neither tax increases nor entitlements are politically attractive, Democratic Liberals have begun to think in terms of 'corporate welfare' schemes. The plan is to enact legislation which requires American businesses to pay for health care, day-care and other liberal programs. Presumably, businesses would cover these costs by raising prices. ... Unless they can push these corporate welfare plans through, the liberals will be stuck for the foreseeable future with the priorities imposed on them by the Reagan administration.
Sunday Times 28 Feb 1988

corporatization *or* **corporatisation** *noun* the process of corporatizing

> More radical still was what [Roger] Douglas [New Zealand Minister of Finance] calls the 'corporatisation' of nine government departments, from April 1 this year, which turned them into independent corporations run by private-sector businessmen.
>
> *Daily Telegraph* 8 Apr 1987

corporatize *or* **corporatise** *verb* (in New Zealand) to convert (a state-owned organization) from direct government control to a commercially orientated management structure

> On April 1 1987, the [New Zealand] government's trading activities in things such as coal, electricity, the post and forestry were 'corporatised'. The resulting nine corporations, which account for $12\frac{1}{2}$% of GDP and 20% of total investment, remain state-owned, but they are to be run like businesses, beyond the grasp of civil servants.
>
> *Economist* 21 Nov 1987

▶ Similar though this process sounds to Thatcher-style privatization, it differs in that although the resultant corporations are run on commercial lines (for example, they have to attract investment through the stock market, rather than being publicly funded), their assets nevertheless remain state-owned. What is perhaps surprising about the policy is that it was introduced not by the (conservative) National party, but by the Labour party (see ROGERNOMICS).

cosmetic bonding *noun* an orthodontic technique in which a plastic resin is used to alter the shape of teeth

> If you don't like the shape of your teeth, or the gaps between them, a new sculpting technique known as cosmetic bonding can now be used to change the whole look of your face. The process is very simple – and costs less than half the price of a cap.
>
> *Living* Feb 1987

▶ The enamel surface of the tooth is roughened in the area where remodelling or repair is necessary, and then a plastic resin is applied which bonds to the tooth. This is sculpted to the desired shape and then hardened by shining a blue light on it.

cosmic string *noun* a hypothetical one-dimensional warp in the space-time continuum which is of sub-microscopic thickness but of immense length and mass

If such a search [for galaxy clusters acting as GRAVITATIONAL LENSES] fails to find an appropriate galaxy cluster, the lens is probably produced either by a single black hole with a mass a million million times the mass of our Sun, or by an even more exotic object called a cosmic string. Cosmic strings are among the latest products of the theorists' fertile brains.

New Scientist 15 May 1986

▶ Cosmologists have postulated that cosmic strings are flaws in the smooth structure of space-time left over from the moment when the universe came into being, and that when these strings form themselves into loops they may form the basis for the creation of galaxies.

cosmopilization *or* **cosmopilisation** *noun* the introduction of elements from various cultures or ethnic groups; making cosmopolitan

But of course all this energy and innovation did not spring at one kangaroo-bound out of a night at the Australian opera. The cosmopilisation of Sydney has many other strands, the most obvious being the rich mix of nationalities from the Pacific, Indian ocean and Mediterranean cultures.

Observer Magazine 13 Dec 1987

▶ The regular formation would be *cosmopolitanization* (and a verb *cosmopolitanize* is recorded in English from as early as 1876). This abbreviated version may have been unconsciously modelled on *monopolization*, and no doubt owes much to the unwieldiness of *cosmopolitanization*.

couch potato *noun, informal, chiefly American* a lazy, inactive, unimaginative person, especially one who prefers watching television to active participation in sport, theatre-going, etc

Costly leisure kit ... is worn by armchair spectators and fans – known in the States as 'couch potatoes' – who watch sport with a beer in one hand and the TV remote control in the other.

Sunday Today 27 July 1986

The so-called midlist book (one which, in America, sells 15,000–50,000 copies and from whose ranks both great books and future bestsellers spring) will vanish. Eventually, you will get literature for couch potatoes.

Economist 26 Dec 1987

A feast may await couch potatoes in the early 1990s. The viewer browses through a dozen channels on tiny preview screens and picks one.

Economist 30 Jan 1988

▶ The potato joins the cabbage as a vegetable exemplifying inertia.

countertrade *noun*   a form of trading in which goods are exchanged for other goods rather than for money

The debt crisis generated a burst of enthusiasm for countertrade ... among companies which saw it as a way to carry on trading with third-world countries that had no foreign exchange. But a survey of American firms has shown that it is remarkably prevalent in industrial countries, too.

Economist 20 Dec 1986

The United Nations Economic Commission for Latin America and the Caribbean (ECLAC) is undertaking a study of countertrade policies and practices in five regional countries, it has been announced in Barbados. ... Once completed, the study will demonstrate the significance of countertrade to the Caribbean region now that there has been an increase in the use of such forms of trading activity internationally, said the UNDP representative.

Caribbean Times 27 May 1988

He sees himself in a few years time heading a small countertrade venture, doing business with eastern Europe and the Far East. 'Vienna is pre-eminent in only one area nowadays, and that's countertrade because of its neutrality and geographical location.'

Excel June 1988

▶ Essentially a form of barter, countertrade is becoming increasingly prevalent as a way of overcoming problems of immediate liquidity or surplus capacity. In 1984, 5.6% of US exports involved countertrade, and in 1986 it was estimated that it accounted for 8–10% of all world trade. It was the international arms trade which first went in for counter-trade in a big way, and it still accounts for the majority of such deals, but other industries (such as cars, electronics, and drugs) are using it more and more. Often, it involves not just a simple exchange of goods, but for example a guarantee by the manufacturer/seller to use components made and provided by the buyer.

cowboy *verb, British informal* to drive recklessly

> The commuter on the Blessed Circle Line ... carries on reading in spite of the fact that she is wedged in so tight between alien bodies that her feet only touch the ground when the driver cowboys over points.
>
> *The Times* 15 Feb 1988

► The current colloquial meaning of the noun *cowboy* covers a broad spectrum of disapproval, from irresponsibility to unscrupulousness, but it seems to have started life (in American English of the 1940s) as a synonym for a reckless driver, a sense carried through into this verbal use.

cowhorn bars *noun plural, informal* DH BAR

> Lennon's one-piece handlebars are called DH Bars. ... The bars resemble cow horns, and have been dubbed by many 'cowhorn bars.'
>
> *Newsweek* 25 Apr 1988

crackhead *noun, slang* a person who smokes or is addicted to the drug crack (purified cocaine in pellet form)

> ... residents and businessmen confronted with crack-heads, dealers and miscellaneous bad actors.
>
> *New York Times* 12 June 1988

> Last week Charlie and two fellow 'crackheads' took me to a vast concrete housing estate in south London where crack is on sale for between £20 and £25 a deal.
>
> *Observer* 24 July 1988

crack house *noun, slang* an establishment from which dealers in the drug crack operate

To go after both the dealers and the 'crack houses' ... New York established yesterday an elite new corps of 101 narcotics agents.
Daily Telegraph 23 May 1986

Street-corner drug dealers show less and less hesitation in drawing on cops, and search-and-arrest missions on heavily fortified crack houses often resemble small-scale military operations.
Newsweek 14 Mar 1988

crack up *verb, slang* to smoke the drug crack

Less than 100 yards away, there are three guys passing a crack pipe. Momentarily stunned, Davy loses his train of thought. It's midafternoon f'f*** sake and, right in front of us, on a sidestreet, they're cracking up.
New Musical Express 6 June 1987

Over there, a pair of dudes crack up on the corner, sucking in poison from a glass pipe, straightening up to the rush of crystallised death.
New Musical Express 10 Oct 1987

▶ The pun on *crack up*, 'have a mental or physical breakdown,' is probably intentional: crack is severely depressant, and can be fatal in the long term.

crash-worthiness *noun* the capacity of a vehicle to withstand a crash without harm to its occupants

In the United States, car companies originally fought the introduction of crash-worthiness ratings but quickly broke ranks when they found the information could be a marketing advantage.
Sunday Times 26 June 1988

creative *adjective, euphemistic* going beyond conventional scope or legal limits

Hollywood is well known for its creative accounting. But even Hollywood at its most inventive has never been able to make a $2 million movie for a mere $150,000.
Guardian 24 May 1984

The miners' debate was marked by some creative chairmanship by Mr Alan Hadden. No doubt with the loyalest of motives, Mr Hadden called both Eric Hammond of the Electricians and Gavin Laird of the Engineers to speak against the NUM, but resolutely refused to call Ron Todd of the Transport Workers.
Guardian 3 Oct 1985

The ruler is also coming down on the knuckles of some of the more 'creative' unit trust advertising and mail shots. Past performance figures quoted must be accompanied by figures showing the trust's performance over a five-year period.

Observer 8 May 1988

▶ This new meaning of *creative*, with its implication of imaginative rule-bending for possibly disreputable purposes, appears to have been coined in the field of accountancy (perhaps an activity ripe with opportunities for such creativity), but has since widened its area of application considerably.

-cred *combining form, slang* popular acceptance among the stated group

▶ This form started its career in the mid 1980s in *street-cred*, an abbreviation of *street credibility* – popular approval in urban working-class culture – but is now beginning to show signs of developing into a buzz-suffix in its own right: **force-cred**

All these qualities make him [Peter Imbert, Metropolitan Police Commissioner] a copper's copper. He has force-cred, and therefore is as well placed as anyone could be to make the Newman structural reforms actually work in practice.

Guardian 18 Mar 1988

creeping takeover *noun* a takeover of a company effected by the gradual secret purchase of its equity

Hongkong has announced plans for a law to force those holding 10 p.c. or more of a listed company's equity to disclose the holding. Announcing details of the Securities (Disclosure of Interests) Bill 1987, David Nendick, Secretary for Monetary Affairs, said the Bill was aimed at curbing insider trading and would make 'creeping takeovers' harder to conceal.

Daily Telegraph 29 May 1987

crinkly *noun, slang* an older person; CRUMBLY, WRINKLY

This paddle in Bennett Bay is refreshing in the way that it elicits sympathy for the crinklies while still acknowledging their vices.

Time Out 4 May 1988

Rosamond ended our day together by saying, 'You've certainly inspired this "crinkly" into fashion action!'
Good Housekeeping June 1988

crossfader *noun* a device used by discjockeys to transfer smoothly from one record to another on a double turntable, gradually decreasing the volume of the first and increasing that of the second

The final main ingredient in the DJ setup is the mixer, which is where things start getting complicated. The mixer all homeboys check for is the GLI ('Derek B's hands are quicker than the eye/The crossfader flies on the GLI').
City Limits 24 Mar 1988

▶ This originated in the language of backstage technology, where it refers to the fading out of one set of lights and the simultaneous bringing up of another.

cross-marketing *or* **cross-selling** *noun* (in banking and insurance) the selling of additional services to existing customers

If an insurance company wishes you a happy birthday, take it as a sure sign that they view you as a target for a touch of cross-marketing. In other words, having sold to you once or twice before, they would like to do it over and over again.
Daily Telegraph 20 Feb 1988

If financial institutions are to succeed in diversifying the services offered they need to succeed in cross-selling – that is selling a range of products to existing customers, as well as attracting new ones.
Money Management May 1986

cross-over store *noun* a self-service shop featuring health foods, organically farmed fruit, vegetables, meat, dairy products, etc, and health products as well as a range of standard household essentials

Spring Foods in Brighton is not quite a health food shop and not quite a supermarket. It's the first of a new style store, neatly termed a cross-over store, a brand new concept in healthy food shopping.
Here's Health Mar 1988

▶ The term *cross-over* probably originated in the popular music business, where it refers to music that is a blend of two styles, especially when one of them is a minority taste and the other more broadly popular.

cross training *noun* physical training involving a mixture of sports and exercises designed to improve various aspects of bodily condition

Cross training involves combining different sports and exercises for optimum health, with improved overall performance. Try mixing racquet sports for more flexibility, aerobics for stamina and weight training to improve strength.

Cosmopolitan Aug 1988

crumbly *noun, slang* an older person; CRINKLY, WRINKLY

During the past week Simon Dee had made reference to the 'crumblies bus pass' in his trailer for the programme *Sounds of the 60s*. ... I cannot tell how many others find the word totally offensive. ... [letter]

Radio Times 28 May 1988

crumb rubber *or* **crumb** *noun* rubber pulverized for reuse

Tires, a perennial waste problem, are crushed into 'crumb rubber' by machines like Tom Buchanan's Tiregator in Houston. The crumbs can be used in road pavement or rubber substitutes such as TIRECYCLE, a substance that its inventors claim can be better than virgin rubber.

Newsweek 14 Mar 1988

If cheaper and more efficient methods of shredding radial tyres could be achieved, then 'crumb,' produced by grinding the material again and again, could have a far greater use in road-making and in a wide range of rubber and plastics products.

Daily Telegraph 12 July 1988

crumpet *noun, British slang* a man or men considered solely from the point of view of being sexually attractive

His performance as a trendy and hung-up LA painter in 'Heartbreakers' made him the thinking woman's West Coast crumpet. In a film that has just opened here, 'Outrageous Fortune,' he plays the unthinking woman's crumpet too, seducing Bette Midler as well as Shelley Long.

Observer Magazine 13 Sept 1987

It's Paul Newman – the older woman's crumpet.
Double First, BBC1, 13 Sept 1988

▶ The use of *crumpet* by men to refer to women goes back at least to the 1930s, but its appropriation by women to refer to men is a phenomenon of the 1980s.

cruzado *noun*   the basic monetary unit of Brazil, containing 100 centavos, introduced in 1986

On February 28, 1986, in a surprise decree, he [José Sarney, president of Brazil] slapped a radical anti-inflation package on the nation – the Cruzado Plan. He lopped three zeroes off the cruzeiro currency and declared it the cruzado, froze prices and wages, and established Brazil's first unemployment-compensation program.
National Geographic Mar 1987

▶ The cruzado has replaced the former Brazilian currency unit, the cruzeiro (which itself supplanted the milreis in 1942). Its name is taken from that of a former Portuguese coin and, like *cruzeiro*, derives ultimately from the Portuguese word for 'cross.' Its introduction was part of a package, the Cruzado Plan (mentioned in the above extract), to achieve a measure of economic stability in Brazil (which suffered a 16.2% rise in its inflation rate in January 1986).

cryoextraction *noun*   a technique of extracting juice from wine grapes by freezing them before they are pressed, so that more highly concentrated juice (which has a lower freezing point than the water content) can be obtained

Negociant Yvon Mau's Château Ducla Entre-Deux-Mers and the Bordeaux Institut d'Oenologie have been experimenting with cryoextraction and the results have been interesting.
Wine June 1988

▶ Essentially this is a technologization of a process which occurs naturally in the production of German eiswein, where grapes are left on the vine until the middle of winter and pressed when frozen to produce a very concentrated sweet wine. Initial tests of cryoextraction suggest that it produces a wine which is very fruity, but perhaps deficient in acidity.

cryptozoology *noun* the scientific study of creatures whose existence has not been scientifically proved

Neither King Cheetahs nor the Loch Ness monster, nor the so-called Kellas Cats are accepted by conventional scientists as a sub-species. But they have been taken very seriously by members of the International Society of Cryptozoology, who have been meeting in Edinburgh. Its members are interested in unknown or un-classified animals, creatures like the yeti, the sasquatch, Bigfoot and the Queensland tiger. ... It may be that the cryptozoologists need to believe what cannot be demonstrated.

Daily Telegraph 10 Aug 1987

▶ This somewhat portentous term for monster hunters in-corporates the Greek-derived prefix *crypto-*, meaning 'hidden' or 'secret.'

crystal meth *or* **crystal** *noun,* *slang* a stimulant drug con-sisting of powdered crystals of methamphetamine

For a total investment of less than $5,000, an underground chemist can make approximately 10 pounds of 'crystal meth,' one of the most potent and sought-after forms of amphetamine on the street.

Newsweek 25 Apr 1988

'Well, maybe I can go a few more hours. How much can you spend?' 'Cash or crystal?' Most kids say they hate crystal dates.

Newsweek 25 Apr 1988

▶ Crystal meth first appeared on the streets of the USA in the early 1980s. Its effects are similar to those of ampheta-mine, but their onset is much quicker and they last longer. It is easily made in backstreet laboratories from cheap in-gredients (ephedrine, red phosphorus, and hydriodic acid), although this is a hazardous process, as it can explode.

CTC *noun* CITY TECHNOLOGY COLLEGE

Cuppie *noun* a wealthy middle-class devotee of (the social, fashionable aspects of) yacht racing

> Now there are Cuppies ... in the streets of Freemantle, wearing expensive French sunglasses which dangle from their tanned necks on black corded chains. Their feet are adorned with trendy deckshoes, ranging in colour from tan to raspberry.
>
> *International Herald Tribune* 31 Jan 1987

> Following America's full sail to victory in the America's Cup, a new social group has emerged. Camouflaged at work by the unanimity of their city suits, at leisure they are easy to recognise in their Gucci yachting shoes, Saint Laurent sailing smocks and Lapidus life-jackets. Relaxing with a regular broadside of champagne corks at the exclusive New York Club, these nautical newcomers to the style scene somewhat self-consciously refer to themselves as 'Cuppies.'
>
> *Daily Telegraph* 23 Apr 1987

▶ The America's Cup races for 12-metre yachts had proceeded quietly for well over a century, arousing no more than a passing interest among the general public, when in 1984, out of the blue, the US boat was defeated, and for the first time the prestigious trophy was lost to the New York Yacht Club. The US efforts to regain it, which culminated in success in Australia in 1987, were launched on an ocean of hype which attracted to the sport many who couldn't tell a spinnaker from a spanner but loved the glamorous, jet-setting milieu in which the races took place. Compare YOTTIE.

cut *noun,* *slang* a single song or other item on an LP; a track

> The album's gonna be more like Cameo, like 'Word up'. Definitely not less rap. So far we've just started writing it. There's only one cut I have a name for yet, 'Career Girls'.
>
> *New Musical Express* 15 Aug 1987

> Pete Gillet ... is left with his debt to society undiminished thanks to a debut album, single cuts of which were shamelessly plugged by the whistling Gillet during a Sri Lankan island 'survival' item on *Network 7* recently.
>
> *Independent* 22 July 1988

cutting-room journalism *noun, derogatory* the practice of compiling news or background stories by researching old newspaper cuttings and similar sources rather than gathering first-hand information by field work

Big Brother Birt has also introduced a new Orwellian language into the BBC. His current affairs and newspeak vocabulary, fast being adopted by ambitious subordinates, includes strange phrases like 'Lexpo' and 'Bexpo.' For the uninitiated viewer (and BBC staff member), they mean 'Long exposition' and 'Brief exposition.' There's also something called 'cutting-room journalism.'
Observer Magazine 26 July 1987

cyberphobic *noun* a person who does not understand and is afraid of computers

Three specific visitor groups have been identified: computer-naive visitors or cyberphobics ..., computer-literate visitors, and specialists. A strategy has been evolved to serve the separate needs and interests of each group.
Guardian 1 Oct 1987

▶ For *cyberphobia*, 'fear of or hostility towards computers,' see *Longman Guardian New Words*.

cyberpunk *noun* **1** a genre of science fiction which envisages a bleak violent future society in which the world is controlled by a computer network

And this, along with those computer absorption stories, leads directly to the newest sf development. The Americans, who love labels, have dubbed it 'cyberpunk.' The term embraces the work of John Shirley and Bruce Sterling – the latter's Schismatrix ... is a pretty fair example – and, pre-eminently, William Gibson.
Guardian 12 June 1986

Cyberpunk was the science fiction mode of the 1980s.
Times Literary Supplement 12 Aug 1988

2 a writer of cyberpunk

While major contemporary writers like Don Delillo depict human lives cast uneasily adrift in this 'white noise' of 'technic' rationality, fashionable 'cyberpunks' (last year's radicals in this year's designer jeans) seem to be generating nothing but more static.
City Limits 24 Mar 1988

▶ Cyberpunk blends the automated control processes of *cybernetics* with the sleaze and garishness of *punk* to produce a hard-bitten critique of the world's descent into a computerized dictatorship. The work of leading cyberpunk author William Gibson, which includes *Neuromancer* 1984 and *Count Zero* 1986, has been described as 'Raymond Chandler rewritten for the computer age.'

cyber-space *noun* (in cyberpunk fiction) the three-dimensional space made up of all the world's computer networks

> Both books are set in sleazy future societies in which the electronic network is what makes the world go round. ... Both books feature computer cowboys, not jocks whose consciousness can enter cyber-space ... directly. They do this by plugging a terminal directly into the brain via a prepared skull socket.
> *Guardian* 12 June 1986

cytobrush *noun* a small brush for collecting cells from the cervical canal in order to carry out cervical cancer checks

> At the Marie Stopes clinic in London, smears are taken using both the traditional spatula and the new cytobrush. ... The cytobrush looks like a small pipe-cleaner and makes it easier to collect cells from inside the canal. The brush is not yet widely available to GPs and family planning clinics. It should be.
> *Guardian* 2 Aug 1988

▶ *Cyto-* (from Greek *kutos*, 'hollow vessel') is a prefix used in words relating to cells.

cytoscreener *noun* a person who examines smear-test slides for signs of cervical or other cancer

> A major issue is the training of the laboratory staff who carry out the smear checks. Jan Gauntlett, speaking for the Institute of Medical Laboratory Services, is highly critical of present policies, which permit the use of untrained low-paid staff as 'cytoscreeners,' as in the Manchester laboratory.
> *Daily Telegraph* 15 July 1988

dallymony *noun, American* an allowance paid by order of a court to one partner in a former sexual relationship by the other partner whose professions of affection and announced intentions have been established as insincere

In this country we like to laugh at the quarrelsome Americans with their absurd over-fondness for legal action. They sue for alimony, palimony and dallymony.

Daily Telegraph 6 Mar 1987

▶ The quaintly old-fashioned notion of *dalliance* provides a convenient rhyme for the coinage of this term alongside the now fairly well established *palimony* (which first appeared around 1979 and is based, of course, on *alimony*).

dataflow *noun* (in computing) a technique of parallel processing in which the computer's operations are broken down into separate units known as 'processes,' between which data flow

One of the reasons for dataflow's low profile ... is that, so far, dataflow research has concentrated on scientific number-crunching. But there is no reason why the techniques ... should not be applied to processing images, speech or text.

New Scientist 25 Sept 1986

dawn raid *noun, British* a sudden unexpected attempt to buy a significant proportion of a company's equity, typically at the start of a day's trading

British Petroleum yesterday bought a 14.9 per cent stake in Britoil ... after a dawn raid, then announced that it planned to increase its holding to 29.9 per cent. BP refused to comment on speculation that the move was a prelude to a full-scale bid.

Daily Telegraph 9 Dec 1987

▶ The ploy of the dawn raid first appeared on the stock-market scene in the early 1980s. Essentially it is a tactic employed by a company; it comes into the market as soon as it opens for the day and buys up to 14.9% of the target company's shares, usually at well above the going rate, in order to give it a springboard for later acquisition. From the outset the manoeuvre was widely criticized, mainly because it did not give target companies time to assess bids and advise their shareholders, and the Stock Exchange and the Council for the Securities Industry have since 1980 issued various rules limiting the proportion of shares that can be bought in this way, and delaying the speed with which such acquisitions can be made; nevertheless, in the late 1980s dawn raiding is still rife.

ddC *noun* DIDEOXYCYTIDINE

de-accession *verb, euphemistic* to sell or otherwise dispose of (an article that is in a museum, library, etc)

> Although London's museum officials like saving things for a rainy day, the Americans have a more practical approach. Most museums in the United States believe that collections are strengthened by pruning. They see 'de-accessioning' as part of good museum management.
>
> *Economist* 12 Sept 1987

> The year's most regretted sale went ahead amid protests yesterday when Sotheby's sold 97 magnificent medieval and Renaissance books from the John Rylands Library, Manchester. ... The library broke with a century's convention that British public collections do not deaccession their holdings, the principle being that the terms of bequests will dry up if they are not accepted in perpetuity.
>
> *Daily Telegraph* 15 Apr 1988

▶ The coy euphemism of this word betrays a trace of guilty conscience among the advocates of enforced commercialization of public collections. The selling-off of items supposedly surplus to requirements has joined admission charges as one of the most controversial issues in museum administration in the government-funding-starved 1980s. Opponents see it discouraging potential donors from giving over art treasures for public exhibition.

dead-ass *adjective,   American slang* depressingly dreary and insignificant

> It [Terry McMillan's novel *Mama*] starts in a thinly-disguised Port Huron, a 'dead-ass' town in Michigan, enough to make you give up in itself, but Mama had drive.
>
> *Guardian* 9 Apr 1987

dead-cat bounce *noun, informal* a deceptive temporary recovery of share prices in a stock market whose price-level is generally low

> Formerly upwardly mobile City types are mining seams of black humour to try to alleviate the pain of what's known in the trade as a 'dead-cat bounce' by share prices.
>
> *Listener* 27 Oct 1987

▶ A gruesomely graphic phrase that originated on Wall Street. It suggests that even a dead cat will bounce up from the ground if dropped from a sufficient height.

dead parrot *noun,   British informal* something completely and irrevocably moribund

> At that point, Mr Steel's future – like his document – was widely regarded as a 'dead parrot.' Surely this was the end of his 12-year reign as Liberal leader?
>
> *Observer* 8 May 1988

▶ The concept of the dead parrot as a metaphor for utter unrevivability originated in a comic sketch in the legendary BBC TV series 'Monty Python's Flying Circus' of the early 1970s, in which a disgruntled customer returns to a pet shop with a parrot he bought there which turned out to be dead, and the shopkeeper tries to convince him it is not. But its current vogue started with the so-called 'dead-parrot document,' the joint policy statement, entitled *Voices and Choices for All*, issued by David Steel and Robert McLennan on 13 January 1988 as the basis for a merged Liberal–Social Democratic party. It was roundly reviled by both sides as being a completely inadequate document, representative of few of the views of either side, too right-wing and Thatcher-ite (it included support for the Trident missile, the phasing out of mortgage tax relief, and the imposition of VAT on food, fuel, and children's clothes, and was generally re-garded as having been slipped by Mr McLennan under the guard of Mr Steel, notorious for his impatience of detail), and offering no hope whatever of joint action, so the two party leaders were told to go away and try again. See also SOCIAL AND LIBERAL DEMOCRATS.

death star *noun* a weapon consisting of a small thin metal disc cut into a star-shape, with sharp-edged points – called also *throwing star*

> Shopkeepers selling 'death stars' in London's West End reluctantly pledged to comply with any ban on potential weapons last night, but protested that concern over the issue had been exaggerated.
> *Daily Telegraph* 8 Oct 1987

▶ Death stars are one of the range of street-weapons, mostly of Oriental 'martial-arts' origin or inspiration, that have come to prominence in recent years (see under SURVIVAL-IST). As their alternative name suggests, they are designed to be thrown, and rubber versions are used by genuine mar-tial-arts enthusiasts. Those favoured by football hooligans and the like have viciously sharp points which can inflict horrifying injuries. In August 1988 the British government announced its intention to ban the manufacture, sale, and import of death stars and various other offensive weapons.

deccie *noun* a person who is obsessively interested in in-terior decoration, and compulsively redecorates his or her house

> Surely Yuppies, Foodies and Peter York's Deccies belong under a bigger umbrella which shelters ambition, food and decorating – they are Housies.
> *Observer* 3 July 1988

▶ A notorious clue to the imminent yuppification of an area is the appearance of a large number of builders' skips in the roads. These often betray the presence of the deccie, single-mindedly intent on incorporating all the trendiest interior decoration techniques into his or her new home (see RAG ROLLING). For the really obsessed it is an ongoing process, every new style whim being experimented with hot off the magazines.

The word *deccie* seems to have been coined by Peter York, a sharp-eyed observer of the social scene who brought the Sloane Rangers to public attention.

decompress *verb*   to rid oneself of feelings of tension and anxiety

> For employees who want to learn how to decompress, experts recommend several forms of relief. Allen Elkin, program director for Stresscare, suggests abdominal breathing, meditation, and 'imaging.'
>
> *Newsweek* 25 Apr 1988

dectet *noun*   a group of ten singers or instrumentalists

> Ladysmith Black Mambazo: Skilled and charming *a capella* dectet who brought houses down all over Europe on Paul Simon's 'Graceland' tour.
>
> *Daily Telegraph* 18 July 1987

▶ This useful coinage does not appear in Grove's *Dictionary of Music and Musicians*.

def *adjective, slang*   wonderful, marvellous

> They said I was def and I said 'Really! You think I'm deaf?' Then someone told me def means brilliant.
>
> *New Musical Express* 20 June 1987

> When Danny speaks approvingly of certain lettering he says it is 'def.'
>
> *Guardian* 14 Oct 1987

▶ This voguish term of approval among the young (a late 1980s equivalent of the 1960s *fab*) arose in the Hip Hop youth culture and appears to be an abbreviation of *definitive*, with some suggestion too of *definite*. A television slot for teenagers on BBC2 has been designated *DEF II*.

defensive medicine *noun*   the adoption of cautious, conservative, or exaggeratedly fail-safe methods in the treatment of illness in order to minimize liability if sued by a dissatisfied patient

British obstetricians increasingly worry that the threat of being sued is forcing doctors into practising 'defensive medicine.'

Listener 6 Feb 1986

▶ The notorious litigiousness of American patients gave birth to defensive medicine in the USA, but it is now a growing phenomenon in Britain. Its main negative effects are twofold: as doctors become disinclined to adopt any procedure that is in any way risky, in case it goes wrong, research into new techniques is stifled and fewer patients may actually recover; and in order to cover themselves against any eventuality, doctors demand every conceivable test to be carried out on patients, no matter how marginally appropriate, which pushes NHS costs up unwarrantably. The British Medical Association has suggested the adoption in Britain of the system used in Sweden and New Zealand, in which a patient who suffers as a result of medical treatment is automatically compensated, without the need to establish whether the doctor has made a mistake.

dekalogy *noun*   a series of ten connected works

The magnum opus and crowning achievement of one of the grand storytellers of our time, the Mission Earth series [by L. Ron Hubbard] is a work of such scope and magnitude that the new term of 'dekalogy' (meaning 10 volumes) had to be coined to describe it. [advertisement]

Bookseller 17 Apr 1987

▶ This word has been formed on the analogy of *trilogy, tetralogy* (series of four books), and so on. Given the work's authorship (L. Ron Hubbard was the founder of Scientology), it may be more than a coincidence that *dekalogy* is cognate with *decalogue*, an alternative name for the Ten Commandments.

delist *verb* to remove from a list of acceptable or approved items; withdraw from a range of products offered or handled

Powerful supermarket chains could 'delist' a manufacturer's whole range if it refused to provide part of it as own-brand goods.
Economist 16 Apr 1988

demerge *verb* to split up (a conglomerate formed by a previous merger) into separate companies

Lonrho, however, is pushing ahead with its resolution on demerging Harrods.
Financial Times 2 Nov 1982

Originally the group had planned to bolster its demerged insurance business by joining forces with fellow broker Fenchurch, part of the Guinness Peat financial services conglomerate. But the two groups said yesterday that talks had broken down and were now off.
Guardian 26 June 1987

demerger *noun* an act of demerging a company

If the merger boom is now nearing a close, will it be followed by a demerger boom? And will that demerger boom be to the forthcoming bear market what the merger boom has been to the past bull market?
Guardian 24 June 1986

The demerger will split Hogg Robinson's travel and fast-growing estate agency business from its core insurance activities to create two separately listed companies.
Guardian 26 June 1987

dependency culture *noun, derogatory* a social environment in which people have become accustomed to relying on state benefits, such as the National Health Service, free education, and social-security payments

The welfare state was criticised last night by Lord Young, Trade and Industry Secretary, for weakening individual responsibility and creating a 'dependency culture.' Emphasising his own passionate belief in private enterprise, he said he thought that previous governments had gone too far in developing the role of the State in relation to the responsibilities of individuals.
Daily Telegraph 3 Mar 1988

▶ The notion of a society enervated by decades of reliance on handouts from the nanny state is central to the Thatcher government's concerted campaign in favour of economic self-reliance (see ENTERPRISE and compare LEARNED HELP-LESSNESS).

depowerment *noun* removal of people's control over their own lives

> The enthusiastic apostles of progress, including many on the left, have been so mesmerised by the altered decor of postwar society, have been so impressed by the version of abundance conceded by capital on its own terms, that they have seen nothing of the depowerment, disabling and loss that have accompanied these processes.
>
> *New Society* 25 Mar 1988

deprofessionalization *or* **deprofessionalisation** *noun* removal of professional standards or status

> For local comprehensives, a different cause for their better performance must be sought. Perhaps it is the professional competence and commitment of their staffs? This hypothesis is supported by the slight drop in the steady upward curve in 1983-84... when the government started its deprofessionalisation campaign.
>
> *Guardian* 8 May 1987

derecognize *or* **derecognise** *verb* to withdraw official recognition from

> But in choosing instead to capitalise on the fears and dissatisfactions of some of his crew and derecognise the union, he [Peter Ford, chairman of P&O European Ferries] has taken a more radical course.
>
> *Financial Times* 26 Apr 1988

DERL *noun* derived emergency reference level: the point in any given situation at which action should be taken to counter a potentially dangerous rise in radiation levels

> A complex structure of emergency reference levels have been derived. These are called Derived Emergency Reference Levels (DERLs) which are calculated on the basis of the most sensitive members of the public – generally infants below one year.
>
> *Guardian* 7 May 1986

deselect *verb, euphemistic* to remove from participation, availability, etc; exclude

Her books may have been banned by grown-ups – or 'deselected' as contemporary librarians prefer to say – but Enid Blyton is still the most popular choice for many school children.

Times Educational Supplement 21 Aug 1987

▶ As noted in *Longman Guardian New Words*, *deselect* first came to public attention in the early 1980s in the context of Labour party politics: sitting MPs, councillors, etc who got on the wrong side of their constituency party face the possibility of having their candidature revoked before the next election. Its application in other circumstances is no doubt in part a conscious ironic reference to this.

des res *noun, British informal* a house with many features (e g of design or location) attractive to prospective purchasers

Those enjoying the perks of being perfectly des. res. positioned in London include Gabrielle Crawford with The Frock Exchange in fashionable Fulham and Dominique Cousins at Designs in Hampstead.

Independent 8 May 1987

A tiny des res has been fitted out to sell British aid for Africa. [headline] Elizabeth Young ... has helped to mastermind Designer Aid with the best of British and an intricate, miniature house in the Adam style, which stands little over four feet high but will ... raise £1m for a little-known charity in Africa.

Independent 8 May 1987

▶ It seems that this estate agent's abbreviation (for 'desirable residence') is about to join *mod con* as a fully-fledged English word.

detox *noun, informal* removal of the effects of substances harmful to the body, especially drugs and alcohol; detoxification

HGB: 'What was the hardest thing when you got to the clinic?' LT [Liz Taylor]: 'Saying goodbye to my brother and sister-in-law.

Walking in the dark to the little house where I would be a patient. I was waiting for a nurse who was going to help me through detox.'
Cosmopolitan Sept 1987

John, a ragged-looking 46, said 'I'm an alcoholic; funny, isn't it?' As he was taken into the detox centre, with blood on his face and saliva dribbling out of his mouth, he laughed, shouted 'I want a bottle of metho,' and tried to pick a fight.
Sydney Morning Herald 13 Apr 1988

de-ward *verb* to rescind the official custody order applying to (a ward of court)

On Tuesday December 7 the family assembled at Middlesbrough High Court to hear Mr Justice Eastham's scathing judgement: 'I am satisfied that these children were not sexually abused by their father; I am satisfied that they were not sexually abused at all.... These children are about to be de-warded by me because I am satisfied that they have caring and loving parents who have not harmed them in any way whatsoever. The wardship is going to be terminated. ...'
Sunday Times Magazine 29 May 1988

dewomb *verb* to take away (a woman's) child-bearing capacity by removing the womb or destroying its function

For seven years, I have suffered in the consciousness that I am dewombed and yet remain a woman. ... Seven years ago I had cervical cancer. ... The treatment offered was radiotherapy. An alternative would have been a hysterectomy. The result for my fertility was the same, the only difference being that the dewombing happened over the course of three exhausting months rather than in the hours of a single operation.
Guardian 11 Feb 1987

DH bar *noun* bicycle handlebars configured in such a way that the hands grip upwardly curving ends while the forearms and elbows rest on a padded horizontal section – called also *cowhorn bars*

Every prominent triathlete in the world now uses the DH bar – or one of 10 similar designs – in competition.
Newsweek 25 Apr 1988

109

▶ DH stands for 'downhill,' and the name comes from the resemblance borne by the rider, leaning forwards with his hands in front of his face, to a downhill ski racer in tuck position. For both skier and rider this position, with the elbows pressed in to the sides, helps to reduce wind resistance and increase speed.

diacerhein *noun*   an anti-inflammatory drug used to counter osteoarthritis

> Much of the trouble [from arthritic inflammation] is caused by the very active oxygen radicals released by white blood cells in their efforts to degrade foreign materials. As a quinone, diacerhein seems able to combine with these radicals and deactivate them.
> *New Scientist* 21 Nov 1985

▶ Diacerhein (tradename Artrodar) was developed by Charles Friedmann, of the University of Florence. It is a derivative of anthraquinone. Standard anti-inflammatory drugs, such as fenbufen, work by reducing the body's synthesis of prostaglandins; a common side-effect of this is bleeding and ulceration of the stomach. Diacerhein, on the other hand, actually increases prostaglandin synthesis, so this side-effect is avoided.

dicastery *noun*   a Roman Catholic tribunal

> The Italian-language discussion group at the synod comprised 33 members from 14 nations. It had 14 cardinals ..., 10 heads of Curial dicasteries ..., and two founders of 'movements.'
> *The Tablet* 13 Feb 1988

▶ This is a reapplication of a term (Greek *dikasterion*) used for a court of law in ancient Athens, for which 6000 citizens were chosen annually to try cases.

dickhead *noun, slang*   a foolish or incompetent person, especially male

> 'Socialism has got to be useful and attractive to the relatively affluent,' he [Neil Kinnock] bellowed over spasmodic rage from the Left ('dickhead' came soaring over).
> *Daily Telegraph* 30 Sept 1987

The other dickheads here will sneer and rant.
Melody Maker 24 Oct 1987

Then disaster strikes when you find you have to deal with 'the dickhead on the set who suggests you shoot things with a zoom lens when you have spent hours setting up a track shot'.
Campaign 1 July 1988

▶ An insult modelled no doubt on *thickhead, fathead,* etc, with the substitution of *dick*, 'penis'. See also AIRHEAD, MEATHEAD, RUBBLEHEAD.

dideoxycytidine *noun* (*abbreviation* **ddC**) a nucleoside analogue drug related to zidovudine (AZT) which is being tested for use in the treatment of AIDS

A team of 18 doctors and researchers has published the results of a preliminary trial of dideoxycytidine (ddC) in 20 patients with AIDS or severe disease caused by HIV infection.
New Scientist 21 Jan 1988

▶ Dideoxycytidine works by blocking the formation of viral DNA in cells infected by the human immunodeficiency virus (HIV), and is therefore a potential AIDS drug. It does, however, have toxic side-effects.

dieman *noun, West African* a dead person whose existence is fictitiously maintained in order that his or her wages or other benefits may continue to be drawn

Each month [Sierra Leone] pays out some £2.5 million pounds to its Civil Service. A good chunk ... goes to what are called 'diemen'.
Daily Telegraph 19 Nov 1987

digital *adjective* of computers and computerization

'As word processors are indispensable for writers, a computer will be a necessary part of an artist's studio.' And not just for painters. Musicians, dancers, cartoonists and even poets are all going digital.
Newsweek 25 Apr 1988

▶ As the above extract suggests, *digital* is fast outgrowing its specific computing sense of 'using digits to represent quantities,' and to the layman is becoming a broad-brush term for referring generally to the world of computers. The process is no doubt helped by digital clocks, digital recording, and the like, which the man in the street perhaps perceives as vaguely part of the same phenomenon.

digital subtraction angiography *noun* (*abbreviation* **DSA**) a computerized technique for studying blood vessels by comparing X-ray photographs of them before and after they have been injected with dye

An artery at the base of the brain balloons with a dangerous aneurysm ... in an X-ray view enhanced by digital subtraction angiography (DSA).

National Geographic Jan 1987

▶ This new tool for studying veins and arteries that may be blocked or otherwise diseased works by computationally storing several 'before and after' X-rays of the vessel and digitally 'subtracting' the one from the other, to highlight differences revealed by the dye.

dink *noun, American slang* a fool

There is now a delay of up to three months for delivery of a $26,000 luxury sedan and clients have been sent letters asking them to accept the company's apologies and a $20 Cross pen and pencil set. Terry Smith, industrial relations manager at the Wixom, Michigan, plant is not pleased with his masters. 'Those dinks,' he said. 'We're building as fast as we can.' Dinks might be a suitable description. Sending furious customers the Cross package may prompt them to put their costly pens to paper and write further letters of complaint.

Daily Telegraph 31 Mar 1988

▶ As with many other words for 'fool,' *dink* first meant 'penis.' It is probably an alteration of *dick*, although there may be some connection with German *ding*, 'thing.'

Dinky *noun* either member of a (married) partnership in which both members have a job and there are no children

The average Dinky couple is just turned 40 with combined annual income in excess of £50,000. One or the other is usually working at the weekend. When they shop, it's at Waitrose, late night. When they go out, it's to a snatched film after work with both of them dozing off in the final reel. And with Mrs Dinky (BA Cantab) on the brink of an associateship at the office, maternity leave is positively unthinkable.

Daily Mail 22 Dec 1986

▶ The term *Dinky* was coined in the USA (with a sidelong glance, no doubt, at the adjective *dinky*, which in American English has negative connotations of smallness and insignificance), based on the first letters of 'double *or* dual income, no kids' (the *y* is sometimes taken to stand for 'yet', but for many Dinky couples that addition is inappropriate). The niche occupied by Dinkies in the narcissistic self-classification of the professional middle class in the 1980s is that of the slightly greying, or balding Yuppie, arrived now in the antechamber of the boardroom by dint of hard work which has left time for marriage but not for the procreation of future Yuppies.

dirty dancing *noun* a form of dancing to pop music based essentially on the mambo, involving close gyratory hip-to-hip contact – called also *touch dancing*

'Dirty Dancing is good clean fun really,' insists Peggy Spencer, MBE, the spry 67-year-old who runs a chain of dance studios in South London suburbs.

London Evening Standard 20 Oct 1987

▶ Dirty dancing was immortalized in a highly successful 1987 film of the same name, directed by Emile Ardolino.

disadaptive *adjective* tending to make something badly adapted or unfitted

This [homosexuality] is unusual among primates and mammals generally, and should be disadaptive in Darwinian terms if considered alone, but it is a universal finding as is a sprinkling of left-handedness.

Guardian 22 July 1988

113

▶ Randle Cotgrave records the verb *disadapt* in his *Dictionarie of the French and English tongues* 1611, but *OED* notes it as 'obscure and rare.'

disimprove *verb, euphemistic* to make or become worse

Should he need lessons on how to put a gloss on bad news, Mr Lawson might learn from Tony O'Reilly, the Irish international rugby player best known for running HJ Heinz. Wearing his hat as chairman of Atlantic Resources ... he yesterday reported half-time results which 'show a disimproved revenue position.'

Daily Telegraph 5 Nov 1987

diskinaesthesis *noun* lack of muscular coordination and of an awareness of the position and movement of one's limbs

Everyone knows the clumsy child – the boy with the permanently-grazed knee who cannot tie his shoelace, is forever breaking things and always drops the cricket ball. Until very recently it was thought that such children were backward or just plain mischievous. Now it is known they are suffering from a genuine disorder called 'diskinaesthesis.'

Daily Telegraph 9 Sept 1987

▶ The term *kinaesthesis*, referring to the sense of muscular movement, has been extant since before World War II, but this negation is a new development.

diss *verb, slang* to reject or dismiss contemptuously; put down

Roxanne Shanté is the Alexis of Rap. ... She entertains the suitors of her Rap Dynasty, only to diss them.

New Musical Express 15 Aug 1987

On 'Tramp,' Carla Thomas' '60s soul original is spliced to Salt'n'Pepa's declaration: 'Homegirl, what would you do if a stranger said 'Hi'? Would you diss him or would you reply?'

City Limits 18 Feb 1988

▶ Apparently an abbreviation of *disrespect*, originally in Black American Rap culture.

do *verb, slang* to take (drugs or a drug)

> I suppose we do as much drugs as the next bunch of friends, not very much really. We like a good smoke ... or a spot of acid if there's any around.
>
> *New Musical Express* 23 July 1987

dockny *noun* a person who lives in the redeveloped dock-land area of East London

> The new community of 'Docknies' that has emerged often work 15 hours a day. When they meet for a social drink, they talk not of families or holidays, but of the pounds per square foot their Dock-land home is worth.
>
> *Daily Telegraph* 18 Nov 1987

▶ The docknies are the new yuppyish tendency in London's docklands rather than the original inhabitants of the Isle of Dogs and contiguous areas. Given the derivation from *cock-ney*, the *-ny* ending is anomalous.

dockominium *noun, American* a boat mooring which can be bought outright

> Hip New Yorkers, who certainly wouldn't buy the Brooklyn Bridge, have been paying up to $70,000 this summer for patches of water. Welcome to the wonderful growth industry of 'docko-miniums.'
>
> *Daily Telegraph* 19 Aug 1987

▶ Moorings in marinas and harbours are standardly rented rather than sold, but an American developer evidently gauged the property-owning instinct of yuppie YOTTIES aright when he decided to sell them off instead. The word is a blend of *dock* and *condominium*, American English for an owner-occupied flat.

docu-fantasy *noun* a television presentation which uses factual elements as the basis of a far-fetched dramatic reconstruction or projection of events

> Tonight a special treat, as actual Queensland [politicians] take part in a docu-fantasy based on the last days of Joh in which the shamb-ling old stager joins the ALP.
>
> *Sydney Morning Herald* 13 Apr 1988

▶ The overt encroachment of speculation and dramatization into documentary programmes, and of documentary techniques into drama, began with the *docudrama*, but with the advent of the docu-fantasy seems to leave the tiresome world of facts behind altogether.

dog *noun, British slang* the telephone

> Get on the dog; invite old Arthur down here for an evening on the river.
>
> *Minder*, Thames Television 1983

▶ *Dog* is short for 'dog and bone,' Cockney rhyming slang for 'phone'. It is one of several colourful expressions from the world of small-time London crime popularized by the television series *Minder*; see HER INDOORS.

dog-and-pony *verb, American informal* to attempt to influence by extravagant claims or high-pressure salesmanship

> He's very straightforward. He doesn't dog-and-pony you.
>
> *USA Today* 23 July 1987

▶ The verb has been coined from *dog and pony show*, an American expression for a perhaps overelaborate sales-pitch or publicity presentation.

dollar shop *noun* a shop in a Communist country in which goods may be bought for US dollars or other hard currency rather than the local currency

> The few [shops] open seem to concentrate on books on Marxist philosophy, apart from the 'dollar shops' where imported whisky and tinned European delicacies are on offer.
>
> *The Times* 4 Mar 1988

domino *noun* a multiple transplant operation in which patient A is given a new heart and lungs from a brain-dead donor and patient B is given patient A's old heart

'There's such a shortage of organs here,' says Julieta Gonzalez, spokeswoman for the university medical centre in Tucson, Arizona, where the country's fifth domino was carried out last month.

Sunday Times 8 May 1988

▶ The domino operation was pioneered at Harefield Hospital, West London, by a team led by Professor Magdi Yacoub. It involves one patient who needs a lung transplant and one who needs a heart transplant: the first is given new lungs *and* a new heart from a dead donor, because transplanting the lungs alone often does not succeed; and the second is then given the first's old, but perfectly healthy, heart.

The source of the metaphor is presumably not a falling domino's propensity to knock its neighbours over, as in *domino theory*, but the division of a domino's face into two equal parts.

donkey crushing *noun*   the practice of riding a donkey hard until it collapses from exhaustion

Many readers want to support the campaign to stop the sport of 'donkey crushing' in Spain. ... The Donkey Sanctuary in Devon is spearheading the campaign to stop donkey crushing.

Saffron Walden Weekly News 11 Feb 1988

▶ One of a range of activities taken by the British as proof of the unspeakable behaviour of the Spaniards towards their animals (others include drugging and maltreatment of monkeys kept to be photographed with tourists), donkey crushing is engaged in by the young men of the town to prove their machismo.

doomsayer *noun*   a person who forecasts misfortune or disaster, especially overpessimistically

The chairman of Merrill Lynch, Mr William Schreyer, appeared on television advertisements proclaiming 'We believe in America'. At the same time, doomsayers noted that stockmarket crashes of this magnitude have 'always' been followed a year or two later by the onset of an economic depression.

Economist 31 Oct 1987

Drug stocks have been strong because the doomsayers who were suggesting that the Medicare Bill was going to be a major negative for the industry are being proved wrong.

Business Times [Malaysia] 3 June 1988

▶ This formation is probably based on *soothsayer*. See GLOOMSTER.

dork *noun, American slang* a fool, idiot

'That's based on this book ... it's our first pretentious song! I can't remember the name of the story but it's about those dorks that live on Staten Island, they pick names out of the phone book and call them up for a joke.'

Underground Jan 1988

▶ In common with many other words for 'fool' (e g *prick, plonker*), the primary meaning of *dork* is 'penis.' The 1975 supplement to Wentworth and Flexner's *Dictionary of American Slang* defines its usership in this anatomical sense as 'adolescents and students.'

dorkish *or* **dorky** *adjective, American slang* stupid

Then she pours some Sno-Wite into the machine and just stands there in front of all these dumb, dorkish guys.

Guardian 6 Feb 1986

Tony O'Dell from 'Head of the Class' was really upset we described his jacket as 'dorky' in the April 'What He Said.'

Sassy June 1988

dot ball *noun* (in cricket) a delivery not scored from

And Greenidge lets that go by outside the off stump, and that's what they proudly call a 'dot ball' these days.

Test Match Special, Radio 3, 8 Aug 1988

▶ The term derives from the fact that balls unscored off are noted in the scorebook by means of a dot.

double-breasting *noun, Canadian* a ploy to circumvent a trade-union closed shop by which a unionized company sets up a non-unionized subsidiary and subcontracts work to it

The law bans secondary picketing, curbs unions' disciplinary powers and permits 'double-breasting.'

Economist 8 Aug 1987

double zero *noun* ZERO-ZERO

Because the LRINF proposal had been called the 'zero option', the joint scheme has come to be called the 'double zero'.

Daily Telegraph 21 May 1987

Nato will, after the nail-biting, accept the 'double zero' solution.

Economist 30 May 1987

downside *noun* a negative or adverse aspect

A documentary from Granada TV which attempts to look at the downside of the ecological battle with a profile of the plight of a community of Norwegian fishermen.

Time Out 16 Mar 1988

But although the decision to fill the gap left by the longserving Don Arlett appears a brave one, it does have its downside.

Campaign 6 May 1988

▶ The metaphor derives from the language of the stock market, in which the downside is a fall in prices following a peak. A share delicately described as having 'downside potential' is one whose value is likely to fall.

downsize *verb, euphemistic* to reduce (a workforce) in size by redundancy

Many of them will start the new year in fear of their well-paid jobs, as what is typically called 'downsizing' sweeps through the securities industry. ... Salomon Brothers inaugurated the recent wave of lay-offs by firing 800 staff.

Economist 26 Dec 1987

'Downsizing' is today the buzz word of a securities industry which only a year ago hummed to the tune of golden hellos, golden handcuffs and golden parachutes.

Guardian 22 Jan 1988

downspin *noun* a continuously accelerating deterioration

A streak of bad luck, some poor decisions and the general down-spin of the northern Indiana economy threaten to close the school.
Chicago Tribune 11 Mar 1988

dragon *noun* a newly-industrializing country in eastern Asia

Japan's chasers are the newly industrialised 'dragons' – Taiwan, Singapore, South Korea and Hongkong.
Economist 23 Jan 1988

America 'graduated' South Korea, Taiwan, Hongkong, and Singapore from its Generalised System of Preferences – ie, stripped them of trade concessions. The dragons will now face tariffs averaging 5%.
Economist 6 Feb 1988

▶ Sometimes also known as 'little dragons,' these are Asia's NICS, nations which over the past couple of decades have progressed rapidly from largely agricultural economies to ones capable of making an impression even on the commercial might of Japan.

dragon light *noun* an intensely bright mobile light used by police for immobilizing potentially violent suspects

Last week's dawn raid by the crack PT18 police unit on an illegal drink and drug party in East London unveiled a remarkable new weapon in Scotland Yard's armoury: the dragon light.
Daily Telegraph 18 Apr 1988

The raid was undertaken by the 48-strong elite unit codenamed PT18, which is identified by its all-black 'riot' garments, dragon-light torches and plastic 'lassoo-type' handcuffs.
Caribbean Times 27 May 1988

▶ These million-candle-power lamps have such a devastating effect on anyone they are aimed at that the most recalcitrant villain is instantly subdued.

drama-com *noun* DRAMEDY

The latest comedies on American TV, including some of the new 'drama-coms,' have done away with laugh tracks altogether.
Sydney Morning Herald 11 Apr 1988

dramedy *noun, American* a television comedy-drama

NBC Entertainment President Brandon Tuarukoff tried to bury the hatchet over his recent negative remarks about this season's trendy 'dramedy' genre.

USA Today 8 Feb 1988

draw-down *noun* (in economics) a diminution in quantity caused by depletion; a reduction

According to latest estimates from the ITC ... 1986 world production may fall to 127,200 tonnes from 158,200 in 1985 – just over 30,000 below estimated Western consumption, which is forecast to rise marginally. This implies a draw-down in stocks to about 55,000 tonnes by the end of this year, compared with probably more than 100,000 at their 1985 peak.

Guardian 27 Oct 1986

Mr Lester Brown, president of the Worldwatch Institute in Washington, said ... 'Consumption [of grain] this year will be about 152 million tonnes above production – and we have never before experienced a draw-down on stocks on that scale.'

Daily Telegraph 6 Aug 1988

drive *verb* to be the determining factor in (something)

But Richard Ellis' City expert ... stresses: 'Rents in the City are driven by availability – or the lack of it in terms of walk-in space. There is a very low vacancy rate in the City.'

Observer 12 June 1988

▶ This sense of *drive* seems to derive from the use of *-driven* as a combining form meaning 'having as a basis' (as in 'a data-driven system').

drive-by *adjective* (of a killing) committed by shooting from a moving car

Los Angeles gangs killed more than 200 people last year in drug and territory wars; this year is even worse. Gang members have started shooting people at random from cars, a practice called drive-by murder.

Sydney Morning Herald 13 Apr 1988

> Long before its premier over the weekend, the movie 'Colors' was intensifying jitters about the gang fights and 'drive-by' murders that have terrorized the city.
>
> *Newsweek* 25 Apr 1988

► Drive-by shootings are no new phenomenon, of course – they were a notorious tactic in gangland battles during Prohibition – but they seem to be undergoing a new wave of popularity in the USA, and they have acquired a new epithet to go with it.

driza-bone *noun, Australian* a waterproof coat worn by those who live and work in the Australian bush

> The Queen, on walkabout in the port of Geelong ... walked over to Spud's owner, Peter Sharp, a bearded, laconic 38-year-old dressed in slouch hat and a bushman's all-weather coat, known locally as a 'driza-bone.'
>
> *Daily Telegraph* 29 Apr 1988

► In the mid 1980s these overcoats-cum-mackintoshes became suddenly fashionable in the USA (partly, no doubt, on the strength of the Crocodile Dundee craze for all things Australian), and smart 5th Avenue stores were selling them at prices which would faze a bushman.

drogue bomb *noun* a home-made guerrilla weapon consisting of a grenade fitted with an improvised parachute

> A policeman killed in a terrorist ambush in Belfast was the first victim of a lethal new IRA armour-piercing bomb. Security sources said the weapon – called a drogue bomb – was the most frightening device in the hands of the terrorists.
>
> *Western Mail* 27 Jan 1988

► Drogue bombs, filled with several pounds of plastic explosive, have binliners attached to them, which act like parachutes in giving the armour-piercing grenade a certain amount of stability in flight after it is thrown. 'Drogue' is a name given to any baglike contrivance (such as a sea anchor or a windsock) which streams out in the wake of something or in the flow of wind or water passing something.

druggie *noun, informal, chiefly American* a drug addict

> So I asked Capt Lesley Fraze of USAF Public Affairs if there was a
> problem at the base. 'No.' Not even a single alcoholic or druggie?
> 'No.'
>
> *Independent* 16 Apr 1987

> The shooting clearly demonstrated the druggies' willingness to
> attack police authority head-on.
>
> *Newsweek* 14 Mar 1988

> Get some of the whores, some of the druggies, chase them away.
>
> *New York Times* 12 June 1988

DSA *noun* DIGITAL SUBTRACTION ANGIOGRAPHY

DTP *noun* desktop publishing

> A year after DTP was launched, it was apparent to rival companies
> that their inertia in the field was costing them money. IBM in-
> vested heavily in DTP development, eventually adopting Post-
> Script, the same DTP language used by Apple, as its favoured
> solution.
>
> *The Times* 19 Jan 1988

▶ Desktop publishing, the production of printed material
by means of a personal computer, appropriate software, and
a laser printer, has been widely adopted in the last couple of
years.

duke *verb* – **duke it out** *American slang* to fight with one's
fists

> Never has this city's mayor been caught duking it out in public
> with an alderman – at least not like North-lake Mayor Gene Doyle
> and Ald. Reid Paxson were Tuesday night.
>
> *Chicago Tribune* 11 Mar 1988

▶ The verb derives from the noun *dukes*, 'fists,' as in 'put up
your dukes,' which in turn is short for *Duke of Yorks*, 19th-
century rhyming slang for 'forks' (i e 'fingers' or 'fists').

dump on *verb, slang, chiefly American* to criticize
severely

> For some time now it's been open season for dumping on the United
> Nations. Mayor Ed Koch of New York called it a 'cesspool.'
>
> *Newsweek* 18 Apr 1988

▶ *Dump* is an American slang term for 'defecation.'

dumpster *noun, American* a large receptacle in which rubbish is disposed of

> Like, so many kids don't know where they're going to sleep each night. I've slept in carpet dumpsters from here to Salinas, so I feel for those kids.
> *Newsweek* 25 Apr 1988

▶ *Dumpster* is a trademark in origin.

dysergy *noun* (in business) the tendency of two individual organizations to be less successful, efficient, etc when joined together than either of them had been on its own

> Mr Klesch says that the two firms will be kept separate and argues that their positions in the market place are complementary. Others disagree; Marshall and Martin, they say, overlap. ... On that view, Marshall plus Martin would be a merger with dysergy.
> *Daily Telegraph* 24 Aug 1987

▶ This coinage reverses the meaning of SYNERGY, a City buzzword of the 1980s, using the prefix *dys-*, 'impaired.'

dyskaryosis *noun* an abnormal or diseased condition of cell nuclei

> New terminology to standardise cervical screening reports and eliminate current confusion has been recommended by a working party of the British Society for Clinical Cytology. They recommend that the term 'dyskaryosis' should be universally used to describe abnormalities that are greater than inflammation. Dyskaryosis should be termed mild, moderate or severe. Where abnormalities on a smear fall between inflammation and dyskaryosis, the smear should be termed borderline.
> *Cosmopolitan* Sept 1987

▶ The term is based on *karyo-*, a combining form derived from Greek *karyon*, 'nut, kernel.'

dystrophin *noun* a protein, the absence of which is thought to cause the disease muscular dystrophy

Louis Kunkel and Eric Hoffman at Harvard Medical School in Boston and their colleagues have found a protein that is present in normal muscle, but is absent from the muscles of boys suffering from the inherited disease Duchenne muscular dystrophy (DMD). ... They have named the missing protein 'dystrophin.'

New Scientist 14 Jan 1988

▶ The identification of lack of dystrophin as the key factor in the development of muscular dystrophy was a first step towards an understanding of this degenerative disease. More recent research in Canada, Japan, and America has found that it is located in the outer membrane of normal muscles and that its function is probably to strengthen the muscle cells so that they do not tear when the muscle contracts.

E *noun, slang* the drug ECSTASY

> Ecstasy, known as 'E' in the clubs, is currently on sale at £20–£25 a tablet, but the price is expected to fall as demand grows.
>
> *Observer* 28 Aug 1988

earcon *noun* an audio signal produced by a computer, representing a particular activity that can be or is being carried out by the computer

> One of his [Dr Buxton's] projects is to devise sound cues which the computer can give its user to let them know what it is doing. These 'earcons,' a sound equivalent of icons, would tell the user how much memory is left, which task it is performing and how close it is to finishing, for example.
>
> *New Scientist* 23 June 1988

> Audio signals or 'earcons' are about to supersede icons as the latest user aid to getting the most out of PCs when research at Rank Xerox's new Europarc lab is commercialised.
>
> *Computer Weekly* 23 June 1988

► This punning coinage is the work of Dr William Buxton, developer of the earcon itself. Icons are visual cues for computer users (a stylized book on the screen could be used for selecting a diary facility, for example), and so signals that operate via the ear rather than the eye are naturally earcons. Various sorts of sound are proposed; they may be directly symbolic, like the noise of a dustbin being emptied when the computer dumps data, but less easily representable activities may be denoted by brief musical phrases.

ear-sight *noun* sensitive hearing able to pinpoint the source of faint sounds

> You thought owls were bemused intellectuals? In fact they are deadly killing machines, with terrifying talons ..., advanced 'ear-sight' and cunningly silent flight.
>
> Chris Mead, *Owls* 1987

EC *abbreviation* European Community *or* Communities

... access to the lucrative EC market.
The World This Week, Channel 4, 10 July 1988

▶ The association of European nations formed under the terms of the Treaty of Rome has gone under a bewildering array of names, of which the latest is *EC*. This has been used officially for some time with reference to the European *Communities* – that is to say, not just the EEC but various other bodies such as the European Coal and Steel Community and the European Atomic Energy Commission – but its widespread use as a virtual synonym for the EEC seems to have been started by the *Independent* newspaper in 1987. It reflects the fact that the EEC is increasingly not just about economic cooperation, but envisages also a gradual coming together in other areas, notably political.

Echo Boom *noun* a significant surge in the US birth rate which occurred in 1987

The new baby wave – with 3,800,000 babies born in America last year, more than any year since 1971 – is known as 'Echo Boom.'
Daily Telegraph 2 Mar 1988

These films all dramatise the unforeseen effects of 'echo boom' babies on adults long ensconced in childless self-indulgence.
Economist 12 Mar 1988

▶ This mini-boom echoes the major postwar birth-rate explosion of 1946–64 (see BABYBOOMER). It has prompted a rash of baby films from Hollywood (such as *Baby Boom*, starring Diane Keaton, and *Three Men and a Baby*).

echogenicity *noun* the capacity of a particular type of tissue to reflect sound when scanned ultrasonically

Cuckle and Wald will be looking at two variables: the size of the abnormal ovary, and the echogenicity of the mass. They hope to be able to set guidelines based on these variables that will determine which women need further investigation.
New Scientist 14 Jan 1988

▶ Ultrasound scanning, or echography as it is also called, depends for its diagnostic value on the fact that different types of bodily tissue – for example tumours and cysts – reflect sound differently.

economical *adjective, euphemistic* deliberately withholding something from public knowledge

> In the face of all this why, I wonder, are the bishops so defensive? Why are so many of them managing in their public statements to be economical with their memories about what they do and say in private?
>
> *New Statesman* 26 Feb 1988

> Whether you're being economical with the truth or just boiling inside, body language can be a terrible giveaway.
>
> *Daily Telegraph* 25 Apr 1988

> During four days in the witness box, Mr Meacher strenuously denied the allegation that he had been 'economical with the truth'.
>
> *Daily Telegraph* 11 June 1988

▶ This circumlocution was introduced to the language by Sir Robert Armstrong, former head of the British Civil Service, when giving evidence in an Australian court on behalf of the British government in the Peter Wright *Spycatcher* case on 17 Nov 1986. When challenged with making misleading statements in correspondence, he sidestepped with a piece of elegant Mandarin-speak: he admitted being misleading, but denied telling untruths, defining the act of misleading as being 'economical with the truth'. The British public took this euphemism to their hearts (it is after all only a metaphorical extension of an existing euphemism for 'stingy') and applied it to a range of other concealments and subterfuges.

Various sources of Armstrong's phrase have been suggested, in the works of R S Surtees, Cardinal Newman, and 'Somerville and Ross', but none has been confirmed.

Economy Class Syndrome *noun* a tendency to form thromboses as a result of sitting immobile for long periods in the cramped conditions of an aircraft

The 'Economy Class Syndrome' is highlighted in today's edition of
the Lancet by leading heart and neuro specialists Dr John Cruick-
shank and Professors Brian Jennett and Richard Gorlin.

Today 26 Aug 1988

▶ A connection has recently been made between cases of
heart attack and air travel. Sitting hunched up in economy-
class chicken coops (first-class passengers do not suffer)
stops blood circulating in the legs and can lead to the formation of clots which may later cause a heart attack. Doctors
advise getting up and walking around occasionally on long
flights.

ecotoxicology *noun* the scientific study of the toxic effects
of pollutants on the environment

The vacancy exists as head of the Ecotoxicology Section which is a
part of the Environmental Team of the Laboratory. You will lead a
research group of seven scientists working on problems associated
with the assessment of the effects of the pollutants around the
coasts of Scotland. [advertisement]

New Scientist 17 Mar 1988

ecstasy *noun* a powerful amphetamine-based synthetic
stimulant drug, methylene dioxymethamphetamine
(see MDMA)

Three women were bailed yesterday at Horseferry Road Magistrates' Court in London, charged with conspiring to supply a ...
drug known as ecstasy.

Guardian 15 May 1987

Two former models wept in Southwark Crown Court yesterday as
they were cleared of supplying the powerful sex drug Ecstasy.

Daily Telegraph 28 Jan 1988

Ecstasy is officially known as MDMA. ... It originated at showbiz
parties in California and was first noticed in Britain two years ago.

The Sport 17 Aug 1988

▶ The drug ecstasy dispels inhibitions and is often used as
a sexual stimulant, but its aftereffects, especially from large
doses, can be extremely unpleasant (research suggests that
it damages nerve paths in the brain), and it has been banned
in the USA and Britain.

It was first made in 1914 by the German drug company Merck, and patented as an appetite suppressant, but then was forgotten about for nearly seventy years, reappearing as a street drug in the USA in the early 1980s. Its slang name is *Adam.*

Ecstatic *noun* a user of the drug ECSTASY

> The car park at the YMCA in Tottenham Court Road is crammed with 1,500 people ... all dancing at 3 in the morning of 31 July. ... They are Ecstatics and they have just quit the last night of the popular acid house club, the Trip.
>
> *Observer Magazine* 11 Sept 1988

EDI *noun* electronic data interchange: a computerized system for sending and receiving information about business transactions (such as an order or invoice) electronically via telephone lines, satellites, etc

> Paperless trading – the jargon is electronic data interchange (EDI) – is growing fast in Britain and North America.
>
> *Guardian* 13 Apr 1987

> To enable firms to cut out the mountains of paper that clog up commercial transactions, several computer groups have taken advantage of de-regulation in the telecommunications industry to set up networks for electronic data interchange (EDI). These networks receive and transmit data from and to any make of computer.
>
> *Observer* 10 Apr 1988

▶ EDI works in very much the same way as electronic funds transfer (see EFT/POS), except that it involves business rather than financial transactions. Users of the system communicate via a computer network: senders translate their messages into a standardized format and transmit them to a centralized mailbox, from which receivers take them and convert them into a format their computers can understand.

E-fit *noun* Electronic Facial Identification Technique: an electronic system for constructing identikit pictures from a range of computer-stored facial features which can be combined onscreen

The computer-based E-fit ... will be filled with real-life features taken from photographs of members of the public.

Daily Telegraph 14 Sept 1987

E-free *adjective* (of food) without additives, especially artificial preservatives, colourings, etc

Who could have imagined mammoth supermarket chains majoring their promotion campaigns on E-free food as they do now?

She Jan 1988

▶ The *E* in this word refers to E numbers, official EC designations for particular food additives (see *Longman Guardian New Words*).

In 1988, a brand of 'natural' sweet was advertised in Britain with 'Thr arn't any E's in Panda licoric.'

eft/pos *noun* electronic funds transfer at point of sale: a financial transaction using credit or debit cards rather than cash, with the amount being electronically registered; cashless shopping

As the [national] system gradually develops ..., the shape of electronic shopping will inevitably change. As one leading retailer put it: 'What happens to eft/pos once the devolved service gets going is anybody's guess.'

Observer 10 Apr 1988

▶ In the most fully developed form of eft/pos, using debit cards, details of a transaction are fed into the system together with the purchaser's card, and the amount to be paid is transferred automatically from the purchaser's bank account to the seller's. In France and some other European countries eft/pos has been in place for some years. In Britain, the first experimental eft/pos services were set up in various places in 1985-86; these used credit cards as well as debit cards, and were run by banks and credit-card companies. Development has been slow, but by 1988 Barclays, for example, had installed 3000 terminals throughout the country, and a body called Eft/pos UK, comprising eleven banks and three building societies, has been set up to organize a national system.

electoralism *noun,* *usually derogatory* (in politics) consideration of electoral advantage in formulating one's policies

Mr Neil Kinnock told the parliamentary Labour Party yesterday that he pleaded guilty to 'electoralism', but not to the charge that the party was drifting loose from its democratic socialist moorings. ... He said: 'Our sentence for not being electoralist is lack of power.'
Guardian 5 Nov 1987

▶ Unprincipled vote-grabbing is a charge that has often been aimed at the Labour leadership in Britain over the years by the keepers of the party's conscience on its left wing; criticism of Neil Kinnock in the late 1980s by Tony Benn and his supporters is merely the latest example. Those on the centre and right of the party, on the other hand, accuse the left-wing purists of naivety in adhering to policies that have repeatedly proved unpopular with the electorate.

electoralist *adjective* practising or favouring ELECTORALISM

electronic virus *noun* a bug deliberately and maliciously inserted into a computer program in order to spoil it

Home computer enthusiasts are falling victim to a more thoughtful kind of vandal. ... He destroys computer games belonging to complete strangers by devising ingenious electronic viruses. These viruses infect the magnetic discs which carry computer programs, ruining them instantly or inducing a lingering illness.
Independent 26 Jan 1988

So-called 'electronic viruses' are actually small computer programs, usually developed by mischievous 'hackers' to attack software in mainframes and personal computers.
Turkish Daily News 23 May 1988

▶ These 'viruses' lodge themselves in a computer's random-access memory, and infect any new disk that is inserted. One way in which they can be eliminated is by switching the computer off, but that does not cure the ruined disk. A new development, however, is the so-called 'killer disk', which can seek out and destroy the bug.

El Niño *noun* an upwelling of cold water to the surface of the sea which occurs in the eastern Pacific in most years, producing an abundant catch of fish

El Niño is the most noted example of a cyclical fluctuation in the surface temperature of the sea.

Guardian 29 July 1988

▶ *El niño* is Spanish for 'the child.'

encounter parlour *noun* an establishment where a customer pays for a session in company with a naked woman

Police and customs officers yesterday began a sweeping purge of London's Soho area. They raided dozens of unlicensed sex shops, peep shows, and nude encounter parlours in a drive to identify the property owners behind the sex and pornography businesses.

Guardian 18 June 1985

▶ The Greater London Council (General Powers) Act 1986 (designed to 'clean up Soho') defines sex encounter establishments as premises where services or entertainments 'are provided by one or more persons who are naked or who expose their breasts or genital, urinary or excretory organs.' The reality of encounter parlours is rather less lurid than this suggests: the most the punter usually gets for his money is desultory conversation with a more or less naked hostess separated from him by a window – actual sex is seldom on offer.

end-stop *verb* to bring to an abrupt or conclusive halt

Russell once end-stopped a rarefied discussion about a thinker of whom he (and, therefore, many others) had never heard by musing, 'It's his mother I feel sorry for.'

Independent 9 June 1988

▶ *End-stopped* is a technical term in prosody, referring to a line of verse that has a distinct break or pause in meaning at the end. The emphasis provided by the apparent semantic reiteration made it an irresistible target for a despecialization in meaning.

enterprise *noun* initiative and self-reliance directed towards the creation of wealth

But these positive findings about Mrs Thatcher's 'enterprise culture' were offset by other results: 48 per cent of people were 'more unhappy' today than ten years ago, 21 per cent believed people were 'happier.'

Observer 22 May 1988

Designer businessmen with phoney phones are obvious customers for the current spate of books extolling the 'enterprise culture.' ... Many teach-yourself enterprise books are decked out with charts and diagrams and written in Amerenglish.

Guardian 22 July 1988

▶ 'Enterprise' has become a key word in the promotion of the Conservative government's economic philosophy in the late 1980s: the Department of Trade and Industry, for example, has taken to calling itself the Department for Enterprise, and has instituted what it refers to as 'enterprise initiatives' to encourage the setting up of new businesses, etc. The term has the avowed purpose of gingering up people's attitude to wealth creation and making it seem a more positive activity, though some would see it as euphemistically enthroning acquisitiveness as a virtue (see LOADSAMONEY).

The institutional changes for which 'enterprise' is a code word were set in train by Lord Young when he took over as Secretary for Trade and Industry in the autumn of 1987. The DTI was seen as dissipating its resources in the indiscriminate propping up of large inefficient businesses, and the government wanted to rechannel its efforts. Lord Young declared his object to be to cut red tape and build up an open competitive economy in which all can trade freely:

Lord Young's memorandum reminds his staff that wealth creation must be their prime objective. To this end there should be less emphasis on supporting big business and more on people and enterprise.

The Times 13 Oct 1987

There is, incidentally, no direct connection with *Enterprise Zones*, which are separate entities under the aegis of the Department of the Environment: certain towns (e g Corby, Dudley, Hartlepool, and Wellingborough) are exempt from planning and other restrictions for ten years to encourage them to develop economically.

entry-level *adjective* (especially in computers) suitable for learners or first-time users

The entry-level Amstrad PC will offer a single 5.25 inch disk-drive, 256k of RAM, bundled office software, a keyboard, and black and white monitor.

Daily Mail 2 Sept 1986

Looking for an entry-level, multi-user computer that will perform and grow with your business? Talk to CCS Business Systems. [advertisement]

Sunday Times Magazine 7 Sept 1986

Adopting all the tactics he had learned at NCR, Watson aggressively bullied his way into a massive 90 per cent share of the rapidly expanding computer market. Using profits from more expensive machines, he subsidised the price of entry-level systems.

Listener 2 July 1987

▶ Comparable terms for more advanced machines are *mid-range* and *top-end*.

ephemerist *noun* a collector of ephemera (printed material not originally intended for long keeping, such as advertising leaflets and handbills)

Bookmarks move up in the world this week, when the prestigious London Antiquarian Book Fair ... will feature an exhibition of 200 decorated bookplates, some of a vast collection made by Hilary Sturt, a 23-year-old student of the violin and devoted 'ephemerist.'

Daily Telegraph 20 June 1987

ergonomy *noun* the study of the ways in which human beings can operate efficiently in their environment; ergonomics

As Nixdorf's watchdog in California, Günther Frommel, recently put it: 'Ergonomy is still a foreign word in Silicon Valley. You see products here that for reasons of human efficiency you just couldn't sell in Europe.'

Language Technology Sept/Oct 1987

▶ *Ergonomy* is probably still a foreign word in the rest of the English-speaking world too: the speaker in the above extract being apparently German, it no doubt represents German *ergonomie*. It remains to be seen whether it will catch on.

Erops *noun*　extended range operations: that part of a commercial flight which is beyond an officially stipulated distance from a suitable landing point

The Erops portion of a commercial flight is defined as that period when the aircraft is more than a hour's flying time at single-engine speed from its departure or destination airport.

Daily Telegraph 11 Jan 1988

So-called Extended Range Operations (EROPS) rules allow an airline to operate a twin-engined jet up to about 800 miles ... from an airport where it might land in an emergency

Economist 2 Apr 1988

▶ Aircraft which fly beyond the maximum range fixed by the Erops regulations must comply with certain safety requirements (for example, they must have an independently sustainable electrical system which would continue if an engine should fail). As the above extracts indicate, the standard range limit is an hour (or about 400 miles), but specially adapted twin jets are permitted to double this amount.

escrima *noun*　a form of martial art involving fighting with sticks

Martial arts students from all over the country came to study three very different fighting disciplines at BishopSport sports hall, Bishop's Storford. ... They were instructed in escrima, aiki-jutsu and ninjutsu, and shown how each provides different forms of defence against unarmed attackers or assailants using swords, knives, sticks and firearms.

Herts and Essex Observer 10 Mar 1988

▶ Escrima originated in the Philippines.

establishmentology *noun* the study of the institutions and individuals that control public life, and of the way in which they operate

Thus only a reader well-versed in British establishmentology might deduce that Milne regards Mrs Thatcher as a vicious authoritarian, Duke Hussey as her devious henchman and Sir William Rees-Mogg ... as a series of unprintable nouns.
Sunday Times 19 June 1988

▶ The use of the suffix *-logy* to mean the study of a particular political institution is probably modelled on *Kremlinology*, a term (arising in the late 1950s) for the study of the Soviet government.

ethnic monitoring *noun* regular checking to determine the proportion of different ethnic groups within an organization

The ethnic composition of individual units and regiments in the Armed Forces should be monitored to prevent discrimination, the House of Commons Defence Committee recommended yesterday. ... The committee did not, however, recommend that ethnic monitoring should be extended to the promotion process.
Daily Telegraph 26 Apr 1988

▶ The need for constant spotchecking in order to monitor organizations' recruitment policies and ensure that they do not discriminate against blacks or other ethnic groups was most recently highlighted in Britain in 1986, when remarks by the Prince of Wales about the relatively small numbers of blacks in the armed forces aroused a certain amount of controversy.

ethno-medicine *noun* the study of the techniques used in folk medicine

Each year the Conservation Foundation helps fund young scientists who want to visit tropical rainforests to further their studies in ethno-medicine. ... James Gilman and Philip Gothard ... pave the way for their team of nine ... to travel deep into the Indo-Malayan forest on a 12-week survey to ... detail the ethno-medical potential of the local flora.

Environment Now Dec 1987

▶ A better-known term for this study is *ethnobotany*, which more broadly encompasses the plant lore of a people.

-eur *suffix* (in the financial world) a person who engages in the stated activity; -er

▶ We may be seeing the first signs of the emergence of a new suffix. At the moment it is restricted to the arcane language of stockbrokers, for it originated in *arbitrageur*. This word, borrowed from French, has been in the English language for over a hundred years (and an Anglicized form, *arbitrager*, has developed), but the rash of takeover activity in the past decade, from which arbitrageurs make a profitable living, has given the term a much higher profile (and a colloquial abbreviation, *arb*). Now some new formations are beginning to appear in which *-eur* is being used where *-er* might have been expected:

Daimler puts the customary case for its acquisitive drive, making much of the 'synergy' all conglomerateurs promise to foster between different parts of their empires.

Economist 12 Dec 1987

everything *pronoun* (in physics) the totality of natural phenomena and physical forces in the universe, from the cosmological scale of gravity to the behaviour of subatomic particles

It's been called the theory of everything, a way of describing the very nature of matter. But will superstring theory really tie up all the loose ends?

Radio Times 16 Apr 1988

▶ It is the dream of physicists to formulate a grand unified theory which will account for all the forces acting on matter in the universe, namely the strong force, the weak force, gravity, and electromagnetism (supersymmetry and the SUPERSTRING theory were the flavours of the mid-1980s, but the latest contender is the SUPERMEMBRANE theory). This particular use of *everything* to characterize the object of this search may well owe something to the title of Douglas Adams's humorous novel *Life, the Universe and Everything* 1982.

executive *adjective* of the highest standard of luxury and exclusivity

> Special Pre-Christmas Shoppers to the French Hypermarkets – Caen and Bayeux Departs Wednesday, 2nd December to 4th December £30 inclusive of executive coach travel, luxury ferry travel and free litre of gin or whisky.
>
> *Bridgwater Mercury* 18 Nov 1987

▶ This adjective seems to be passing rapidly from specific equation with the supposedly enviable jet-setting lifestyle of business executives to the generally 'luxurious'; with the best will in the world it is hard to imagine the chairmen of multinational corporations abandoning their executive jets for 'executive coaches'. The broadening in meaning seems to have begun in American English in the early 1980s.

exmatriculate *verb* to remove (a pupil) from a school roll

> Fehamettin Akingüç, the President of the Association of Private Schools, said inflation was running at a rate of 70 percent in the country and the raise of 45 percent in the fees will not cover the increasing expenses. However, he also admitted that many families were unable to pay the tuition fees even before the increases and were obliged to exmatriculate their children.
>
> *Dateline* 21 May 1988

exon *noun* a small section of DNA which carries the genetic information for synthesizing proteins

> Molecular biologists have become used to the idea that genes often come in bits. Small stretches, called exons, that code for proteins are separated by long, apparently meaningless, introns. In the chain from DNA to protein the whole gene, introns and all, is first translated into RNA. Special enzymes then snip out the introns and splice the exons together to make the messenger RNA (mRNA). This messenger carries the final code that will be translated into the protein.
>
> *New Scientist* 17 Mar 1988

exotic *noun, American* a non-indigenous animal imported into a country for the express purpose of being hunted

> Joe Burkett, a veterinarian, owns at least five African lions and keeps them in his back yard. He has numerous kinds of 'exotics' on his 400-acre ranch ... for sale and use by hunters.
> *Sunday Times* 12 June 1988

▶ Exotics are used in CANNED HUNTS, artificial safaris in which the hunted animals are kept within a fenced area. They mainly consist of various species of African and Asian deer and antelope, but there are also much more sought-after 'super exotics,' such as lions.

expatriatism *noun* the practice of living or travelling abroad for an extended period

> But the foundations of the *Trib* (or, to the French, the tongue-tying *Le Herald*) are as deeply set in American 'expatriatism' as are those of *The Times* of London in Victorian diplomacy. ... A history of catering to travelling Americans eager for news from back home leaves a strong legacy.
> *Economist* 8 Aug 1987

explete *verb* to use an expletive; swear

> To its shame, ITV picked up the Miss UK contest, and it is still very boring. So little has changed in the frocks, the cleavage, the rictus grins and the love of horses/windsurfing/rose growing that ITV could have saved a fortune by repeating last year's contest and just changing the winner's name. Maybe that's what they did, without telling Alexandra Bastedo, which would explain why she expleted off-screen at some point.
> *Sunday Times* 28 Aug 1988

▶ This is essentially a back-formation from *expletive*, which established itself firmly in the general vocabulary with the 'expletives deleted' affair during the Nixon scandal of the early 1970s. But in fact the verb has existed before in English, meaning 'to complete' (it is formed from the stem of the Latin verb *explere*, 'fill out'). It first appears in the early 15th century, but has not been heard of since the mid 17th century. The noun *expletive* originally meant an extra word or phrase added to fill in a line of verse or complete a sentence, without adding anything to the meaning – hence, in due course, it has also, and chiefly, come to mean 'an obscenity.'

exploding head syndrome *noun* a sensation of explosive noise deep in the centre or back of the head, waking the sufferer from sleep

> A previously unreported medical condition known as the Exploding Head Syndrome in which patients experience a bomb-like explosion in the back of the head, is described by a consultant neurologist in the weekly medical journal the Lancet today.
>
> *Daily Telegraph* 30 July 1988

▶ People who suffer from this alarming condition tend to be middle-aged or elderly women, but it does not appear to be linked to any other form of ill health (not even, as its name might suggest, to having one too many the night before), and its cause is so far unexplained.

exput *noun* the extraction of information from a computer database

> Its [a new form of electronic mail for use by botanists] special quality is that communications are independent of hardware and software – just requiring 'input' and 'exput' programs to be written into and out of individual garden databases.
>
> *Guardian* 12 Nov 1987

extensification *noun* the reduction of intensive production in the EC of agricultural items (such as cereals and beef) which are in surplus

> Mr John MacGregor, the Minister of Agriculture, is even now putting the finishing touches to a consultation document on how Britain is to implement the EEC's directive on 'extensification' (a deliberately meaningless bureaucratic word).
>
> *Daily Telegraph* 31 Oct 1987

> I think one sees ... the necessity to put into effect the EEC extensification proposals.
>
> *Environment Now* Dec 1987/Jan 1988

▶ This is apparently intended as an antonym of *intensification*, on the model of *intensive:extensive*. It faces competition, however, from *deintensification*:

> Agricultural deintensification ... is likely to push more farmers into forestry.
>
> *New Society* 8 Apr 1988

externality *noun* an incidental effect of an activity

> In nineteenth-century London, railway companies could buy the slums that stood where Euston, St. Pancras and King's Cross station now do, and run their trains into the city centre without offending the grandees of Kensington. Airports shower their 'externalities' on great and small alike. The busiest one in Europe incessantly rattles the Queen's tea-cups at Windsor Castle.
>
> *Economist* 27 Feb 1988

extract *verb* to publish an extract or extracts from (a piece of writing)

> Glenn Savan quit the advertising business to wait tables – and to write his first novel, White Palace, extracted here.
>
> *Elle* Mar 1988

extremilexic *noun* a person whose surname begins with any of the letters A-F or U-Z

> Not only am I a statistic; I am a ranked statistic. The world, I now understand, is divided into summilexics, whose names begin with A-M, and fundilexics, whose names begin with N-Z. Another grouping, the mediocre, is the medilexics, G-T, while A-F and U-Z make up the extremilexics.
>
> *New Scientist* 22 Oct 1987

▶ See ALPHABETISM.

eyelyser *noun* a device for gauging alcohol consumption by measuring the level of alcohol in vapour given off by the eyes

> They advocate replacing the 'breathalyser' with the 'eyelyser'.
>
> *New Scientist* 10 Sept 1987

▶ The eyelyser was developed by scientists at the Addiction Research Foundation in Toronto, Canada. It consists essentially of a funnel, which is placed over the eyeball for 15 seconds, and a gas sensor which analyses the vapour collected by the funnel. It is claimed that it can measure the alcohol intake even of people who are unconscious.

The term is, of course, a blend of *eye* and *analyser*.

eyeprint *noun* a measurement of the pattern of veins in an individual's retina, used for purposes of identification

> The days of the hotel key are numbered, he said. Credit cards and other magnetic cards are already being used in some hotels though eventually 'biometric' systems will be introduced. One type uses an electronic finger-print reader. Another takes an 'eyeprint.'
> *Daily Telegraph* 19 May 1988

▶ The pattern of veins in someone's retina is as individual a mark of identity as fingerprints.

fabby *adjective, British informal* wonderful

> Christmas is hip, cool, ace, fabby – NOT rubbish. Think of all those discos, parties, concerts and films which are ace.
> *Patches* 19 Feb 1988

> But not when it's three lucky Jackie readers! We brightened up their February with a fabby new look.
> *Jackie* 20 Feb 1988

▶ A usage restricted mainly to pre-adolescent girls, based apparently on the now venerable *fab*.

face-time *noun, American slang* a period of duty by a US secret service agent accompanying and guarding a VIP

> 'How come you're always doing the face-time?' complained one of the plastic-ear brigade to his colleague. ... Face-time is from the jargon of the US Secret Service, whose men sweep and freeze the vicinity of the big candidates before their arrival. The agents who stare steely-eyed into the crowd from just in front of their man are doing face-time.
> *The Times* 17 Mar 1988

fade cream *noun* a cosmetic cream containing the compound hydroquinone, which inhibits production of the skin pigment melanin and thus makes the skin paler

> 'Fade creams' are popular with women (and men) to even out skin tones and regulate the colour of the complexion.
> *Cosmopolitan* Mar 1988

family credit *noun* (in Britain) a social-security payment for low-income families with one or more children

> One of the key strengths of family credit is that whether or not parents are unemployed, they can claim the same amount for their children, if they are poor.
> *Sunday Times* 10 Apr 1988

▶ Family credit was introduced on 11 Apr 1988 under the terms of the Social Security Act 1988, to replace the previous family income supplement. It is available to those on low incomes who work at least 24 hours a week and have at least one child. It differs from family income supplement by being based on net income rather than gross income. See also INCOME SUPPORT, SOCIAL FUND.

fan club *noun* a group of individuals or companies that favours the taking over of a particular company and buys shares in that company in order to vote in support of the takeover bid

> There is also a looser version of the concert party known as a fan club. Companies in favour of Ebenezer's takeover for their own reasons might buy Scrooge shares just to vote for the takeover.
> *Cosmopolitan* Sept 1987

▶ As the above extract suggests, the fan club has much in common with another City phenomenon, the concert party (see *Longman Guardian New Words*). The essential difference is that whereas a fan club simply acts in a generally supportive role towards the prospective bidder, and does so in its own interests, a concert party is usually got up by the bidder himself, in order to acquire shares in the target company which it can then hand over to him.

fat transfer *noun* a cosmetic surgery technique in which fat is removed from the hips, thighs, etc by vacuum pumping and then injected into facial tissues to swell them and thus reduce skin wrinkling

> The American Society of Plastic and Reconstructive Surgeons has called fat transfer an 'experimental procedure' that needs more study.
> *USA Today* 8 Feb 1988

▶ Fat transfer originated in the USA around 1982, but as the above extract suggests, it has yet to be fully accepted by the medical establishment as a valid treatment. The main difficulty to be overcome is ensuring that the tissue transferred does not simply get absorbed and disappear.

fattyism *noun, informal* discrimination against or ill-treatment of fat people

Grange Hill ... – the programme that single-handedly convinces entire generations of schoolchildren that they aren't *living* unless their classrooms resound with parody, criminalspeak, uninventive abuse, bullying, racism and fattyism.

Observer 10 Apr 1988

faxbox *noun* a computerized document storage facility for a fax machine

When operating as a computer printer for the IBM-PC, the Omega has a 10-megabyte memory that can store some 200 documents, filing some of them in special 'faxboxes' (for transmission to a single location) if necessary.

Newsweek 4 Apr 1988

▶ The term is possibly modelled on the *electronic mailbox*, the receiving and storing facility for data sent via electronic communications systems such as Prestel.

feeder *verb* to convey by means of a subsidiary transport system linking with a main transport centre

But the final push to move out of Sembawang came this year when the American carrier decided to make direct calls at Singapore instead of feedering the cargo from here to Kaohsiung.

Business Times (Malaysia) 3 June 1988

▶ A *feeder* is a railway, airline, shipping route, etc that serves outlying areas, joining them up to a main transport system.

feller-buncher *noun* a machine used in forestry to cut down trees and remove their branches

Lawrence says that the researchers have successfully completed phase one of a project to develop a remotely operated 'feller-buncher' which is used to fell and de-limb trees.

New Scientist 17 Mar 1988

feminal¹ *adjective* (of a man) displaying certain behavioural or psychological characteristics traditionally assigned to women

> The Henley Centre for Forecasting ... says it has found that men are, increasingly, behaving like women when shopping. The new man is called a 'feminal consumer,' which has nothing to do with being effeminate. In the course of field-work at my local Sainsbury's, I was able to identify a Labour MP and two BBC/TV producers, steering their trolleys through the displays, as specimens of this new breed.
>
> *Daily Telegraph* 11 Apr 1987

▶ Compare NEW MAN.

feminal² *noun* a feminal man

> The feminals seemed to be shopping with great authority.
>
> *Daily Telegraph* 11 Apr 1987

feni *or* **fenny** *noun* a spirit distilled in Goa from cashew nuts or coconuts

> Western tourists have been accused of spreading Aids and ruining the economy of the small Indian state of Goa, famous for years as an exotic seaside paradise on the hippie trail. The inhabitants say the state is no longer 'a land of fun, frolic and feni.'
>
> *Daily Telegraph* 24 Feb 1988

▶ Feni is the powerful local brew of Goa, the former Portuguese colony on the west coast of India. It is made into a variety of fanciful cocktails for visitors, but the Goans tend to take it neat.

fertigation *noun* a method of agricultural fertilization in which plants are continuously fed via a drip irrigation system with water that has nutrients added to it

> In co-operation with the Research Station for Fruit Growers in Holland, the researchers at DSM have developed a completely new fertilising technique for north-west Europe. They call it 'fertigation.' [advertisement]
>
> *Economist* 11 June 1988

147

filmization *or* **filmisation** *noun* a film version of a book, play, etc

'My Fair Lady' (1964). Smooth 'filmization' of the Alan Jay Lerner and Frederic Loewe musical from Bernard Shaw's *Pygmalion*, with Rex Harrison as Professor Higgins.

Daily Telegraph 30 May 1988

filofiction *trademark* novels published in a format suitable for incorporation in a PERSONAL ORGANIZER

Filofiction – best-selling novels by authors such as Jeffrey Archer scaled down to fit a chapter at a time into a filofax – is on the way. The slimline novels are to be launched in September.

Independent 22 June 1988

It may have seemed that publishing conglomerate Octopus could not come up with a less appealing idea than 'filofiction,' novels in loose leaves with holes down the left margin, that fit into Filofaxes.

Sunday Times 24 July 1988

fire-flash *noun* a very rapid spread of flame across a burning surface

Much of the modernisation on platforms and around escalators [in underground stations] consists of putting in false walls and ceilings of panels and tiles. ... It would be hard to detect any initial smouldering, but there would be extensive space for a sudden fire-flash.

Daily Telegraph 24 Nov 1987

▶ *Fire-flash* and the more familiar *flash-over* were two items of fire brigade terminology brought forcibly before a wider audience on 18 Nov 1987, when a fire in London's King's Cross underground station killed 31 people.

fiscal *noun* an accounting period of 12 months; a fiscal year, especially as related to the stated calendar year

For fiscal 1986, the administration wanted the budget reduced from $164 million to $70 million – the steepest cut yet. ... Budgets will probably be even tighter in fiscal 1987.

New Scientist 20 June 1985

▶ This usage is of American origin, and in British English is still largely used in US contexts, but it could well become completely naturalized.

flag out *verb* to register a ship under a flag of convenience rather than in the owner's home country

> Shipowners 'flag out' because the convenience flag registers are cheaper, the safety and employment standards are lower, unions weaker, and the tax advantages enormous.
>
> *Guardian* 5 Jan 1987

> Cost cutting pressures ... have led to much of the rest of the developed world's fleets registering under flags of convenience ('flagging out').
>
> *Financial Times* 26 Apr 1988

▶ Compare REFLAG.

flake *noun, informal, chiefly American* an unstable or unreliable person

> [Gary] Hart scares the Democratic party big-wigs as a liberal 'flake.'
>
> *Daily Telegraph* 13 Apr 1987

> Nagyvary's findings have been scrutinised by the American Chemical Society. And he himself, according to a society member, is 'not a kook or a flake. He is a legitimate guy.'
>
> *Daily Telegraph* 26 Jan 1988

▶ The noun is formed from the adjective *flaky*, which came into the spotlight in Britain when used by Ronald Reagan in 1986 to describe Colonel Gadaffi (see *Longman Guardian New Words*).

flan *verb* to assault with a custard pie

> The actors hit the headlines in 1983 when Prince Charles visited them on a tour of Jubilee Trust-sponsored groups, and was 'flanned' in an exchange of custard pies.
>
> *Observer* 1 Mar 1987

flash-bang *noun, informal* a grenade intended to stun its victims by means of its flash and loud report; a stun grenade

Others of the SAS assault team, preparing their way with flash-bangs ..., were able to reach the critical rooms.

The Times 4 Feb 1988

flesh *noun* – **press (the) flesh** *informal, chiefly American* to shake hands, especially with large numbers of people

I was sitting with Norman Mailer, Chuck Pfeifer, and our women, when Koch suddenly appeared in front of our table and began pressing flesh in the graceful manner of Tip O'Neill, i.e. shaking hands while looking around the room to see where more important people were sitting.

Spectator 24 Jan 1987

There was a rush to press flesh as the verdict [the result of the Booker Prize] was announced, with Deutsch director Anthony Thwaite leading the way.

Publishing News 6 Nov 1987

▶ The phrase is very closely associated with politicians, for whom shaking every hand in sight is second only to kissing babies as a campaign-trail ploy. There is increasing evidence, as in the second quote above, of a widening application, but still the underlying note is negative: to shake so many hands argues against sincerity.

flesh-pressing *noun, informal* large-scale hand-shaking, especially as a political campaign ploy

President Reagan plans several meetings with Soviet citizens during his summit trip to Moscow next month, but White House officials have ruled out any campaign-style flesh-pressing.

Newsweek 18 Apr 1988

▶ See previous entry.

flight *noun* a particular sequence of wines evaluated at a wine-tasting session

Gault Milau ... magazine ... organized a so-called wine Olympics ... with a jury of 32 tasters from several countries ... For reasons of convenience the wines were examined in four sessions – what the Americans call 'flights' and the French call *séances*.

Observer 1 Mar 1987

The tastings took place at the University Club, Chicago, and consisted of two sessions, each of four 'flights' of vintages.

Decanter July 1988

▶ *Pace* the first extract above, the term *flight* refers to an individual sequence of wines tasted, typically linked by some characteristic, rather than an entire session, and is rapidly becoming adopted into British wine-tasting terminology.

flip-flop *noun, informal, chiefly American* a sudden complete change or reversal; a U-turn

The President, in his first meeting with the Tower Commission, agreed with McFarlane. Then he was persuaded by Regan to change his story, leaving the impression in Washington that the Chief of Staff was covering himself by getting the President to alter his account. This flip-flop was perhaps the most damaging blow to the President's credibility amid the welter of charges of cover-up.

Daily Telegraph 28 Feb 1987

Gephardt mocked Dukakis's 'battlefield conversion', and his staff groused that Dukakis had somehow gotten away with just the sort of 'flip-flop' on the issues that Gephardt himself had so often been criticized for.

Newsweek 4 Apr 1988

▶ The metaphor derives from another American sense of *flip-flop*: 'a backward somersault.'

floatel *noun* a hotel in which accommodation is provided in chalets constructed on semi-permanently moored barges

The calm blue waters [of the Bay of Islands, New Zealand], sheltered anchorages and deserted beaches are the setting for one of the most novel forms of self-catering I have come across. Floating Scandinavian-style wooden chalets called 'floatels' cannot really be described as houseboats, since they're far more house than boat.

Daily Telegraph 4 June 1988

▶ Floatels should not be confused with boatels (a coinage of the mid-1950s), which are waterfront hotels with facilities for boat owners.

flume ride *noun, chiefly American* a fairground amusement consisting of a water chute down which people ride

There are [at Florida theme parks] roller coasters, scream machines and flume rides.

Time Out 4 May 1988

▶ A *flume* is a sloping channel for conveying water, for example to a hydroelectric plant. Compare *aquatube* (*Longman Guardian New Words*).

foetal reduction *noun* the abortion of one or some of the foetuses in a multiple pregnancy

For she is one of a small band of women who have undergone foetal reduction, a new procedure in which one or more foetuses are destroyed in a multiple pregnancy.

Observer 1 Nov 1987

▶ The technique of foetal reduction is a logical, but controversial, consequence of many modern methods of combatting infertility, such as the artificial implantation of fertilized eggs, which result in multiple pregnancies. Once the pregnancy has been established, the number of foetuses is reduced by abortion in order to minimize or eliminate the risks of giving birth to several babies at one time. This has enraged the pro-life lobby, who view the process as the creation of life only to destroy it.

fontanometer *noun* a device for measuring pressure inside a baby's skull

This device offers for the first time the possibility of routine monitoring of this kind of pressure. It's called a fontanometer and it doesn't have any probes or needles at all.

Tomorrow's World, BBC1, 21 Apr 1988

▶ The build-up of pressure in the fluid surrounding the brain of premature babies, potentially causing brain damage, has hitherto been detectable only by inserting a probe into the skull. The fontanometer, however (the term derives from *fontanelle*, the membrane-covered space between the bones of a baby's skull), works non-intrusively: a small air-filled container with a membrane is placed against the fontanelle, and any movement on the membrane ensures that the air pressure within the container is equalized with the pressure inside the head, which can thus be measured.

foothold buying *noun* the gradual acquisition of small amounts of a company's equity with a view to later making a takeover bid for it

> While Mr Jarrell would not dispute that insider trading accounts for some of the rise, he thinks that matters like press interest and 'foothold buying' ... account for a large and wholly legitimate part of the market movements.
>
> *Economist* 20 Dec 1986

footprint *noun* the area within which the warheads of a multiple-warhead missile land

> Trident's footprint is considerably large and each warhead can be targeted more accurately.
>
> *Independent* 26 Jan 1988

▶ This is the latest variation in a closely related set of meanings of *footprint*, including the area in which a spacecraft is to land and the area covered by the signal from a geostationary communications satellite.

Footsie *noun, informal* (quasi-acronym for the) Financial Times-Stock Exchange 100 share index

> Footsie runs out of steam. [headline]
>
> *Sunday Times* 1 June 1986

> Take an investor who is convinced that Footsie – currently around the 1600 mark – is destined for better things by Christmas.
>
> *Daily Telegraph* 4 Oct 1986

▶ The Financial Times-Stock Exchange 100 share index monitors the ups and downs of the share prices of the hundred largest public companies in Britain, according to market capitalization. It was set up on 3 Jan 1984. The acronym-like nickname comes from the initial letters FT-SE.

forest therapy *noun* a psychotherapeutic technique involving breathing in sedative chemicals given off by trees

Forest therapy is another popular de-stressor. It has its origins in Japan where scientific research has shown health benefits from breathing the chemicals and aromas given off by trees like the Sugi and the Hinoki which are similar to the pine tree.

Cosmopolitan Sept 1987

forfaiting *noun* the practice of buying and selling debts outstanding in international trade

Other securitised-debt markets have mushroomed in the past 20 years but not forfaiting, a business where competition is fierce. Although the market has grown by more than 20% since 1982 to $20 billion–30 billion of outstanding debts, it accounts for less than 0.25% of the value of world trade.

Economist 27 Feb 1988

▶ A forfaiter will buy, at a discount, IOUs held by the exporters in respect of goods supplied to other countries, and eventually sell them on in the form of tradeable securities to banks and other financial institutions. In French, *vente à forfait* is 'selling of futures.'

fragile X syndrome *noun* a severe mental handicap transmitted genetically and characterized by a break or fragile area in the X chromosome

The children are victims of Fragile X Syndrome, a genetic deficiency, which is the second most common genetic mental handicap after Downs Syndrome.

Daily Telegraph 10 Apr 1987

▶ It is only in the past ten years that fragile X syndrome has come to be recognized by doctors. The chromosomal defect is usually transmitted by the mother, but its effects show themselves in male children. Sufferers from the syndrome exhibit a mental age of two.

free-fall *noun* a sudden severe decline (especially in stock-market prices or foreign exchange rates) which shows no sign of stopping

Lawson, in his first statement since shares went into freefall, said that the underlying economy was strong.
London Evening Standard 20 Oct 1987

All morning the Stock Exchange has been in freefall.
Daily Telegraph 21 Oct 1987

This has propelled the ... island economy into free fall.
Financial Times 26 Apr 1988

One Republican senator ... said that unless Mr Bush performed amazingly well at the convention, he was in danger of going into 'free fall'.
Daily Telegraph 9 Aug 1988

▶ In general physical terms, *free-fall* is unrestrained motion in a gravitational field, but this metaphor more likely comes from the parachutist's free-fall, the period between jumping out of the aircraft and actually opening the chute. The term enjoyed a particular boom with the stock-market crash of October 1987. It is also used as a verb:

But the main surprise in dealing yesterday was the resilience of the dollar, which most foreign-exchange traders expected to free-fall after Friday's sharp drop.
Daily Telegraph 27 Oct 1987

frisée *or* **frisé** *noun* endive

Unusual salads from the supermarket cabinet include Sainsbury's fennel and water-cress or crinkly frisé; radicchio, chicory and lambs' lettuce provide contrasting colours and textures.
Daily Telegraph 3 July 1987

▶ Endive, which resembles a dishevelled spidery lettuce, is one of a bewildering array of salad leaves which have invaded the supermarket shelves of Britain over the past decade. It suffers from a potentially crippling name problem, however. Confusion is rife over which of a range of fairly similar vegetables should be called 'endives,' and which 'chicory.' This is compounded by American speakers using 'chicory' for what British speakers usually call 'endive.' It is therefore a welcome development that traders, probably following the lead of restaurateurs, have cut through the muddle by starting to use the French term *frisée* for 'endive' (one hesitates to add the further complication that this is short for *chicorée frisée*, 'curly chicory').

frit *adjective, British dialect* frightened

> On Black Thursday, a week before polling, Margaret Thatcher
> seemed frit – to use her own Lincolnshire dialect word for 'fright-
> ened' – and some admirers were even more frit by signs that she
> was accident-prone.
>
> *Listener* 18 June 1987

▶ This humble dialectal past participle of the verb 'to fright'
sprang from obscurity to stardom on 19 April 1983, when
Margaret Thatcher used it in the House of Commons. She
was answering questions on inflation when Denis Healey
intervened to accuse her of 'cutting and running' in
preparation for a general election. Stung by the taunt, she
rounded on Labour, saying it was they who were 'afraid of
an election – frightened – frit!'

This unfamiliar locution was gleefully seized on by the
press and soon became part of the baggage of Thatcher folk-
lore, as being a word of ancient Lincolnshire origin. In fact,
it is common to many parts of England (Joseph Wright's
English Dialect Dictionary records it from Nottingham-
shire, Northamptonshire, Warwickshire, Herefordshire,
Oxfordshire, Bedfordshire, Hertfordshire, Huntingdon-
shire, Suffolk, Sussex, Hampshire, and Devon as well as
Lincolnshire), but to give a genuine Lincolnshire example,
from Mabel Peacock's *Taales fra Linkisheere* 1890: 'He was
to be frit wi' nowt.'

fromage frais *noun*　a fairly liquid variety of curd cheese

> Plain or flavoured with fruit, *fromage frais* tastes fine on its own or
> is great used for cooking or on cereals.
>
> *Cosmopolitan* May 1988

> It's always interesting to try out a new food, especially when it
> comes from France – but what is this *fromage frais*, and how do you
> use it?
>
> *Family Circle* July 1988

▶ Meaning literally 'fresh cheese' in French, this is a form
of cheese simply made by heating milk with buttermilk
until it coagulates and then briefly draining it. It is a traditional French accompaniment to fresh fruit, and in recent

years has become increasingly popular in Britain, often in a rather commercialized version with sugar and fruit flavour added.

front-line *adjective*　at the point of most acute conflict

> During angry Commons exchanges which followed yesterday's State Opening of Parliament, the Prime Minister confirmed that she would be visiting the front-line inner city area herself.
> *Daily Telegraph* 26 June 1987

> The Prince and Princess of Wales toured 'front-line' Brixton yesterday, venturing into what has been described as the most violent and racially sensitive [area] in Britain.
> *Daily Telegraph* 8 July 1987

fudge and mudge *noun*　avoidance of definite commitment; equivocation; fudging

> It remains possible that the fudges and mudges [in the Fowler review], which were so glaringly obvious to almost everyone … will be retracted later.
> *Guardian* 10 June 1985

> Fratricide and matricide play much the same part in their societies as fudge and mudge do in our own.
> *Guardian* 8 May 1986

▶ This expression (which is also used as a verb) seems to have first been popularized by the politician Roy Jenkins, and has perhaps become chiefly associated with the Liberal and Social Democratic parties, accused by critics of failing to arrive at definite and agreed policies. Commenting on a policy proposal by David Steel, a writer in the *Guardian* (9 June 1986) said 'That doesn't sound too fudge and mudgy.'

Mudge gives the appearance of being merely a nonsense word, formed by repeating *fudge* with an alteration of the initial sound. This sort of repetition with slight variation is quite a common way of reinforcing the meaning of a word, although it is rather more usual for the variation to occur in the vowel (*flip-flop*, *criss-cross*). Change of the first consonant seems less frequent; *humdrum* and *hocus pocus* are examples, and *hugger mugger* may well be too. The second part of this last compound comes from a Middle English verb *mukeren*, to conceal or hoard; and coincidentally its old Scottish form is *hudge mudge*. So maybe *mudge* is not a nonsense word after all; 'conceal' is close in meaning to 'fudge,' and *fudge and mudge* could (like *moil and toil*) be a case of a compound formed from rhyming synonyms.

An alternative source of *mudge* may be the obsolete Scottish and Northern English verb *mudge*, to move or budge (the *English Dialect Dictionary* gives a Northumbrian example: 'Aa canna mudge 'd; it's ower hivvy'), but the sense relationship here is a little less convincing.

See also MUDGER.

full-frills *adjective* having a wide range of additional desirable features

> The new carrier is an attempt (the third, so far) to introduce a full-frills, first-class service to America's skies.
>
> *Economist* 12 Sept 1987

▶ The opposite of NO-FRILLS (often in itself a term of approval) is felt, interestingly, to be not *frilly*, but *full-frills*.

fundilexic *noun* a person whose surname begins with any of the letters N-Z

> Not only am I a statistic; I am a ranked statistic. The world, I now understand, is divided into summilexics, whose names begin with A-M, and fundilexics, whose names begin with N-Z.
>
> *New Scientist* 22 Oct 1987

▶ See ALPHABETISM.

fuzzy matching *noun* a computerized cross-checking technique which can identify parts which are similar rather than strictly identical

> Now computers, sophisticated software, 'fuzzy matching' ... and other techniques will be used to try to trap people making illegal multiple applications [for new issues of shares]. ... Data received from the Rolls-Royce Share Information Office about people who

registered their interest in advance will be checked against
applications. Helping out will be 'fuzzy matching.'

Daily Telegraph May 1987

▶ In computing and mathematics, *fuzzy* is used to refer to
data which is imprecise or has uncertain boundaries.

fuzzy navel *noun* a cocktail made from peach schnapps and
orange juice

Every age gets the drinks it deserves. ... It's quite possible that our
own time will be remembered for the peach schnapps and orange
juice concoction known as the Fuzzy Navel.

Esquire Mar 1988

Gi

gado-gado *noun* a Singapore dish consisting of a cooked vegetable salad with hard-boiled egg and a peanut sauce

Most Singaporean/Malaysian restaurants in London offer some Indonesian fare as well. ... The by now ubiquitous satay ... and gado gado are common to all three countries.

City Limits 18 Feb 1988

There were prawns lightly fried in hot sambal sauce ..., noodles fried with bean sprouts and the famous gado-gado.

Time Out 11 May 1988

▶ Malay cuisine, making great use of peanuts, has recently become fashionable on both sides of the Atlantic.

gai-ge *noun* (in the People's Republic of China) a fundamental and revolutionary reordering of the economic and social basis of the state

The Chinese have their own version of *perestroika*: gai-ge. These two words could change the shape of the world, so it is worth being clear about their meaning. *Perestroika* has a slight suggestion of moving things about. Gai-ge is stronger: it means getting rid of things as well as changing them – radical reform.

Daily Telegraph 20 Apr 1988

One sign of how far *gaige* – Chinese *perestroika* – has already advanced is that China's peasants are now far richer than official per capita dollar incomes suggest.

Economist 9 July 1988

The word '*gaige*' – Chinese for *perestroika* – is on the lips of every official from the lowliest party secretary to the most senior member of the Politburo.

Daily Telegraph 23 Aug 1988

▶ The Chinese word *gǎigé* means 'reform'. Compare PERE-STROIKA.

gain sharing *noun*   a form of profit sharing in which employees receive additional payments in direct proportion to economies or gains they are able to make on behalf of their company in the course of their work

A majority of employees in America say they do not see much connection between effort and subsequent pay rises. To strengthen the link, companies are devising a number of schemes that tie financial rewards more closely to performance than do traditional bonuses and profit-sharing. Particularly popular is 'gain-sharing.' This is an idea ... tried out by a number of large corporations including General Electric, Motorola and Bank of America. In a gain-sharing scheme, operating units share with the company in savings for which they are responsible. At GE, 5% of whose American workforce now participates in gain sharing, schemes typically are run by groups of 500-600 employees. Rewards are always in cash and paid quarterly, monthly or weekly.
Economist 13 Feb 1988

galleonic *adjective*   like a galleon in majestic but no-nonsense belligerence

He [John Smith] is very intelligent and analytical. His parliamentary style ... is 'galleonic.' The proud sail of his interrogation alarms the Tories. They very much want him *not* to become the opposition leader.
Sunday Times 26 June 1988

gameplan *noun*   a strategy for achieving an objective by a series of steps

Auty deserted these towers for the rarefied atmosphere and the tweed jackets of the BBC four years ago, and a neatly formulated gameplan took him from script editor to producer in no time at all.
Time Out 4 May 1988

▶ The term probably originated with the convoluted tactical manoeuvrings of American footballers, but its metaphorical use is now beginning to make itself felt in British English.

garbology *noun,   American*   the scientific study of waste disposal

Each year every American produces, on average, around a tonne of rubbish; and American industry churns out about 250m tonnes of hazardous wastes. ... Hence the burgeoning science of garbology.

Economist 13 Feb 1988

▶ This apparently serious coinage is based, of course, on *garbage*.

gastrodrama *noun*   a theatrical production in which food plays a prominent part, especially one in which the audience participates by eating

Given the variety of French cooking, the Comédie de Caen's successful gastrodrama, 'P'tit Albert,' to be served up at the Edinburgh Festival this summer, may come as a bit of a shock. ... The host of this one-course, one-man show is not a lonely waiter but a hyperactive loony intent on telling his captive guests about life in an asylum. Seated the length of a narrow refectory table, the 40 or so diners watching the performance will uneasily spoon their lentils while a slightly manic cook and kitchen boy regales them with tales told by an idiot.

Observer Magazine 14 Aug 1988

-gate *suffix*   a political scandal involving some sort of corruption

▶ A decade and half after the Watergate affair launched this suffix on its career, it is still going strong, and indeed after a fallow period seems to be coming back with renewed vigour in the late 1980s. In the USA the impetus for this probably came largely from *Contragate* and *Irangate* (a scandal involving the supply of arms to Iran and the use of the profits to help fund the Contras in Nicaragua), while in Britain *Westlandgate* (see *Longman Guardian New Words*) perhaps helped the relaunch. It has now spread throughout the English-speaking world:

senior officials [in Sierra Leone] whose wholesale involvement in corruption is generally referred to as the 'Milliongate' scandal

Daily Telegraph 19 Nov 1987

And it offers ample opportunity for puns:

Incidentally, [Oliver] North will be asked about his accepting the gift of a security gate at his home, a sub-plot that has become known as Gategate.

Daily Telegraph 1 July 1987

The Oral Roberts affair was a mere curtain-raiser to the main event of what is now becoming known as Gospelgate (or Godscam or Pearlygate) [scandal surrounding the wrongdoings of US TELEVAN-GELISTS].

Daily Telegraph 10 Apr 1987

gazetting *noun, Singapore English* the placing of an official restriction on the sales or distribution of a newspaper or similar publication

The government has severely restricted the distribution of publications that it deemed to be delving into Singapore's domestic politics or presenting a distorted view of the country. The Asian Wall Street Journal, Time, Asiaweek and the Far Eastern Economic Review have all had their distribution slashed. Gazetting, as it's called, is a powerful weapon; Singapore, with its highly educated and prosperous population, is one of Asia's largest media outlets.

Newsweek 15 Feb 1988

gazwelcher *noun, British* a person who undertakes to buy a house but withdraws from the transaction just before contracts are to be signed

A new term I have recently heard is the 'gazwelchers,' which is the opposite of gazumping. It refers to the purchaser who leads the vendor 'up the garden path,' withdrawing from the purchase at the last moment.

Essex Countryside Magazine Mar 1987

▶ A blend of *gazump* and *welch*, 'evade one's obligations.' The word *gazump*, which refers to defaulting by the vendor rather than the buyer, has been around since the 1920s, although it then referred to swindling in general, and its specific application to house purchasing does not seem to have developed until about 1970.

geddit *interjection, British informal* (used facetiously or ironically for drawing attention to a pun, innuendo, or other supposedly witty rhetorical or linguistic device)

'40 Minutes' had made a sympathetic and reasonably unexploitative film about what dwarves think of the rest of us, called it 'Short Stories' (geddit?) and then spent the rest of the time trying to make up for the title by referring to dwarves throughout as 'persons of restricted growth.'

Daily Telegraph 16 Jan 1987

Dr Owen ... has coined a new campaign slogan: 'Confidence and concern, competitiveness and compassion, competence and cohesion.' These he calls 'the six key ingredients of a coalition' – another 'C,' geddit? – 'for the national interest.'

Daily Telegraph 12 May 1987

Radio 4's Department of Silly Titles has been at it again, coming up with a new science series called *SO4* (*Science on 4*, Geddit?).

Listener 11 June 1987

▶ This attempt to represent the casual pronunciation of *get it?* seems to have begun, or at least been popularized, in the Glenda Slag column of the satirical magazine *Private Eye*, a cod version of a certain Fleet Street column in which a series of rather lame nudge-nudge, wink-wink allusions are regularly punctuated by *geddit?*

geep *noun* a cross between a sheep and a goat produced by genetic engineering

Other teams have fused goat embryos with sheep embryos, to produce a new life-form they call a geep.

Listener 30 Apr 1987

The now-famous 'geep' ... inherited horns from its parent goat and a shaggy coat from its parent sheep.

Economist 30 Apr 1988

▶ The geep was first produced by Cambridge scientists in 1984. It is a chimera – that is, an animal created by artificially combining DNA from parents of two distinct species. It cannot reproduce.

gender *verb* to associate (something) stereotypically with one sex or the other

The most important thing is that the sex discrimination legislation ... is applied. The scheme could use what it is often criticised for, its very closeness to employers, to challenge their practices and influence them to change patterns of recruitment and the gendering of jobs.

Guardian 26 Nov 1986

gender gap *noun* the difference between the political issues with which men and women are concerned, and the consequent tendency of one sex to vote differently from the other

A substantial gender gap has opened up on defence. Among men, the Tories have a 15-point lead over Labour as the party trusted most; among women, the lead is just two points.

Observer 5 Oct 1986

Vice-President Bush ... struggles to overcome his lagging popularity among women voters. ... Unless narrowed, the gender gap alone could lose the election for Mr Bush.

Daily Telegraph 12 Aug 1988

▶ The not altogether surprising existence of this difference has been confirmed and quantified by pollsters in the 1980s. They have found that women are mainly concerned with social and environmental issues, whereas men attach more importance to defence and foreign affairs. And this can translate into differences in party support: in the US congressional elections of 1982 it was estimated that the women's vote diverged from the men's by about 10% in favour of the Democrats.

genderist *adjective* involving unfair discrimination between male and female

This is not to say that men do not exhibit similar or worse tendencies, but rather to suggest that the problem is one of how people relate together as people and not a genderist issue.

Guardian 3 Feb 1987

▶ This term probably represents an attempt to express rather less emotively the same essential notion that *sexist* conveys. *Sexist* has become so strongly linked with anti-female prejudice that it is scarcely available to denote discrimination against either sex.

genethliadeltiology *noun* the hobby of collecting birthday and Christmas cards

Connoisseurs of genethliadeltiology ... will be aware of the deep significance buried in some of the designs.

Daily Telegraph 14 Dec 1987

▶ *Deltiology*, the term for collecting postcards (*deltos* is Greek for a writing tablet), is first recorded from 1947; it seems to have originated in the USA. The word for this even more esoteric refinement of the hobby has been formed from Greek *genethliakos*, 'of one's birth or birthday'.

genetic mother *noun* the woman who donated the egg from which a baby developed in another woman's womb

> The VLA was concerned that the child might one day find out that its aunt was its genetic mother.
>
> *Guardian* 8 May 1987

gennaker *or* **genniker** *noun* an asymmetrical spinnaker sail

> The recovery of the Colin Beashel-captained Australia IV was helped by the use of a rarely seen 'gennaker,' a cross between a genoa and a spinnaker.
>
> *Daily Telegraph* 7 Jan 1987

> Without seeming to disturb the water around her, [the yacht] New Zealand accelerated to 12 knots. Her joint skippers, David Barnes and Peter Lester, now ordered the downwind headsail to be hoisted; not a conventional spinnaker, but a masthead 'genniker.'
>
> *Guardian* 25 Mar 1988

▶ Standard spinnakers are cut so that the two long sides of their triangle are of equal length. A gennaker, however, has one of these sides longer than the other. Its shape is modelled on that of the Genoa jib, a larger than usual jib (sail rigged forward of the mast) used on some boats, and the name is a blend of *Genoa* and *spinnaker*.

gentrify *verb* to make or become more in conformity with middle-class standards and values

> After 1 billion televiewers had watched the last world cup in 1982, it was hoped that ground attendances would increase and gentrify everywhere.
>
> *Economist* 28 June 1986

> In the Middle Ages, the exaction of excessive interest was condemned as 'usury.' Now it's been gentrified as 'servicing.'
>
> *Daily Telegraph* 8 Dec 1987

In preparation for his presidential campaign the leader of France's far-right National Front, Mr Jean-Marie Le Pen, was advised to gentrify his image. ... The burly ex-paratrooper duly went on a brutal diet and bought a wardrobe of the sort of clothes French people tend to associate with English squires.

Economist 12 Mar 1988

► This verb started life describing the influx of middle-class inhabitants into traditional working-class areas, and the various changes, social and architectural, resulting from it; but it was only a matter of time before metaphor broadened out its application.

geopathic *adjective*　produced by the effects of harmful radiation from the earth

I am quoted, in a recent Alternative Health feature by Simon Martin – 'Danger Underground' – as saying that if a patient is adversely affected by geopathic stress ..., there is no point in them having medical treatment. [letter]

She Feb 1988

► The ground is a dangerous place, as those who live in granitic areas, such as Dartmoor, with carcinogenically high levels of background radiation, know only too well. In this case the lurking threat is the electromagnetic radiation of the Earth, which is claimed to have adverse effects on people, such as causing depression and sleeplessness. The remedy is apparently to align one's bed with the Earth's magnetic field or, should this not prove practicable, to shield oneself by putting a sheet of aluminium foil under the bed.

Gerbil *or* **GERBIL** *noun, informal*　great education reform bill: the education bill enacted by the British parliament in 1988

Mr Kenneth Baker has done quite well so far in persuading people that his Great Education Reform Bill is 'user-friendly.' Even the cuddly acronym of 'Gerbil' does not seem grotesquely inappropriate. The aim is, after all, one which ought to be popular: to rescue education from the clutches of local politicians and bureaucrats and union militants, and to offer to all schools and parents something resembling the control over their own destinies that at present only independent schools and well-to-do parents enjoy.

Daily Telegraph 22 Jan 1988

How does the British government's new Education Reform Bill (GERBIL) propose to deal with Britain's educational facts-of-life?

New Scientist 19 May 1988

▶ The chief provisions of the 147-clause Education Reform Bill are: a national curriculum, with all pupils in state schools taking stipulated courses in three core subjects (English, mathematics, and science) and seven foundation subjects (history, geography, a modern language, technology, music, art, and physical education); compulsory open enrolment of pupils; devolution of financial management to the level of the schools themselves; the creation of new types of school (see CITY TECHNOLOGY COLLEGE and GRANT-MAINTAINED SCHOOL); and the requirement to teach Christianity in religious instruction lessons.

gilt warrant *noun*   a warrant giving an investor the right to buy a particular government-issued security at a fixed price on or before a particular date

The Bank of England has given the go ahead for the issue of gilt-edged warrants from July 20, thus opening the way for the creation of a new kind of hedging instrument in the gilts market. The gilt warrants will resemble gilt options, but will be tailor-made to suit individual investors.

Daily Telegraph 7 July 1987

gimme *or* **gimmie** *noun, informal*   **1** something achieved with little effort

Cardus snorted: 'The Sussex bowlers did their best to make Hallows's task easy. Was it cricket? Nobody would wish to be a spoilsport in this hour of Hallows's splendour ... still, the game is the game; besides, Hallows is quite capable of dealing with *good* bowling.' Hick will have no gimmes.

Guardian 18 May 1988

2 something acquired for nothing; a free gift

The secret of these socks is that, like 90 per cent of the Edmonds' wardrobe, they are 'gimmies'. ...'Most of it comes from Austin Reed because they sponsor us,' says Edmonds....Messrs Austin Reed are kind enough to kit out the entire Middlesex team. But while most of the players wouldn't be seen dead in their 'gimmies' once off duty, Phil Edmonds lives in his.

Daily Telegraph 6 June 1987

▶ This nominalization of *gimme*, the colloquial contraction of *give me*, is first recorded in the 1920s as meaning 'acquisitive greed.' The much more recent uses illustrated here occur quite frequently in sporting contexts, and may even have originated in golf, where it is often used for a putt so straightforward that the player might say to his opponent 'You may as well give it to me' – that is, concede it:

There are no gimmes in this. You have to sweat out every hole.

Tony Jacklin, BBC TV golf commentary, 19 July 1986

glam *noun, informal* a well-off middle-aged person

These people are GLAMS. They're Greying, Leisured, Affluent and Married, and they are aged between 45 and 59. They are *the* key socioeconomic group. They have a whacking disposable income (£15 billion). The typical Glam couple bought their first home 20 years ago for £10,000.

Daily Mail 26 June 1987

In an increasingly consumerist society, it is reassuring to discover that one sector of society positively revels in its lack of material ambition. The Glams ... 'dislike the constant urge to buy which they detect in younger people,' says a new Euromonitor report on the attitudes of the over-50s.

Daily Telegraph 6 July 1988

▶ Compare WOOPIE.

glasnost *noun* the opening up of an institution formerly closed or secretive, making it easier of access for all

Watching 'Hamlet' in any language other than English may sound a daunting prospect but not, it seems, to Glaswegians, who are spending £2000 underwriting a production of the tragedy in Russian by a touring Soviet theatre company. 'It will be a box office hit,' says Labour leader councillor Patrick Lally. 'We are operating a policy of glasnost – opening up to the world.'

Daily Telegraph 30 June 1987

BBC journalists are expecting the corporation's new deputy director-general, Mr John Birt, to announce senior news appointments
in the new directorate to run the BBC's news programmes within
three days. This follows Mr Birt's five-day seminar with senior
programme executives at a Surrey hotel last week. Proposals put
forward at the gathering have now been transmitted to newsrooms
and programme staff throughout the BBC, who have now dubbed
them 'John Birt's Glasnost.'

Daily Telegraph 8 July 1987

▶ It has not taken long for Mikhail Gorbachev's *glasnost*,
the policy of greater openness in Soviet affairs (see *Longman Guardian New Words*), to find metaphorical applications in fields far from international relations (compare
PERESTROIKA).

glasnostian *adjective* relating to glasnost, the Soviet policy
of openness and frankness

Poland's best-known underground satirist – the 'Will Rogers of
Warsaw,' plus an unexpected streak of Slavic Lennie Bruce –
yesterday completed a sell-out, 15-state tour of Polish-American
communities. ... Many Polish-Americans were left wondering what
glasnostian brainstorm within the top Polish leadership resulted
in Pietrzak's being permitted to travel abroad.

Daily Telegraph 5 Apr 1988

gloomster *noun, informal* a pessimistic person, especially
one who foretells misfortune

Since August Chemical Bank, Sheerson Lehman and Salomon
Brothers have each shed 150–170 people. Post October 19th, gloom-
sters predict that many more equity jobs will be lost.

Economist 26 Dec 1987

▶ Compare DOOMSAYER.

goal hanger *noun, derogatory* an opportunist

When Hatton was in his first year at the Liverpool Institute he
shared detention with a sixth former by the name of Paul McCartney. Unlike McCartney, Cilla, Tarbuck, Boardman and the rest of
the Scouse goal hangers, however, he believes in putting some of
his ability back into the city he loves.

Blitz Mar 1988

▶ In soccer, a *goal hanger* is someone who, rather than running about the pitch taking part in the ebb and flow of the game, simply hangs around the opponents' goal hoping to score from opportunities created by less selfish team-mates.

goalposts *noun plural* – **move/shift the goalposts** *informal* to change the conditions or rules under which something is done, especially surreptitiously or dishonestly, in order to disqualify what was formerly permissible or vice versa

Mr Tony Griffin ... accused the DoE and Nirex of 'moving the goal-posts'. In the first planning guidelines the department had talked about the clay for the dispersal site needing to be 30 to 40 metres deep. When it was realised that the clay at Elstow was only 17 metres deep this requirement disappeared.

Guardian 17 Apr 1986

It is beginning to look as though the Inland Revenue is quietly trying to move the goalposts in the game of the taxation of pooled investments.

Daily Telegraph 12 June 1987

Ludovic Kennedy ... justified his claim as a reliable detumescent by asking 'Has time shifted the moral goal-posts?'

Guardian 26 Aug 1987

gobsmack *verb,* *British informal* to take utterly aback; overwhelm

She has been gobsmacking the punters in a recent cluster of Personal Appearances in gay clubs, straight clubs and 'kids clubs'.

Melody Maker 24 Oct 1987

Aghast, concussed and altogether gobsmacked I find myself this week, having just listened to a most extraordinary documentary.

Listener 21 Apr 1988

Patsy [Puttnam] was unrattled. Slim, blonde and gutsy, she remains a proud Sixties girl who rarely wears make-up or moderates her demotic candour. ... Her conversation crackles with cockney slang. They weren't merely surprised by Coke's financial manoeuvre. In Patsy parlance, they were 'gob-smacked.'

Sunday Times 24 Apr 1988

▶ Despite the implication contained in the third extract above, there is no direct evidence that *gob-smack* is of exclusively 'Cockney' origin: *gob* is 'mouth' in many different varieties of British English.

gob-struck *adjective, British informal* gobsmacked

> Bonham's publicity director Jill Mindham said: 'We were gob-struck. This is the sort of thing you might expect in eastern Europe.'
>
> *Observer* 7 Aug 1988

gofer *noun* an assistant employed to do menial duties or act as intermediary

> BRIGHT BRAT FOR LONDON PR COMPANY Young person required to be gofer, tea maker and administrative assistant. Some keyboard skills preferred.
>
> *Guardian* 21 Apr 1986

> David Hart, the journalist-cum-political-fixer who was 'gofer' between the UDM and Sir Ian MacGregor, has weighed in with a Times article comparing the parents' protest to that of the working miners.
>
> *Daily Telegraph* 3 Feb 1987

▶ *Gofer* is of American origin, but is finding its way into British English. It is a fanciful alteration of *go for*, alluding to the gofer's task of running errands for his or her boss, consciously based, no doubt, on *gopher* (as it is also spelled), an American burrowing animal.

go-get *verb, informal* to be ambitious or go-getting

> Additionally, the government's drive to reduce Holland's budget deficit provides even greater incentive for the young to go-get, particularly since the ceiling for the minimum salary will be increased from 23 to 27-year-olds.
>
> *Excel* June 1988

gold card *noun* a credit card whose holder is entitled to various benefits (e g unsecured overdraft facilities and various sorts of insurance cover) not available to holders of standard credit cards

As status symbols go, gold cards are more fuel efficient than a Rolls Royce, less offensive to animal rights campaigners than mink coats, and cheaper to insure than a fistful of diamonds.
Sunday Times 13 Apr 1986

Travellers get 'special' treatment whichever gold card they use.
Sunday Express 17 Aug 1986

▶ Gold cards first appeared on the scene in Britain around 1982, and three main brands are currently available: American Express, Gold MasterCard, and Visa Premier card. Useful as the fringe benefits they offer can undoubtedly be, they do not of course come free (there is a joining fee for all gold cards, and an annual subscription), and sceptics have come to regard the cards' snob value as higher than their cash value: with a minimum-income qualification (currently about £30,000), flashing a gold card around is an instant status-statement. In 1986 there were 180,000 gold-card holders in Britain, each with an average annual salary of £45,000.

The cachet of the gold card has spread beyond its original application: British Rail offer a 'Gold Card' which confers various travel advantages on its purchaser. And indeed, 'gold' is the 'in' epithet of the late 1980s for the most exclusive grade of product or service: LRC call their most expensive condoms 'Durex Gold' because of their superior quality, not because of what they are made of.

American Express have subsequently raised the stakes still further by introducing a platinum card (on the use of *platinum* as a metaphor for even greater wealth and exclusivity than gold, see PLATINUM HANDSHAKE).

golden cross *noun* the moment when a line on a graph representing 75-day average share-price movements on the Tokyo Stock Exchange intersects with that representing 200-day movements

On average, a golden cross is apparently followed by a 51% rise in share prices over the following nine months.
Economist 16 Apr 1988

▶ The golden cross is a phenomenon identified by and beloved of CHARTISTS, people who con financial statistics in much the same way as Roman augurs probed the entrails of animals, looking for hints of future market movements.

For various other 'golden' phenomena that attach themselves to financial institutions (for example *golden hello, golden parachute*) see *Longman Guardian New Words*.

golden goodbye *noun*   a golden handshake given on retirement

> Elderly corporate grandees now regard pay-offs as a final tithe. At Kleinwort Benson, two directors shared a payment of £805,000 as they headed off to retirement. ... But how do shareholders benefit when their chairmen receive golden goodbyes?
> *Economist* 16 July 1988

> A £750,000 'golden goodbye' to Sir Robert Crichton-Brown, 68, retiring chairman of the tobacco group Rothmans International, was pushed through at the group's annual meeting in the gilded splendour of the Dorchester Hotel, London, yesterday.
> *Daily Telegraph* 30 July 1988

▶ Compare PLATINUM HANDSHAKE.

golden goose *noun*   a source of unlimited prosperity

> I had a close friend, an executive of the bank, and he had asked me if I would help one of their clients, a Frenchman, who wanted to transfer 20kg of gold from France into Switzerland. ... My friend made it clear ... that a successful conclusion would be regarded very favourably by his bank. There was, he added, a lot more where this was coming from: 'This Frenchman's a golden goose.'
> *Sunday Times Magazine* 6 Mar 1988

▶ The term derives from the expression 'kill the goose that laid the golden egg,' a metaphor used by Aesop to illustrate the foolishness of destroying one's prospects of long-term prosperity for the sake of instant gratification. Its ellipsis into the quite illogical *golden goose* is presumably due simply to the need for a more manageable expression; 'a goose that lays golden eggs' is rather a mouthful. A similar process can be seen in the devaluing of the *$64,000 question* to the *$64 question.*

golf formation *noun* a method of naval minesweeping in which only one side of the vessel is used for sweeping

The Ministry of Defence says that the four vessels will sweep for mines in 'golf formation.'

New Scientist 20 Aug 1987

▶ 'Golf' here is simply the communications code word for the letter *g* (compare INDIA FORMATION). The techniques and terminology of minesweeping came to considerably increased public notice in consequence of the American and British operations in 1987 to clear the Persian Gulf of mines during the Iran-Iraq war.

goofproof *verb, American informal* to render (someone) less likely to make blunders

Reagan went through 'inoffensiveness training' with behavioural psychologists who, in the process of goofproofing their candidate, soon learned that his limitation was attention to detail and that his asset was his buoyant good humour.

Listener 25 Feb 1988

goserelin *noun* a hormone-blocking drug which has the effect of reducing sex drive

They [a sex offender's lawyers] will also ask for an emergency declaration allowing injections of the drug goserelin ... to go ahead pending the court hearing.

Guardian 7 Jan 1988

▶ Goserelin (better known under the trade name Zoladex) is used as a form of biochemical castration for persistent sex offenders. It is more powerful than the libido-reducing hormone drugs Depo Provera and Androcur. It is administered by placing beneath the skin a minute biodegradable sponge containing the drug, which is slowly released into the bloodstream.

goth *noun* (a pop musician favouring) a serious, rather austere style of rock music

> We've gone from complete goth to total bright pop and the things that I've learnt as I've gone along have stayed in my mind. If I come across a song that needs something poppy, I'm not frightened to incorporate it.
>
> *Melody Maker* 10 Jan 1987

> I don't know any 'goth' who would condone the lyrics and/or videos of the metal bands.
>
> *Guardian* 5 July 1988

▶ The goth musical cult of the mid to late 1980s favours dark, gloom-laden music (the derivation from *gothic* is obvious), and its eschewal of all frivolity is reflected in its strict all-black dress code.

gothic *noun* an adherent of the GOTH music cult

> The drape-jacketed septet did their best to smile as they came out before a packed and intense audience of punks, gothics and neo-hippies.
>
> *Daily Telegraph* 9 Sept 1987

gouger *noun, Irish* a young ruffian

> Yet it is a mystery how any young street tough, known here as a 'gouger,' would tackle the police; so big are Dublin's policemen that it is easy to believe the myth that they were tempted down from the Kerry Mountains with hunks of raw meat.
>
> *Economist* 8 Aug 1987

go with *verb, chiefly American* to take (something) up and pursue it, especially because it reaches a satisfactory standard

> It's amazing, when the networks first saw the outline [of *Star Trek – The Next Generation*] they insisted that the proportion of the sexes should not be 50/50, because audiences would feel that they'd always be up to something. So they decided on a 70/30 ratio male to female, and then they decided not to go with it anyway.
>
> *Time Out* 4 May 1988

When we came to plan our 'en primeur' offers for 1988, we felt that the 1987 vintage in Bordeaux had little to offer our customers. ... We therefore looked to other areas, and decided to go with Burgundy and California.

Le Journal (Les Amis du Vin) No. 9, June 1988

graceful degradation *noun* the property of continuing to function satisfactorily even when some components are damaged

They [computers which mimic the brain] would also be ideal in high-reliability applications in nuclear reactors or spacecraft because of their brain-like property called 'graceful degradation': their processing power is shared among many neurons so they still work when some are damaged – a feat that is impossible with a conventional computer.

Daily Telegraph 8 Feb 1988

▶ The term was first coined with reference to the way the brain itself works, but is equally applicable to computers which function on biological lines; see NEURAL NETWORK.

graf *noun, slang* graffiti as a form of artistic expression

But there was no mistaking the 22-year-old ex-postman's sincerity as he explained the lurid 'graf' was an improvisation on the word, legal. The canvas for Paul's 'piece' – the graf short for masterpiece – was a 40 foot brick council wall.

Daily Telegraph 7 Dec 1987

gram *noun* an embarrassing greeting delivered to its recipient in public

Any costume, any gram, anywhere. ... ALL GRAMS MINIMUM 20 MINUTES.

Ms London 27 May 1986

Suddenly it's all over. ... The strippagram is left, a lonely spotlit figure, pulling on his clothes as if he has just got out of bed. For Philip Hudd, it was one of four grams in the evening. ... Grams came to this country from America about five years ago. 'Singing grams were a favourite then, but when I started Satinglow three years ago, kissagrams were already popular.' ... [Fiona's] most enjoyable gram was 'a domination gram for a 60-year-old paraplegic in a wheelchair. He loved it.'

Guardian 11 Feb 1987

▶ The booming trade in kissagrams, strippagrams, and the like in Britain over the past half dozen years (they began in the USA) has been well documented in *Longman Guardian New Words*, but it is interesting to note that, at least among those professionally concerned with them, their shared suffix *-gram* has been promoted to a fully fledged word, filling a presumably widely-felt need for a generic term that can encompass both the gorillagram and the boobagram.

granite-wash *noun* an effect of pale streaking on blue denim, achieved (as if) by distressing the fabric in water containing rough stones

> They also say that the jewel in Levi's crown ... isn't selling too well, and that this year's look is the granite-wash, a new name for that old favourite of blue denim streaked with white.
> *Guardian* 13 Apr 1987

granny farm *noun*, *British* an old people's home, especially one which charges exorbitant rates for minimal services

> Mr Cook employed an undercover granny, a doughty American journalist, to do his research. She sampled eight granny farms as a paying customer and emerged scarified by the experience. 'Even the good ones,' she reported, 'scared me to death.'
> *Observer* 29 May 1988

▶ This formation follows in the line of *granny* compounds coined in the 1970s and 1980s, such as *granny flat* and *granny glasses*. It reflects an increasing awareness of the scandal of the rest home industry, which is being moved in on by unscrupulous proprietors intent on exploiting their clients up to the hilt; with the growing number of old people in the community, there are rich pickings to be had.

grant-maintained school *noun* (in Britain) a proposed form of secondary school funded by central government rather than by a local authority

A new form of State school, the Grant Maintained School, will be created for governors or parents who want to opt out of local education authority control.

Daily Telegraph 21 Nov 1987

▶ The grant-maintained school is one of a package of educational reforms put forward by the Conservative government in the late 1980s whose general drift was to centralize control over schools (another is the proposed national curriculum). In response to the supposed dissatisfaction of parents with the standards achieved by schools controlled by local education authorities, new arrangements will from 1989 enable schools to opt out of this system and become self-governing with government funding. See also CITY TECHNOLOGY COLLEGE.

graviphoton *noun*   a hypothetical particle of spin 1 which is thought to carry forces between matter

If supersymmetry is a valid description of the Universe, some theories hold that it should produce two analogues of the graviton – the as-yet-unobserved particle thought to carry gravitational force. The graviton has spin 2; the other particles would have spins of 1 and 0, and like gravitons would carry forces between matter. Bars and Matt Visser of USC suggest that these forces combine to form the 'feeble force.' Terry Goldman, Richard Hughes, and Michael Nieto at the Los Alamos National Laboratory have proposed similar ideas and suggested names for the particles, 'graviphoton' for the spin 1 particle and 'graviscalar' for the spin 0 particle.

New Scientist 5 June 1986

▶ The 'spin' possessed by these elementary particles is their intrinsic angular momentum.

graviscalar *noun*   a hypothetical particle of spin 0 which is thought to carry forces between matter – see GRAVIPHOTON

gravitational lens *noun*   an object in space (e g a galaxy or black hole) whose mass is so huge that it bends light gravitationally

American astronomers have confirmed a claim that a cluster of galaxies is acting as a gravitational lens, and focusing the light from a more distant galaxy into a ring.

New Scientist 10 Dec 1987

▶ The notion of the gravitational lens is predicted in Einstein's General Theory of Relativity, but it is only in recent years that astronomers have been finding experimental evidence for it. It accounts for observational phenomena such as the so-called 'triple quasars,' which are really only multiple images of single quasars, produced by gravitational lenses.

graze *verb* **1** to eat continuously in small amounts throughout the day, rather than at set meal times

Traditional meal times are 'blurred' and consumers 'graze' – 'a nibble here and a nibble there, spread unpredictably across the day.' The growth of 'grazing,' says the report, has developed in the last 10 years, and its potential has not yet been recognised by the catering industry.

Daily Telegraph 9 Dec 1987

We eat on the run, on average $6\frac{1}{2}$ times a day, grazing through packet after packet of crisps, nuts and savouries.

Guardian 29 Apr 1988

2 *American* to pick up and eat items of food while shopping in a supermarket

The practice of eating produce while going around a supermarket is known in America by the mild name of 'grazing,' but in the daughter's case it is more like wholesale pillage.

New Society 22 May 1987

▶ The metaphor derives, of course, from the eating habits of cattle and similar animals, which simply chew away all day.

grebo *noun, British slang* (a member of) a youth cult whose adherents adopt a deliberately scruffy appearance and boorish manner and favour aggressively crude rock music

Grebo! The dirty denims! The sweaty armpits! The crappy songs! The *crazy* names! ... Despite all being in their (early) 20s, the grebos do exacerbate an ever widening generation gap, are as much a breakaway from the boring, effete Indie/Anorak pop bands... as they are a revolt against the traditional enemy, the rich, the old, and the fat.

New Musical Express 23 July 1987

Sadly Grebo has meant only a merging of the dog end of punk (loutishness, inane aggression) with the rump of hippiedom (what they used to call 'hippy gumbo' – grunge, self-neglect, getting blasted).

New Statesman 13 Nov 1987

▶ The *gre-* element presumably derives from *greaser*, 'a long-haired member of a motorcycle gang', while *-bo* is probably an arbitrary suffix.

greenbacking *noun, informal* provision of funds for something

A team of psychologists at ... the University of Texas have been attempting to find out to what extent the ordinary guy ... is able to suppress forbidden thoughts. ... More likely it was a sudden idea that seemed attractive and could get greenbacking.

New Scientist 11 Feb 1988

▶ *Greenback* is a colloquial Americanism for 'dollar bill'.

greenroader *noun* a person whose hobby is driving on unmetalled country roads and trackways

The great passion in the life of greenroaders is to hammer around on unsurfaced country tracks, bouncing from pot-hole to pot-hole with 4 × 4 surefootedness.

Daily Telegraph 13 Jan 1988

▶ The actual driving of a vehicle along such roadways is merely the culmination of the greenroader's work, the high spot of his hobby. First, extensive research has often to be done in old parish records and the like to establish that the routes, for long the preserve of hikers and riders, have in the past been used by vehicular traffic, and that a precedent therefore exists to go bombing along them.

grey *verb* (of a population) to come to have an increasingly large proportion of old people

At current birth rates the populations of Finland ..., of Norway ... and of Sweden are set to grey and then to decline in the twenty-first century.

Economist 21 Nov 1987

grey market *noun* trading in a company's shares before it has been officially quoted on a stock exchange

Hong Kong share prices drifted to a mixed finish in moderate trading. ... Subscription for Cathay Pacific's shares starts today. They were quoted at over HK$5 on the grey market against an issue price of HK$3.88.

Financial Times 22 Apr 1986

The company was set up in 1962 and has been one of the major licensed dealers operating in the 'grey market' which trades in shares before they are officially listed.

Independent 24 Dec 1986

▶ The grey market in shares has become particularly active in Britain in recent years with the public flotation of previously nationalized industries by the Thatcher government. In particular, a large amount of trading is done in free shares allocated to the employees of the privatized companies and in those bought by small investors interested in a quick profit.

gridlock *noun, American* a complete halting or breakdown of a system or organization

Two new major reports say the crash ... came within a whisker of paralyzing the world's financial system. ... The presidential commission ... said the system came 'close to gridlock.'

USA Today 8 Feb 1988

The crowded poverty of the masses and the social and economic gridlock of class distinctions in Europe made both wilderness colonies [USA and Australia] seem utopian.

National Geographic Feb 1988

▶ In American English, a *gridlock* is literally a serious jam in which all traffic comes to a halt.

groovox *adjective,* *slang* fashionable; cool; groovy

No, these aren't the latest Martian paper clips. In fact, these 'Le Twists' are the most groovox new way to hold back even the thinnest hair.

Sassy June 1988

GUI *noun* graphical user interface: interaction between a user and a computer which displays data pictorially

Apple's implementation shows some of the benefits and some of the pitfalls of what ... has come to be called the graphical user interface (or GUI, pronounced 'gooey').

Economist 30 Jan 1988

gumboot *noun,* *East African* a condom

In the rural, backwater villages of Rakai [in Uganda] most people do not believe Aids ... is sexually transmitted. ... Roman Catholic teaching and the belief in producing as many children as possible have made condoms – which are given names such as 'American socks' or 'gumboots' – all but taboo.

Daily Telegraph 5 June 1987

gutted *adjective,* *British slang* devastated; shattered

[Jimmy] White was obviously disappointed when he said: 'I am absolutely gutted – I really wanted to win this title three years on the spin.'

Daily Telegraph 27 Mar 1987

Emma Allen ... is a living case study, admirably nonchalant and witty about the psychological trauma of fighting cancer. 'I was gutted,' she said, echoing an expression she heard while on a story.

Observer Magazine 5 June 1988

▶ Jonathon Green's *Dictionary of Contemporary Slang* 1984, which defines the word as 'sick and tired,' identifies it as UK prison slang.

gynergy *noun* spiritual energy inherent in women

Modern witchcraft offers an alternative psychology. It focuses on spirituality or 'gynergy' and concentrates on healing the split or estrangement between spirit and flesh, mind and body.

Guardian 3 Feb 1987

▶ Greek *gyne* is 'woman,' forming compounds in English such as *gynaecology*.

gynocidal *adjective* tending to kill women

This explains how the word 'witch' became synonymous with evil in man-made language. Such fallacious, mythical association imposed on adherents of the pre-agricultural Old Religion was founded and perpetrated by a most explicit misogyny, expressed particularly in the 'gynocidal' Middle Ages.

Guardian 3 Feb 1987

gynopathy *noun* a pathological condition brought on in men who feel under threat from women

At a recent conference in West Germany, a researcher put forward the hypothesis that if in any given area of technical work, women colleagues come to number more than 50 per cent, men inevitably contract gynopathy. ... The first symptom of gynopathy is probably a comment along the lines of 'My goodness, you girls seem to be taking over!', at which point the man in question can still usually laugh. But the ability to make jokes about girls soon goes.

New Scientist 22 Jan 1987

haar *noun* a cold sea mist with drizzling rain

It's haar, it's clag, it's drizzle – all pretty depressing.
Breakfast Time, BBC1, 18 Apr 1988

▶ *Haar* is a dialect word of Northern England and Scotland, probably of Dutch origin (there is a Dutch dialect *harig*, meaning 'damp and misty'); it has recently, however, been reaching a national audience via the weather forecasts of BBC weatherman Francis Wilson.

hacked off *adjective, informal* fed up

McCormicks' problem was finding a successor to its 1985 campaign for 17 with tastefully made up young men. 'Our research showed that teenage girls were hacked off with seeing very glamorous models in ads,' says Moira.
Campaign 4 Apr 1986

During the coffee break you bump into an Army Air Corps officer who's just flown in the Brigade Commander by helicopter. He's hacked off that a unit he was due to do abseiling exercises with next week has suddenly been redeployed. [Army recruitment advertisement]
Guardian 2 Mar 1987

haemorrhage *noun* a severe loss due to continuous depletion

The unions say that in spite of their repeated warnings, nothing has been done to stop the haemorrhage of nurses from the NHS.
Somerset Evening Post 10 Dec 1987

The party also risks facing a new haemorrhage of members.
Financial Times 26 Apr 1988

hands-off *adjective* allowing people or affairs under one's control much latitude for action, rather than involving oneself closely at all stages

Mr Robert Maxwell is withdrawing from day-to-day management of his main company, British Printing & Communications Corporation, which he has dominated for six years, to concentrate on strategic planning and takeovers. ... However, sources close to Mr Maxwell doubt whether he will be able to adopt a hands-off approach.

Guardian 22 May 1986

Some China experts believe the Central Committee's call for a hands-off policy with regard to the economy could have a dark side, too.

Newsweek 13 Oct 1986

He [Ronald Reagan] will find the report uncomfortable reading. The three-man commission finds much to fault in his hands-off management style.

Daily Telegraph 27 Feb 1987

hands-on *adjective* involving practical experience or active personal involvement

Peter Cadbury is very much a hands-on leader and that is how he sees his involvement with Working Woman.

Working Woman Apr 1986

The Sinclair QL got off to a bad start by being oversold at its launch party, where perhaps dozens of impressionable journalists ... wrote cheques to ensure early samples. But as hands-on experience quickly showed, the Basic and operating system were bug-ridden [and] the keyboard was awful.

Guardian 8 May 1986

The trust has created an aggressive image in the sector, with a 'hands-on' management style.

Independent 30 Oct 1986

▶ The original, practical meaning of the adjective (of obvious derivation) is used now particularly in the field of computers. Starting life in the USA, *hands-on* has recently become well established in British English.

hashing *noun* a version of hare and hounds played largely by expatriate Britons throughout the world, in which someone lays a trail of paper, flour, etc which is then pursued by the main group of runners

> Hashing began in Kuala Lumpur, where some high-spirited Britons and Australians used to end their evening's exercise at a restaurant known as the Hash House.
>
> *Economist* 8 Aug 1987

▶ Hashing, a uniquely British mixture of paper chase and fox hunt (pursuers indulge in a good deal of tally-hoing), must be viewed askance by locals in the four corners of the Earth where it manifests itself. As with golf's 19th hole, a crucial feature of the pursuit is the roistering which follows its successful conclusion.

haut ton *noun*   high society

> But with the perfect timing that comes from a lifetime spent in the socially attuned air of the haut ton, Fiona, 55, left – just before Tita, 44, made her entrance.
>
> *Daily Express* 18 Mar 1988

▶ Literally translated, this French phrase means 'high tone.' Although it was current during the first half of the 19th century, the OED says that it is 'now [1898] little used in English,' and it here makes a return in, perhaps unexpectedly, the pages of the *Daily Express*.

Hawaii *noun,   British slang*   a banknote, variously £5 or £50

> Latest jargon from streetwise elements on the trading floor.... Five pounds, of course, is still a Hawaii.
>
> *Daily Telegraph* 30 Mar 1988

> Yesterday's item on City jargon has met an inflationary response from the big spenders of BZW. 'A Hawaii' ... in their book does not mean a fiver but a £50 note. Moreover, they say, the term 'Hawaii' is passé. 'We call a £50 note a Jack,' they say. Why? The star character in Hawaii Five-O is played by Jack Lord.
>
> *Daily Telegraph* 31 Mar 1988

▶ Inflated City salaries appear to have pushed up the value of a Hawaii to a level more appropriate to its name, since it is based on the popular American television series *Hawaii Five-O* (1968-79) about the Hawaiian police. See also PLACIDO.

heads-up *adjective, American* confident and of high quality

She [Martina Navratilova] has played heads-up tennis this week.
Christine Evert, BBC TV, 1 July 1987

healie-feelie *noun, informal* an adherent of a theory which holds that certain mineral crystals possess therapeutic properties

Mineralogists confirm that the healie-feelie craze has spread to Britain: Brian Lloyd of Gregory, Botley & Lloyd in London says that in the last few months there has been a sharp increase in the number of people buying quartz crystals for healing. And the Geological Museum shop in Exhibition Road has never done such good business. Simon Harrison, a mineral dealer based in Bath, is delighted. 'Healie-feelies will pay thousands of dollars for a gem crystal like tourmaline. The demand in France and Germany is also getting bigger; Britain tends to be slower because people aren't prepared to pay such high prices.'
Observer 1 Mar 1987

▶ Compare TOUCHY-FEELY.

health tax *noun* a tax whose proceeds are devoted to the funding of health services

Sir Raymond Hoffenberg, president of the Royal College of Physicians, called for a health tax on tobacco and alcohol to provide a new source of income for the NHS.
Daily Telegraph 7 Dec 1987

▶ The idea of a health tax has been much mooted in Britain in recent years, with the growing crisis in the funding of the NHS. Among many alternative sources of income suggested, taxation has received a significant measure of support in several quarters, particularly taxation of the type which targets unhealthy indulgences such as smoking as a source of revenue.

heightism *noun* discrimination on the grounds of height; *specifically* unfair treatment of tall women and short men

It's exciting to discover you're the victim of the brand-new 'ism,' though you won't be surprised to learn that this one comes from the States. Speaking as a 5ft 11in female, 'heightism' … is something I've suffered from for most of my life. … Researchers' studies have confirmed what I've known all along: in the romance stakes heightism is rampant. Short men and tall women don't even get out of the starting gate.

Good Housekeeping Feb 1988

Heightism could be a factor in the US presidential election.

Guardian 13 June 1988

At the beginning of the convention, the newspapers said Mr Dukakis measured 5ft 8in. A day later his height was put at half an inch shorter. Now he is said to be 5ft 7in. … But the height question needs to be put into perspective. … The Democratic party is resolutely opposed to racism, sexism, ageism and heightism.

Daily Telegraph 22 July 1988

heightist *adjective* guilty of HEIGHTISM

Where would you draw the line in making children taller in what Professor Michael Preece at the Institute of Child Health in London calls a 'heightist' society? As a general rule taller people get a better deal.

Daily Telegraph 22 Sept 1987

heliculture *noun* snail farming

Heliculture … is attracting two classes – farmers who want to diversify from traditional lines, and professionals seeking rewarding early retirement.

Guardian 27 June 1988

▶ The Roman or edible snail's Latin name is *Helix pomatia*. See also SNAIL PARK.

heli-skiing *noun* skiing in which the participants are conveyed to the starting point, typically a remote and crowd-free spot, by helicopter

Europe's first permanent heli-skiing centre lies 30 kilometres from Courmayeur, in Italy, in the Aosta valley.

Sunday Times 27 Mar 1988

Most intermediate skiers think that heliskiing is way beyond their wildest dreams.

Daily Telegraph 13 Sept 1988

▶ The concept of heli-skiing apparently originated in Canada in the mid 1960s, but it remains a novelty in Europe.

herbivory *noun* the practice or habit of eating plants; herbivorousness

This is exactly the problem that ecologists face in trying to explain how the abundances of interacting species in a community are co-determined by competition, predation, herbivory, disease, parasitism, mutualism and disturbance.

Nature 7 Aug 1986

▶ This word has not been recorded before, but it is quite regular in formation: adjectives ending in *-ic* or *-ous*, particularly in scientific or technical areas, frequently have corresponding nouns ending in *-y* (*synchrony*, for example, was formed from *synchronous*).

her indoors *noun, British informal* one's wife, especially thought of as exercising tyrannical behind-the-scenes influence; *broadly* a domineering woman in a position of control

Last week, Bernard Ingham, the Prime Minister's personal press secretary no less, was making soothing noises to the lobby with assurances that what 'er indoors really had in mind were nasty foreign programmes and not our own dear broadcasters at all.

Time Out 11 May 1988

▶ This is one of a range of colourful vocabulary items from the world of small-time London crime popularized by the Thames TV series *Minder* (1979–). Many have already found a footing in the mainstream language, notably *minder* itself and *earner*, 'something profitable,' and *her indoors* may join them, at least temporarily. In the television series the term refers to the unseen wife of used-car salesman Arthur Daley, the inexorability of whose commands has suggested its application in more rarefied spheres.

heritage *adjective* nostalgically emphasizing traditional customs and institutions, especially in the context of tourism

British general elections have become as archaic as silent movies and seaside postcards. They evoke a world of Victorian school-rooms, stubby pencils, flag-draped platforms and politicians standing in high streets, grinning like village idiots. ... Yet even as a heritage event, the election held on June 11, 1987, was a low-key affair.

Sunday Times 24 Apr 1988

▶ The proliferating use of this word in the tourism industry is viewed by many as devaluing its 'real' meaning, a perception reflected in ironical noun uses as well as the all-pervasive adjective:

If you're interested in history, or heritage, as we're supposed to call it today, you can have a good day out today, as all the National Trust properties are open for free.

Breakfast Time, BBC1, 11 May 1988

The phenomenon has been studied by Robert Hewison in *The Heritage Industry* 1987.

Hero *noun* hazards of electromagnetic radiation to ordnance: the danger that some form of electromagnetic radiation, such as an electrostatic discharge, will accidentally trigger the electrical fuse of a missile warhead, causing it to explode

In fact, Pershing IIs, along with the air-launched cruise missile, the B1 bomber, the imaging infra-red maverick missile,... must all be considered potentially Hero-vulnerable in the absence of adequate testing. Understandably the military have made genuine anti Hero attempts including filters, containers, shielding and grounding, and safing and arming mechanisms but these measures are far from foolproof, and on occasion have actually triggered Hero incidents.

Guardian 26 June 1987

high-five *noun* a gesture of exultation, congratulation, or greeting in which two people join hands above their heads, palms together

The teacher exchanges the 'high-five' slapped-hands greeting of the American city with the card players.

Daily Telegraph 31 May 1988

▶ The practice of high-fiving, essentially a feature of black culture, seems to have started, or at least begun to be popularized, among American basketball players. Its spread has reached the West Indian cricket team, which greets the capture of a wicket with a vigorous display of overhead hand slapping.

highwaywoman *noun* a woman who holds up and robs passengers in road vehicles

A 'highwaywoman' from Waterford, Ireland, who pleaded guilty to using an imitation firearm to carry out five robberies, was sentenced to three years' youth custody at the Old Bailey yesterday.
Daily Telegraph 19 Feb 1988

Hildaberry *noun* a fruit resembling a large raspberry, a cross between the tayberry and the boysenberry

The most remarkable new fruit introduced at Chelsea this year is most certainly a hybrid bearing the unlikely name 'The Hildaberry.'
Daily Telegraph 21 May 1987

▶ The Hildaberry was called into being accidentally by retired London taxi-driver Eric Cornwell in his Devon garden, when seeds from a fruit trodden into the ground suddenly sprouted, and in due course produced berries of gigantic proportions. He named the new cross after his wife Hilda.

hip pocket *verb, American* to retain possession of something (as if) by putting it in one's hip pocket

Because Continental, unlike other carriers, pays pilots only for flight time, some pilots say they 'hip pocket' maintenance write-ups until they reach the end of a four-day trip so that they don't lose money while on the ground.
Newsweek 25 Apr 1988

hippohaulage *noun* transportation using horses

The mechanical replacement of horse transport did not really replace hippohaulage for some time.
Times Literary Supplement 26 Feb 1988

▶ *Hippos* is Greek for 'horse.' This formation is purely facetious, but in the first decade of the 20th century, shortly after their introduction, motor vehicles (or 'horseless carriages') were for a time quite seriously called *hippomobiles*.

HIV-2 *noun*   a virus similar to but distinct from HIV-1, the human immunodeficiency virus which causes AIDS

The second human immunodeficiency virus – HIV-2 – has finally made its expected appearance in Britain. Scientists at the Middlesex Hospital in London found the virus, which is sufficiently distinct from HIV-1 to warrant a different name, in a blood sample taken anonymously from a homosexual man attending a clinic for sexually transmitted diseases.

New Scientist 31 Mar 1988

▶ HIV-2 was discovered at the Institut Pasteur in Paris in 1986. There are fears that it may provide a second AIDS-like epidemic, although it has also been speculated that someone injected with it might thereby become immune to HIV-1. Belgian scientists claimed in the summer of 1988 to have discovered a third human immunodeficiency virus, which they called HIV-3, but it has not been confirmed that it is sufficiently different from HIV-1 and HIV-2 to be given independent status.

hold 'em *noun*   a version of seven-card stud poker in which each player is dealt two cards face-down, followed by a round of betting, and a further five cards are dealt face-up in lots of three, one, and one, with a further round of betting after each

Among the many variants of the game [poker], the current favourite in Las Vegas, which is played in the world championship, is called 'Hold 'em.' It has only recently been introduced to players in this country; but anyone who wants to win out West had better master it.

Daily Telegraph 16 May 1987

home banking *noun* a computerized system which enables a bank's customers to have access to their accounts via a terminal at home, which can be used to make balance inquiries, pay bills, order chequebooks, transfer money, etc

But while investment in such systems by the banks is high and indeed crucial if they are to remain competitive, other more futuristic battles look like being fought in areas such as cash-less shopping and home banking.

Observer 10 Apr 1988

▶ In France, where there is a high incidence of households with an interactive television set (the system is known there as Minitel), no fewer than two in a thousand already use home banking. The British equivalent, Prestel, is far less widely used, and hopes for home banking here currently rest on adapting telephones to perform the necessary functions.

homeobox *noun* a piece of the genetic material DNA that controls the organization of certain structures in an embryo and is common to both vertebrate and invertebrate animals

Perhaps, Harvey suggests, homeobox genes are part of the basic machinery for creating the body pattern in multicellular animals. ... What it probably does reflect is that multicellular organisms have a limited palette of developmental mechanisms with which to solve the pattern problem, and homeobox genes are part of this repertoire.

New Scientist 18 Aug 1988

home parole *noun* a system of parole practised in the USA in which the parolee wears a wristband or ankleband which emits an electronic signal, so that any movement away from home or other place designated by the parole order can be detected

Criminal Justice officials in 20 US states are using electronic tracking devices to put more than 900 offenders under home parole programmes. There are 45 such programmes in the US.

Guardian 3 Feb 1987

▶ Proposals have recently been made to introduce some sort of home parole system in Britain, largely to relieve overcrowding in prisons, but the notion has been received with considerable disquiet on the grounds of its 'Big Brother' aspects. See also RECEIVER-DIALLER.

homophobia *noun* fear of and/or hostility to homosexuals

> To homophobia we can now add racism and sexism in our culture's irrational response to this serious disease [AIDS].
>
> *Guardian* 11 Feb 1987

▶ Scarcely a new phenomenon, homophobia gained considerable impetus from the spread of AIDS, which in the first instance attacked mainly the homosexual community. Press scare stories about the 'Gay plague' were more than enough to arouse latent prejudice, and there were various manifestations of an increasing desire to ghettoize homosexuals (notably, in Britain, Clause 28 of the 1988 Local Government Bill, which seeks to prevent the 'promotion' of homosexuality).

honcho *noun, informal* a controller, boss

> The earliest opportunity will be later this year when Lord Thomson – the IBA's chief honcho and an ex-Labour minister – retires.
>
> *Time Out* 4 May 1988

▶ The word is well established in American English (it is first recorded from 1947), but is now showing signs of crossing the Atlantic. In origin it is a Japanese compound, from *han* 'squad' + *cho* 'head, chief.'

'hood *noun, informal* a neighbourhood

> Once every kid in the 'hood lusted for a guitar – then it was Casio keyboards.
>
> *City Limits* 24 Mar 1988

hoof *noun* – **on the hoof** in an impromptu, improvised manner, while engaged in something else

> Like so many of Thatcher's ideas this [the Broadcasting Standards
> Council] was thought of on the hoof and announced last autumn
> and is now being refined.
>
> *Time Out* 11 May 1988

▶ This standardly refers to live cattle, etc as opposed to slaughtered ones. The above rather far-removed use probably owes its origin to *hoofing around*, 'to go on foot,' and to *thinking on one's feet*.

hook *noun, informal* a repeated, typically catchy melodic phrase in a popular musical composition

> The intellectual capacity of people is getting shorter. They demand
> hooks.
>
> *Melody Maker* 24 Oct 1987

> Hurby experimented early on with snatches of familiar vintage
> hits like 'Tramp' – to provide hooks for the over-35s, as well as for
> kids in the projects.
>
> *City Limits* 18 Feb 1988

hoolivan *noun* a van specially adapted to carry video cameras, for use by police in crowd control, especially at football matches

> The 'hoolivan' ... was unveiled at the Chelsea-Luton match at
> Stamford Bridge last night.
>
> *Daily Telegraph* 9 May 1985

▶ The hoolivan is one of the range of recent ideas dreamed up by the police to counter soccer hooligans (hence the name). Its cameras, roof-mounted and equipped with zoom lenses, sweep the terraces looking for troublemakers.

horse pill *noun, humorous* a large medicinal pill

> After four hours Jeni had had enough of her mantra. 'I was just
> about to take one of my homeopathic horse pills, when the midwife
> said, "You can push now." So I started to push like this,' says Jeni,
> screwing up her face and making grunting noises, 'and the midwife
> said, "No, not from the throat, dear, do it from *down below*".'
>
> *Woman* 18 July 1987

▶ This term, evocative of the unsophisticated medical practices of yesteryear (one can almost picture it being administered via a funnel), is not new, but it does not seem to have been captured by the dictionaries of English before. 'Horse' used to be quite a common epithet for large, coarse things (*horse radish, horse laugh*, and so on), although here of course the reference is simply to the size of the boluses administered by vets to horses.

hot housing *noun* highly intensive techniques of teaching and training young children in order to produce people of exceptional intelligence

> A group of California women give lessons to their unborn children in hopes of enhancing their intelligence; and one set of hot-housing parents produced four daughters, all geniuses.
>
> *TV Times* 23 July 1988

▶ As the above extract shows, some parents go to the lengths of giving their children lessons while still in the womb, but even the less extreme forms of hot housing leave the child little breathing space. Scarcely a minute of young girls' and boys' waking existence is left untutored to the end that the backward may catch up, the ordinary become geniuses, and the exceptionally gifted have their talents properly developed.

The notion of hot housing (the name comes from the forcing of plants in hothouses) began in the USA in the late 1950s; shocked out of complacency by the Soviet Union's successful launching of Sputnik, the nation decided it must do all it could to bring on its talent. A notable centre in the States is Walter Reed Junior High, North Hollywood, where highly able pupils are given the sort of intensive stimulating tuition that enables 14-year-olds to take college courses. But the less advantaged are not ignored: the federal Project Headstart was begun in the mid 1960s, to give poor preschoolers an opportunity to progress. Japan, not surprisingly, embraces hot housing enthusiastically, cramming 18 hours of lessons per day into selected pupils, and the Soviet Union has a hothouse in Siberia, but it has not caught on to such an extent in Britain.

House *noun* a style of pop music originating in Chicago, featuring electronically simulated or modified effects and intended chiefly for dancing to

House is far bigger than anyone imagined it would ever become, so big that in Britain five major labels have signed career contracts with House acts.

New Musical Express 15 Aug 1987

Split-level drum programmes, sequencer motifs, minimal, costive basslines: the trad idea of the band grooving off one another, of flesh hitting wood and metal, has been superseded by machines talking among themselves, with the producer as chairman. The singer in House is even more of a puppet than in oldstyle disco: the voice is vivisected by editing and vocoderisation. House is not susceptible to a hijacking of its form by 'content,' radical or authentic.

New Statesman 22 Jan 1988

▶ House is pop music's answer to muzak. Lyrics are perfunctory and, as the second extract suggests, the record producer's knob-twiddling has a much greater influence on the final sound than what the musicians actually play. The name appears to derive from the Warehouse, a club in Chicago at which House was originally played by Frankie Knuckles. Compare ACID HOUSE.

hub and spoke *noun* a system of organizing air-traffic routes in which certain major airports act as centres to and from which all flights from outlying airports operate

Eventually, the 'hub and spoke' system, in which travellers fly between hub airports and then take a branch line, would be supplemented by more secondary hubs.

Economist 2 Apr 1988

Third-level, or commuter, operators feed traffic from smaller towns into their base airports from which their main-line services fly. 'Hub-and-spoke' operations, as these are called, have become widespread in the United States over the past decade and are starting to be established in Europe and other parts of the world.

Observer 10 Apr 1988

▶ The hub and spoke system can be frustrating when one would like to fly direct from A to B, 100 miles apart, but has to go via a hub airport C which trebles the length of the journey. In part it is a response to operating restrictions placed on oversea flights.

hubba *noun, American slang* a chip or pellet of crack (form of cocaine)

> Jennifer, an 18-year-old transvestite, is smoking hubbas. ... So when Starr leaves to find more drugs for herself, the other two routinely care for the baby during the night.
> *Newsweek* 25 Apr 1988

▶ The derivation of the word is not clear, but it may have some connection with the American interjection *hubba-hubba*, used as an exclamation of enthusiasm or excitement.

huffer *noun, British* a long roll or section of French bread with a sandwich-style filling

> Come on – be a glutton and proud of it! Tuck into some profession-ally-made goodies like sausage and onion huffer, or cheese, ham, egg and onion all in one jaw-stretcher they call 'The Gulf' or per-haps just a classy bacon and avocado sandwich! ... There is a choice of 18 sandwiches and huffers with prices ranging from 85p.
> *Herts & Essex Observer* 17 Mar 1988

▶ Huffers are quite commonly encountered nowadays as pub food. The origin of the name is not clear, but there may be some connection with *huffkins,* a sort of tea cake former-ly made in Kent, or with *huff*, a Gloucestershire word for light pastry or pie crust (perhaps from its huffing or puffing up).

humanware *noun* people, considered as part of a system analogous to a computer

> This [gilts] market has 26 hungry firms of market-makers to sup-port, all with expensive hardware and humanware.
> *Daily Telegraph* 19 Mar 1987

humidifier fever *noun*　a condition affecting office workers in buildings with sealed windows and humidification systems, characterized by headache, eye irritation, flu-like symptoms, and lethargy

> That well-known feeling of lethargy suffered by office workers at the start of the week could be more than a hangover from the weekend excesses or just plain idleness. ... Dr Charles Pickering, a consultant chest physician, said yesterday that it had been identified by doctors as a clinical illness, sometimes known as humidifier fever.
>
> *Daily Telegraph* 24 Mar 1988

▶ The illness, more commonly known as *sick building syndrome* (see *Longman Guardian New Words*), is caused by tiny organisms which live in the water of office humidifiers and are dispersed from there into the air, producing symptoms of mild fever and headache. People are at their most susceptible after a weekend away from them.

humorology *noun*　the scientific study of humour

> Disciplinary Boundaries in Humorology.
> Title of paper by Mahadev L Apte in *Humor: International Journal of Humor Research* 1/1 1988

▶ Humour has long been a target for forays of solemn scientific research, but it is now evidently about to be elevated into a field in its own right, with the full interdisciplinary panoply of linguists, psychologists, sociologists, anthropologists, and historians being deployed to probe its mysteries.

The term *humorology* has actually been used before, in the 1830s, but in an entirely different context; it then meant 'the doctrine of the humours' – that is, a person's disposition as accounted for by the bodily humours blood, phlegm, choler, and melancholy – and was virtually the equivalent of what we would now call psychology.

hybrid chip *noun*   a computer chip in which a layer of super-conducting material is fused to a base of silicon, making possible much higher working speeds than for standard chips

> The next challenge is to build micron-size circuits on the hybrid chips, to see if they can serve as computer innards. Says Bellcore's Venky Venkatesan, 'Industry needs to couple superconductivity with chip technology to get the best of both worlds.'
> *Newsweek* 18 Apr 1988

▶ Breakthroughs in superconductor research, in which materials have been discovered capable of superconducting at far higher temperatures than once thought possible, have been combined with more sophisticated laser-bonding techniques to make possible the hybrid chip, which promises to revolutionize the performance of computers.

hyper *adjective, informal*   excessively active and excitable

> *Who Will Love Billy* concerned a slightly hyper 13-year-old orphan who so badly wants a family that he stops people in the street and asks them to be his mum and dad.
> *Sunday Times* 10 Apr 1988

> Adragon (who was looking zonked when he met me at the airport three hours ago) is now all bright-eyed and bubbly – almost hyper.
> *Sassy* June 1988

▶ This is a shortening of *hyperactive*, but there may also be echoes of *hyped-up* in it.

hyperdrive *noun*   extreme intensity of activity

> As the Reagan administration increases the pressure on Tokyo to lift quotas on imported U.S. agricultural products, Japan's powerful farm lobby has shifted into hyperdrive.
> *Newsweek* 4 Apr 1988

▶ A raising-the-stakes formation based on *superdrive*.

hypermedia *noun*   (in computers) the facility for creating a mixture of text, sounds, video, and graphics from various packages

Back in the lab, researchers are already working on a successor to hypertext. Called hypermedia, [it] promises to link video and music as well as text and computer graphics. So you could have your computer play Beethoven's Fifth as you read his biography.
Economist 30 July 1988

▶ See HYPERTEXT.

hypertext *noun* (in computers) the facility for creating a network of texts from various packages (e g word processor, database, spreadsheet, graphics store) each of which can be accessed from within any other

The hyping of 'hypertext' has, understandably, aroused some suspicions among the computing industry's ever-growing brood of cynics.
Guardian 24 Mar 1988

A type of software called hypertext ... organises information more flexibly than a traditional database. Enthusiasts say it will revolutionise the way people work with computers and, eventually, the way they think. Critics say that hypertext is just a buzz-word to be pronounced with an accent on the hype.
Economist 30 July 1988

hysteresis *noun* (in economics) a tendency for high long-term levels of unemployment not to lead immediately to lower wage levels

Wage settlements in Britain refuse to react to high unemployment by falling in real terms. ... This stickiness in wages – hysteresis in econospeak – baffles and disappoints Mrs Thatcher's government.
Economist 9 Aug 1986

▶ The term *hysteresis* was originally introduced in 1881 by J A Ewing, in the field of magnetism. Deriving it from Greek *hysteresis*, 'a falling short, deficiency,' he used it for the phenomenon of a magnetic effect lagging behind its cause. Since then its use has broadened out into various other areas of the physical sciences, with the general sense of a delay between the production of an effect and the event producing it. The notion behind its recent application to economics is that if someone is unemployed for a long time, he or she gradually becomes a less attractive prospect for an employer and eventually, discouraged, stops looking for a job; therefore the unemployed do not exert any significant downward pressure on wage levels, and unemployment fails to lead directly to what, in simple economic logic, might be expected to be its result, lower wages.

I

ikat *noun* a silk fabric traditionally made in Asia, in which the weft threads are tied and dyed before weaving to produce a distinctive blurred pattern

> The Crafts Council Gallery has a splendid show of late nineteeth-century ikats ... from what is now Soviet Central Asia.
>> *Time Out* 4 May 1988

▶ The *OED* restricts the range of ikats to Indonesia and Malaysia, and indeed the word comes from the Malay for 'to tie, fasten,' but the above extract shows the application to be somewhat wider. The term is first recorded in English as early as 1931, but is now becoming more generally known.

IKBS *noun* INTELLIGENT KNOWLEDGE-BASED SYSTEM

illiterature *noun* writing without literary pretensions

> He [Jack Trever Story] is uneducated and proud of it. ... He continues to write illiterature – because that's *him*.
>> *Listener* 5 Mar 1987

▶ Compare ALITERATE.

imaging *noun* a therapeutic technique for relieving stress by summoning up mental pictures of pleasant things or activities

> For employees who want to learn how to decompress, experts recommend several forms of relief. Allen Elkin, program director for Stresscare, suggests abdominal breathing, meditation, and 'imaging.'
>> *Newsweek* 25 Apr 1988

immoralization *or* **immoralisation** *noun* the practice of regarding something as immoral

In Britain, the 'immoralisation' of certain drugs – mostly those used by the young – is leading us down a similar road. A growing number of policemen, magistrates and doctors regard hard drug criminalisation as a disaster.

Sunday Times 29 May 1988

immuno-compromised *adjective* having a defective immune response

I was obviously immuno-compromised but to what degree no-one could say since there is no measure for immuno-suppression. If I had Aids I had to accept that without treatment I was going to die.

Guardian 3 June 1987

▶ The problems of those affected by impaired function of the body's immune system have of course been highlighted in recent years by the onset of AIDS. This rather euphemistic use of *compromised* puts it almost in the same class as *challenged* (see *Longman Guardian New Words*).

income support *noun* (in Britain) a social-security payment for the poor and unemployed

'Young people leave home for a wide variety of reasons,' the [social security advisory] committee said. 'We regret that the structure of income support ... will deprive many young people of this option.'

Sunday Times 10 Apr 1988

▶ Income support was introduced on 11 Apr 1988 under the terms of the Social Security Act 1988, to replace the previous means-tested social-security payment, supplementary benefit. It is less complex than its predecessor, with many of the additional special-needs allowances consolidated into a smaller number of broader categories (for example, additional payments for the disabled and the old). See also FAMILY CREDIT, SOCIAL FUND.

index arbitrage *noun* near-simultaneous purchase and sale of a stock listed on a share-index, and of futures in that stock, in such a way as to take advantage of a discrepancy in price between the two

> Profitable index arbitrage is still popular and may have been responsible for a big part of last Friday's plunge.
>
> *Time* 18 Jan 1988

> Goldman, Sachs & Co. said it suspended index arbitrage trading for its own account, becoming the third major Wall Street firm to take such a step.
>
> *Wall Street Journal* 8 Feb 1988

▶ As the above extracts suggest, index arbitrage, while not against the rules, is frowned upon by those who regulate stock exchange dealings. It has been accused of contributing to uncomfortably wide share-price fluctuations, and has been implicated in the market crash of Oct 1987.

India formation *noun* a method of naval minesweeping in which both sides of the vessel are used for sweeping

> All the boats sailing in India formation sail into water that has not been swept of mines.
>
> *New Scientist* 20 Aug 1987

▶ 'India' here is simply the communications code word for the letter *i* (compare GOLF FORMATION).

infomercial *noun* a short film produced by an advertiser giving information about goods which it has for sale, to be shown on television

> Two years ago, W. H. Smith Television Services ... ran a pilot programme of 'infomercials' on a cable-television channel in Glasgow.
>
> *Economist* 16 Jan 1988

> This autumn Consumer Channel will be launched showing 'infomercials' on anything from cars to life-insurance policies.
>
> *Daily Telegraph* 18 Apr 1988

▶ A blend of *information* and *commercial*.

intelligent knowledge-based system *noun* (*abbreviation* **IKBS**) a computer system with problem-solving and decision-making capacity within a particular area of expertise; an expert system

Hence the terms 'knowledge engineering systems' and 'intelligent knowledge-based systems' (IKBS) are becoming the expert system world's buzz words.

Mini-Micro News Feb 1988

▶ The term seems to have been coined around 1985, in response to a perception that 'expert system' lacks precision.

interactive fiction *noun* stories stored on computer disk which have branching sets of alternative plot lines from among which the reader can choose, using the computer's software to create a version of his or her choice – called also *computer fiction*

The computer could also change fiction. For several years software writers have been producing works of 'interactive fiction,' which are read on computers. ... Critics sniff that these are overgrown computer games, but the genre is now attracting serious attention: the first university course on writing computer fiction started this semester at Carnegie Mellon.

Newsweek 25 Apr 1988

Linking machinery – the most concrete expression of human reason possible – with Surrealism may seem perverse ... but it has helped to pave the way for what could be one of the more significant literary developments of the coming decades: interactive fiction.

Listener 7 July 1988

interleukin-2 *noun* (*abbreviation* **IL-2**) a protein produced by the body's immune system, which is used in ADOPTIVE IMMUNOTHERAPY

Unfortunately, large doses of LAK cells and IL-2 are needed for treatment. Both substances are in short supply, and IL-2 has serious side effects.

New Scientist 25 Sept 1986

▶ See LAK CELL.

interline *verb* to transfer from one vehicle to another en route

Mr Alan Haslehurst ... said it would be difficult for London to remain competitive if people were required to inter-line by taking a bus around the M25.

Guardian 6 June 1985

The busiest [airport] in Europe incessantly rattles the Queen's tea-cups at Windsor Castle. A quarter of the passengers roaring in over her head will roar straight out again; Heathrow is an 'interlining' champion.

Economist 27 Feb 1988

intifada *noun*   an uprising by Palestinian inhabitants of Israel which started at the end of 1987

On separate sides of the border, the lives of two extended families, one Arab and the other Jewish, show how much the intifada ... has transformed the relationship between the rulers and the ruled.

Newsweek 2 May 1988

At last week's Arab summit in Algiers the PLO received heaps of praise for the *intifada*, the Palestinian uprising in the Israeli-occupied West Bank and Gaza Strip.

Economist 18 June 1988

▶ Tension had been rising among Palestinian inhabitants of the occupied territories in the final months of 1987, culminating in an outcry when four Palestinian labourers were killed on 8 December when an Israeli taxi crashed into them. The following day an uprising (Arabic *intifada*) started in Gaza, and it spread to the West Bank on the 10th. It continued to escalate during the early months of 1988, with much world attention being focussed on the heavy-handed treatment of Palestinian demonstrators by armed Israeli soldiers.

into *preposition*   on the subject of; about; on

We don't think that each public enquiry should take the form of a national debate into nuclear.

Cecil Parkinson, *Panorama*, BBC1, 6 June 1988

▶ The preposition *into* has long been standard usage with words suggesting metaphorical 'probing' which overtly contain the element 'in' – *enquiry*, for example, and *investigation* – but it is now commonly used with the nouns *report* and *study* ('the report into the Cleveland child-abuse case'), and cabinet ministers, as in the above extract, are even applying it to *debate*.

intron *noun* any of the long, apparently functionless sections of DNA which are interspersed with exons

Molecular biologists have become used to the idea that genes often come in bits. Small stretches, called exons, that code for proteins are separated by long, apparently meaningless, introns. In the chain from DNA to protein the whole gene, introns and all, is first translated into RNA. Special enzymes then snip out the introns and splice the exons together to make the messenger RNA (mRNA). This messenger carries the final code that will be translated into the protein.

New Scientist 17 Mar 1988

ivermectin *noun* an antibiotic proposed for the treatment of the disease river blindness

The battle against river blindness in West Africa has been going on for more than a decade. ... Now a drug called ivermectin, which can stop infected people going blind, has opened up a second front.

Economist 18 June 1988

Ivermectin prevents the blindness caused by the build-up of microfilariae in the eye. It will not, however, reverse severe eye disease and so will not restore sight to the 340 000 people already blinded by onchocerciasis.

New Scientist 7 July 1988

▶ River blindness, or onchocerciasis, is a form of filariasis, a group of diseases caused by filarial worms and spread by bloodsucking flies. It affects over 40 million people in Africa and tropical America. The antibiotic ivermectin is derived from the bacterium *Streptomyces avermitilis*; it was discovered in the mid 1970s and has been used by vets to treat worms in farm animals, but will surely become more prominent now if it proves to be a safe treatment for river blindness.

J

Jack *noun, British slang* a £50 note

▶ See HAWAII.

jangle *verb, British informal* to gossip

> If I catch you jangling about my family again. ...
> *Brookside*, Channel 4, 17 Feb 1987

janny *noun, informal, chiefly Scottish* a school caretaker

> All you need to do is sack the janny!! He is one of these Victorian, short-back-and-sides merchants who takes the hedging shears to everything in early spring and, in the process, removes all the flowering wood from your lovely Berberis, Flowering Currant, Forsythia etc.
> *Scottish Field* Apr 1987

▶ An abbreviation of *janitor*.

jazz ballet bottom *noun* the formation of an abscess or abscesses on the lower back or between the cheeks of the buttocks, caused by pressure

> Cambridge surgeons have called attention to a little known, but potentially painful consequence of jazz ballet, which they have called 'jazz ballet bottom.' Some jazz ballet exercises demand that dancers sit on the floor and rest most of their weight on the base of the spine. Such exercises can cause an abscess to form under the skin in the natal clefts, or more colloquially, between the cheeks.
> *New Scientist* 10 Feb 1988

▶ This condition is by no means new – in the past it has been called 'jeep disease,' from the constant jarring of a jeep's seats on its driver's or passenger's posteriors – but the surge in popularity of jazz ballet has apparently led to an increased number of cases.

jazzerati *noun plural* celebrated or distinguished jazz musicians

> Legend has it that Gonella was the British Armstrong of his day. ... Among the contemporary jazzerati playing their tributes to him will be the evergreen Harry Gold, George Webb, Ronnie Scott, and Humphrey Lyttleton.
>
> *Daily Telegraph* 26 Sept 1987

▶ On the *-erati* suffix, see NUMERATI.

jazzercise *noun* exercise to a musical accompaniment of jazz

> A Jazzercise group kept parents and children on their toes at Wood Green School fete in Witney on Saturday. The group put people through their paces and showed them how to keep in trim to a musical backing.
>
> *Oxford Star* 30 June 1988

jet-ski *noun* a small powered vehicle that glides across the water on a flat keel shaped like a water ski

> I've promised to take part – jet-skiing on the Clyde. That'll be my favourite bit of the festival. ... Glasgow makes a great base for a visit to the Highlands. I come out here at the weekend. Give me a jet-ski on Loch Lomond and I'm in heaven.
>
> *Essentials* Apr 1988

jet skiing *noun* the sport of riding jet-skis

> Jet skiing is a cross between water-skiing and riding a motorbike. You can stand, kneel or sit on your craft, compete in races or just do it for fun.
>
> *Cosmopolitan* Aug 1988

JIT *adjective, noun* JUST-IN-TIME

job search *noun* attempting to find employment

> The emphasis will inevitably be upon the most basic of skills – including job search skills and the development of motivation and personal effectiveness.
>
> *New Statesman* 26 Feb 1988

▶ As higher levels of unemployment become institution-alized, the vocabulary of joblessness takes on a more codified aspect. What in the past might have been loosely referred to as 'job hunting' is today identified as a discrete skill with teachable techniques, and dignified with its own designation.

Joey *noun, British slang* a schoolchild coerced into steal-ing and other criminal acts by older children, typically members of teenage gangs

> A gang of six black teenagers bullied and terrorised four younger schoolboys, nicknamed 'Joeys,' into carrying out a series of muggings, the Old Bailey was told yesterday.
>
> *Daily Telegraph* 19 Mar 1988

jokestress *noun* a female comedian

> I don't think I'd get on well with the Joan Rivers type of female jokestress. Too aggressive. Victoria Wood is almost perfect. Lovely lady, pity about the voice.
>
> *Cosmopolitan* Feb 1987

Joshua *noun* a test for detecting the disease sickle cell anaemia

> Scientists in California have developed a simple and highly sen-sitive test to detect sickle cell anaemia, an inherited disease of the blood that frequently affects people of African, Mediterranean and Asian descent. The test, called Joshua ..., is based on a monoclonal antibody specific for sickle cell anaemia.
>
> *New Scientist* 31 Mar 1988

▶ *Joshua* is an acronym for Joint Sickling Haemoglobin Universal Assay.

Jostaberry *noun* a hybrid plant of the currant family which produces fruit resembling large blackcurrants

> Autumn is the best time to plant the Jostaberry because the soil is warm and will stimulate root development.
>
> *Sunday Times* 8 May 1988

▶ The Jostaberry is the result of a cross between a black-currant/gooseberry hybrid and a blackcurrant/Worcester-berry hybrid; it is high-yielding and disease-resistant. *Josta* derives from the initial syllables of the German words *Johannisbeere* 'currant' and *Stachelbeere* 'gooseberry'.

jump-rope *noun* skipping

> Skipping has had a facelift and, like Sellafield, it's got a new name. It's now called jump-rope. And the jump-rope girls are popping up all over the place with the kind of wacky uniforms and rosy cheeks that have me drafting a sick note in my head. 'Please excuse Laura from jump-rope today. ...'
>
> *Daily Telegraph* 16 Mar 1987

▶ This word may be new to British English, but it is standard in American English.

junk debt *noun* MEZZANINE debt

> But of greater long term importance than the drama of Storehouse was the structure of the £2 billion bid package by Shearson Lehman. It marks the first appearance of junk debt, so long a vital feature of corporate America, on the British takeover scene.
>
> *Daily Telegraph* 26 Sept 1987

▶ This term is first cousin to *junk bond*, a high-yield speculative security (see *Longman Guardian New Words*), which are one form of mezzanine debt.

Juppy *noun, informal* a Japanese yuppy

> Mr Oda, head of marketing, and seven colleagues from advertising and design, were banished from the Toshiba Skyscraper near the docks to the Aoyama district, a select residential area for the Juppy.
>
> *Daily Telegraph* 25 Mar 1988

just-in-time *adjective, noun* (*abbreviation* **JIT**) an inventorying technique which enables industrial production to be keyed in precisely to rises and falls in demand, rather than building up large stocks in advance of orders

In flexible production factories the aim of JIT is more than simply trimming inventories. It is to allow production to be quickly responsive to demand rather than merely to build for stock in the hope of later sale. In JIT factories machines and production workers are organised into clusters doing many different jobs, instead of being strung out along production lines doing a single task.

Economist 16 Apr 1988

The Japanese ... give workers more responsibility for production decisions. They learnt to do so when they introduced their 'just-in-time' system of inventory control.

Economist 21 May 1988

kanga cricket *noun,* *Australian* KWIK CRICKET

Keith's mum *noun,* *British humorous* (used as a stereotype of a well-meaning but dim middle-aged woman of representatively average views)

> The Guardian, Screen Guardian, Financial Guardian ... you are splintering faster than the SDP. Please stop it at once. Keith's mum and I don't like it. [letter]
> *Guardian* 14 May 1988

▶ This mythical average person first surfaced as the eminence grise of E J Thribb's deathless verse in the satirical journal *Private Eye*, where her judgments, retailed at second hand, on the recently deceased were cautious but conclusive. (E J Thribb is a pen name of Christopher Logue.)

kelim *noun* a flatweave carpet with decorative patterns made in Turkey, Kurdistan, and neighbouring countries

> Some things are sold as they were found, others are transformed; kelims for example are used to cover sofas and armchairs.
> *Time Out* 4 May 1988

▶ Kelims were first mentioned in an English text as long ago as 1881, but as the above extract suggests, they are now becoming more widely known as interior decoration accessories. The word derives from Persian *kilim*, via Turkish.

keprom *noun* keyed-access erasable programmable read-only memory: a computer chip's erasable reprogrammable memory with an electronic lock to protect programs

America's Intel ... announced its keyed-access, erasable, programmable, read-only memory, or keprom for short.
Economist 23 Feb 1985

khozraschot *noun* (in the Soviet Union) economic accoun-
tability; the notion that industrial and other under-
takings should be responsible for their own finances,
and not depend on state subsidies

Khozrachiot [sic] means the end of huge subsidies to inefficient
enterprises, which will result in closures and lay-offs.
Daily Telegraph 5 Jan 1988

'If they don't let me go private, then let's go khozraschot,' he [a
Russian jazz-club manager] says, using Gorbachev's buzzword for
a new system of 'profit-and-loss accounting' which aims to increase
individual incentives in state enterprises.
Daily Telegraph 16 Feb 1988

Despite his brutally frank words on the economy, Mr Gorbachev ...
also avoided the question of unemployment– and bankruptcies as
the 'profit-and-loss' system (khozraschot) begins to bite.
Daily Telegraph 30 June 1988

▶ *Khozraschot* joins *glasnost* and *perestroika* as a Russian
word contributed by Soviet leader Mikhail Gorbachev to
the languages of the world. It is a key element in his plans to
revitalize the Soviet economy. Centralized control of
industry has led in the past to a sort of fatalistic inertia in
which lack of initiative has dragged down production rates
and stifled innovation. Gorbachev wants to put the responsibility for factories back into their own hands, freeing them
to sink or swim as best they can. Two-thirds of Soviet industry was put onto a self-financing basis at the start of 1988,
amid opposition from more conservative quarters; social
unrest is forecast, as a result of inevitable price rises.

Khozraschot is a conflation of the Russian phrase
khozyaistvenny raschot, meaning 'self-supporting running'.

kick-start *verb* to provide an initial impetus in order to set
an activity going

The Netherlands, too, seems to be trying to 'kick-start manufacturers into the wind energy industry,' according to one British turbine designer. It is said to be offering a 40 per cent subsidy on investment to Dutch developers of new wind farms.

New Scientist 17 Mar 1988

▶ The metaphor derives from the method of starting a motor cycle engine by pushing down on a pedal.

kiddie condo *noun, American* an owner-occupied flat in a block purpose-built as student accommodation

Real estate people call them 'kiddie condos' ... and they have turned out to be about the worst property investment since the era of the Florida swamp salesmen.

Daily Telegraph 3 Nov 1986

▶ The idea of the kiddie condo took off in the USA in the late 1970s. It supposedly had a dual advantage: parents would buy one for their son or daughter attending university, to circumvent the problems of finding rented accommodation, enjoying certain tax advantages at the same time, and when the time came to vacate the flat, it could be sold for a small profit. However, tax changes in the mid 1980s made them more of a liability than an asset.

Condo is short for *condominium*, an American term for a flat that is individually owner-occupied rather than rented.

killer cell *noun* a white blood cell which attacks cancer cells

Now, however, Rosenberg has found another type of killer cell that is 50 to 100 times more potent and requires very little IL-2 to be effective.

New Scientist 25 Sept 1986

▶ See LAK CELL.

kiss-and-tell *adjective* (especially of memoirs) revealing intimate secrets relating to former associates

Though kiss-and-tell books have been composed about other administrations, it is as a rule considered polite to wait until a president is out of office.

Economist 14 May 1988

The British cannot do kiss-and-tell books the way Americans do.

Sunday Times 19 June 1988

Françoise Gilot (now Mrs Salk) has written a reasonably good-humoured 'kiss and tell' about her life with Picasso which came out in 1964.

Observer 3 July 1988

▶ The term originates in American English, and refers to secrets of the boudoir and other intimate locations revealed autobiographically when the lure of royalties overcomes the ties of loyalty. See also SNORT-AND-TELL.

kissy *adjective, informal* inclined to kiss

In the moments before the show began in the vomit-peach space of James Stirling's Tate auditorium, an uncertain cocktail party atmosphere prevailed. The punters got kissy.

Blitz May 1988

kitchenalia *noun plural* collectible items of antique or bygone kitchen equipment

I wish people would refrain from calling kitchen antiques Kitchenalia.

Sunday Telegraph Magazine 5 June 1988

▶ Although the ending *-alia* appears in a few English words (such as *marginalia* and *paraphernalia*), the usual suffix for 'collected objects' is *-ana* (as in *Victoriana)*; 'kitchenana', however, would be hopelessly clumsy.

kletten prinzip *noun* a method of crowd- and riot-control developed by the West German police, centred on constant supervision of potential troublemakers by uniformed policemen throughout a particular event

Stuttgart, last weekend, was to be the first test for the *kletten prinzip*. Thousands of peaceable Irish fans were arriving to watch the Republic play England in the Neckar stadium on Sunday afternoon and the British police 'spotters' had identified scores of known English hooligans from seven notorious gangs.

Sunday Times 19 June 1988

▶ The *kletten prinzip* – it literally means 'burr principle' – has three principal thrusts: first, identify the people or groups likely to cause trouble at public events, such as football matches, rallies, or demonstrations; second, ensure that they are constantly kept under police observation – stuck to like burrs – for as long as the event lasts; and third, keep riot squads in reserve for rapid deployment to stop minor disturbances from developing into major trouble. The technique came under the spotlight during the European Football Championships in West Germany in 1988, which were marred by several outbreaks of rioting by hooligans.

kwik cricket *noun*   a version of cricket adapted for young children

The launch of Kwik Cricket by the England cricket team on the day they flew out to New Zealand in January, was a great boost for the promotion of this new and exciting form of the game for primary school children.

Cricketer Mar 1988

Welcome back to Headingley, where kwik cricket, the children's game, is in progress all round the ground.

Test Match Special, Radio 3, 22 July 1988

▶ Kwik cricket was officially introduced into Britain in January 1988, although it had been in existence for some years previously in Australia, under the name *kanga cricket*. Its object is to introduce youngsters to the techniques of cricket in a manageable and enjoyable context: equipment includes lightweight plastic bats and balls, the pitch is shorter than for adult cricket, and it is played in a variety of formats, such as 'singles,' 'pairs,' 'continuous,' and 'mini,' in many of which the person batting has an innings of fixed duration, with runs deducted for dismissals. Exhibition games are often played during the lunch interval in Test matches in England. Compare SHORT TENNIS.

L

laddish *adjective, British*   having the quality of macho un-
couthness and aggression exhibited by male groups

> The Irish, delighted by their side's surprise one-nil win, were
> predominantly boozy and laddish, too.
> > *New Statesman & Society* 17 June 1988

▶ The term comes from the notion of being 'one of the lads,'
an accolade among those who aspire to male in-groups and
the approval of their peers; of being 'a bit of lad' (that is,
behaving wildly and irresponsibly); and perhaps also of being 'Jack the lad,' someone who thinks a lot of himself.

laddishness *noun, British*   the quality of being laddish

> The well-heeled yobs on the youth fringes of the Conservative
> party who regularly smash up their conference venues, the Left-
> Wing MPs chanting like bovver boys in the Commons, striking
> miners taking up the hooligans' cry of 'Here we go,' are all
> depressingly convincing evidence of the universalisation of
> 'laddishness.'
> > *Daily Telegraph* 16 Apr 1988

lag *verb*   to lag behind (someone or something)

> The US lags Japan in implementing robot technology.
> > *New Scientist* 14 Nov 1985

> The moral conventions of the royal family lag those of society by
> about one generation.
> > *Economist* 12 Dec 1987

▶ This transitive use of *lag*, with a direct object rather than
followed by *behind*, is a new development.

LAK cell *noun*   lymphokine-activated killer cell: a form of
white blood cell used in adoptive immunotherapy to
attack cancer cells

> When the NCI [National Cancer Institute] announced its success with LAK cells last December it was deluged with requests for treatment, which is still not approved because of the toxic side effects.
>
> *New Scientist* 25 Sept 1986

▶ LAK cells are removed, incubated with interleukin-2 (a protein produced by the immune system), and then returned to the body along with some interleukin-2. They attack cancer cells, and may reverse the spread of the disease. This technique, known as adoptive immunotherapy, was discovered in 1980 by Steven Rosenberg at the National Cancer Institute in Maryland, USA, and has been continually developed since then. Its main drawback is that the interleukin-2 has severe and distressing side-effects, so much of the research effort has gone into ways of minimizing the amount needed. Recent developments have suggested that this aim may be achieved using a different sort of white blood cell, called a tumour-infiltrating leucocyte.

Lake Wobegon effect *noun* a tendency to overestimate quality

> The treachery of statistics is nowhere as evident as in the 'Lake Wobegon effect'. ... West Virginia physician John Cannell noticed that all 50 states were claiming that their students performed above average on standardized tests – an impossible phenomenon.
>
> *Newsweek* 2 May 1988

▶ The term is a reference to *Lake Wobegon Days* 1985, by American novelist Garrison Keillor, where in the town of that name 'the women are strong, the men good looking and all the children above average.'

lan *or* **Lan** *noun* local area network; an interconnected group of word processors, workstations, etc within a small area (e g a set of offices), each capable of independent operation but linked to each other and to centralized resources such as a large disk storage facility and fast laser printing

Compared with multiple standalone systems, Lans provide economies of scale in both peripherals and communications lines and equipment.

Computer Weekly 27 Nov 1986

Spidergate X100 from Spider Systems is an Ethernet to X.25 Gateway which provides a link from lan to wans. ... Logic Replacement Technology (LRT) has developed a direct-connect Megastream wide area network (WAN) bridge of communications between remote Ethernet lans.

Mini-Micro News Jan 1988

▶ Lans are more economical to install than conventional networks, in which a number of terminals are linked to a standard mainframe or minicomputer. Compare WAN.

landsailing *noun* the sport of racing land yachts

Landsailing was a sport I had rarely heard of, let alone seen, and I never imagined that just 40 minutes away from Bishop's Stortford, intrepid pilots were blown along at up to 70 miles an hour.

Herts & Essex Observer 6 Aug 1987

▶ Land yachts first appeared on the scene as long ago as 1928, but the term *landsailing* seems to be a comparatively new development.

lane rental *noun* a method of financing motorway repair and maintenance in which the contractor is charged rent for the section of road being worked on

Motorway maintenance has benefited since 1984 from a new pricing technique called lane rental.

Economist 12 Apr 1986

▶ Daily rates for such rental are in the £2000 range; they are calculated on the basis of how much is lost to the national economy by keeping the lane closed.

lap pool *noun* a long thin swimming pool about three feet wide and four feet deep, used for exercise

In Beverly Hills the palm trees have grown so tall they obscure the blue sky. ... No one uses a swimming pool any more. They have 'lap pools' instead.

Daily Telegraph 9 Apr 1988

▶ In California, the sybaritic days of lounging in several acres of heart-shaped pool are apparently on the way out. The watchwords now are fitness and austerity, and the sedate early-morning dip has been replaced by earnest laps up and down these new lap pools.

laser card *noun* an optical storage device the size and shape of a credit card, on which data are stored in the form of microscopic holes burned into the surface, which can be read by scanning with a laser beam

Two new controversial optical storage devices – the interactive videodisc and the laser card – are at last coming into the limelight after six or seven uncertain years of costly development.
Listener 8 Jan 1987

▶ The laser card is the brainchild of California scientist Jerome Drexler. Its advantage is that since it can be produced very quickly and accurately in large numbers, it will enable very large packages of data (up to 5 megabytes) to be sold very cheaply.

lasertripsy *noun* a technique for eliminating stones in the bladder, kidney, etc in which laser pulses tuned to the specific wavelength of the stone are fired at it and shatter it

Hope is at hand for people afflicted with kidney stones. Using a technique called 'lasertripsy,' even stones impacted in walls of the ureter, or kidney tube, may be removed without the need for major surgery or a general anaesthetic.
New Scientist 18 Feb 1988

▶ The word is based on *lithotripsy* (or more usually *lithotrity*), the term for the process of crushing stones in the bladder in order to eliminate them. Operations of this type have been performed since the early 19th century, but it was not until the early 1980s that a noninvasive method was devised. In this, the high-energy sound waves are fired at the stones through a water-filled bag laid against the patient's back, breaking them up. Lasertripsy has refined the technique even further by using lasers to produce the shock waves.

The second element in the word, *-tripsy,* derives ultimately from Greek *thruptein,* 'to crush.'

last hurrah *noun, informal* a final or farewell act; a swan song

It [Tony Benn's and Eric Heffer's contesting of the Labour leadership] is hardly the youthful politics of the future; more like an episode from Last of the Summer Wine. For Benn and Heffer, this is the Last Hurrah.

Observer 27 Mar 1988

This was only the start of Mr Reagan's Last Hurrah. He has promised to appear at least twice a week during the campaign.

Daily Telegraph 16 Aug 1988

▶ The phrase is of American origin, and comes, by somewhat delayed action, from John Ford's 1958 film *The Last Hurrah,* in which the political boss of a New England town (played by Spencer Tracy) fights his last campaign.

laugh track *noun* a soundtrack containing prerecorded laughter

The formula is an unusual one – a drama-cum-comedy rather than an out and out sitcom ..., it purports to tackle serious issues of feminism, racism and exploitation and is made without a studio audience or laugh track.

Time Out 11 May 1988

lawn dart *noun* a long metal dart used in a garden game based on conventional darts, in which the players attempt to throw the darts into a target on the grass

Sometimes, as in the case of lawn darts, the regulatory process can be moved because the hazard is so unusual. Accidental stabbings from the foot-long metal darts ... send an average of 680 people to emergency rooms each year and have killed three.

Newsweek 18 Apr 1988

▶ As the source of the above extract suggests, the game of lawn darts originated in the USA, and it does not appear yet to have reached Britain.

leading-edge *adjective* of or being the most advanced or up to date, especially technologically

Three-dimensional holographic output, computer graphics with artificial intelligence and a computer screen manipulated by eye are just three of the leading-edge projects underway at MIT's newest research centre.

Guardian 5 Nov 1987

▶ The metaphor derives from the front edge of a sail or of an aircraft wing. Originally in its nominal form, it has been one of the main terms of techno-approval of the 1980s, used whenever thrusting innovation needs to be suggested:

At Smiths Industries in Cheltenham, 'leading edge' is not a term we bandy round lightly. Ever since 1911 … we've remained in the avionics forefront.

Guardian 6 June 1985

learned helplessness *noun* gradually acquired dependency caused by prolonged reliance on others

Once it is admitted that the quality of life matters, then all kinds of work become 'proper' jobs, and it no longer makes sense to spend money on unemployment pay, thus prolonging 'learned helplessness,' rather than on public service projects and amenities.

Tablet 29 Mar 1986

▶ Compare DEPENDENCY CULTURE.

least-worst *adjective* unsatisfactory but preferable to any available alternatives

But the BBC remains the least-worst way of running (reasonably) independent public-subsidy broadcasting. We can criticise poor programmes, superfluous pop music, the eccentrics of Radio 3, inflated headquarters staff and too many local stations, but we still have a product that is outstandingly good.

Sunday Times 19 June 1988

▶ Logic (of the sort that condemns 'double negatives') would seem to demand *least-bad*, but the rhetorical force of the successive superlatives carries more weight.

lethal *adjective, chiefly American* (of foreign aid) in the form of, or for the purpose of buying, weapons

The president radically cut back his request ... and he asked for only $3.6 million in 'lethal' military aid. On the eve of the vote Reagan compromised still further, offering to keep the lethal-aid portion in escrow until April.

Newsweek 15 Feb 1988

▶ The term could scarcely be more explicit, but nevertheless 'lethal aid' still manages to sound somehow euphemistic. More common, if anything, is its opposite, *non-lethal*:

The Senate bill, on the other hand, had included $9m in 'non-lethal aid' (food, clothing, shelter and medical supplies) to the contras, plus $7m to transport military equipment already purchased.

Economist 26 Dec 1987

Gore ... backed the invasion of Grenada, the bombing of Tripoli, 'non-lethal' aid to the Contras and the Gulf operation.

Daily Telegraph 15 Mar 1988

liberation priest *noun* a priest who engages in politically committed community work of the type advocated by liberation theology in Latin America

Both [Derek Foster MP and the Bishop of Durham] share a radical solution to the problem, which would bring more than a touch of Third World politics to that corner of North-east England. They are attracted by the idea of 'liberation priests' – priests who work with the people like the Catholic priests in South America.

Guardian 3 Feb 1987

▶ On liberation theology, a theory that sees the eradication of social and political injustice as central to the Christian message, see *Longman Guardian New Words*.

lick *verb, slang* to smoke the drug crack

Sometimes I still buy it [crack] at five or six in the morning. When you are licking ... with your friends you get the flavour. You don't want to go home. You can't sleep. You only want more, more, more.

Observer 24 July 1988

life-expired *adjective* obsolete

Life-expired buses can breathe again. ... The sale of 534 former Greater Manchester Transport vehicles ... was greeted like manna from Heaven by sections of the transport industry.

Guardian 27 Oct 1986

lifestyle *noun* a marketing concept in which a range of products is designed and packaged (typically with co-ordinated features) in such a way as to fit in with the potential customers' self-image and the sort of life they think of themselves as leading

Next, Britain's bounciest 'lifestyle' retailer, is developing a taste for other companies.

Economist 18 July 1987

The report, which is written in marketingspeak and illustrated with a farrago of colour snapshots ... features eight 'lifestyle leaders' and some Gallup statistics which are intended to 'paint a picture of modern-day life.' It contains all sorts of aggravating information. For example, putting a 'Haunted House' label on a tin of spaghetti is called 'fun concept lifestyle packaging.' As part of its baffling campaign to convince us that it is not *just* a paint manufacturer, Crown Berger is also searching for yet more 'lifestyle leaders,' and is mounting an award 'for those who shape the lifestyle of the majority of the British people.'

Observer 14 Aug 1988

lift-slab *noun* a method of installing pre-cast concrete slabs to form the floor of a building by lifting them between four vertical columns and fixing them at the required height

The lift-slab method cuts costs for builders. No scaffolding is needed. But it has to be executed carefully.

New Scientist 30 Apr 1987

lig *noun, British informal* a fashionable place to be seen at

By keeping a relative distance from the lights and ligs of London and by presenting a very fresh and approachable image live The Primitives have won themselves an audience.

New Musical Express 15 Aug 1987

▶ This word is a nominalization of the verb *lig*, 'to freeload' (see *Longman Guardian New Words*).

liming *noun* a technique of decorative surface treatment for wood in which lime paste is applied and then brushed off when dry, giving a silvered effect

> Liming is time-consuming and craftsman-based, not suited to mass production. Along with other special finishes, therefore, it highlights the natural grain.
>
> *Homes and Gardens* Mar 1988

▶ In common with other surface decoration techniques popular at the turn of the century (see RAG-ROLLING), liming is now making a comeback. The lime works its way unevenly into the grain; most dries out on the surface, leaving a pale, understated effect when brushed off.

line *noun, slang* a quantity of cocaine arranged in a long narrow strip on a small mirror, ready to be sniffed up

> He first encountered coke when a business meeting with a Wall Street banker ended and he was offered a cocktail or a line of cocaine. They had both, with the man from Wall Street taking out his little sachet from his waistcoat pocket and chopping the lines on his glass-topped table with a gold American Express card.
>
> *Daily Telegraph* 26 June 1987

> She is of course as high as a kite on lines of cocaine.
>
> *Times Literary Supplement* 15 Aug 1987

▶ This word has been current in the subculture of drug users for 15 years or more, but it is now more and more putting in an appearance in general English.

linkage *noun* (in international relations) reciprocal dependency of two sometimes diverse elements in negotiations, so that agreement on one of them is conditional on agreement on the other

> But the plan has been stalled for the past five years, since the introduction of the element of 'linkage' – a precondition, laid down by Washington and Pretoria, that Cuban troops must leave Angola before the timetable begins to roll.
>
> *Observer* 13 July 1986

Reagan ... allowed linkage between the cases of Daniloff and the alleged spy Zakharov; ... he broke linkage between Daniloff and a summit.

Newsweek 29 Sept 1986

▶ Linkage is scarcely new as a bargaining tactic, but dignifying it with a term of its own seems to be largely a product of the growing international relations industry, which is busy putting the minutiae of international negotiations (among many other things) under the microscope and neatly categorizing all the ploys and stratagems used.

load *verb, Australian slang* to frame (a suspect) by planting an illegal substance or object on him or her

A former police sergeant accused a detective chief superintendent yesterday of threatening to shut his mouth for good by planting heroin on him. ... Mr Hook said he asked: 'Are you going to load me?' [Chief Superintendent] Shephard had replied: 'I will shut your mouth for good.'

Daily Telegraph (Sydney) 13 Apr 1988

loadsamoney *noun, British informal* extensive and conspicuous wealth

According to America's influential Fortune magazine, Britain is booming as never before. Moreover, we are living longer and spending more. Even the old are identified as sitting on loadsamoney in the form of frozen equity on their homes.

London Evening Standard 26 Apr 1988

It might of course be some pangs of conscience as she realises the consequences of her actions and attitudes which have deliberately encouraged a society in which the poor get poorer and the rich get richer, and social responsibility takes second place to the 'loadsamoney' mentality.

Neil Kinnock, *Observer* 22 May 1988

Tory MPs cheered Mrs Thatcher and jeered at Mr Kinnock. One shouted, 'eatyermoney', a reference to Mr Kinnock's attack at the weekend on the 'loadsamoney' economy.

Independent 25 May 1988

Any claim that the Conservatives want to see the newly tax-cut flaunting their wealth in a vulgar, 'loadsamoney' fashion would horrify her [Mrs Thatcher].

Daily Telegraph 25 May 1988

A holiday flat, a car, a jewel-encrusted map of France and loads-amoney are among the tasty goodies, totalling £130,000, awaiting the winner of the Tour de France which starts tomorrow.
Sunday Times 3 July 1988

▶ This expression first came to public attention as a character invented by alternative comedian Harry Enfield, satirist of the new plutocracy. It caught on, ironically, as a catchphrase used by the high-earning yobbish tendency in southern English football crowds to taunt visiting supporters from the less well-off North, thus neatly reinforcing Mr Enfield's point. It was taken up in May 1988 by Labour leader Neil Kinnock in a speech attacking the Conservative government's policy of encouraging the creation of wealth for its own sake, and promised to make at least a temporary place for itself in the language, albeit not always with the demotic spelling:

Luckily Mr Lawson has his own resources to fall back on. He can make loads of money in the City, or so it is said.
Observer 22 May 1988

There are signs, too, that the initial *loadsa-* is taking on a temporary life of its own as a prefix:

Loadsa-sermons won't stop the Thatcherite rot [headline].
Sunday Times 29 May 1988

Loadsaglasnost [headline].
Independent 22 July 1988

There's loadsaspace at your nearest Hackney Council car park along with better security and new pay-and-display ticket machines.
Hackney Herald Aug 1988

It [Clare Short's bill to outlaw certain sorts of pornography] stands no chance and would deprive loadsa people – men and women – of a lot of pleasure.
The Sport 17 Aug 1988

lofting *noun* a bombing manoeuvre in which the aircraft performs a steep climb at the moment of releasing the bomb

To deliver a nuclear bomb at the moment, RAF pilots use the tactic known as lofting. The pilot pulls into a sharp climb and releases the bomb, flinging it more than three miles. The plane flips over and speeds away, staying just ahead of the bomb's shock wave.

Panorama, BBC1, 16 May 1988

lombard *noun,* *derogatory slang* a rich but brainless individual

A reader in Yorkshire describes watching a young man making calls on a portable telephone while standing in a queue at King's Cross station; one observer apparently made a predictable remark about 'flash yuppies', but another stated: 'He's not a yuppie, he's a LOMBARD'.

Guardian 12 Nov 1987

Jealous onlookers outside the Square Mile talked gleefully about Lombards.

The Times 1 Jan 1988

▶ Of all the welter of facetious acronyms coined in the late 1980s to characterize the variety of life-styles of contemporary city types and the like, lombard is one of the few to gain more than a fleeting currency. It is formed from the initial letters of 'Lots of money but a real [or right] dickhead.'

longbeard *noun,* *informal* an older person

The longbeards among us remember how Brit-punk largely bypassed America, though suburban kids later picked up on the fall-out, refined it into a style of crack-like purity and called it hardcore.

Sounds 16 Apr 1988

looksmanship *noun* the art of maximizing one's visual appeal

Ever since the dawn of the television age, when John F. Kennedy wiped the floor with Richard Nixon before he had opened his mouth (a lesson in 'looksmanship' that Nixon never forgot) American politicians have been hitting the hair dye bottle and hiring 'image consultants.'

The Times 15 Feb 1988

loop *noun* – **out of the loop** *American* not within the inner circle of those directly concerned with a matter

'Loyalty to the president' prevents him [George Bush] boasting about his part or saying where he disagreed, and on one issue it leaves him trying to square a circle: claiming intimate knowledge of everything going on in the White House yet being 'out of the loop' on the Iran-Contra affair.

Economist 12 Mar 1988

His [Mr Dukakis's] supporters have taken to chanting 'Where was George?' – a reference to Mr Bush's assertion that he was 'out of the loop' when money from the shipments was used to purchase arms illegally for Contra rebels in Nicaragua.

Daily Telegraph 6 Aug 1988

loose cannon *noun,* *chiefly American* someone not attached to any particular faction, who acts independently and disruptively

Gung-ho, loose cannon, cowboy, Jesus freak – there is already a cottage industry manufacturing Ollie epithets. Lynching North is quickly becoming a national sport.

Observer Magazine 26 July 1987

Mr Jackson, the loose cannon of the Democratic party, signalled to reporters to begin, and questions zeroed in on the conundrum that has fascinated and frustrated the United States for months: What does Jesse really want?

Daily Telegraph 18 July 1988

luau *noun,* *American* a sudden source of large profit; a bonanza

The Hazardous Waste Treatment Council warns that sham 'exemption enterprises' have been set up to avoid federal disposal requirements. Richard Fortuna, executive director of the HWTC, says that the 'regulatory limbo' created by Congress when it temporarily exempted recycling enterprises from hazardous-waste-disposal laws pending EPA rules 'turned into a regulatory luau.'

Newsweek 14 Mar 1988

▶ The original meaning of *luau* is a 'sumptuous Hawaiian feast.'

lunch *noun* **– out to lunch** *informal* completely lacking in common sense or cogency; crazy

Most alternative approaches [to medicine] don't stand 'scientific' analysis; some are dangerous. Some, too, are so beyond the fringe as to be 'out to lunch' – radionics, for example.

Daily Telegraph 8 July 1986

Is this guy out to lunch?

New Musical Express 26 Sept 1987

lunch-bucket *adjective,* *American informal* working-class; blue-collar

And when will Dukakis prove he can appeal to lunch-bucket democrats? Certainly not in Connecticut, the white-collar state he is expected to win this week. 'Michael Dukakis is having trouble carrying Democrats who sweat,' says Mark Siegel, a member of the Democratic National Committee.

Newsweek 4 Apr 1988

▶ The metaphor derives from manual workers' tendency to consume packed lunches rather than take themselves off to the nearest restaurant.

Lyme disease *noun* an infectious disease with symptoms including a rash, fever, and pains in the joints, and in the longer term chronic fatigue, partial paralysis, and in rare cases death from infection of the heart muscle

Today no continent except Antarctica is free of Lyme disease.... There is no sure cure for Lyme disease and, at least for now, no vaccine in sight.

Economist 10 Oct 1987

Scientists have found that a newly-discovered disease, carried by blood-sucking ticks, is far more widespread than previously supposed. ... Many who have suffered mysterious bouts of 'summer flu,' rashes, joint pain, prolonged lethargy or even paralysis may have been the victims of a bacterial infection called Lyme disease, researchers say.

Sunday Times 26 June 1988

▶ The worldwide Lyme disease has probably been around for many centuries, but it was first pinpointed as an identifiable entity in 1975, following an outbreak of arthritis among children in the town of Old Lyme, Connecticut, USA (hence the name). In 1982, the bacterium responsible for the disease was discovered in ticks, who pass it on when they bite their human victims. In 1987 there were 1000 new cases reported in Britain.

M

M&A *noun* mergers and acquisitions: the business of advising firms which are being threatened with takeover

Then came Wall Street's great takeover splurge and the rise of the mergers and acquisitions superstars. The top specialists in M&A ... may not have become more famous than their firms, but they were certainly better known than their bosses.

Newsweek 15 Feb 1988

MacGuffin *or* **McGuffin** *noun* something (e g an object or event) which provides the impetus for the plot of a film, book, etc

But the whole structure of a novel like 'The Influence' or my 'The Damnation Game' has at its centre the supernatural MacGuffin. Now supposing the mainstream reviewer says: 'Well, the problem is that the very introduction of a supernatural dimension somehow undercuts the reality of what you've created'.

Time Out 16 Mar 1988

In the 20 years since I attended my first [US political] convention, issues have faded in significance while images have increased in importance. Indeed, issues have become the equivalent of Hitchcock's 'McGuffin'. ... Few devoted time in Atlanta to analysing the 'McGuffin' of policy differences between Michael Dukakis and Jesse Jackson. Most delegates and viewers were far more keen to know how Jesse would react to being snubbed.

Daily Telegraph 27 July 1988

▶ *MacGuffin* was coined by the film director Alfred Hitchcock for something, often quite irrelevant to the actual point of the film, on which the plot of one of his films hung. For example, *The Thirty-nine Steps* 1935 (made around the time that Hitchcock invented the term) is ostensibly about the unmasking of a spy ring, but the essential point of the film is the pursuit of the man trying to do the unmasking, and the audience is told no more about the spy ring than is necessary to make the pursuit seem plausible. In its recent more general application, it seems to have lost its implication of potential irrelevance.

Hitchcock himself liked to account for *MacGuffin* as coming from an old Scottish shaggy dog story in which a train passenger with a large mysterious-looking parcel is asked by his fellow passenger what is in it. 'A MacGuffin.' 'What's a MacGuffin?' 'It's for trapping lions in the Highlands.' 'But there are no lions in the Highlands.' 'Well then, there's no MacGuffin.'

magainin *noun* a peptide with antibiotic properties

> Patents on magainins have been applied for by the American Government, which will license their production to drug companies.
>
> *Economist* 5 Sept 1987

▶ Magainins were discovered in 1987 by Dr Michael Zasloff of the US National Institute of Child Health and Human Development. He noticed that an experimental frog with skin lesions did not develop an infection despite being in a germ-ridden environment. Investigating this, he isolated from the frog's skin anti-bacterial substances, which he named magainins, from the Hebrew word for 'shield.' They appear to attach themselves to the surface of bacterial cells and then burst them. It is envisaged that they will be of particular use in the treatment of burns.

magalog *noun* a large magazine-format catalogue advertising mail-order goods

> Two new words have entered the fast-expanding vocabulary of mail-order fashion. We can thank Kit, the cheap and cheerful fashion division of Great Universal Stores, for 'magalog' and 'videolog,' natural offspring of the now superseded catalogue and specialogue. The new Kit offering for this summer is packaged as a glossy, full-colour 143-page fashion magazine, or magalog, available at 7,000 newsagents, including major branches of W H Smith, for £1.50.
>
> *Daily Telegraph* 19 May 1988

▶ A blend of *magazine* and *catalog*. The spelling -*log* (rather than -*logue*) suggests an American provenance.

magnetic resonance imaging *noun* (*abbreviation* **MRI**) a technique for viewing internal organs of the body in which pulses of radio waves momentarily reverse the magnetic alignment of nuclei of certain elements, especially hydrogen, enabling the tissues in which this reversal takes place to be scanned and an image produced

Payments of more than £3 million ... are being made by the British Technology Group to the universities of Nottingham and Aberdeen and to 20 scientists who have been involved in the development of magnetic resonance imaging (MRI) over the past 15 years, one of the major breakthroughs in medical diagnosis this century.
Daily Telegraph 3 Mar 1988

Magnetic resonance imaging gives doctors detailed information and does so without injections, operations, or harmful radiation.
Sunday Times 26 June 1988

▶ A particular advantage of MRI is that it can penetrate bone and scan body structures lying underneath. The first commercially available system came on the market in 1983.

magnet school *or* **magnet** *noun* a school which places special emphasis on the teaching of a particular group of subjects (e g science)

Even the U.S. Department of Education does not know just how many magnet schools there are in America. The one thing that is known is that the movement is spreading rapidly, though not always without growing pains.
Independent 30 Oct 1986

The Inner London Education Authority is to discuss proposals to open American-style 'magnet schools' as inner-city centres of excellence, in response to public condemnation of its performance.
Daily Telegraph 16 Oct 1987

School officials last year introduced a desegregation plan that included ... the development of magnet schools offering enriched curriculums.
New York Times 12 June 1988

▶ Magnet schools began in the USA as a response to the consequences of the 1954 Supreme Court ruling banning racial segregation in schools. Children were bussed from one district to another to achieve racial balance, but this only led to white families moving out of inner cities altogether, so that their children could be sure of going to all-white schools. In an effort to attract them back, the authorities decided in the 1970s to offer the incentive of schools (in black areas) that were centres of excellence in a particular field, concentrating resources and high-quality teachers on a certain subject area. They have now gone beyond, if not outlived, their original purpose, and advocates of their introduction in Britain see them as offering an alternative to neighbourhood schools which attempt to teach everyone the whole range of subjects, perhaps none of them outstandingly well.

mahi-mahi *noun* an edible fish of tropical and temperate seas, of the genus *Coryphaena*

> This 20-year-old fish place, run by two generations of the Berkowitz family, has become a chain of six: and what was once a no-frills atmosphere has given way to mahi-mahi and a computerized wine list. But the fish remains peerless.
>
> *Newsweek* 2 May 1988

> My companion [at a Cajun restaurant] had a mixed Mesquite grill ... The mixture was beef, chicken, shrimp and a fish called mahi mahi, which is a little like a sea bass.
>
> *Daily Telegraph* 6 Aug 1988

▶ *Mahi-mahi* is the Hawaiian and Tahitian name for the fish more generally known in English as the dolphin fish. It grows up to six feet, and when hauled on deck and dying its skin displays dazzlingly iridescent colours.

marginality *noun* the condition of being removed from the mainstream of society

> He [Jean Genet] died two years ago in a small Paris hotel after being given a state Grand Prix ... to wipe out years of marginality and was buried in Morocco where he usually lived.
>
> *Guardian* 14 May 1988

marginalize *or* **marginalise** *verb* to remove from the centre of affairs, so as to be ignored or rendered powerless

Last week, his wing of the party was in effect marginalised and reduced to splenetic outrage on the fringes of the conference. But on the defence issue, members of the hard Left believe that time is on their side.

Observer 5 Oct 1986

Unfortunately the present system encourages the securing of delegates' credentials rather than the support of the membership. It leads to manipulative practices which effectively marginalise political debate at the grassroots.

Guardian 26 June 1987

Old hands drew in their breath in awe at how Neil Kinnock has marginalised Tony Benn, is isolating Ken Livingstone as an eccentric, and has left Arthur Scargill to wither on the vine.

Listener 26 Nov 1987

Black teachers remain stuck on the lowest rungs of the professional ladder, are passed over for promotions, steered into shortage subjects and 'marginalised,' says a disturbing report published ... by the Commission for Racial Equality.

New Society 25 Mar 1988

▶ See also MARGINALITY.

market-maker *noun* a person whose business is buying shares, securities, bonds, etc and selling them on, usually at a marginal profit

Wine and rumour flowed in equal quantities in City dealing rooms yesterday as market-makers braced themselves for the Christmas festivities.

Today 24 Dec 1986

Interestingly, the evidence is that private investors, having seen the chaos of Black Monday, quickly turned into buyers, reasoning that what came down must go back up again. Market-makers, having been forced to take an awful lot of stock on to their books on October 19, were happy to oblige them.

Business Mar 1988

▶ The term *market-maker* was current at the end of the 19th century, when it referred to the slightly frowned-on activity of trading in a stock in order to arouse buyers' interest in it. Today's market-maker, however, closely resembles the pre-Big Bang stockjobber, who officially disappeared in October 1986.

For the record, the official definition of a market-maker in the Financial Services Act 1986 is 'a person (whether an individual, partnership or company) who (*a*) holds himself out at all normal times in compliance with the rules of a recognised stock exchange as willing to buy and sell securities at prices specified by him; and (*b*) is recognised as doing so by that recognised stock exchange.'

market-making *noun* the activities of a MARKET-MAKER

Coping with good and bad markets is what market-making is all about.
Business Mar 1988

marmelize *or* **marmelise** *verb, British humorous* to defeat or destroy utterly; annihilate; spifflicate

In 1984 England were marmelized by West Indies and then faced apparently second-rate opposition in Sri Lanka. When the Sri Lankans nearly won, a Guardian leader writer suggested that English cricket had reached its nadir.
Guardian 19 Aug 1988

masculinism *noun* advocacy of a dominant role for men in society, and of qualities traditionally thought of as characteristically male

My sources include the University of Pennsylvania and Dr Bryce Rankine, a top wine academic in that bastion of masculinism, Australia.
London Evening Standard 12 Apr 1988

masterclass *noun* a session in which a distinguished expert in a particular field gives instruction, typically to young professionals or advanced learners in that field, especially by analysing and criticizing their performance

241

Students, some of whom have been active in animated film-making for nearly a decade, were able to work for two days with a variety of masters of the medium. In addition to a masterclass in model animation at the Aardman studio ..., there was one masterclass in computer and two in drawn animation at Bristol Polytechnic.

Guardian 5 Nov 1987

▶ The concept of the masterclass started in the world of music, and has now become such an established part of the scene that it virtually constitutes a performance category in its own right. Audiences pay handsomely to attend masterclasses given by the likes of Elisabeth Schwarzkopf, Alfred Brendel, Julian Bream, and Geraint Evans, as much in some cases to observe the masters' occasional idiosyncratic behaviour or listen to anecdotes about their career as to see them put their temporary pupils through their paces.

Recently, however, a whole range of disciplines have spawned masterclasses – or perhaps it would be more accurate to say have discovered that the term *masterclass* can be applied to a form of teaching which they have all used from time to time.

maxi-series *noun* a television drama presented in a large number of sequential episodes

The ABC was filming scenes for its 30-part 'maxi-series' *The Last Report* at Bondi last week, and the crew was using special effects to create rain. That's showbusiness.

Sydney Morning Herald 13 Apr 1988

▶ An inflated version of the miniseries, so popular with television companies in the 1980s. These consist of three or four episodes, typically shown within the space of a single week, but maxi-series promise to test viewers' patience far more severely.

MDMA *noun* methylene dioxymethamphetamine: the synthetic stimulant drug ECSTASY

Recent research at the Johns Hopkins University in America revealed that monkeys injected with MDMA showed a marked drop in the level of serotonin, a vital brain chemical, and damage to nerve paths in the brain.

Observer 7 Aug 1988

ME *noun* MYALGIC ENCEPHALOMYELITIS

meat and potatoes *adjective, informal* of central or basic importance

> The 12 member-states of the European Community consider their Mecca of co-ordination to be at community headquarters in Brussels rather than at the OECD offices in the tranquil 16th Arrondissement of Paris. Given this, it is not surprising that the prestigious body of the industrial nations is in the throes of a major transformation – moving away from meat and potatoes economic issues in favour of such side dishes as tax policy, technological change, financial market liberalization and extended shopping hours.
>
> *Globe and Mail* (Toronto) 17 May 1988

meathead *noun, slang* an idiot

> The things about Head that wouldn't appeal to an NME journalist are (a) they're sexist; (b) they play sludgy pub rock, and (c) they're one of that long line of meatheads who thinks anyone in a pair of filthy leathers is cool.
>
> *New Musical Express* 22 Aug 1987

> John Demjanjuk ... looks the archetype of blue-collar, middle-aged America with his ill-fitting suit and weight problem, a denizen of the shopping mall and the bowling alley. That this suburban meathead could be Ivan the Terrible requires a considerable feat of imagination.
>
> *Daily Telegraph* 20 Apr 1988

> 'Everyone thinks we're one-hit wonders,' says bassist Craig Logan. 'But we're not a bunch of meatheads. We're here to stay.'
>
> *Radio Times* 28 May 1988

▶ *Meathead* has been common in American English since the 1940s, but it now seems to be finding its way into British English. In this context *meat* may mean 'penis' (compare *dickhead*). See also AIRHEAD.

mechatronics *noun* the application of electronic engineering, especially computers, to the design and operation of machines

Most Japanese institutes have a mechatronics department which focuses on designing machines to move precisely – with an accuracy of one micrometre. The microelectronics centre now does its own precision mechatronics.

New Scientist 14 Nov 1985

The term 'mechatronics' refers to a synergistic combination of precision mechanical engineering, electronic control and systems thinking in the design of products and manufacturing processes.

Daily Telegraph 29 Feb 1988

▶ Mechatronics is a term coined by the Japanese for a field in which they are world-leaders: essentially, the automated factory, office, etc, in which machines monitor and correct their own functions.

mediagenic *adjective* calculated to convey an attractive or positive image via the news media

Yesterday, as the Prime Ministerial cavalcade headed south to Tblisi ... for a final day of highly 'mediagenic' sightseeing, the jumbled pieces of a kaleidoscope of dazzling images were still falling into place.

Independent 2 Apr 1987

▶ *Photogenic* has produced a steady trickle of offspring since it first appeared on the scene in the late 1920s. First in the field was *radiogenic*, followed as early as 1939 by *telegenic*, 'presenting a good appearance on television.'

medigap *noun, American* private health insurance intended to cover payments for treatment not included under government schemes

But medigap insurance doesn't cover nursing home care, either. In fact, a congressional committee says that the elderly waste $3 billion a year buying unnecessary medigap policies, hoping to prevent catastrophic illness from bankrupting their families.

USA Today 22 May 1987

▶ These health schemes are aimed primarily at the elderly: the federally-funded Medicare system for the over 65s does not cover chronically expensive items such as home nursing care and extended periods of hospitalization, nor can it be used to pay for prescription medicines.

medilexic *noun*   a person whose names begin with any of the letters G-T

> Not only am I a statistic; I am a ranked statistic. The world, I now understand, is divided into summilexics, whose names begin with A-M, and fundilexics, whose names begin with N-Z. Another grouping, the mediocre, is the medilexics, G-T, while A-F and U-Z make up the extremilexics.
>
> *New Scientist* 22 Oct 1987

▶ See ALPHABETISM.

mega *adjective,   informal*   impressively large or comprehensive

> The handsome blond rep in his navy blazer smiles benignly. 'The club sports facilities out there are mega,' he continues. 'There's the gym, Jacuzzi and sauna, trampolining, snooker, wind-surfing, water-skiing and subaqua.'
>
> *Guardian* 29 June 1988

▶ *Mega-* has been the buzz prefix of the 1980s (*Longman Guardian New Words* lists 16 compounds, including *megablockbuster, megasulk,* and *megawally*), so it was probably only a matter of time before, like *super*, it came to be used as an adjective.

megathon *noun*   an event of impressive size or length; *specifically* a very long television programme

> The BBC has rung to say it is miffed by this column's reporting of the MI5 megathon on Monday night. The Beeb insists that the Panorama programme which was to investigate allegations by Peter Wright was not killed off by the new deputy director-general, John Birt.
>
> *Guardian* 17 Sept 1987

▶ This curious word appears at first sight to be that fairly rare phenomenon, a compound formed from two affixes: in this case two very characteristic of the 1980s, the prefix *mega-* and the suffix *-athon*, 'something very long requiring great endurance' (see *Longman Guardian New Words*). That may be so (its formation perhaps suggested by *telethon*), but in fact the absence of any notion of fund-raising, which is a usual characteristic of *-athon* words, suggests that this may simply be an adaptation of *marathon*.

Meltdown Monday *noun* BLACK MONDAY

> It was last October's appalling trade figures which helped to trigger the world stockmarket crash which led to Meltdown Monday on October 19.
>
> *Daily Telegraph* 16 Jan 1988

▶ Use of the nuclear-reactor meltdown metaphor in financial contexts predates the massive price falls of 19 October 1987:

> With the Japanese elections over, the prospect of a speculative 'meltdown' of the dollar against the yen confronts the authorities.
>
> *The Times* 7 July 1986

But its specific application to this event may well have been due to a comment by John Phelan, chairman of the New York Stock Exchange, after the crash: 'Maybe this is the big meltdown.'

memorial *noun,* *American* a charitable donation in memory of a dead person

> In lieu of flowers memorials may be made to Roanoke County #5 Rescue Squad, Hollins, or to the Baptist Children's Home, Salem.
>
> *Roanoke Times and World-News* 11 Apr 1988

memorious *adjective* having a retentive memory

> Memorious followers of this column perhaps recall that more than once I have displayed mild reproachfulness towards London's Underground system.
>
> *Times Literary Supplement* 17 July 1987

▶ This word enjoyed a brief currency in the first half of the 17th century, but has scarcely appeared since. Its revival is welcome, filling a gap in the language for a single word meaning 'long-memoried' (another candidate would have been *memorative*, which survived from the 15th century to the end of the 17th).

merchant banking *noun, American* the practice of banks investing their own money in the takeover of companies

Before October's crash, American investment banks had eagerly put their capital at stake as a means of grabbing business in take-overs and buyouts. Afterwards, it seemed that this enthusiasm for the risky business that Americans call 'merchant banking' would wane.

Economist 23 Jan 1988

▶ This sort of high-risk financing is not to be confused with British usage, in which *merchant banking* denotes a range of rather more staid activities including the buying of stocks and shares and the accepting of foreign bills of exchange.

mergerite *noun* a person who favours a merger

After Dr Owen, the biggest thorn now in the flesh of the SDP's 'Mergerites' is probably a 28-year-old computer consultant, Miss Marina Carr. Barely six weeks ago, she took out a £7,500 bank loan and placed an advertisement in a national newspaper condemning the Liberals' sudden call for a merger.

Daily Telegraph 3 Sept 1987

Both mergerites and anti-mergerites hurried forward to claim their share of the blame, knowing that nothing in British politics succeeds like apology.

Daily Telegraph 4 Sept 1987

The aim of Green Voice is ... particularly to provide liberals disaffected with mergerite politics an alternative closer to true Liberalism.

Green Line Feb 1988

▶ As the above extracts indicate, this term has been coined to cover not commercial mergers but the combining of the former Liberal and Social Democratic parties (see SOCIAL AND LIBERAL DEMOCRATS), a lengthy and rancorous process which took place in late 1987 and early 1988.

mersh *adjective, American slang* commercial

Today, Watt, Crawford and Hurley are Firehoses, a band that continues the Minutemen's tradition of unpretentious innovative rock, made a bit more 'mersh' ... by Crawford's frequently R.E.M.-influenced crooning.

New Musical Express 6 June 1987

mesoeconomic *adjective* of the functioning of medium-sized economic entities, such as large business companies

That mesoeconomic firms should alter the way in which other firms' decisions are made is none too surprising, but can they influence national aggregates such as GNP?

Times Literary Supplement 4 Mar 1988

▶ The terms *mesoeconomic* and *mesoeconomics* were apparently coined by the economist and Labour politician Stuart Holland, and introduced in his book *Towards a New Political Economy* 1988 (Vol I: *The Market Economy: from micro to mesoeconomics*; Vol II: *The Global Economy: from meso to macroeconomics*). He used them to denote economic groupings intermediate between small (micro-) ones such as households and small firms and large (macro-) ones such as nations and regions of the world.

metamessage *noun* an implied message conveyed nonverbally in addition to and often contradicting an overt written or spoken message

And it's metamessages that we react to most strongly. If someone says, 'I'm not angry' but his jaw is set hard and his words seem to be squeezed out in a hiss, you won't believe the message that he's not angry; you'll believe the metamessage. Comments like, 'It's not what you said but the way that you said it' or 'Why did you say it like that?' or 'Obviously it's not nothing – something's wrong' are responses to metamessages.

Cosmopolitan June 1987

mezzanine *adjective* being a form of financing for the takeover of a large company made up of unsecured subordinated loans at a high rate of interest repayable only after the main 'senior' loans have been repaid in case of bankruptcy

So far, only American insurance companies have acted as big providers of mezzanine finance. So-called junk bonds (below what credit agencies consider 'investment grade') are one form of mezzanine debt. Finance for a typical buy-out might be broken down thus: managers 1%; other equity investors 9%; senior bank debt 45%; and mezzanine debt 45%.

Economist 3 Jan 1987

But the most interesting portion of the package was the £500m of 'mezzanine' finance which was to be put up by Shearson itself.

Daily Telegraph 26 Sept 1987

▶ This form of high-risk, high-return lending has proliferated with the spiral in corporate takeovers and buy-outs over the past decade. Such large companies are now targeted that even the main banks cannot provide enough money to fund their acquisition, so a new 'lower' level of lending (*mezzanine* is literally a storey between two main storeys) has evolved. The providers of this capital have to accept that if anything goes wrong (such as a bankruptcy) they will be last in the queue to get their money back, but in return for this risk they get a higher yield, and often also share warrants or options as an added incentive.

micromachine *noun* a machine of microscopic size

The technology that launched the microchip will soon lead to the development of 'micromachines' – mechanical devices the size of a speck of dust – a scientist claimed yesterday. ... Prof Richard Muller, co-director of the centre, believes that within a few years they will be able to construct 'micromachines' capable of performing delicate surgery in the body.

Daily Telegraph 25 Apr 1988

▶ This ultimate in miniaturization produces mechanical parts so small that 60,000 could fit on a postage stamp. The term has also recently been applied to tiny thumbnail-sized toy cars and other vehicles.

micropropagation *noun* a technique for producing a large number of hormone-induced clones from a single plant bud

Now the work has gone one step forward thanks to 'micropropaga-tion' ..., which Dr Leakey's team is using to mass-produce mahogany trees.

Daily Telegraph 13 July 1987

▶ Part of the new growth area of plant molecular biology, micropropagation promises to revolutionize agriculture over the next decade. The sheer prodigality with which clones are produced is astounding: it is estimated that 10 million new plants could be made in a year in a small laboratory. Other advantages are that the plants are uni-form and have the known good qualities (e g freedom from disease) of their parent.

microsponge *noun* a tiny sponge with microscopically small holes, used for the slow release of medication, cosmetics, etc

Unlike microcapsules, which discharge their contents in one go, microsponges are designed to release gradually. The miniature sponges, developed by Advanced Polymer Systems of Redwood City, contain vast networks of channels. One gramme of micro-sponge contains 240,000 miles of pores.

Daily Telegraph 26 Mar 1988

▶ Microsponges respond to pressure by discharging small amounts of their contents: thus the action of smiling or pouting could be enough to release sufficient gloss to revive flagging lips.

microwaveable *adjective* suitable for cooking in a micro-wave oven

The pudding is always execrable. So is the word 'microwaveable,' though I admit that its meaning is clear and I cannot think of an alternative to signify foods that are specially prepared for micro-wave cooking.

New Scientist 28 May 1987

middlemarket *adjective* between upmarket and downmar-ket in status or appeal

Cuisine 2000 is an airline-similar eating system where food is con-
tainerised and brought to your seat. Don't groan. Middlemarket
designer touches are there to mollify; linen napkins, flowers, chocs
with your coffee.

Guardian 21 May 1987

milk round *noun* a form of graduate recruitment in which
large companies tour universities and colleges giving
information about themselves to job seekers and inter-
viewing applicants

Graduate employers are becoming much more competitive in their
recruitment methods. The most noticeable indication of this has
been the extension of on and off-campus recruitment activities well
before and well after the traditional Lent term milk round.

The Times 3 Mar 1986

After graduating from Magdalen College with a 1st class degree in
Human Sciences, Sarah Carter joined Unilever. 'I wanted to go into
marketing, and having done the milk round of interviews I'd
decided that industry would provide me with the best training and
the widest choice.'

Working Woman Apr 1986

Usually the agency will only recruit people with advertising experience, or via the elitist university 'milk round.'

Company Jan 1987

▶ This term has been current since at least the early 1970s
(it derives, of course, from the milkman's regular round of
calls), but does not seem up to now to have come to the
notice of lexicographers.

mindfuck *noun, slang* a state of heightened emotion and
excitement; freak-out

But, unlike them, we don't leap around or put on a big stage show,
so we're even more dependent on volume to help push the music
out, to help create the mind••• k

New Musical Express 23 July 1987

minehunter *noun* a naval vessel which searches for mines
and destroys them with explosives

> Although the Royal Navy has several 'minehunters' which can locate mines within 50 metres of the surface, at deeper levels ... the most effective vessels are regular minesweepers.
>
> *Daily Telegraph* 11 Aug 1987

> The boats, Brocklesby, Bicester, Hurworth and Brecon, are 57 metres long, which makes them smaller than the average vessel in the Royal Navy, but still the largest minehunters in the world with plastic hulls.
>
> *New Scientist* 20 Aug 1987

▶ The term *minehunting* was first used as long ago as 1915, but the distinction generally drawn today between minehunters and minesweepers is that the latter destroy mines by setting them off with a towed wire rather than with explosives.

minibreak *noun* a brief pause or respite

> It seems they believe I took a minibreak from the book to bump off an American in East Berlin.
>
> *Punch* Feb 1988

▶ This term was originally coined by the travel industry to promote short 2–4-day holidays, but now seems to be on the point of spreading to the general language.

mini-supercomputer *noun* a compact, relatively inexpensive supercomputer (very powerful computer which can perform calculations at very high speed on very large amounts of data)

> The term 'mini-supercomputers' (not to be confused with superminicomputer) has been coined to describe the 'low cost' computers which will enable even small to medium-sized companies to carry out complex, high speed mathematical analysis.
>
> *Mini-Micro News* Mar 1988

▶ Compare SUPERMINICOMPUTER.

misery index *noun* a statistical expression of the degree of economic suffering and deprivation within a society, calculated on the basis of the rates of inflation and unemployment

This suggests that much will be heard of the 'misery index'...,
impotence in the face of assorted foreign demons, and Mr Carter's
'malaise' contrasted with Mr Reagan's 'walking tall.'

Financial Times 26 Apr 1988

misfortuned *adjective* having suffered misfortune;
unlucky

In fact, 'Mortimer in Tuscany' was a paradigm of a certain kind of
'literary' travelogue in which the BBC seems to specialise. The
misfortuned Russell Harty's 'Grand Tour' is another recent
example.

Observer 22 May 1988

▶ The OED calls *misfortuned* 'now *rare,*' and gives no
quotations later than 1881.

mixer *noun* a disc jockey skilled in presenting music from
a pair of turntables, with frequent use of techniques
such as rapid intercutting from one to the other, manipulating the needle to repeat phrases, 'playing' the
record with the needle to produce scratching sounds,
etc

The undisputed highlight was the annual mixers and rappers con-
test on the final afternoon, when real New York sweeps in and
takes over.

News on Sunday 26 July 1987

Mockney *noun* a person who tries to put across a proleta-
rian image (for example, by affecting a working-class
London accent)

Like most senior advertising agency people, Dave isn't *really* a
'Mockney' (Mock-cockneys, like the older generation of creative
directors, copywriters and so on) or a Plastic Toff (like the older
account directors, the front men who manage the client's account).

Observer 14 Aug 1988

money-centre bank *noun* any of a loosely defined group of
US banks that are the largest in the country in terms of
assets

Money-centre banks should, on the face of it, be America's qualifiers for the banking superleague. But compared with such Europeans as Deutsche Bank and National Westminster, and such Japanese as Sumimoto Bank, Fuji Bank and Industrial Bank of Japan, most American money-centre banks are feebly capitalised and weakly managed.

Economist 8 Aug 1987

▶ There is no official listing of such banks, but there are usually reckoned to be between eight and nine of them, mostly in New York. Leading examples include Citicorp, JP Morgan, and Bankers Trust.

moneyman *noun* a man professionally concerned with financial dealings; a financier

Although the pound's slide began last year for two good reasons – weaker oil prices, a bounding dollar – it continued against every major currency for the most avoidable one: moneymen were scared that Mrs Thatcher had gone soft.

Economist 19 Jan 1985

▶ Although by no means a new word (the OED's first record of it is from 1575), *moneyman* has enjoyed a resurgence in the finance-obsessed 1980s.

monnet *noun* a hypothetical European currency unit

By 1992, when Europe hopes to become a truly common market, its people will have become familiar with an idea which today still seems outlandish: that before long the cash in their wallets might not be D-marks, francs, lire and so on, but, let us say, monnets – a single European currency for a single European market.

Economist 25 June 1988

▶ By a happy chance this coinage – or rather proposal – combines the name of Jean Monnet (1888-1979), the French economist who was one of the progenitors of the Common Market, with the notion of *money*. A form of European currency already exists – the *ecu* (European Currency Unit), inspired no doubt by the former French coin, the *écu* – but it is simply a notional unit, used for pricing goods traded within the EC. But, as the above extract suggests, when trade barriers fall in 1992 it could be the signal for the introduction of real Euro-folding money.

monopoem *noun* a monologue written in poetical form

Calvin Simpson, who performs Ali's monopoem [*Slipping Into Darkness*], is superb as the self-appointed history man. Pumping the audience up with skilful jumps of tone and by loitering around his caged set with unpredictable intent, he racks his audience by treating them as confessor and accused.

Time Out 4 May 1988

MOR *adjective, informal* (in pop music) middle-of-the-road; stylistically unadventurous

Ouch! The Leather Nun have written a dance hit. Spliced around a typically MOR guitar solo you're treated to an awkward Swedish rap.

New Musical Express 22 Aug 1987

moral majority *noun* those members of a society who uphold traditional moral values, reputedly a numerical majority of the population but underrepresented among those who hold power; *specifically* those Americans who support right-wing policies underpinned by Christian fundamentalist dogmas

The appointment of the Revd Andrew Young as United States Ambassador to the United Nations may be said to have consecrated the civil rights movement. The moral majority seeks to bury it.

Times Literary Supplement 24 May 1985

▶ In the USA, the moral majority is a crusading movement aimed at pushing back the tide of liberal reform, which it sees as corrupting the soul of America. It is fanatically opposed to such things as abortion and antidiscriminatory legislation for gays, and is seen by many commentators as being influential in the election of Ronald Reagan to the presidency. Interestingly enough, though, the term moral majority seems not to have become so firmly linked to right-wing reaction, at least in British English, that it cannot still be appropriated by those who espouse a more liberal philosophy:

In his speech to the party conference Neil Kinnock said that Labour would mobilise a compassionate 'moral majority,' a majority which opposed the meanness of Toryism and abominated its dual standards.

Guardian 27 Oct 1986

morphogen *noun* any substance which acts on embryonic cells to determine what body structures they will develop into

Prof Eichele stressed his experiment provided good, but not absolute confirmation, that retinoic acid is a morphogen.

Daily Telegraph 18 June 1987

Enthusiasts for the idea suspected that morphogens diffuse through an embryo, establishing a gradient of concentration. Cells in different places would then respond according to the concentration of morphogen around them, developing in a particular way to produce polarised structures such as the digits on a limb.

New Scientist 2 July 1987

▶ The first morphogen to be tentatively identified is retinoic acid, a derivative of vitamin A. Work by Christina Thaller and Gregor Eichele at Harvard Medical School has recently shown that this morphogen is released in minute amounts into an embryo's limb buds, and the different concentrations of the substance in different areas of the bud trigger growth of various components of the future limb (e g little toes or kneecaps).

moshing *noun* frenzied energetic dancing engaged in by SPEED-METAL fans

Upfront, there is the usual but still-incredible spectacle of the hardcore fanatics thrashing, dive-bombing off the stage, writhing ('moshing') in an uninhibited physical mania.

New Musical Express 21 Mar 1987

Thrash metal fans ... participate at concerts by 'moshing': dirty-tackling each other in a mass body-slam dance.

Daily Telegraph 24 Apr 1987

▶ Compare SLAMDANCING.

mouthfeel *noun* the tactile impression made by food on the mouth of the eater

Watch out, too, for polydextrose, a bulking agent for ice-cream, instant puddings and candies which can reduce calories by up to 90 per cent without sacrificing texture, palatability or 'mouthfeel.'
Listener 31 Mar 1988

movers and shakers *noun plural, chiefly American* people of power and influence – called also *shakers*

Bill Blass, Oscar de la Renta and Geoffrey Beene cater chiefly to the ladies who lunch: Nancy Reagan, Nancy Kissinger, Pat Buckley, Brooke Astor and their friends, the movers and the shakers in fund-raising galas and behind-the-scenes politics.
Guardian 10 Nov 1986

But the appointment of political virgins [by Ronald Reagan] brings other problems. It contributes to a high turnover in the top jobs, with no one staying long enough to master his task, let alone ensure continuity of purpose. ... Many of the advertised movers and shakers soon resign in disgust, or bolt back to the private sector once their Washington experience can be cashed in.
Economist 7 Nov 1987

Its movers and shakers know this cosmopolitan scene faces stiff challenges.
New Statesman & Society 17 June 1988

▶ The source of the phrase is Arthur O'Shaughnessy's 'Ode' (1874), a piece of wistful escapism in which its use is rather less worldly than it has since become:

> We are the music-makers,
>
> And we are the dreamers of dreams,
>
> Wandering by lone sea breakers,
>
> And sitting by desolate streams;
>
> World-losers and world forsakers,
>
> On whom the pale moon gleams:
>
> Yet we are the movers and shakers
>
> Of the world for ever, it seems.

MRI *noun* MAGNETIC RESONANCE IMAGING

MRM *noun* mechanically-recovered meat: low-quality meat removed from a carcass by mechanical means (e g high-pressure jets) after the main cuts have been conventionally removed, and used for example in sausages

> Telford magistrates ruled that the firm broke the Food Labelling Regulations Act of 1984 when it failed to disclose on labels that mechanically recovered meat (MRM) was contained in the products.
>
> *Guardian* 19 July 1988

mudger *noun, informal* an equivocator; a prevaricator

> Mr Kinnock is showing himself to be a lovely mudger on the home front too. True, it is Mr Bryan Gould who holds the Shadow Mudging portfolio, but the enabling rhetoric which is to sway the party conference is Mr Kinnock's own.
>
> *Daily Telegraph* 13 May 1988

▶ On the possible derivation of this term see FUDGE AND MUDGE.

mule *noun, slang* a courier employed to smuggle drugs, especially South American cocaine, into a country

> For the past five years or so, since the first real attempts at cocaine trafficking were recognised in Britain, the 'mules' have relied on concealment of small portions of the drug in baggage or on, or within, their bodies. They have concentrated on air routes, often transitting through countries with close South American ties, such as Spain and Portugal.
>
> *Guardian* 12 Nov 1987

mush-mouthed *adjective, American informal* tongue-tied

> 'I'm not a natural-born speaker,' she said with a recurring sense of amazement at her activities in the campaign. 'I get all mush-mouth-ed.'
>
> *Chicago Tribune* 11 Mar 1988

muso *noun, derogatory slang* a pop musician who is pedantically concerned with technical minutiae of performance, to the detriment of the spirit of the music

Why is the vast majority of the first side devoted to a nine-minute
version of 'Light My Fire' which only goes to prove the tedious
muso strain that lurked in Morrison's musicians?

New Musical Express 20 June 1987

As you probably know, the majority of deaf musos claim that
there's been nothing good in the music scene all year ... apart from
Dylan coming over, oh yeah, and Clapton on the South Bank Show.

Underground Jan 1988

must- *adjective combining form, chiefly American* (used
for suggesting that something is absolutely necessary
or highly desirable)

▶ The conversion of verb phrases using the auxiliary *must*
into attributive adjectives (*must have, must do, must see,
must buy*) is a current linguistic fad in American English
but does not seem to have made much of an impact on
British English as yet:

Nicholson and Streep are so incredible, they make Ironweed a
must see film.

ABC-TV, New York, quoted in *Sunday Times* 15 May 1988

Even better is the Ribeaupierre Vendange Tardive. This is a 'must
have' wine for connoisseurs, for it is as rich, opulent, and complex
as the greatest Yquem or German Eiswein.

Robert Parker [American author], *The Wine Buyer's Guide* 1988

myalgic encephalomyelitis *noun (abbreviation* **ME***)* a
viral disease which affects the nervous system and
produces long-lasting effects of fatigue and poor coordination

The disease is Myalgic Encephalomyelitis or ME, which was unknown 20 years ago. ... It would appear that whichever virus or
viruses is implicated in ME the patient may present with neurolo-
gical symptoms, while depression, lethargy, inordinate fatigue,
mood swings, paranoid feelings, hallucinations, forgetfulness, inability to concentrate and nominal aphasia are psychological.

Guardian 1 Oct 1987

It is very difficult to describe ME, and we all look so well a lot of us,
and it's only when people are chronically ill with ME that they
start getting the muscle wastage.

Clare Francis, Thames TV, Apr 1988

► The true nature of this disease is only now becoming understood, and indeed it is still controversial. The generalized malaise it produces has led in the past to its being called the 'malingerer's disease,' because doctors could not find anything physically wrong with people suffering from it. The discovery that a virus seems to be implicated in it has led to the coinage of the less disparaging name of *post-viral syndrome* for the set of distressing and disabling symptoms which can blight sufferers' lives for very many years. There is no cure, but treatment with antibiotics can alleviate the symptoms. Many doctors still believe that there is a psychosomatic element to the syndrome, inasmuch as its extreme duration has a depressant effect on sufferers, which makes them feel even worse. With increased knowledge of the condition, an ME Action Campaign has been formed in Britain to provide support for those with the disease.

N

N *abbreviation* nuclear

> Army blows up mines on test site for N-waste.
>
> *Guardian* 28 Aug 1986

▶ This abbreviation is now quite widespread in the written language, especially in newspaper headlines, but does not yet seem to have entered the spoken language.

NAI *abbreviation* non-accidental injury

> I knew that the Dobbs family had a social worker all to themselves. Stepfather had been in prison, the older boys were delinquent and an older sister had been taken into care. The younger ones, still in the primary school, had been the subject of NAI inquiries.
>
> *Guardian* 7 July 1987

nailarium *noun, American* a manicurist's salon

> All she wants is to get her nails done, which is all New York suddenly wants. Each corner seems to have a nailarium. ... Haircutters retreat, useful shops are beaten out by the cost of leases, amenities are all replaced by franchises; and all that's left is the manicure.
>
> *Observer* 6 Mar 1988

NAIRU *noun* non-accelerating-inflation rate of unemployment: the level of unemployment at which the rate of inflation stays stable

> But not all of the rise in the NAIRU can be explained by labour-market rigidity: the OECD reckons that real wages in Europe have become less rigid during the 1980s.
>
> *Economist* 30 Aug 1986

> Every economy has a rate of unemployment at which inflation is stable. This rate is inelegantly termed the non-accelerating-inflation rate of unemployment, or NAIRU.
>
> *Economist* 12 Mar 1988

▶ The attention of economists has been drawn to this laboriously named figure in recent years by the phenomenon that high unemployment has been failing to depress wage levels (see HYSTERESIS). This fact contradicted the orthodox belief, enshrined in the 'Phillips curve' invented by A W Phillips in 1958, that higher employment produces a corresponding wage inflation.

namecheck *verb, informal, chiefly American* to refer to someone specifically by name

It's no accident that Lloyd should namecheck Roxy Music and U2.
Sounds 21 Nov 1987

As for what the band say lyrically, the words are a celebration of music's antidepressant qualities – ... Chuck Berry, Howling Wolf and Little Richard all get namechecked – laced with surrealism.
New Musical Express 16 Jan 1988

nanotechnology *noun* the technology of manufacturing and measuring objects of microscopically small size

The Department of Trade and Industry is offering to give grants to teams of workers involved in nanotechnology projects.
New Scientist 17 Sept 1987

▶ The prefix *nano-* denotes 1 thousand millionth part of a particular unit of measurement. Nanotechnology deals with objects that are between 0.1 and 100 nanometres in size. Compare MICROMACHINE.

narcodollars *noun plural* US dollars earned by the export of cocaine or other illegal drugs

Cocaine existed before the new economic policy, of course. But officials admit that drug income [in Bolivia] is growing in spite of a high-profit four-month campaign by US Air Force helicopters and troops last year. Mr Paz's government has also been more successful in channelling the 'narcodollars' into the economy than its predecessors.
Guardian 9 May 1987

▶ The basis of this coinage is no doubt the strictly legitimate *petrodollars*, foreign exchange earned by the export of petroleum.

nashi *noun* a variety of Japanese pear

> The nashi ... is just the kind of up-market fruit the New Zealanders have been looking for since their worldwide triumph with the hairy green, curiously tasteless Kiwi fruit.
>
> *Sunday Times* 10 Apr 1988

▶ The nashi is a close relative of the Tientsin pear, which achieved a certain vogue in the mid 1980s. Large-scale cultivation of it has started in New Zealand, and a New Zealand Nashi Council has been set up to market it abroad.

natural auralism *noun* a technique for the treatment of those born deaf but with some residual hearing, in which at as early an age as two months they are given hearing aids and encouraged to listen, and in due course speak, to those around them

> We, too, have a daughter born severely deaf, but fortunate to come under the care of professionals dedicated to what you describe as natural auralism at the age of 10 months.
>
> *Sunday Times* 17 Jan 1988

▶ This form of therapy, in which the child is encouraged to develop its hearing as naturally as it can, without being segregated as 'deaf,' is still a subject of considerable controversy in the medical world. Proponents point to cases where sufficient useful hearing is developed to understand and talk without using sign language or lipreading, but opponents have branded it a middle-class cult backed by the hearing-aid industry.

necessity defence *noun* a defence in law which seeks to justify an illegal action by showing that it was done to prevent a greater wrong

> President Carter's daughter and President Reagan's policies went on trial together yesterday in a court case which evoked the passions and personalities of the turbulent Sixties. ... They [the defence] will deploy them [the witnesses] on behalf of what is known as the 'necessity defence' – that they violated the law to prevent a greater wrong, namely covert US foreign policies in Central America and elsewhere which subvert democracy at home and abroad.
>
> *Guardian* 9 Apr 1987

The 'necessity defence' is having its most public test in Northampton. The defence says trespassing and disorderly conduct are sometimes necessary to prevent commission of greater crimes, such as apartheid, or the killing of civilians in Nicaragua.

Independent 16 Apr 1987

▶ This defence had its origins in various 18th- and 19th-century cases in which shipwrecked sailors charged with eating their dead shipmates pleaded that it was necessary for them to do so in order to survive. It has been revived recently by political protestors.

neo-poverty *noun* impoverishment of people previously comfortably off, due to changing social conditions (for example, changes in the pattern of employment or of welfare benefit payments)

... reckons that about a fifth of all [Swedish] families with two children are members of the 'new poor.' He says that of the few families with more than two children, over a half are in neo-poverty.

Economist 7 June 1986

neovascularization *or* **neovascularisation** *noun* the development of blood vessels in an area previously lacking them, or of new vessels in an area where they already exist

Most contact lenses also reduce the amount of oxygen reaching the cornea, and this can be exacerbated if you wear your lenses for long periods every day, year in, year out. In extreme cases, the eyes respond by growing blood vessels into the cornea (a process known as 'neovascularisation'). But you can't see this change without specialist equipment.

Which? June 1987

nerdish *or* **nerdic** *adjective, American slang* tiresomely gormless

Charles Nelson Reilly directs this new American comedy about a beleaguered midwestern architect unexpectedly playing host to the stranger who once saved his life, his nerdish guest who refuses to leave.

Where: Chicago Mar 1988

Not wishing to libel his former employers, Swerdlick has trans-
posed the experience to a high school ... with the nerdic Ronald
buying the affections of the blonde cheer-leader Cindy ... so that his
status will soar.

Sunday Times 5 June 1988

▶ *Nerd* has been the 'in' American term of abuse of the
1980s for the ineffectual or unpopular individual. In origin it
may arise from an attempt to represent in spelling a variant
pronunciation of *nut* (*nerts* was American college slang for
'nuts' in the 1930s and 40s); *turd* could well have played a
part in its formation, too. Merriam-Webster's *12,000 Words*
1986 mentions the derivative *nerdy*, but *nerdish* and *nerdic*
have not yet appeared in mainstream dictionaries.

network *verb*   to establish a set of contacts with people in a
similar business or situation as oneself, to provide for
interchange of information, furtherance of one's own
prospects, etc

Consultant surgeon Margaret Ghilchik ... is a member of various
societies which specialise in her area of interest, breast cancer. She
also meets people through being on hospital committees. But you
can also network with clients and associates in a semi-formal
setting.

Company June 1987

All the bands on Ruthless have been trying in the traditional way
to get a record out. Either they're total f**k-ups ..., on acid all the
time, in another world, or they won't suck dick. They don't network. They don't meet people, don't make connections.

New Musical Express 20 June 1987

▶ The noun *networking* is now fairly well established in
British English (amongst the earliest to adopt it were femin-
ists, who saw the need to put in touch with each other
women whose situation was worsened by isolation: 'The
N[ew] D[irections] F[or] W[omen] encourages women who
attend to set up their own self-help groups and to extend the
work by informal networking' – *Guardian* 1 Aug 1984), and
its conversion to verbal use is a logical next step.

networker *noun* a person who networks

> Albini resents what he sees as the evils of the networking system, which enslave bands to a lifetime of ass-kissing and being ripped off. He is plagued with his own personal swarm of networkers.
>
> *New Musical Express* 20 June 1987

neural network *or* **neural net** *noun* a type of computer function which works by processing separate pieces of information all at once rather than in a step-by-step manner

> Dr David Bounds of the Royal Signals and Radar Establishment, Malvern, described how the next generation of computers, called neural nets, mimics the brain. ... Neural nets are patterned after the complex interconnections between brain cells.
>
> *Daily Telegraph* 8 Feb 1988

> Researchers in the new field of neural networks are bringing together work in neuroscience, computer science and other fields such as the cognitive sciences. Models of neural networks help the neuroscientist to understand how the brain works ... and they also provide the computer scientist with a model of how a computer might work.
>
> *New Scientist* 26 May 1988

> Although the neurocomputer cannot exactly emulate the brain, it does have electronic neural networks which can achieve results through learning and correction, rather than number crunching.
>
> *Financial Times* 17 June 1988

► As their name suggests, the way in which neural network computers function mimics that of the brain. Not only is their circuitry interconnected in such a way that they can perform multiple operations simultaneously, they are actually capable of 'learning' on the basis of tasks that they have already carried out. See also CONNECTIONISM.

neurocomputer *noun* a computer which operates by means of NEURAL NETWORKS

> IBM and TRW ... have developed prototypes of general-purpose neurocomputers, and many computer companies in the US, Japan and Europe are now building experimental machines. ... Researchers are also considering the development of neurocomputers based on optical or even biological components.
>
> *New Scientist* 26 May 1988

Hollywood's version of computers – beeping, talking androids that always outwit the bad guys – are already on the drawing boards in Japan. They are called neurocomputers, or computers that think. Conventional computers can add up columns of numbers in a split second, but they cannot instantly recognise a face, learn from past experiences or make a judgment based on prior knowledge. Neuro-computers, like the human brain, should be able to do all these things one day.

Financial Times 17 June 1988

neurogenetics *noun* the study of the genetic basis of the nervous system

This discovery, described in the last issue of the Journal of Neuro-genetics, may give scientists an important clue in their hunt for the molecular machinery responsible for our own body clock.

Daily Telegraph 17 Nov 1986

new man *noun* a man who does not adopt an aggressively male social role, but participates in activities tradition-ally regarded as more appropriate to women (e g look-ing after children, cooking, and housework)

To some limited extent, then, it is possible to detect the emergence of a 'new man,' less sure of himself perhaps, having to rethink his place in society at large and at home, accepting the inexorable trend towards equal opportunities for the sexes in the workplace, and learning how to adapt to changing circumstances without necessarily feeling that his essential 'maleness,' 'masculinity' or 'manliness' is being eroded.

Listener 4 July 1985

The New Man ... sounds suspiciously like one of those fictional stereotypes dreamed up by an adman after a long lunch.

Guardian 30 Nov 1987

▶ The new man – caring, gentle, self-aware, anti-sexist, and not weighed down with traditional male stereotypes – is in origin a creature of the late 1970s, a by-product of the women's movement. As women revised their role in society, the other side of the equation was that some men moved into what used to be exclusively female preserves.

The term 'new man,' however, seems not to have arisen until the mid-1980s. It is of course modelled on the 'new woman,' a phenomenon of the late 19th century, the earlier phase of women's emancipation, defined by the *OED* when she first appeared as 'a woman of "advanced" views, advocating the independence of her sex and defying convention.' The earliest known example comes from George Gissing's *Odd Women* (1894): 'A strong character, of course. More decidedly one of the new women than you yourself – isn't she?'

See also FEMINAL.

NIC *noun* newly-industrializing country: a country which during the past two or three decades has developed rapidly from a relatively poor agricultural economy to one in which industry (particularly light industry, such as electronics) plays a major role

The debate centers on the policies of three of the so-called newly industrialized countries (NIC's) – Taiwan, Hong Kong and Singapore.

Newsweek 14 March 1988

The Asian NICs have invaded Japan's heartland, and they've come to stay.

Money Programme, BBC2, 8 May 1988

▶ Low unit labour costs have been a key to the mushrooming of industry in many Third World countries. In the Far East, for example, NICs such as Korea, Taiwan, Singapore, and Malaysia are beginning to muscle in on Japan's stranglehold on the electronics industry; they now take 5% of Japan's total home market in electronic goods.

The word NIC can be pronoununced like 'nick', rather than like its three component letters.

Nilky *noun,* *informal* an out-of-work person with a large family

Following hard on the heels of 'Yuppies' and 'Dinkies' ... comes the latest in acronym categories, one familiar to many, perhaps; 'Nilkies,' standing for no-income-lots-of-kids.

Daily Telegraph 1 June 1987

nimbyism *noun, derogatory* selfish opposition to new building or other developments in one's vicinity which one would not object to if they were elsewhere

Britain's environment secretary, Mr Nicholas Ridley, has increased by a third ... his department's forecast of the number of new households needing accommodation in south-east England by the turn of the century. As a result, over 90 Tory backbenchers, including some keen Thatcherites, have joined a parliamentary group dedicated to Sane Planning: doublespeak for 'not-in-my-back-yard,' or nimbyism.

Economist 21 May 1988

▶ The acronym *nimby* arose in the mid 1980s to express the attitudes of people protesting against the siting of a nuclear power station, military installation, etc near their own homes (see *Longman Guardian New Words*).

911 candidate *noun, American slang* a candidate who is put up for election at the last moment when another candidate or candidates from the same party seems unlikely to be successful

If no candidate manages a break-out, then party elders may have recourse to a 911 candidate – code for Mr Mario Cuomo.

The Times 17 Mar 1988

▶ The US equivalent of Britain's 999 is 911 – appropriate for an emergency candidate.

Nizinny *noun* a breed of medium-sized Polish sheepdog

But the Nizinny is shaggy and playful, and to the lay observer it looks like something between the less yappy of Yorkshire terriers and the most amiable of Old English Sheepdogs cut down to manageable size.

Daily Telegraph 1 Aug 1987

▶ The Nizinny is a breed recently introduced from Poland. In full its name is Polski Owczarek Nizinny, literally 'Polish lowland sheepdog.'

no brainer *noun, American informal* something that can be achieved without much intelligence, thought, or skill

There is a new expression in American golf. It is called a 'no brainer,' and it was one of these that enabled Tom Watson to get a better glimpse of what would be his second United States Open Championship.

Daily Telegraph 22 June 1987

In developing their ... strategy, McDonald's officials quickly focused on the family. Traditionally, children hated stuffy French restaurants as much as the restaurants hated having the children. 'When we started positioning ourselves, there was no other restaurant in France that went after families,' said Mr Allin .... 'It was a no-brainer.'

New York Times 12 June 1988

▶ The notion behind this coinage's use in the first extract above is that the putt is so long and difficult that even if it does go in the hole, success must be attributed to luck rather than the golfer's cleverness.

noddy suit *noun* a garment worn by soldiers for protection against gas and chemical attack

First came the BBC's nine-to-five world of the briefcase brigade, balancing budgets and showing us pretty pictures of the sun glinting on the armour of a brand new frigate and soldiers in 'noddy' suits and respirators working off their lunch on the assault course.

Today 10 Apr 1986

But if the wind shifts or the troops are equipped with protective suits and masks, chemical attacks may not do much (although the cumbersome protective 'noddy suits' will cut the soldiers' effectiveness).

Economist 10 July 1987

no-frills *adjective* basic, without any additional (desirable) features

If a husband and wife take on a no-frills mortgage of £90,000, at an interest rate of 11%, their monthly interest payments ... will be roughly £750.

Economist 18 July 1987

▶ Compare FULL-FRILLS.

-nomics *suffix* economic theory or policy

▶ *Economics* began to take on a new career as a suffix with the coinage of *Nixonomics* to characterize the economic policies of the Nixon administration in the USA, and its popularity became greater when Ronald Reagan's policies became widely known as REAGANOMICS. For the precise connotation of the first of the following formations, see BIMBO:

> **bimbonomics** [Eric] Morley, meanwhile, is a former Tory candidate and expert in bimbonomics who has made a fortune from what was anathema to the News on Sunday worthies: the beauty contest.
>
> *Daily Telegraph* 7 June 1988

> **Dukakonomics** the economic policies of Michael Dukakis, US Democratic presidential candidate in 1988

> Dukakonomics just doesn't have the same ring to it. [cartoon caption]
>
> *Daily Telegraph* 18 May 1988

> **Lawsonomics** the economic policies of Nigel Lawson, British Chancellor of the Exchequer

> Hot and cold summer of Lawsonomics [headline]
>
> *Daily Telegraph* 27 Aug 1988

See also ROGERNOMICS.

nonet *noun* a group of nine related things

> Dessert wines are coming back into favour, and there are many styles to choose from. We have selected a broad and unusual nonet of classic mature examples.
>
> La Réserve wine-tasting brochure May 1988

▶ In common with its fellow terms for pieces of music written for a particular number of performers (*septet, octet*, etc), *nonet* has been ripe for metaphorical transfer, and indeed in the early 1960s it was applied to a group of nine subatomic particles, but this appears to be its first recorded use in a more general sense.

non-lethal *adjective, chiefly American* (of foreign aid) in the form of, or for the purpose of buying, food, clothing, and medical supplies

▶ See LETHAL.

non-performing *adjective* (of a loan) not paying interest

> Of all the loans Citicorp has made, 3.2% ... are 'non-performing.'
> *Economist* 8 Aug 1987

noodle *verb* to doodle at a computer keyboard, hitting keys at random

> An award-winning program from Broderbund called Jam Session plays jazz, rock and classical tunes through a personal computer's built-in speaker, as little animated musicians perform on screen. The operator plays along by hitting keys on the computer's keyboard, and the program seamlessly integrates the noodling into the music; it sounds like jamming with the band.
> *Newsweek* 25 Apr 1988

nose *verb* to smell (especially wine) in order to evaluate it

> If you are a newcomer [to wine tasting], and especially if you are female, I'm afraid you yourself run the risk of being surreptitiously – and sometimes not so surreptitiously – 'nosed' (winespeak for smelt).
> *London Evening Standard* 22 Mar 1988

nostalgiast *noun* a person with a sentimental attachment to the past

> In post-Butskellite Britain, rival doctrines jostle for control of our hearts and minds. But there is one doctrine which transcends both class and party: that of nostalgia. ... Far from being passive, the 'nostalgiasts' are on the march, their banner proudly borne by the Prince of Wales, scourge of the mindless modernists.
> *Daily Telegraph* 30 May 1988

nuclear *noun* nuclear power

> Nuclear's charm [headline]. Only by investing heavily in nuclear power today can the world be sure of avoiding highcost energy in the 1990s and beyond.
> *Economist* 29 Mar 1986

We don't think that each public inquiry should take the form of a national debate into nuclear.

Cecil Parkinson, *Panorama*, BBC1, 6 June 1988

nuclear autumn *noun* a global drop in temperatures sufficient to have a severely detrimental effect on agriculture, caused by the blocking of sunlight by fallout from a nuclear explosion

Several tactical weapons, amounting perhaps to as little as one megaton, would produce sufficient soot to create a nuclear autumn.

New Scientist 4 May 1987

▶ The notion of a 'nuclear winter' following a nuclear war, in which a blocking of sunlight for several months would lead to freezing temperatures and widespread famine, was first postulated in 1983. Further research tended to show that these initial predictions were overpessimistic, but many scientists nevertheless believe that sun blockage will be serious enough to lower temperatures to a level (say 10° below average) that would decimate the Earth's agricultural production.

nugget *noun* an item of interesting or instructive information

The quality of 'tutors' [at wine tastings] varies enormously. I must say I can listen to a string of inanities so long as they are pronounced with a French accent (not that Paul Pontallier of Chateau Margaux, or Henri Krug had anything but nuggets to impart to us at Gleneagles).

London Evening Standard 22 Mar 1988

▶ The metaphorical sense of *nugget* (a unit or item of something non-material) is by no means new, but this specific application (evidently inspired by the common collocation 'nugget of information') seems to be a recent development.

nuke *verb, informal* to destroy conclusively

The real gardening intellectual can tell a selective weedkiller from a non-selective one. Dee-Weed, for example, will nuke everything in sight, and nothing will grow for three years.

She July 1987

▶ The verb *nuke*, meaning to attack and destroy with nuclear weapons, was coined in the middle 1960s, but this alarmingly cosy metaphoricization is a new development.

numerati *noun plural, informal* financial whizzkids

> Amid the tales of corporate woe and personal ruin following the Stock Market crash, there is a promising medical prognosis from American doctors who have been monitoring the fallen numerati.
> *Daily Telegraph* 2 Jan 1988

> All the clichés about the golden numerati falling from grace and selling the Porsche have a ring of truth.
> *Daily Telegraph* 23 Feb 1988

▶ The immediate source of this formation is no doubt *literati*, with a conscious reference to the pair *literate/ numerate*; but it is *glitterati* which, as *Longman Guardian New Words* notes, appears to have started the minor vogue for the suffix *-erati* (it records also *slopperati*). The word presumably alludes to their skill at juggling figures.

See also JAZZERATI.

nurdle *verb, informal* (in cricket) to score runs with small pushes and deflections rather than flamboyant stroke-play

> Edrich opened with Compton and, as he took guard, Bradman warned him, 'You're going to have to fight for them, lad'; and he directed Waite and McCabe to bowl flat out. But Edrich nurdled his tremulous ten [to achieve 1000 runs before the end of May].
> *Guardian* 18 May 1988

nurturance *noun* caring for, looking after, and bringing up other people; nurturing

> You talk about a long tradition of separate women's values – nurturance, co-operation and so on – as opposed to male values of aggression and domination.
> *New Statesman* 26 Feb 1988

▶ A word which seeks to fill what some would view as one of the gaps in male-dominated language, in which activities engaged in by women go unnamed and therefore unregarded. Unhappily the term chosen is not distinguished by its euphoniousness.

nutmeg *verb, British informal* (in sport) to deceive a player or make him look foolish by passing the ball between his legs

Indeed, had Essex ... not been quite so shoddy in the field – Pringle was nutmegged and Topley dummied to concede fours – Sussex might not have reached 130.

Sunday Times 12 June 1988

▶ *Nutmeg* has been current for some time with reference to soccer, although not recorded elsewhere, but the reference to other sports (cricket, in this case) seems to be a new development. The word probably derives from the colloquial use of *nuts* for 'testicles.'

oatsy *adjective, American and Canadian informal* full of vigour and self-importance

> Amendments ... will probably emerge as a public consensus, aided by furious behind-the-scenes lobbying and another locked-door federal-provincial conference. When all provinces are feeling oatsy with power, there is little opportunity for Ontario to throw its weight around.
>
> *Globe and Mail* (Toronto) 17 May 1988

▶ This derives from the expression 'feel one's oats,' implying a mixture of friskiness and self-satisfaction.

ob-gyn *noun* an obstetrician and gynaecologist

> According to the American College of Obstetricians and Gynecologists, 73% of its 24,500 members have been sued for malpractice at least once. To escape the soaring cost of malpractice protection, some 3000 ob-gyns have abandoned the specialty.
>
> *Time* 24 Mar 1986

> The smug-faced appearance of a well-known ob-gyn photographed between the upside down torsoless legs of a model in lewd underwear in a glossy magazine drove one journalist to write a furious piece recently which culminated with the ringing exhortation: 'Women, choose women.'
>
> *Guardian* 16 Aug 1988

Obscuranto *noun, humorous* wilfully obscure language intended to conceal or mislead

> All this jargon can be found in official EEC documents, and yesterday a British Euro-MP, Dr Caroline Jackson, supported by consumer groups, began a campaign to get rid of it. The campaigners have a word for it: 'Obscuranto,' chosen to convey their view that as well as being long-winded, the mandarins of Brussels are deliberately unintelligible.
>
> *Daily Telegraph* 2 Feb 1988

▶ The sort of Eurobabble against which the coiners of this term are campaigning includes such brain-numbing formations as 'non-edible vegetables' for flowers and 'mammary secretions' for milk. The word *Obscuranto* is of course based on *Esperanto*, the artificial international language.

off-balance sheet financing *noun*   those areas of a company's financial affairs which are not properly recorded on a balance sheet

Mining company Burnett and Hallamshire revealed net liabilities of £4 million in its 1985 accounts. The previous year it showed net assets of £108 million but indicated potential problems in an obscure note. Tighter accounting standards would have required the company to reveal a very different picture in 1984, the authors suggest. They say that off-balance sheet financing is now a major problem.
Guardian 2 Mar 1987

office *verb, American*   to work in an office

One of the worst examples is the use of the word 'office' as a verb, said Mr Jim Seymour, a distinguished consultant, writing in the latest issue of the American journal, PC Magazine. People say: 'Where do you office?' or 'I office in 42nd Street.'
Daily Telegraph 22 Sept 1987

off-limits *adjective*   out of bounds

In 1980, MI6 saw Graham's double-glazing business as an ideal way of penetrating the Soviet Trade Delegation in Highgate ..., which was thought to be a nest of spies. The 650-strong Trade Delegation, like the Soviet Embassy, is off-limits. So for diplomatic purposes, every stick, stone and s-bend is on Russian soil.
News on Sunday 26 July 1987

▶ This word has been current in American English since at least the early 1950s, particularly with reference to military installations, but there are now signs of its becoming established in British English.

one-stop *adjective*   offering a comprehensive range of services or facilities within a single package

Commodore introduces the one-stop office – new Amiga System 500 [advertisement].

Daily Telegraph 13 Apr 1988

Businesses in NSW ... will soon need only one licence to operate. ... At present some businesses have to get up to 17 licences. The new one-stop system will be operated by the Business and Consumer Affairs Department.

Daily Telegraph (Sydney) 15 Apr 1988

▶ The metaphor derives from one-stop shopping, the concept of the hypermarket housing every conceivable sort of merchandise under one vast roof, so that one can drive to it, park there, and do all one's shopping at one fell swoop. The notion was originally extended to the provision of a wide variety of financial services from a single source:

One-stop shopping is on the way in financial services, so a bank must be able to offer the full range under one roof.

Economist 26 Mar 1988

and has spread from there to more general applications.

orgasmatron *noun* a device for inducing orgasm

Billed as the ultimate Motorhead bash, it will feature the band's infamous Orgasmatron and legendary Bomber together on stage for the first time.

New Musical Express 19 Dec 1987

▶ The concept of the orgasmatron has a long and rather dubious history. It could well be that it has its origins in Wilhelm Reich's orgone box. This was a sort of cubicle in which physically or mentally ill patients could sit and be restored by the vital forces of the universe, a portion of which had been collected and stored in the box. The fact that Reich held that such energy was discharged through sexual release no doubt led to speculation as to what actually went on inside the boxes. In 1954 they were banned by the US Food and Drugs Administration. The orgasmatron proper made a fully-fledged appearance in Woody Allen's futuristic film *Sleeper* (1973), in which people in need of sexual satisfaction enter a superloo-like capsule and emerge after a short while with a look of inane bliss.

outsource *verb* to subcontract work to another company

> Job security is just as big an issue at Chrysler, which has pushed constantly to 'outsource,' or move work to lower-cost outside suppliers.
> *Roanoke Times and World-News* 11 Apr 1988

▶ Compare SOURCE.

ovenable *adjective* able to be used in an oven without damage; ovenproof

> This ramekin is not ovenable or flameproof.
> Packaging of Marks and Spencer chocolate mousse, 1987

▶ Although it is not unprecedented to form *-able* adjectives from nouns rather than verbs (*saleable* is an example, and so possibly is *clubbable*), *ovenable* is a rather outlandish creation. It does seem that the suffix *-able* needs at least some hint of a verb in the air if it is to do its job ('to club together' might have contributed to the formation of *clubbable*, and even *sale* has the closely related *sell*), and there is no trace today of a verb 'to oven'. There used to be one, however, meaning 'to bake in an oven': 'A Jannock [oatmeal bread] is Ovened very soft,' R Holme, *The Academy of Armory* 1688.

overhoused *adjective* living in a house too large for one's needs

> ... people who bought a £4000 family house in 1951, and who are now sitting overhoused in a £100,000 house with no incentive to let in lodgers.
> *Economist* 6 Apr 1985

overstayer *noun* a foreign national who stays in a country for longer than he or she is entitled to (e g after the expiry of a visa or work permit)

> The applicant had a chequered immigration history which culminated in his departure from the United Kingdom in 1984 following his detention and arrest as an overstayer.
> *Independent* 13 Oct 1986

over-the-toppery *noun* exaggeratedly flamboyant behaviour

Big John's over-the-toppery can be aggravating but I find that it has grown on me.

Observer 29 May 1988

own goal *noun* an act which results in harm or disadvantage to the doer

Opponents of Labour Party policy on Northern Ireland have scored an own goal with their attempts to remove the Ulster Unionists' 'veto' on constitutional change, according to leading Labour MPs.

Independent 6 Feb 1987

For Karpov, who committed a horrible blunder in a good position shortly before the end of the first session of play, the game was a tragedy. A careless 35th move led to his having to give up his rook for a bishop, the kind of 'own goal' which would make even a casual club player hang his head in anguish.

Daily Telegraph 11 Nov 1987

▶ A metaphorical extension of the term used in soccer and other sports for a goal scored for the opposing team when a player accidentally hits the ball into his or her own net. Compare SHOOT ONESELF IN THE FOOT.

oxygen of publicity *noun* advantage conferred on an illegal or disapproved activity by publicizing it

Not to mention the fact that in the current climate Thatcher may well start bandying phrases like 'the oxygen of publicity.'

Time Out 11 May 1988

▶ This phrase was coined by Margaret Thatcher in response to the screening of *The Edge of the Union*, a documentary on the IRA in the *Real Lives* series on BBC in the summer of 1985. She disapproved strongly of giving any coverage of their views, arguing that this only encouraged them, and that if you ignored them they might go away:

Despite a speech by Mrs Thatcher earlier this month in which she demanded that terrorists be starved of the 'oxygen of publicity,' the BBC director-general, Alasdair Milne, has given the go-ahead for the interview with Martin McGuinness, a senior IRA man, to be shown next week.

The Times 31 July 1985

padbolt *noun* a bolt with a padlock incorporated for securing the bar in the staple

Where appearance doesn't matter use a padbolt. ... Neater are key-operated bolts (surface mounted) or mortice rack bolts, which are concealed from view.

Good Housekeeping Nov 1987

Pameton *noun* a pain-killing drug consisting of a combination of paracetamol and methionine

The Drugs and Therapeutics Bulletin ... yesterday recommended that Pameton should be the painkiller used in homes where there is an emotionally unstable teenager or a depressed member of the family who may take an overdose in a desperate moment.

Independent 15 Dec 1987

▶ The methionine component of this new drug counteracts the harmful effect on the liver which paracetamol may have when taken in large doses.

paneer *noun* a crumbly North Indian curd cheese

There are many vegetarian and fish dishes to choose from and particularly moreish is paneer: chunks of fresh cottage cheese with capsicum, cherry tomatoes and onions in a marinade.

Options Apr 1988

▶ Paneer is a delicately flavoured cheese and hence (rather like bean curd in Chinese cuisine) tends to be used as a background for other flavours, chiefly vegetarian, rather than on its own (e g *saag paneer*, cheese with spinach). The above extract suggests in fact that in British usage the distinction between the cheese and the dish is becoming blurred.

panelology *noun* the hobby of collecting comics

> The English author, Alan Moore, is a superstar, although few people outside the hobby of comic collecting ('panelology' is the neologism coined by the committed) have yet heard of him.
>
> *Listener* 18 Dec 1986

▶ The word is probably based on the individual panels of drawings of which the page of a comic is made up.

parachute candidate *noun, derogatory* a political candidate drafted in to stand for election in a place where he or she does not live

> Paul Martin Jr. ... took the plunge yesterday and announced he will seek the party's nomination in the new Montreal riding of LaSalle-Emard. Martin ... drew accusations he's a parachute candidate. 'He doesn't have any connections' with the area, said Claude Lanthier, Conservative MP for LaSalle riding.
>
> *The Gazette* (Montreal) 17 May 1988

▶ The more customary term for such a person in British and American English is *carpet-bagger*.

parachutist *noun, American derogatory* an incompetent person who holds his or her job as the result of a favour

> Is the bureaucracy overblown? Yes, indeed. It is choked with deadwood – many national civil servants who have been unloaded on the United Nations as the result of political favor-paying back home. The able and diligent staff members in the United Nations, who are there on their own merits, find these parachutists a tiresome drag.
>
> *Newsweek* 18 Apr 1988

parenting *noun* looking after someone as a parent does

> Parenting creates its own emotional issues, and being a 'parent' to an elderly parent puts strain on a marriage, posing a risk to sexual relations. ... The marriage must deal with the parenting-parents issue. If one spouse takes on the responsibility, then the other will end up resentful or isolated.
>
> *Good Housekeeping* Mar 1988

▶ The term *parenting* to describe the role of a mother or father in relation to a child is now fairly well established (it is first recorded from 1959), but we are now beginning to see its application being broadened out to cover other situations in which an analogous relationship obtains, notably the mirror-image in which a grown-up son or daughter takes on the responsibility of looking after their own aged parent or parents.

park home *noun* a large caravan installed on a site as a permanent home

A decent park home with two or three bedrooms, bathroom, sometimes an extra loo, fully-equipped kitchen, furnished parlour, curtains, lampshades and mattresses, can be bought on site, already connected to mains water and sewers, electricity, and bottle gas, for between £40,000 and £60,000.

Observer 24 July 1988

▶ Park homes were given a boost in Britain in 1983 by the passing of the Mobile Homes Act, which guaranteed security of tenure. In 1988 it was estimated that throughout the country there were about 100,000 families living in them on 1284 sites.

parmales *noun* any of an order (Parmales) of microscopic single-celled algae of polar regions

The parmales may be small – they can be seen only in the electron microscope – but they can reach populations of 750,000 cells a litre at depths of between 75 and 120 metres.

New Scientist 8 Oct 1987

▶ Parmales form part of the planktonic population of the polar regions, and are a primary source of food for krill. They were first discovered in 1980, and were then thought to be single-celled animals, but they have more recently been shown to be algae. Their name comes from Latin *parma*, 'small shield,' and was given because the walls of the algae consist of shieldlike silica plates.

patsy *noun,* *informal* a person who is easily exploited, cheated, or defeated; a sucker

> While remaining aware of the nature of one swallow and its relationship to a spring, Sussex's early wins in the Britannic and Refuge [cricket] competitions suggest that they may not be the patsies of past seasons.
>
> *Time Out* 4 May 1988

▶ Until recently this word was restricted to American English; it may derive from Italian *pazzo,* 'fool.'

payroll giving *noun* a form of charitable donation in which an employer regularly deducts a certain amount from an employee's pre-tax salary and passes it on his or her behalf to an agency charity

> A new scheme starts on 6 April called payroll giving. ... You can give up to a maximum of £120 in each tax year from your before-tax pay.
>
> *Which?* Mar 1987

pêcher *noun* a peach-flavoured alcoholic drink, especially sparkling wine

> While France is the source of the pêchers sold in Britain, it can only be a matter of time before other countries cash in and start making their own.
>
> *Sunday Times* 28 Aug 1988

▶ The vogue for the misbegotten peach champagne hit Britain in the summer of 1988. The term *pêcher* is a direct borrowing from French.

pencil whipping *noun,* *American* the practice of falsifying certification

> Union members often accuse the airline of 'pencil whipping' – signing off on repairs that have been done improperly or haven't been done at all. Some Lorenzo employees say that corner cutting accounts for many of the problems.
>
> *Newsweek* 25 Apr 1988

people's court *or* **people's courtroom** *noun* an unofficial tribunal in which a plaintiff and defendant present their cases and agree to abide by the 'judge's' decision, the proceedings forming the basis of a television programme

Sher is Shylock, the villain in question, in what remains one of the Bard's more distressing pieces, despite being made up of famous quotations, and contains not only the Elizabethan equivalent of a game show ..., but also a people's-courtroom drama, and a soap-style epilogue full of revengeful spouses and craven, errant hubbies.

Time Out 4 May 1988

▶ The notion of staging a 'real' trial as a television show began in the USA, and *The People's Court*, presided over by Judge Joseph A Wapner (an actual judge, now retired from the bench), attracts considerable audiences. It is now shown in Britain. The issues tried are usually minor civil cases, of the sort that would be settled in a small-claims court.

Pepsification *noun* American-style commercialization, especially the introduction of branded junk food

On the summit fringe there is new evidence of what has become known as the Pepsification of Moscow. An enterprising New Orleans restaurateur has brought in huge stocks of Cajun food. ... This augments the New Jersey pizza van which was selling 280 slices an hour in Red Square yesterday.

Daily Telegraph 30 May 1988

▶ Mikhail Gorbachev's programme of reforms in the Soviet Union has included a considerable relaxation of trading relations with the West. American exporters in particular received a notable boost from Ronald Reagan's visit to Moscow in May 1988; they did not fail to take advantage of the attendant publicity. Stalls selling pizzas, burgers, etc (not to mention cola drinks) appeared on the streets of the Soviet capital.

perestroika *noun* the far-reaching programme of reform in the Soviet Union undertaken by Mikhail Gorbachev

Some led by Dr Andrei Sakharov accept Mr Gorbachev's sincerity and think his 'perestroika' ('restructuring') should be encouraged.
Daily Telegraph 2 July 1987

The scope of the reforms outlined indicates a political triumph for Mikhail Gorbachev in his struggle with conservative opponents of his strategy of perestroika to modernise and revitalise Soviet society.
Independent 27 May 1988

▶ Behind the simple term *perestroika* (it means literally 'rebuilding,' 'reconstruction,' 'reform') lies a huge ambition: to grab the ossified institutions of the Soviet Union by the scruff of the neck and shake them until they work efficiently. Mikhail Gorbachev has set himself the task of cleansing Augean stables untouched since the days of Lenin. Party placemen and backscratching hacks are to be swept aside, outdated and restrictive methods to be done away with, and a new spirit of self-reliance and enterprise to be instilled (see KHOZRASCHOT). No wonder Margaret Thatcher is an admirer.

Mr Gorbachev revealed the full, breathtaking, scope of the reforms he hopes to achieve in his keynote address to the Soviet National Communist Party conference on 28 June 1988: he envisages, for example, disbanding the Supreme Soviet, replacing it with a smaller legislative body to which delegates will be elected strictly on merit (the notion of quotas for workers, peasants, and intellectuals, enshrined since the Bolshevik revolution, will be done away with); a president of limited term will be elected, with powers similar to those of the US president; and the legal system will be reformed to include such concepts as presumption of innocence.

Along with *glasnost* (see *Longman Guardian New Words*), *perestroika* has been the Russian buzzword of the 1980s, and has well and truly colonized English. Its real impact probably began when Mr Gorbachev published his book *Perestroika: Our Hopes for Our Country and the World* in 1987, and it has now established itself to such an extent that it is used by analogy for any sort of (liberalizing) organizational restructuring:

Perestroika in publishing takes many forms, but it did not take the form of Bell & Hyman 'buying' Allen & Unwin. ... The two companies merged their publishing interests and became Unwin Hyman.

Publishing News 23 Oct 1987

Mr Peter Brooke was yesterday morning recovering from a particularly bad press and steeling himself for the task of instilling a little perestroika (reconstruction) into Conservative Central Office in his new role as party chairman.

Daily Telegraph 4 Nov 1987

Stockbrokers, merchant banks and Euromarket firms are hiring management consultants as fast as they lay off idle traders. ... This perestroika should be good for the City's long-term health and reputation.

Economist 25 June 1988

perestroikan *adjective* of PERESTROIKA

Special investigators of the Moscow Directorate General of Bath Houses swing into action [to catch people who have entered without paying]. ... But behind these raids is a story that might make Mr Gorbachev reach for his perestroikan sword.

Daily Telegraph 12 Aug 1988

perfume dynamics *noun* the planned deployment of pleasant aromas in a building in order to make the environment more congenial

Shimizu, Japan's third-largest construction firm, is designing perfumed offices and hospitals which engineers say improve efficiency and relieve stress. 'The era of perfume dynamics has arrived,' says Masakuni Kiuchi, a Shimizu engineer.

Daily Telegraph 18 Apr 1988

Perfume dynamics ... is the use of scents to alter the moods of customers, or to improve efficiency.

New Scientist 26 May 1988

personal organizer *or* **personal organiser** *noun* a file or folder, typically in the form of a small loose-leaf book, containing a variety of page-formats on which one can record details relating to one's business or social life (e g appointments, important addresses and phone numbers, and memoranda)

The people at Filofax headquarters in London call it [a Filofax] a personal organizer.

Language Technology Sept 1987

A London magistrate was puzzled yesterday by the term 'personal organiser.' Mr Eric Crowther said at Horseferry Road Court: 'The only thing I can imagine it to be is a wife.' Mr Christopher Sutton-Mattocks, defending a man accused of stealing three personal organisers, explained: 'They are a type of Filofax.' Mr Crowther, who has complete faith in his old pocket diary, which he consults frequently on the bench, sighed: 'Oh I see.'

Daily Telegraph 10 Mar 1988

▶ Personal organizers, better known by the name of the best-selling and most prestigious brand, Filofax, have become the unmistakable hallmark of 1980s yuppies, who carry these bulging leather-covered talismans with them wherever they go.

phantom bug *noun* a concealed instruction within a computer program which is activated by a particular set of circumstances

Not all phantom bugs are antisocial: they are used by some sections of the computer industry to discourage illicit copying.

New Scientist 28 Jan 1988

▶ These secret instructions are extremely difficult to find, since they are usually disguised as data. They lurk dormant until some preprogrammed event – such as the elapse of a certain number of days – sets them going. Despite the exceptions noted in the above extract, they are mostly inserted for malicious purposes, and cause various sorts of havoc (such as deleting data). See BOGUSWARE.

phoenix syndrome *noun* the phenomenon of the directors of a bankrupted company immediately forming a new one, so as to continue trading freed from the company's debts

The Insolvency Act 1985, which came into effect last month, has been heralded as a major new piece of legislation, designed to 'clean up' the law on insolvent companies. And it contains draconian powers which should help to prevent dishonest or incompetent directors simply forming new companies each time their existing company goes into liquidation with a string of unpaid debts – the so-called phoenix syndrome.

Daily Telegraph 31 Jan 1987

physically different *adjective* physiologically or anatomically atypical or damaged, for example in lacking a limb; physically handicapped

The society we [thalidomide sufferers] were born into is not adapted to physically different people.

David Frost on Sunday, ITV, 24 July 1988

▶ The term is an attempt to get away from words such as *handicap* and *disability* which suggest that people who lack a particular body part or function are less able to cope with the world than 'normal people,' and to promote the more positive attitude that they are simply different, and are perfectly able to take life on on their own terms.

pianophile *noun* a piano enthusiast

The Opus Clavicembalisticum [by Kaikhosru Sorabji], known only to pianophiles and editors of the Guinness Book of Records, will be attempted by John Ogdon, the virtuoso, who will have to play for 220 minutes and negotiate 81 consecutive variations on a theme.

Sunday Times 29 May 1988

picturesome *adjective* attractive to look at; photogenic

A sign of the fair's growing stature was undoubtedly the hefty media coverage, though this was undoubtedly given a helpful massage by the ever-newsworthy and picturesome Duchess of York, who performed the opening ceremony.

Publishing News 1 Apr 1988

pilot *noun* a person who sails a land yacht

Landsailing was a sport I had rarely heard of, let alone seen, and I never imagined that just 40 minutes away from Bishop's Stortford, intrepid pilots were blown along at up to 70 miles an hour.

Herts & Essex Observer 6 Aug 1987

PINC *noun*　property income certificate: (in the Stock Exchange) a document certifying a share in the ownership of a property (e g an office block)

> The Stock Exchange has agreed to consider listing property income certificates and to admit members of the PINCs Association to corporate Stock Exchange membership.
>
> *The Times* 12 Aug 1986

> Unitisation of single properties took a step back this week. Yesterday it emerged that the Department of Trade and Industry had halted the launch of PINCs, the property income certificate route to the division of a single property into tradeable shares. The DTI now says the promoters must prove that PINCs is not a 'collective investment scheme,' a problem which the civil servants have suddenly decided is fundamental to the whole idea of unitisation.
>
> *Daily Telegraph* 19 Sept 1987

▶ PINCs were first mooted in Britain in 1986. The idea behind them is to break up the ownership of large expensive buildings into separate purchasable and tradeable units, so as to encourage investment in the building of supposedly much-needed new ones. It is felt that the current state of affairs, in which an institution which puts up money to build a huge new office block may end up paying over £100 million for a very non-liquid asset, discourages investment, and that more investors could be found if they were allowed to buy just a share in the building, which they could later sell (its price would be determined by a market analogous to the stock market). The scheme is approved in principle by the Government and the Stock Exchange, but various technicalities remain in the way of its implementation.

pinger *noun, informal* a microwave oven

> Timing ... was perfect for the turbot; ... and for a dish of sliced pink duck and dark red pigeon breasts, tasting naturally of themselves. You don't do all this with a pinger; it is a matter of feel and understanding.
>
> *Wine* June 1988

▶ The word is first recorded as applying to the ringing timer device of cookers in 1968 (more or less contemporaneously with the introduction of the microwave oven), but this metaphorical transfer to the oven itself is a new development.

pipe *verb,* *slang* to smoke the drug crack

> I've had to sell everything. Every night I spend at least £60 on rock, sometimes more than that. When you pipe you can't sleep.
> *Observer* 24 July 1988

▶ The 'pipe' used for smoking crack is typically a glass with a piece of pierced aluminium foil on top.

pippie *or* **pippy** *noun* person inheriting parents' property: a person typically of middle age, who undergoes a sudden massive increase in wealth following the death of a parent

> First there were the yuppies ... then the dinkies. ... These were the target groups for the advertisers because they had the disposable income. They were aged from 21 to the upper 30s, and the ad man's dream. Or are they? They do seem to have forgotten that there is life and indeed money over 40. Last week along came the pippies.
> *Observer* 17 July 1988

▶ Pippies are essentially a product of the vertiginous rise in house prices in the late 1980s. It is no new thing to inherit parents' property, but when the legacy represents a sudden seven-figure windfall, it means a serious increase in wealth.

piste *noun* an area of gravel 12–15 metres long and about 4 metres wide on which pétanque (a Fench game similar to bowls, but involving throwing rather than bowling balls at a jack) is played – called also *terrain*

> The Coach and Horses in Thorley Street has re-opened with £360,000-worth of new features, including a floodlit pétanque pitch, known as a piste.
> *Herts & Essex Observer* 10 Sept 1987

▶ Pétanque has become increasingly popular as a pub game in the skittles tradition over recent years (in 1987 there were 3500 licensed players in Britain), so its terminology is likely to become a fairly familiar part of our vocabulary.

pitchperson *noun, American* a person who promotes a product, appeal, etc with high-pressure talk

Wrapped around interminable interludes built in to accommodate forced-march fundraising from public television's pitchpersons, the 'Great Performances' tribute turns out to be an entertaining but, disappointingly, pro forma work.

Chicago Tribune 11 Mar 1988

▶ The word derives, of course, from the salesman's 'pitch' or sales talk.

PIUS *noun* process inherent ultimate safety: a system for the emergency cooling of an overheated core in a nuclear reactor which works by automatically flooding it

The designers of PIUS have replaced equipment subject to 'Murphy's law' with 'a system governed exclusively by the laws of nature.'

New Scientist 3 Apr 1986

▶ PIUS is a theoretical design for achieving what is known as an 'inherently safe' reactor: that is, one which has its own safety systems built into it, which do not have to be actively operated by human beings or even by computers. Developed by ASEA-ATOM of Sweden, it is intended for use in a conventional pressurized-water reactor. It works on the simple principle that the very heat generated by an overheating core causes water to flood in, so cooling it. In addition, the water contains a special chemical (such as boron) which immediately shuts down the reactor.

Placido *noun, British slang* the sum of £10

Latest jargon from streetwise elements on the trading floors: £10 is now known as a Placido.

Daily Telegraph 30 Mar 1988

▶ The term comes from the name of the Spanish singer Placido Domingo, punningly based on his occupation as an operatic tenor (tenner).

plastic *noun,* *informal* (the use of) credit cards

> What caught Sir Gordon's eye [Sir Gordon Borrie, Director-General of Fair Trading] ... was the annual rate of interest accruing to banks from plastic.
>
> *Daily Telegraph* 18 Nov 1987

platinum handshake *noun* a very large or generous golden handshake

> Sir Robert Crichton-Brown, chairman of Rothmans, is understandably rather keen to be awarded the £750,000 platinum handshake which the board will propose to the shareholders at the annual general meeting on July 29.
>
> *Daily Telegraph* 8 July 1988

▶ In the inflationary world of metaphor, gold is losing its mystique. Where once, for example, the gold card was the ne plus ultra of the credit card, American Express have now topped it with a platinum card. Perhaps, on the analogy of wedding anniversaries, diamond handshakes will be next.

pleats *noun plural* – **put someone in pleats** *British informal* to annoy someone

> They said, 'Hey, Rod, got no tax or M.O.T. on this' and burned off at about 200 miles an hour. Things like that put you in pleats. ... But they were just taking the piss.
>
> *New Musical Express* 2 May 1987

ploms *noun,* *informal* poor little old me syndrome: self pity

> And so began lesson three: how to get over the 'ploms'. ... A friend put me on to reading poetry as more soothing and simple than trying, and failing, to concentrate on a book. I discovered that bus rides to museums and art galleries cost little and paid off richly.
>
> *Options* Apr 1987

plonker *noun,* *British slang* a dim-witted ineffectual person, especially a male; an idiot

The band are worried about the production, but I can assure you these songs would stand up even if they were recorded by ham-fisted plonkers like the Jesus and Gravy Train.

New Musical Express 6 June 1987

▶ Like other slang terms for 'idiot' (*prick, schmuck*) a *plonker* was originally (and still is) a 'penis' (the verb *plonk* or *plunk*, which now means 'to put down abruptly and heavily,' used to have the sense 'propel with a sudden push'). From being a localized London dialect word, it shot to popularity in the 1980s with the BBC comedy series *Only Fools and Horses*, in which the fly Del Boy constantly refers to his younger brother Rodney as a plonker.

plugumentary *noun, informal* a film or television pro-gramme which purports to be a disinterested factual documentary, but contains publicity material

To make a film called Shanghai Surprise ... seemed like a good idea to ex-Beatle George Harrison, now head of the production company Hand Made Films. ... The finished film will not be seen here for ten days, but you can get a strong taste of it tonight in Hand Made in Hong Kong, one of those TV plugumentaries, on Channel 4 at 10.55.

Independent 7 Oct 1986

▶ A blend of *plug* and *documentary*.

plyometrics *noun* a muscle-toning technique which in-volves increasing the tension of a muscle as it lengthens

A new form of training now fashionable called 'plyometrics' or 'depth jumping' will also come under scrutiny at the [British Olym-pic Medical Centre]. You can try it out by jumping off a stool and then jumping up as you hit the floor.

New Scientist 31 Mar 1988

podiatry *noun* the treatment of the feet or foot disorders by a trained specialist; chiropody

If the correct choice of sports footwear is your priority, then a podiatrist is highly qualified to advise you on your choice. Podiatry Association, 3 Bridge Avenue, Maidenhead, Berkshire.

Here's Health Mar 1985

▶ *Podiatry* is generally regarded as the American English synonym of British *chiropody*, but signs of its importation across the Atlantic may have to do not so much with linguistic borrowing as with changes in chiropodic practice. For in the USA chiropodists routinely give treatments (such as minor surgery) which are not traditional in Britain, but which in recent years have been increasingly introduced there (often in the face of opposition from orthopaedic surgeons). It would seem therefore that the term *podiatry* is being adopted to reflect this move into respectable mainstream therapy, and banish the old downbeat image of chiropody as the removal of corns.

pogo *verb* to jump up and down on the spot to music

> Adam and Mike hitched up with one Adam Horovitz – at that time fighting for his right to pogo with fellow New York punky types Young and Useless.
>
> *New Musical Express* 15 Aug 1987

▶ This form of stationary dancing originated with the punks. It no doubt owes its name to the pogo stick, whose movements it imitates.

pol *noun, informal* a politician

> Nowadays, ... the [American presidential election] campaign is run by professional advisors who market the candidate. ... These professionals are more technically adept than the old pols who cut those deals in the smoke-filled rooms.
>
> *Economist* 26 Dec 1987

▶ This colloquial abbreviation was, as the above extract suggests, American in origin, but there are now signs of it infiltrating into British English (it is usually fairly affectionate, as one might guess from the rhymish collocation with *old*):

> What a great old pol he [François Mitterrand] is!
> *Breakfast Time*, BBC1, 23 Mar 1988

polarization *or* **polarisation** *noun*   rigid demarcation imposed on banks, under which any branch may act either as a general financial adviser to customers, making impartial recommendations from a full range of financial services offered by various organizations, or as an agent for its own bank's products, but not both

[Sir Kenneth] Berrill [head of the Securities and Investments Board] treated polarisation as a resigning issue and steamrollered it through in the face of intense hostility from the clearing banks who were forbidden from blending in-house and third-party financial products.

Sunday Times 28 Feb 1988

▶ Polarization is essentially a customer-protection device, to prevent any conflict of interest which might mean that the client would not get impartial financial advice: clearly, any bank which is trying hard to sell its own services may be tempted to gloss over the advantages of others. The banks, equally understandably, are chafing at the restriction, imposed by the Securities and Investments Board in 1986, which is holding back their plans to widen their range of financial services.

polar therapy *noun*   a form of alternative therapy which proposes that bodily dysfunction is caused by a blockage of energy, and that this can be restored by a programme of diet, exercise, and psychotherapy (known as 'psychological midwifery')

Mr Schorr-Kon was a teacher and also a student of karate when he had a very serious road accident. After three months' work by neurologists, he found he still couldn't move his neck or his left arm. After a month of physiotherapy there was still no improvement. He then turned to Cindy Rawlinson who had brought polar therapy to Britain. After six visits, he found that all movement had returned.

Cambridge Weekly News 28 Apr 1988

pomp rock *noun, derogatory* pretentious pop music more concerned with making an effect than with being a genuine expression of feeling

I'm sure 'New Mind' would make a great film score or groovy funeral muzak but as pop music it's nothing more than pomp rock.
New Musical Express 22 Aug 1987

pop *verb,* *slang* to consume as if addicted

She can hardly get her hands on him for the laxative-popping gay playwright Lester, who asks him to leave the door of their shared bathroom open as he can't bear to be alone.
New Statesman 29 Nov 1985

The red-necked, blue-collar clientele pop tiny, bitesize burgers by the pungent half-dozen.

Elle Mar 1988

▶ It is a relatively short step from 'popping pills' (i e taking addictive drugs, such as amphetamines, in pill form – the original application of *pop*) to compulsively swallowing any substance, particularly if it is vaguely medicinal.

popmobility *noun* a form of vigorous exercise in which various work-out drills are combined in a continuous dance routine performed to pop music

Members of a High Wych popmobility group were this week preparing to give a keep-fit demonstration at Harlow's premier sporting event.
Herts & Essex Observer 30 Oct 1987

porcinologist *noun* a student of pigs

What do you collect? Is it interesting? Is there a collective noun which applies to your hobby? Here is an example. The perfect porcinologist is Mary Marsh of Edmondshaw, Dorset. Mary's large collection of piggy-things, totalling over 500, includes piggy-banks, jugs, toys, mugs, biscuit barrels, postcards and soap dishes.
The Sport 17 Aug 1988

▶ In Latin, *porcinus* means 'relating to pigs.'

pork-barrelling *noun* the provision of lucrative contracts or other benefits by a government, usually corruptly in return for support

> The excruciating fairness of [Ireland's] proportional-representation electoral system positively encourages pork-barrelling. ... Votes are swung by personalities and promises. So elections become local spending competitions. A voter disgruntled with one party's promises on housing, say, or road-building for the region has every incentive to lobby the other candidates – and they have every incentive to make extravagant commitments.
>
> *Economist* 16 Jan 1988

▶ The pork barrel is a fine old American tradition, but there are now signs that the term is crossing the Atlantic. Originally the metaphor referred to the US Treasury viewed as an easily tapped source from which local aid grants could be drawn as readily as a piece of salt pork from the pickle barrel. But it was not long before such grants, contracts, etc became virtually bribes given in return for votes.

port *verb* (in computing) to transfer (eg software) to another system without the need for modification

> Pascal cross-assemblers, as sold by companies like Real Time Systems and Lattice Logic, are finding growing use for porting applications software from one system to another.
>
> *Computing* 28 Aug 1986

> We wanted a product that increases our output of systems, and we wanted to port those systems across different environments.
>
> *Computer Weekly* 3 Mar 1988

▶ This verb derives from the noun *port* meaning 'a place on a computer to which peripherals can be connected for the input and output of data'. Some confusion may now occur with the derivatives *portable* and *portability*: portable hardware can be carried, whereas portable software can be ported in the sense given above. The two senses are etymologically related, but only distantly: one goes back to Latin *portare* 'to carry' and the other to Latin *porta* 'passage, gate', both Latin words deriving ultimately from the Indo-European root *per-* 'to lead, pass over'.

portfolio insurance *noun* selling of share futures during a decline in stock market prices to guard against losses

The Brady report on the American stockmarket crash must be praised for showing up the shortcomings of the financial fad of the moment: portfolio insurance.

Economist 16 Jan 1988

Since portfolio insurance offered no protection to those who tried it on Black Monday, the technique has fallen into disrepute and relative disuse.

Time 18 Jan 1988

posey *or* **posy** *adjective*   pretentious

Posey it certainly is. Next to The Belvedere in Harbour Yard, a large, glass-roofed, neo-classical building containing the Information Centre, a number of offices, three zippy glass elevators, Indian magnolia trees in giant tubs, and space on the ground floor for four restaurants.

Time Out 3 Aug 1988

These are the folk townspeople call yotties. So does Joe Smith, drinking beer in the Duke of York's pub at the other, 'less posy' end of town.

Guardian 5 Aug 1988

posse *noun*   a gang of Jamaican street criminals in the USA

Jamaican gangs known as 'posses' have emerged as the leading killers in America's increasingly violent underworld of drug users and dealers. The 'posses' have turned up in many major cities.

Daily Telegraph 14 Mar 1988

▶ The meaning of *posse* seems to be turning a somersault. Originally a posse was a body of people summoned to maintain public order or pursue wrongdoers; here, however, it is a group of lawbreakers. Compare YARDIE.

post-viral syndrome *noun*   a set of symptoms affecting sufferers from MYALGIC ENCEPHALOMYELITIS

power-striding *noun, American* vigorous walking as a form of exercise to improve fitness

It's called walking – and it's catching on fast! In America, they're calling it power-striding. We're not talking about the kind of gentle stroll which helps the Sunday lunch go down, but a purposeful, vigorous, sustained walking that gives your heart and lungs a healthy workout.

Living Apr 1987

presale *noun* an exhibition giving prospective bidders and others an opportunity to examine lots before an auction

'It's amazing the number of people who are touched by Warhol and want to view the presale and bid,' says Jeffrey Deitch of the international art advisory service at Citibank.

Newsweek 18 Apr 1988

▶ The term is an elliptical form of *presale view*, *presale tasting*, etc.

preschooler *noun* a child who has not yet started to attend school

It has long been recognised that mothers of pre-schoolers are particularly prone to niggling aches and pains.

Bridgwater Journal 28 Nov 1987

They'll field a wide range of questions about your youngsters that might include: What do I do about a child who can't sleep? How can I know if I'm pushing my preschooler?

USA Today 8 Feb 1988

Nutritionists accept that ... the majority of babies and most pre-schoolers don't need vitamin drops.

Woman 28 May 1988

pret *adjective* (of clothes) sold in standard sizes ready to wear; off-the-peg

Rose Marie Bravo, who recently arrived from New York after the Macy's takeover, tells that Christian Lacroix's pret and luxe collections have been ordered for fall, as well as Thierry Mugler, Stephen Sprouse, Oscar de la Renta, Donna Karan, Isaac Misrahi and Calvin Klein.

San Francisco Sunday Examiner and Chronicle 12 June 1988

▶ An abbreviaton of French *prêt-à-porter*, 'ready to wear.'

print-handicapped *adjective* unable to use books or similar printed material

'We have a whole range of materials which assist children who are "print-handicapped",' explained the director, Beverley Mathias. 'This might be because they have a sight problem or because they have a physical disability that precludes them from turning pages. We also have film strips, videos, cassettes – books which are not necessarily in print form.'

Guardian 19 July 1988

privilegentsia *noun* (in the Soviet Union and associated countries) high-ranking officials who receive certain privileges or perquisites in consequence of the posts they hold

Mr Gorbachev ... has to confront the entrenched interests of the privilegentsia ... and stretch the rules of Marxism-Leninism without appearing to break them.

Economist 9 Apr 1988

One of the striking variables of life across Eastern Europe is the supply of cars. Apart from communist party privilegentsia and smugglers of hard currency, only the Czechs can now order a car without waiting years to get it.

Economist 30 Apr 1988

▶ The term is based, of course, on *intelligentsia*, itself of Russian origin.

proactive *adjective* tending to take the initiative in making things happen, or anticipating events before they happen, rather than waiting until they happen and then reacting

The federation, an umbrella body for 45 trade associations, has shifted from a reactive to a pro-active role. 'We were in a highly negative phase in 1986 and for a large part of 1987, but we have now adopted a pro-active approach,' Mr Mackenzie explains.

Daily Telegraph 20 Apr 1988

Charles couldn't help but be impressed as he listened to Camilla explaining to the client the need to adopt a more proactive stance to raise the company's investor relations profile.

Campaign 1 July 1988

▶ *Proactive* has been used for some time as a technical term in educational psychology, referring to interference in the learning process caused by things learned previously (the literal sense of the Latin-based compound being 'acting forwards'). In recent years, however, it has become a buzzword in management and allied fields, contrasting the thrusting get-up-and-goness of the 1980s enterprise culture with the supine commercial practices of former years when companies (now deservedly defunct) were content to sit back and wait for business.

proceduralist *noun* someone who insists on meticulous adherence to correct procedure

Proceduralists enjoyed a field day, with the serious business of the afternoon sadly taking second place.
Law Society's Gazette 5 Feb 1986

pro-choice *adjective* in favour of making abortion relatively widely available

Some political consultants are hired-guns, willing to work for the candidate or for the cause ('pro-life' or 'pro-choice' in abortion, it makes no difference) that offers the best terms.
Economist 26 Dec 1987

In the 15 years since the landmark U.S. Supreme Court ruling that established women's right to abortion, the battles between pro-life and pro-choice forces have moved beyond the courtroom into the streets, onto the hustings, even into clinics that care for pregnant women.
Newsweek 4 Apr 1988

▶ This term is no doubt deliberately modelled on the analogy of its opposite, the somewhat disingenuous *pro-life* ('antiabortionist'; see *Longman Guardian New Words*). It seems to be a considerably newer coinage; it first appears in the mid 1980s (coinciding, perhaps, with the proabortionists' increasingly embattled position, and constituting a response to it), whereas *pro-life* is a product of the late 1970s. As a formation, it is equally polemical in its way; it contains the proposition that a woman should have the right to choose whether or not to continue a pregnancy.

profit-taker *noun* a person who sells shares in order to realize a short-term profit, typically following a rise in the market and anticipating a fall

With the TSB float likely to favour small investors, institutional investors had been building up sector weighting in alternative stocks. Yesterday the profit-takers moved in, sending Barclays down 5p to 522p, Lloyds 8p lower at 464p and Natwest 8p off at 574p.
Today 3 Sept 1986

project *noun* the long-term set of aims of a political leader

> After 1983, as it turned out, his [David Steel's] party and his project entered a slow decline.
>
> *Guardian* 13 May 1988

protein engineering *noun* a genetic-engineering technique in which proteins (typically enzymes) are artificially mutated by making changes in the nucleotides that form their DNA

> Cetus has manufactured a new type of interleukin, a promising anticancer agent, using a method based on protein engineering.
>
> *New Scientist* 20 June 1985

> British Biotechnology, in Oxford, is using a technique known as protein engineering to redesign TPA [tissue plasminogen activator] and prolong its useful life.
>
> *Economist* 30 Apr 1988

▶ This technique was pioneered at the Cambridge Laboratory of Molecular Biology in the early 1980s, and has far-reaching implications for the simpler and more economical production of drugs and industrial chemicals.

pryzhok *noun* a crossing from one to another; transference; leap

> When Nureyev, Baryshnikov and the Panovs made the pryzhok from a Soviet to a U.S. troupe, they had to defect. This week, for the first time, guest artists Nina Ananiashvili and Andris Liepa leap to the New York City Ballet from the Bolshoi without giving up their citizenship.
>
> *Newsweek* 15 Feb 1988

▶ *Pryzhok* means literally 'spring, leap' in Russian.

PSDR *noun* public-sector debt repayment: repayment of (part of) the national debt

> Fiscal prudence was on parade all right, down to the unveiling of a new acronym. Mr Lawson announced that his future 'norm' for government finances will be a balanced budget, and that this year and next he will actually be running a fat budget surplus, or PSDR.
>
> *Economist* 19 Mar 1988

psychobilly *noun* a style of rock music based on 1950s rock and roll but with an overlay of 1980s violence and frenzy

The Long Tall Texans, Brighton's psychobilly bass slappers, have April and May shows in the UK.

Sounds 16 Apr 1988

pull *verb, informal* **1** to withdraw

In the countries just mentioned, if such a revealing programme were made it would be pulled from the schedules. If any journalist attempted to remind the public that such a programme had been pulled, he would no doubt be severely discouraged.

Listener 12 Sept 1985

As BP's existing shares slipped well below the offer price, many in the City thought the chancellor ... would lose his nerve and pull the issue.

Economist 24 Oct 1987

Sinatra is so inaccessible these days, and the background so clouded by years of conjecture, that we will never know why he pulled what is clearly a very good film.

Sunday Times 21 Aug 1988

▶ The sense of the verb is essentially 'pull out,' and its use without the adverb to convey extraction is somehow reminiscent of an obsolete colloquial sense of *pluck*, 'to eliminate an examination candidate from consideration because of poor work.' However, the immediate source of the usage is not clear; the OED quotes instances of *pull* being used for the official rescinding of documents ('He had moved easily in diplomatic circles until the ... State pulled his visa,' B Hayes, *Hungarian Game* 1973), but these sound rather more like contractions of 'pull in' than of 'pull out'; and it may be that there is some connection with the oil industry use of *pull*, meaning 'to withdraw a casing, drill string, etc from a well.'

2 to arrest

It's the bizzies (*police*) down here that piss me off. I've got pulled nearly every day since I've been here, sometimes twice a day.

Blitz May 1988

pumpkin time *noun,* *informal* the moment at which a period of unusual prosperity comes to an end with a sudden return to a previous condition

The biological clock has struck midnight for the baby boomers, which means pumpkin time for Hollywood.

Daily Telegraph 17 Mar 1988

▶ The reference is to the story of Cinderella, whose fairy godmother by magic turned a pumpkin into a coach for her, which changed back into a pumpkin when midnight struck.

punker *noun* a person who plays or is a fan of punk rock; a punk rocker

They opened a punk rock club in a disused Coca Cola bottling plant and the punk rock world beat a path to their doorstep. El Paso met the punkers and neither would be quite the same again.

New Musical Express 19 Dec 1987

▶ The only derivative of *punk* hitherto recorded is *punkster*.

PWA *noun* a person with AIDS

In three years' time there are likely to be 900 or so diagnosed cases in the London area, and at least that number of buddies per two people with AIDS (PWAs) – a phrase that nobody actually likes but that everybody comes to see as preferable to the alternative ('victim' or 'client').

Cosmopolitan Feb 1987

'A Buddy,' says Joe, a PWA, 'is like a friend, sister, mother, father and brother rolled into one.'

Observer 10 May 1987

pyrography *noun* the art of decorating wood surfaces by burning designs in with a pyrograph, an implement with an electrically heated point

In this, the second in the series of six programmes, presenter Stephen Atkinson discusses and demonstrates the crafts of leatherwork, specifically beltmaking, and pyrography, originally known as pokerwork.

TV Times 7 May 1988

qinghaosu *noun* an antimalarial drug

> Brossi ... and his colleagues have concentrated on producing a chemically very similar derivative of qinghaosu that is more potent and which the body assimilates more easily than the natural drug.
>
> *New Scientist* 31 Mar 1988

> A recent discovery has been *Qinghaosu*, artemisinine, which cures malarial infections resistant to standard synthetic remedies.
>
> *Times Literary Supplement* 12 Aug 1988

▶ Qinghaosu is a product of Chinese medical research. It has been shown to be effective in combatting malaria caused by the parasite *Plasmodium falciparum*, which is resistant to the most commonly used antimalarial drug, chloroquine. See also ARTEETHER.

quali-pop *noun* the use in upmarket 'serious' newspapers of stories and presentational techniques more typical of tabloid newspapers

> Not long after that, the quali-pop strategy [on *The Times*] was abandoned: Rees-Mogg retreated to the opinion sections of the paper, leaving the rest to run itself.
>
> *Observer* 22 May 1988

quality circle *noun* a regular meeting between a small group of employees and managers of a company with the purpose of improving performance through the making of suggestions and the airing of complaints

> Shopfloor power – once the scourge of managements – is increasingly being harnessed to boost firms' performances. A dramatic rise in the number of Japanese-style quality circles, in which bosses and employees at all levels meet to thrash out problems, is proving that the most 'bolshie' and vociferous workers are often the ones to come up with the most constructive ideas.
>
> *Daily Mail* 24 Feb 1986

When sales slump, many American businessmen look to systems rather than to products to put things right. They talk a lot about quality circles, or encounter sessions or corporate culture.
Economist 30 May 1987

▶ The notion of quality circles was invented in the 1960s by two American work study experts, in response to a request from Japanese industrialists for suggestions on how to improve their companies' performance. It met with great success in Japan, and soon caught on in the US too. Britain has been slower to take it up, but there are now over 500 companies in this country which use it, including Rolls-Royce, Jaguar, and Wedgwood.

quietize *verb* to sound-proof

The Genicom 4410 [printer] features a standard cabinet that allows operation at less than 60 dBA. So without the added cost of a quietized cabinet, the 4410 is quiet enough for virtually any office. – Advertisement for Genicom line printers, 1987

▶ Although not entirely a neologism, this word has not been recorded since 1791, well before the days of sound-proofing: 'Solitude, and patience, and religion, have now quietized both father and daughter into tolerable contentment,' Fanny Burney's *Diaries*.

R

racist *adjective, noun*

▶ Racism is no doubt almost as old as the human race itself (although the term itself did not come into use until the 1930s; *racialism* is earlier, first recorded in 1907), but recently its pronunciation has been showing signs of an interesting instability. For *racist* /reɪsɪst/ one increasingly hears /reɪʃɪst/. The pronunciation of *racialist* no doubt plays a part, but it may well also be that a semantic connection perceived to exist between *racist* and *fascist* has brought these two words, already morphologically similar, even closer together phonetically.

RAD *noun*   REFLEX ANAL DILATATION

Radio Data System *noun*   (*abbreviation* **RDS**)   a system of encoded information broadcast on a VHF signal which adjusts the tuning of a radio receiver for optimal reception of a particular radio station

But help is on the way with the electronic magic of something known as RDS – Radio Data System, which will enable the new generation of radio receivers to put choice quite literally at our finger tips.

Observer 5 Apr 1987

▶ RDS has been developed by the BBC. An inaudible tone is transmitted at 57 kilohertz, carrying 16-bit pieces of digital code at the rate of 1200 bits per second. A suitably adapted radio receiver can decode these and use them to find the clearest and most interference-free signal for the station one wants to listen to.

rag-out *noun* an extract from a previous issue of a news-paper photographically reproduced in a later issue, typically shaded and with a ragged edge to make it stand out

Prince Philip's piece in yesterday's paper was, as readers may have seen, a reproduction – known in the trade as a 'rag-out' – of how we reported his famous 1961 remark to British industrialists: 'Gentlemen, it's about time we pulled our finger out.'

Daily Telegraph 3 Jan 1987

rag-rolling *also* **ragging** *noun* an interior-decoration technique involving the application of paint with cloth to achieve a particular surface effect

He [Max Glendinning, interior designer] showed them the various transformations through which he had put his own home in Canonbury – the sort of house where now ... the inhabitants were rag-rolling their period features for dear life.

Guardian 19 June 1986

▶ Rag-rolling produces a surface that looks something like crushed velvet. It is used on walls, ceilings, and even furniture. To the base surface a coat of special paint, known as a glaze, is applied, and this is then textured by rolling roughly-folded-up cloth over it. As the above extract suggests, it is a decidedly 'in' feature of mid- to late-1980s interior design, and many is the rag that has rolled in the wake of the skip in gentrification zones.

Raids *noun, humorous* recently acquired income deficiency syndrome: a sudden diminution in income

In Houston, where money is sometimes equated with manhood, proud Texan businessmen are reluctant to admit they are suffering from what local comedians call 'Raids.'

Daily Telegraph 11 May 1987

Even the disaster of Black Monday has spawned its own grim humour with an outbreak of RAIDS.

Guardian 30 Dec 1987

Ramada Socialism *noun,* *derogatory* Labour policies adapted to make the party more attractive to middle-class voters

Ramada Socialism emerged yesterday as the cornerstone of the new-look Labour party as its conference opened in Brighton.
Daily Telegraph 28 Sept 1987

▶ This term was invented by left-wing Labour MP Dennis Skinner. He derived it from the Ramada Renaissance, a new and expensive hotel in which the great and good of the party stayed during their Brighton conference in 1987. Its luxurious appointments no doubt struck him as in pointed contrast to the situation in which traditional working-class Labour voters find themselves. As a coinage it was well timed to encapsulate the bourgeoisification of the Labour party which has been a feature of the mid to late 1980s. The analysis put forward by Bryan Gould and others on his wing of the party is that Labour's stereotypical constituency, the poor working classes, in fact no longer exists – those with jobs are no longer poor, and the poor are out of work – and that Labour needs to produce policies to appeal to the new and growing middle class. See also CHAMPAGNE SOCIALIST.

ratchet *noun* a means of forcing an irreversible increase

'If we are not sure we can market a package of relationship benefits to obtain a profitable customer, we must make sure that the business/customer relationship is a profit ratchet,' said TSB's Malcolm Hughes, adding in plain English: 'The more we sell, the more we make.'
Daily Telegraph 20 Feb 1988

▶ The literal ratchet on which this metaphor is based contains a bar that engages in the teeth of a wheel so as to allow movement in one direction only.

rat-out *noun,* *slang* a disloyal or contemptible withdrawal

Mr Bond said he had been working on the plan to raise private funding before the Government announcement [of withdrawal of funding]. 'I foresaw a complete "rat-out," and I decided to look for commercial funding months ago.'
Daily Telegraph 16 Aug 1988

ratted *adjective, British slang* drunk

> And then he zipped up his anorak and went out to get ratted with
> the rest of the ice hockey team.
> *Daily Telegraph* 19 Dec 1987

▶ Perhaps derived from the simile *ashed* [i e drunk] *as a rat.*
The synonym *rat-arsed* is also current.

RCD *noun* RESIDUAL CURRENT DEVICE

RDS *noun* RADIO DATA SYSTEM

reactive suspension *noun* ACTIVE SUSPENSION

> He [Nigel Mansell] waited patiently in the pits as boffins scratched
> their heads over the electronic reactive suspension, which seemed
> to have developed a mind of its own. ... Hiding his disappointment
> behind a cheerful smile, Frank Williams admitted that the reactive
> suspension was giving his team trouble.
> *Daily Telegraph* 9 July 1988

ready-wash *noun, slang* the drug crack

> Heroin is a real comedown. I only took it once to see what it was
> like. But you feel dizzy. I don't want no more. Ready-wash is the
> thing now. Sniffing is out.
> *Observer* 24 July 1988

Reagan doctrine *noun* a principle in foreign policy enunciated by US President Ronald Reagan: the spread of
international communism can be checked or reversed
by indigenous anticommunist movements within individual countries

> Colonel Oliver North ... was in reality the 'can-do' man implement-
> ing the Reagan doctrine covertly in places where congressional
> scruples would not go.
> *Guardian* 26 Nov 1986

> The 'Reagan doctrine', as it has come to be known, in fact applies
> anywhere in the third world, perhaps even in Europe too.
> *Economist* 3 Jan 1987

▶ The Reagan doctrine, which its adherents would sum-
marize as 'active support of democratic elements around
the world,' was first enunciated in a speech by Ronald
Reagan to the British parliament on 8 June 1982. At first it
was in practice more exhortatory than active, but following
Reagan's 1985 State of the Union speech, in which he spoke
of the USA recovering from the self-doubt of Vietnam to
assume the role of world leader, it has become more activist,
with the USA playing a role in removing despotic governments in Haiti and the Philippines. But it looms largest, of
course, in Nicaragua, where many critics feel that its promotion of anticommunist insurgency could spill over into
firsthand Vietnam-type intervention.

Reaganomics *noun* the economic policies (e g tax cutting
and deficit spending) of the Ronald Reagan administration (1980–88) in the USA

Kemp is the darling of the conservatives, a man who represents
Reaganomics in its purest form.
Observer 1 June 1986

The 68 months of economic recovery, the 16.8 million new jobs in
the United States, the reduction of taxes – all are proud achieve-
ments of the once denigrated Reaganomics.
Daily Telegraph 17 June 1988

A decade later Bentsen was pushing the supply side tax cuts that
later became known as Reaganomics.
Spectator 23 July 1988

rear-end *verb* to crash into the rear of (a vehicle)

Two of the crewmen spent Saturday night in a Bristol hospital after
a car rear-ended the team's passenger van at a stoplight on U.S.11.
Roanoke Times and World-News 11 Apr 1988

re-beating *noun* reorganization and reallocation of the
rounds worked by someone who covers a particular
area

A report was commissioned which showed the dustmen began work at 7 am, and most were finished by 11.30 am. Very few worked more than a four-hour day. Negotiations took place and some re-beating was organised.

Guardian 1 Sept 1987

rebounder *noun* a small trampoline used for REBOUNDING

One of the best rebounders on the market is the PT Bouncer. It comes with clear instructions and costs £69 for the 40-inch version, £59 for the 36-inch.

Company Mar 1987

rebounding *noun* a form of exercise involving jumping up and down on a small trampoline

If you are new to rebounding start by bouncing gently on the unit so that your heels only just leave the platform.

Cosmopolitan Feb 1987

Muscles are usually strengthened by working against gravity and with rebounding the force of gravity ... is constantly changing.

Company Mar 1987

▶ A fairly modest range of exercises is possible on the re-bounder – nothing like the flamboyant somersaults of the full-size trampoline – but its exponents claim that jumping up and down on it is excellent for toning up the system. Rebounding started in the USA, where there is now even an Institute of Reboundology.

receiver-dialler *noun* a person who monitors the movement of offenders under the HOME PAROLE system by picking up the signal from their wristband or ankleband and informing a central computer by telephone when they break the terms of their parole

In most of the programmes, a receiver-dialler detects electronic transmissions from the ankle or wrist band worn by the offender and calls a central computer when the signals stop, usually when the person goes more than 150 to 200 feet from home.

Guardian 3 Feb 1987

reflag *verb* to alter the country of registration of (a merchant ship)

> Foreign Office ministers and officials are privately contemptuous of the US for not being properly prepared to escort the reflagged tankers.
>
> *News on Sunday* 16 Aug 1987

> For nearly three months, since the US began to reflag Kuwaiti tankers, the world's biggest TV stations have been here [i e in the Persian Gulf] in strength, quartered in air-conditioned hotel suites and spending thousands of pounds every day on getting the pictures and getting them back home.
>
> *Guardian* 8 Oct 1987

▶ The concept of reflagging came to prominence in the summer of 1987, when the growing threat to neutral merchant shipping in the Persian Gulf from the missiles of Iran (supposedly at war only with Iraq) began to disrupt the oil export trade, the lifeblood of the Gulf states. The government of Kuwait asked the USA to take some Kuwaiti tankers under its wing, and this request was acceded to. Accordingly the tanker al-Rekkah (401,382 tons) and the gas carrier Gas al-Minagish (46,723 tons) became respectively the Bridgeton and the Gas Prince, both with the Stars and Stripes fluttering from their sterns and both proclaiming Philadelphia as their home port; and on 22 July they set sail from the Strait of Hormuz on the 550-mile voyage to Kuwait, accompanied by a small armada of US warships and bristling air cover. The outcome of the expedition was a little embarrassing for the Americans, for although neither of the tankers was directly attacked, the Bridgeton was badly holed by a mine which they had failed to clear, and had to limp into Kuwait. The reflagged convoys continued thereafter amid decreasing publicity.

Compare FLAG OUT.

reflex anal dilatation *noun* (*abbreviation* **RAD**) involuntary expansion of the anus on examination, especially as used as a diagnostic indicator of previous repeated anal penetration

Dr Wyatt faithfully followed Dr Higgs because he was convinced
initially that the reflex anal dilatation (RAD) method was accurate
and meant that a child must have been abused.

Independent 15 Dec 1987

▶ Paediatricians looking for a clear clinical indicator of
sexual abuse of children hit on RAD in the mid 1980s. The
technique, which involves parting the patient's buttocks
and ascertaining whether this causes the anus to react by
widening, was written up in *The Lancet* in October 1986. It
sprang to notoriety, however, in 1987, when an avalanche of
child-abuse cases was reported in the Middlesbrough area.
The paediatrician Dr Marietta Higgs, using RAD, diagnosed
78 children as sexually abused out of 102 she examined. The
outrage caused by this in the local community led to a judi-
cial enquiry, in which the doctors' procedures were called
seriously into question. In particular it was pointed out that
RAD can be due to other causes than anal penetration
(severe constipation, for example, and Crohn's disease),
and it is now generally accepted that it is unsafe to use it as
an indicator of sexual abuse unless other signs are present,
such as bed-wetting or disturbed behaviour.

refusenik *noun,*   *informal* a person who refuses to
cooperate

It looks as though he [Rupert Murdoch] may swing it: get the bulk
of his journalists to accept cash inducements and opt for the new
premises (though a brave 30 refuseniks at the *Sunday Times* were
still saying no).

New Statesman 31 Jan 1986

A year ago, 10,000 foreigners [in Japan] briefly refused to be finger-
printed, as part of an organised campaign against the exasperating
practice. About 200 hard-core refuseniks are left, four times as
many as before last autumn's campaign.

Economist 23 Aug 1986

Strengthened by the overwhelming endorsement by the Liberal
party for a merger with the Social Democrats, Mr David Steel last
night moved swiftly to isolate Dr David Owen's breakaway SDP
and a small group of Liberal 'refuseniks.'

Daily Telegraph 25 Jan 1988

▶ The original refuseniks were (and are) Soviet Jews who were refused permission to emigrate, especially to Israel (the word is a partial translation of Russian *otkáznik*, from *otkazát'* 'to refuse'). In the course of broadening its application, the term has undergone an interesting shift from 'being refused' to 'refusing.'

regretfully *adverb* unfortunately; regrettably

> One of my officers suggested naming our first anchorage after one of our favourite hobbies. Regretfully, Numismatics Bay doesn't sound quite right to me.
>
> *Punch* Feb 1988

▶ Although it does not seem yet to have become a cause célèbre, this proliferating usage manages to combine within itself two features which most raise the blood pressure of purists: the disjunctive, or 'sentence adverb,' use of a word which is held (for no linguistically logical reason) to be 'correctly' only a 'manner adverb,' such as the notorious *hopefully*; and the sort of miscegenation between affixes (*-able* and *-ful*) which has beaten down the distinction between *disinterested* and *uninterested*.

relational database *noun* a computer database in which the data can be accessed via various different routes, and using several routes simultaneously as well as individually

> The superiority of the relational database ... is now universally acknowledged, not just by suppliers but by users.
>
> *Mini-Micro News* Jan 1988

> Like Laser Watch, it will run on high-performance workstations and use a relational database.
>
> *Business* Mar 1988

▶ A conventional, 'hierarchical' database can be accessed only 'from the top down,' in a step-by-step fashion. The great advantage of relational databases, as used in fifth-generation computers, is that there are several ways into them; and what is more, these access routes can be combined.

Thus, for example, if the information in the database were the equivalent of that in a telephone directory, it could be accessed by address and phone number as well as by name, and combinations of these data could be found – for instance, everyone with a first name beginning X living in a house numbered 100.

relaunch *noun* a reintroduction of an established product or institution to the public by means of a publicity campaign

As a result, although nobody at the BBC will use the word 're-launch,' Citizens [a soap opera] was ordered to find an injection of vitality: more cliffhangers, fizzier story lines, sharper characterisation.

Sunday Times 15 May 1988

▶ As the above extract implies, the subtext of any relaunch is that the original launch has been a flop, or at least that the product concerned, be it a tin of baked beans or a political party, has failed to grab the public. So the marketing men come in to jazz it up, in an attempt to convince the public that where once they had turned their noses up at it, now they will welcome it with open arms.

The term is of course used as a verb as well as nominally.

relief *noun, euphemistic* sexual gratification

The air is full of the different kinds of 'relief' offered by the masseuses at the Wigmore club.

London Evening Standard 17 May 1988

reproclassicism *noun, derogatory* the superficial use of classical models as decorative devices in postmodern architecture

The pundits are getting restless. Reproclassicism has given post-modernity a bad name. Designers are looking for a way out, an escape from the free-market aesthetics of Docklands which will not involve a return to the drab collectivism of the South Bank.

Sunday Times 24 Apr 1988

reschedule *verb* to postpone the payment of (a debt or the interest on it)

Some powerful banks – most notably West Germany's biggest, Deutsche Bank – are even musing publicly about pulling out of rescheduling altogether. Mr Alfred Herrhausen ... suggested ... that his bank might even consider forgiving a large part of Brazil's debt.

Economist 3 Oct 1987

▶ The problem of what to do about the huge backlog of debts mounting up in the ledgers of Third World countries, in hock to international banks, became increasingly pressing throughout the 1980s. The seeds were sown in the 1970s, based on the precarious premise that 'governments never go bankrupt.' By 1988 the accrued total debt had mounted up to $1 trillion, with Brazil, for instance, owing $12 billion in interest every year. The first sign of breaking point being reached came in 1982, with Mexico ($75 billion of debt) suspending repayment and nationalizing its banks; Brazil acted similarly in 1987. Banks faced huge losses, and the entire world financial system seemd under threat. As debtor nations and creditor banks came up with ever more ingenious schemes for solving the problem, it became clear that in many cases it would be unrealistic ever to expect full repayment, and, as the above extract suggests, several banks contemplated cutting the Gordian knot and writing the debts off altogether.

residual current device *noun* (*abbreviation* **RCD**) a type of very sensitive circuit breaker for rapidly cutting off the supply of electricity – called also *earth leakage circuit breaker*

In Britain, the wiring regulations specify that an RCD should be fitted to any electrical circuit specifically intended for outside use.

Which? May 1987

▶ Residual current devices work by detecting any differences of strength in the current flowing through the live and neutral wires in a lead (such as happens, for example, when someone touches a live wire and the current flows away to earth); when this occurs, the device immediately breaks the circuit. It reacts much faster than fuses and ordinary circuit breakers (the most sensitive work in 40 milliseconds) and so can protect people against electric shocks. Most RCDs are incorporated into plugs or adapters, and are used for giving protection when using electrical devices such as lawnmowers, hedge-clippers, and drills.

respectify *verb* to make respectable

> Wonderful! I thought I had seen it all when 'strike' was respectified by 'industrial action' and 'negative profit' cleaned up 'loss.'
> *Daily Telegraph* 12 Mar 1988

restauration *noun* the running of restaurants; the provision of restaurant meals

> Service is largely unnoticeable, and therefore highly professional, and the country house ambience is now more relaxed than in the Manoir's early days. Expensive as it is, a visit is essential for anyone devoted to great restauration.
> *Decanter* June 1988

▶ *Restauration* was in common usage in 17th- and 18th-century English, in various senses of the word we would now spell *restoration*, and in the late 19th century it was used for 'restaurant' (apparently a borrowing from German), but its use for the 'art or business of a restaurateur' is a new development.

resto *noun, Canadian informal* a restaurant

> I came up short on menus specializing on mush, but in the Italian arena I recalled La Transition. The bright and well-upholstered resto in lower Westmount has been receiving favorable marks for its ambiance and menu.
> *Montreal Daily News* 16 May 1988

retail park *noun* a landscaped area containing a number of shops

Among the largest of the proposed developments is a plan by Bridgend Golf Club to develop a nine-hole golf course, Ocean world style aquarium, drive-in cinema, retail park, craft employment centre, hotel, petrol station and fast food outlets on land north of the M4 motorway.
Western Mail 27 Jan 1987

▶ The notion of a *park* as a centre for a particular sort of activity, comprising sets of buildings relieved by lawns and clumps of shrubs, seems to have originated with the *science park* (first recorded in British English in 1970), progressed to the *business park*, and now threatens to bring a breath of the countryside into the weekly one-stop shopping.

retail politics *noun, chiefly American* electoral campaigning of the traditional variety, in which politicians tour around addressing rallies and meeting people

Next week's New Hampshire primary marks the final days of 'retail' politics before the campaign explodes into a nationwide media-only event.
Newsweek 15 Feb 1988

▶ Compare WHOLESALE POLITICS.

re-tread *noun, informal* a person or thing returned to use or service, typically following refurbishment

Tribune ... will be a group where the new MPs easily outnumber the sitting Labour MPs and the many Tribune 'retreads', MPs now hoping to re-enter Parliament from a new constituency.
Guardian 8 July 1986

There will be some reserves Kinnock could draw upon, such as extra ministerial peers. And among the large intake of new MPs there will be some re-treads, back from a spell in the wilderness, who could be taken directly into government.
The Times 12 Aug 1986

▶ The metaphor derives from worn-out tyres fitted with new treads.

retro *adjective* self-consciously reproducing the fashions of the recent past; nostalgically chic

His black-dot-on-yellow silk pyjamas, shown here, are important, too, because of the trousers. 'Palazzo pants,' he calls them, cut wide, and with a romantic retro feel about them.
Guardian 23 Jan 1986

Jasper Conran's collection harks back to the chic of Dior in the fifties; controlled, upright, very lady-like. Katherine Hamnett, too, sensed the mood, her fashion reflexes responding in spite of her dedicatedly non-conformist nature. She framed her retro look as a kind of send-up but talked seriously of 'Power Dressing.'
Guardian 28 Aug 1986

Alternatively, try retro-dressing. It's here again. One step forward, 30 years back. The 'Fifties look is determined to make a comeback on the shoulders of its two most ardent fans, Jasper Conran and Katherine Hamnett.
Cosmopolitan Feb 1987

The sound may be traditional – retro even – but everything else about Morgan/McVey ... is firmly rooted in the style-conscious eighties.
Company Mar 1987

Very alternative. But all hail retro-leather and sunglasses at midnight.
New Musical Express 2 May 1987

To judge by Hollywood's most recent offerings, we are in for a retro summer and autumn.
Daily Telegraph 12 Aug 1987

rhabdophilist *noun* a collector of walking sticks

The prices of swordsticks sold in the shop range from £500 to £1,500, enough to restrict their sale to what Mr Adeney called 'rhabdophilists,' the small army of people who collect walking sticks.
Daily Telegraph 12 Sept 1987

▶ Greek *rhabdos* means 'rod.'

ribozyme *noun* an enzyme made from a section of the genetic material RNA that is able to cut other molecules of RNA (e g in a virus) at specific sites

Ribozymes enable scientists to chop up RNA in a predictable way, a trick which could be used to destroy viruses such as polio or Aids which store their genetic code in the form of RNA.

Daily Telegraph 20 Aug 1988

The ribozymes are likely to become a standard part of the molecular biologists's toolbox, enabling researchers to produce particular RNA fragments in bulk and to construct physical maps of RNA strands.

New Scientist 25 Aug 1988

ride and tie *noun* a cross-country race between teams consisting of two people and one horse, in which one person runs and the other rides until he reaches a point where he thinks his teammate might need a rest from running, dismounts, tethers the horse to await the runner, and sets off running himself (and so on turn and turn about)

The first modern Ride & Tie, sponsored by Levi Strauss, was held in 1971 between Saint Helena and Sonoma in the wine country of northern California. Now there are hundreds of others all over North America and Europe.

Esquire Mar 1988

▶ The name for this new sport revives a term used in the 18th and 19th centuries, as in this passage from Henry Fielding's *Joseph Andrews* (1742):

They were both setting out, having agreed to ride and tie – a method of travelling much used by persons who have but one horse between them, and is thus performed. The two travellers set out together, one on horseback, the other on foot: now as it generally happens that he on horseback outgoes him on foot, the custom is, that when he arrives at the distance agreed on, he is to dismount, tie the horse to some gate, tree, post, or other thing, and then proceed on foot; when the other comes up to the horse, he unties him, mounts, and gallops on till, having passed by his fellow-traveller, he likewise arrives at the place of tying. And this is that method of travelling so much in use among our prudent ancestors, who knew that horses had mouths as well as legs, and that they could not use the latter without being at the expense of suffering the beasts themselves to use the former.

roam-a-phone *noun* a portable telephone

A cursory stroll around the ground confirms that it [Wimbledon] has gone the way of all important sporting events and become a mere sideshow to the real business of, well, doing business – a world of men jabbering ostentatiously into roam-a-phones, of unctuous commissionaires in peaked caps bowing to 'executive' guests.

Sunday Times 26 June 1988

rocket scientist *noun, slang* a person who assembles and markets financial schemes involving moving between different markets, currencies, etc to take advantage of price differentials

'Rocket scientists' may have played a key role in accelerating the Wall Street crash. They are the ex-scientists and academics who are revolutionising stock market operations with 'program trading'.

Daily Telegraph 21 Oct 1987

With the Hotol space project having only just received the Government's thumbs down, recruitment company Michael Page did not choose the best time to place this week's advertisements for 'Rocket Scientists – Stage 2.' White-coated applicants will quickly find that 'rocket scientist' is City slang for the wizards who can put together the currency rate swaps, fixed-interest arbitrages and similar financial schemes and attempt to sell them to baffled clients.

Daily Telegraph 29 July 1988

rock house *noun, American slang* CRACK HOUSE

Posing as a cocaine trafficker ... I had challenged them to show me a 'rock house,' the name given to drug dens where crack is sold in the United States.

Observer 24 July 1988

▶ *Rock* is one of several alternative words for the drug crack.

rockumentary *noun* a documentary-style film about, and featuring, rock music

This is Spinal Tap ... Hilarious spoof rockumentary about British HM band on ill-fated comeback tour of the US.

Time Out 11 May 1988

Rogernomics *noun,* *informal* the monetarist economic policy instituted by the New Zealand Labour government in 1984

Immediately after Labour regained power from the incumbent Nationalists in 1984, New Zealanders learned what Rogernomics was all about. He [the finance minister] devalued the dollar 20 per cent, removed interest rate controls and slapped on a three-month price freeze – and that was only the start.

Daily Telegraph 8 Apr 1987

► The term was coined from the name of New Zealand's finance minister, Roger Douglas. The economic policies adopted by the incoming Labour government of David Lange in 1984 surprised many with their bracing right-wingish radicalism, almost out-Thatchering Thatcherism in their emphasis on deregulation, privatization, and the like. See CORPORATIZE.

ropeline *noun,* *American slang* greeting and shaking hands with a group of onlookers or wellwishers assembled behind a restraining rope, especially as an election-campaign publicity ploy

Mr Bush, on a happy roll thanks to his big mo, had just hit the tarmac for some well-lit ropeline when his Secret Servicemen started bickering.

The Times 17 Mar 1988

rotortuner *noun* a device for regulating the distribution of mass about the axis of a helicopter rotor, to eliminate vibration caused by imbalance

At Fort Lewis, in Washington State, the RAF has been demonstrating rotortuners which reduce the vibrations of helicopter blades in the minimum amount of time.

Daily Telegraph 15 Feb 1988

Royal Free disease *noun,* *British* MYALGIC ENCEPHALO-MYELITIS

Royal Free disease or myalgic encephalomyelitis has divided medical opinion for over 30 years.

Radio Times 25 June 1988

▶ The name derives from the fact that myalgic encephalomyelitis was first identified when an epidemic affected 220 nurses at the Royal Free Hospital, London, in 1955. The outbreak was subsequently dismissed as mass hysteria, but more recent work on the disease has confirmed the original diagnosis.

rubblehead *noun, slang* an idiot

> Why on earth would Ruth ... fall so completely for a rubblehead like Thomas?
>
> *Time Out* 10 Aug 1988

▶ Compare AIRHEAD, DICKHEAD, MEATHEAD.

Rubik's Clock *noun* a puzzle consisting of a circular box with nine small clock faces on each side which must all be set simultaneously to 12 o'clock by manipulating various wheels and buttons

> Prof Erno Rubik has chosen Britain to launch his Rubik's Clock, and although the computers say it is theoretically possible to unravel, no-one has so far succeeded.
>
> *Daily Telegraph* 25 July 1988

> With the launch of his latest toy, Rubik's Clock, he has proved that his ability to engineer easy-to-use but impossible-to-fathom artefacts is undiminished.
>
> *Listener* 1 Sept 1988

▶ The Clock is the latest brainchild of the inventor of Rubik's Cube, Hungarian Ernö Rubik. Despite its claimed insolubility, more than one young puzzle enthusiast had mastered it within days of its unveiling.

runway *noun* modelling involving displaying clothes while walking up and down a catwalk

> Her height, 5ft 9½ins, meant she could do runway as well as photographic modelling.
>
> *Observer Magazine* 26 July 1987

run with *verb, American* to take the responsibility of handling or developing (something)

The best firms encourage contact with customers and allow employees to run with good ideas.

Newsweek 25 Apr 1988

▶ The metaphor derives from a player running with the ball in American football – breaking free from the opposition tackles and by his own efforts gaining several yards of ground.

S

SAD *noun* seasonal affective depression *or* disorder: a tendency to become depressed and anxious during the short-daylight months of winter

Mild SAD patients feel generally down and without energy, but critical cases often complain of terrible lethargy, deep depression, a desire to sleep late in the mornings and early at night, severely antisocial behaviour and a strange craving for stodgy, sweet food.

Company Jan 1987

It is perhaps not surprising that many of Ibsen's characters were so full of Nordic gloom, according to some psychiatrists. They would argue that the further north we live the greater the preponderance of Seasonal Affective Disorder (SAD), more colloquially known among those who suffer from it as 'winter depression'.

Listener 8 Jan 1987

Special lighting is being used to treat the endogenous manic depression known as 'seasonal affective disorder'.

Cosmopolitan Mar 1987

Springtime ... is a welcome time for workaholics, and perhaps a better time for 'resolutions' than during the cold grim days of January and February. And the recent studies on SAD (Seasonal Affective Depression) seem to confirm this.

Daily Telegraph 17 Mar 1987

▶ The infectiousness of winter's gloom is no new phenomenon – the Finns, for example, have always had to live with it – but it is only recently that psychologists have confirmed its existence clinically and begun to offer physiological explanations for it. It has been shown, for example, that people particularly sensitive to SAD can have their depression alleviated by sitting in bright artificial light, and that the light stimulus acts mainly through the eyes rather than the skin. The precise cause is not yet known, but it is believed to involve a complex reaction between various hormones and neurotransmitters in the brain.

SAEF *noun*   Stock Exchange Automatic Execution Facility: a computerized system for processing small orders on the London Stock Exchange

> The Exchange has already announced that it is developing two systems which will revolutionise settlement. One is for the automated execution of small orders, and will come into operation in 1988. Known as SAEF ...., it will make dealing and settlement simpler, faster and cheaper.
> *Daily Telegraph* 24 Dec 1987

> The Stock Exchange is in the process of introducing ... SAEF to ease the pressure on the telephone system.
> *Business* Mar 1988

▶ Not, as its full form might suggest, a method of disposing of dishonest stockbrokers, SAEF works in conjunction with SEAQ (see *Longman Guardian New Words*), the Stock Exchange's computerized system for displaying share prices on screen. Deals can be executed automatically on the basis of firm prices logged by SEAQ, thus relieving some of the enormous pressure on the City's telephone system.

safing *noun*   the rendering of something safe or harmless

> Understandably the military have made genuine anti Hero [hazards of electromagnetic radiation to ordnance] attempts including filters, containers, shielding and grounding, and safing and arming mechanisms but these measures are far from foolproof, and on occasion have actually triggered Hero incidents.
> *Guardian* 26 June 1987

salami technique *noun*   a form of computerized embezzlement in which an employee recording financial transactions rounds up or down the actual amount involved and diverts the difference into a private account of his or her own

> In a world heavy with its own jargon, the 'salami technique' is one of the fraudster's most popular fiddles.
> *Daily Telegraph* 29 Jan 1987

▶ The name presumably refers to the accumulation of the ill-gotten gains in thin slices. They soon mount up. An earlier coinage (from the 1950s) which exploits the same idea is *salami tactics*, meaning roughly 'divide and rule.' It finds echoes, too, in *salami-slicing*, a notion roughly comparable to *cheese-paring*:

> Since the ending ... of the commitment to increase spending by 3% in real terms, several equipment purchases have been cancelled or delayed. These include new tanks for the army, the upgrading of Britain's air defences and new radars for the navy Lynx helicopters. Critics argue that this salami-slicing approach to Britain's defences is rapidly eroding the country's ability to meet its commitments to NATO and elsewhere.
>
> *Sunday Times* 3 July 1988

sampling *noun* taking extracts from a variety of songs and combining them to form a new one

> Whatever you call it, 'sampling' (or as Mantronix prefer 'subliminal theft') is *the* trick of the moment.
>
> *Cosmopolitan* May 1988

> I think that there's got to be some legislation about the use of sampling. Either that or the fad will pass. Sampling is basically theft, but even within that, there is a degree of creativity – it's cutting and pasting after all – but the creativity involved is not of the highest order, nor of the purest.
>
> *Top* June 1988

> Harry Enfield, the 'yob-with-the-wad' comedian whose catch-phrase and song, Loadsamoney, have made him a fortune, is being sued for substantial royalties by the pop group Abba. The quartet, once Sweden's most profitable institution bar Volvo, claim that lines from one of their hits, Money Money Money, were used on Enfield's chart success without permission.... The Enfield record uses an increasingly popular technique of sampling. ... An extract from Money Makes The World Go Around is among several employed in the Enfield hit.
>
> *Daily Telegraph* 7 July 1988

samurai bond *noun* a bond issued in yen-denominations by a non-Japanese firm

> The World Bank ... has long been one the biggest issuers in Tokyo's market for samurai bonds.
>
> *Economist* 9 Apr 1988

sanpro *noun,* *euphemistic* prevention of the potentially embarrassing consequences of menstrual bleeding

Recently the IBA authorised a trial re-introduction of TV advertisements for Sanitary Protection, or sanpro as it is termed in the neatly packaged world of PR.

Cosmopolitan Sept 1987

Most complainants about 'sanpro' ads are women.

Cosmopolitan May 1988

Sark lark *noun* the proliferation of company directorships and other lucrative benefits among the inhabitants of Sark, one of the Channel Islands, in consequence of the large number of companies based there

There is a danger that we might find ourselves [in Guernsey] with a sort of Sark lark going on onshore, but we don't think so. We shall just have to watch how it develops.

6 O'Clock News, BBC1, 9 June 1988

▶ Since the late 1960s Sark has had virtually no company tax or company law, which means that firms in their droves have set up their registered offices there. In order to make this scheme work, they need to be represented by resident directors, so a lively local cottage industry has grown up in which at least 10% of the population is on the board of companies. The island is reputed to have the world's highest concentration of telex and fax machines. In 1988 Guernsey decided to go down the same road.

savvy *adjective,* *informal* astute

When it's spring again, forget about the tulips. They don't come from Amsterdam anyway, but from the fertile polders that surround it ... the savvy traveller does well to give the bulb fields a miss and concentrate on exploring the city.

Working Woman Apr 1986

Mr Keith recalls a dictum of a savvy mentor of his, a Viennese Jewish banker: 'Never buy bad bonds in good times.'

Economist 11 June 1988

It takes a savvy and sophisticated nation ... to allow you to go topless without someone getting shirty.

Cosmopolitan July 1988

SBKKV *noun* space-based kinetic kill vehicle: a Star Wars weapons system consisting of self-guiding missiles launched from an orbiting satellite against recently launched enemy ballistic missiles

At a secret White House briefing just before Christmas, however, Mr Reagan was told by Mr Caspar Weinberger, US Defense Secretary, that he had a feasible alternative as a result of the intensive and costly Star Wars research. ... Two of the experimental systems had paid off. One would put a cluster of small missiles on a space satellite. Guided by infra-red sensors, they could be fired to home in on the launching of Russian ICBMs, destroying them in the boost phase. The system is officially known as SBKKV.

Daily Telegraph 19 Jan 1987

scaf *noun, American informal* self-centred-altruism fad: a currently-popular product (e g a garment or cosmetic) which as well as being attractive purports to have a beneficial effect on the user

No respectable skiing condo is complete without a hot-tub, and the latest line in thermal underwear, heavily and predictably advertised, is sheer silk, a real 'scaf.'

Economist 20 Dec 1986

▶ The curious oxymoron of self-centred altruism sounds like trying to have one's cake and eat it; and indeed it turns out largely to be a marketing ploy by firms trying to make the purchase of luxurious and expensive items seem a touch less self-indulgent by promoting their invigorating or health-giving properties. In practice, as the above extract suggests, the element of self-centredness usually scores heavily over altruism.

screwdriver factory *or* **screwdriver plant** *noun, derogatory* a factory in which units are assembled from parts made elsewhere, rather than manufactured from scratch

The Common Market Commission has authorised France to bar the import of 300,000 Japanese colour television sets worth £86 million. The sets are assembled in Europe at 'screwdriver factories' from components exported from Japan.

Daily Telegraph 25 July 1988

Commission officials ... assert ... that they want the great market's trade policy towards the outside world to be a liberal one. Recent anti-dumping actions and crack-downs on Japanese 'screwdriver plants' make one wonder.

Economist 9 July 1988

scuzzball *noun,* *American slang* an unpleasant or disgusting person

In the two years I was waiting tables here, everybody I ever met came in at some point. You get all types here. The hip, the square, the scuzzballs.

Elle Mar 1988

▶ The noun is apparently a derivative of the American adjective *scuzzy*, 'squalid,' which may be an alteration of *disgusting*. The formation of compounds ending in *-ball* referring to eccentric or undesirable individuals goes back to the 1930s, with *screwball* (originally a baseball term for a type of pitch), and has progressed via *oddball* in the 1940s, and more latterly *goofball*.

seajack *noun* the hijacking of a ship at sea

The hijacking of the Italian cruise ship Achille Lauro. ... The seajack followed hard upon the bombing of the headquarters of the Palestine Liberation Organization in Tunis.

Economist 12 Oct 1985

▶ The hijacking of the Achille Lauro by four Palestinian guerrillas on 7 October 1985 provided an interesting case study of instant word creation based on existing models. The usual target of such political hijackings is of course aircraft, and the word *skyjacking* was coined in 1961 to describe the activity. When, for a change, a ship was attacked, *skyjack* was available as a model for *seajack*, and this was often preferred journalistically to *hijack*, even though *hijack* can standardly be applied to incidents at sea, and indeed was first used in such contexts:

The duties of American coastguards are confined to seizing rumships; they cannot seize a Hi-Jacking ship unless it has pirated.

Daily Mail 22 Dec 1924

See also SHIPJACKER.

serious *adjective,* *informal* in (excessively) large amounts

Who will be left as the final credits roll? I wouldn't put serious money on Mick Belker, who has always carried the mark of the martyr, and Davenport isn't looking too well.

Sunday Times 20 Mar 1988

To say that the uninhibited pursuit of serious money has lost its old stigma already sounds trite.

Guardian 22 July 1988

▶ This facetious usage seems to have started life among the fast-burning earners of the post-Bang, pre-Bust city of London, who when speaking of salaries in the six-figure bracket would concede that this was 'serious money' (a phrase immortalized and satirized in Caryl Churchill's play *Serious Money* 1987). But it soon spread to other activities where quantity is equated with quality:

Will it be the function of the 'guide' to put flesh on such shorthand shouts as 'get back to Annie's' (a bar favoured by serious drinkers)?

Sunday Times 28 Aug 1988

You catch smells of a summer night, fennel, a reek of leeks, diesel oil. Weight, quantity, quality, *logistics.* Cans of *confit* of poultry, 12–14 ducks or 6–8 geese per tin. We are in the business of serious supply.

Guardian 27 Aug 1988

set *noun* a group of jokes and stories comprising a comedian's act

He's not one of those stand-up comedians whose mission is to shock. ... The social observations in his set are about Woolworth's shop assistants, Sunday footballers, the bizarre questions put by pub barmen ..., that kind of thing.

Time Out 4 May 1988

▶ This use of *set* appears to derive from the jazz musician's set, the music played in one session, and belongs to the world of alternative rather than mainstream comedy.

sexy *adjective* **1** attractive, enjoyable

Research among the world's leading airports indicated to the designers that airports were becoming inhuman places, losing their accessible scale. 'They should be sexy and fun places,' says Fitch consultant and airport specialist Alan McKinnon.
Financial Times 10 Apr 1986

Mr Brazier ... went on to describe the potential ... for 'a massive explosion of effort that can change the fuddy-duddy, introverted image of book buying into a trendy, exciting and sexy activity'.
Bookseller 26 Feb 1988

2 fashionable or trendy, and therefore desirable

For the first time in anyone's memory pensions are a sexy subject.
The Times 24 Feb 1986

Horizon (8.05) is devoted to air safety, a 'sexy' topic in television terminology, and one to which the medium devotes disproportionate time and effort.
Financial Times 10 Feb 1986

Radio ... isn't cool, or sexy, or whatever quality it is that gets people in brasseries excited.
Listener 31 Mar 1988

Seymour *noun, British slang* a six-figure salary

Dave told me, six months ago – before promotion ... – that he was on 60K, so he must be pushing *his* 'Seymour' now. And he must have a pretty good stock option too.
Observer 14 Aug 1988

▶ This coinage is apparently based on the name of a creative director of the advertising agency Saatchi and Saatchi in the early 1980s. This Mr Seymour was reputed to have been the first to step into the £100,000 bracket in the advertising industry.

shag *noun* a fast dance involving complex footwork and much intertwining of arms

At the height of the enforced monogamy surrounding the AIDS crisis, the state of South Carolina has generously declared that a local pop craze, 'The Shag,' should become the official state dance.
New Musical Express 5 Sept 1987

▶ The shag appears to be a derivative of such US 1930s black-culture dances as the jitterbug, which migrated southwards from Harlem to the southeastern seaboard and became an essential component of the local BEACH MUSIC. As its name indicates, its movements are decidedly suggestive, but nevertheless the great and good of South Carolina, recognizing a bankable commodity, have recently declared it the official state dance, and it is bidding to become the latest international pop craze.

shakers *noun plural, informal* influential people; MOVERS AND SHAKERS

> Puttnam, 1963 edition, a 22-year-old proletarian meteor photographed by ... David Bailey as one of a portfolio of Sixties shakers like Paul McCartney and Michael Caine.
> *Sunday Times* 24 Apr 1988

▶ With the widening currency of *movers and shakers*, convenience as well as hipness dictates the abbreviation to simply *shakers*.

shareowner *noun* a person who owns shares

> If you like, you could share in a bank. The TSB Group is looking for as many shareowners as possible, among people in all walks of life.
> *Sunday Express* 17 Aug 1986

▶ The coining of this alternative to the long-established term *shareholder* seems to be a by-product of the Thatcherite drive for a shareowning democracy in Britain. It avoids the accretion of associations that has built up around shareholding – as being something only rich people do – and helps to make it seem a less forbidding, more accessible activity for the ordinary person. One cannot yet though, from a grammatical point of view, be a shareowner *in* or *of* a company; perhaps an indication of the shareowner's second-class-citizen status as far as shareholders are concerned.

shell-like *noun,* *informal* someone's ear

> Which broadcaster is going to demur when Mrs T's man whispers in his or her shell-like?
>
> *Time Out* 11 May 1988

▶ The now clichéd application of *shell-like* to ears goes back at least to the early 19th century (it is first recorded in Thomas Hood's *Bianca's Dream* 1827: 'Her small and shell-like ear'); but this elliptical use of the adjective as noun is a more recent development, at least in print, which may well have been popularized by the television series *Minder* (compare HER INDOORS).

shin-sock *noun* a sock that reaches approximately halfway up the calf

> This way, that way. Swish Swish. Black thighs in bright white shin-socks.
>
> *Blitz* Mar 1988

shipjacker *noun* a person who hijacks a ship at sea

> The American navy's skyjacking of the aeroplane carrying the four PLO shipjackers on October 11th. ...
>
> *Economist* 26 Oct 1985

▶ On the coinage of new terms based on *skyjack* see SEA-JACK. *Shipjacker* is something of a new departure in that it is based on the form of transport attacked rather than the place where the attack took place.

shit *noun,* *American slang* something excellent

> 'It's the ultimate record for me, it's shit.' 'Oh! 'scuse me! Over here when we say yo, that's shit, we mean yo! that's good, that's hot. The one.'
>
> *New Musical Express* 15 Aug 1987

▶ This is hip-hop usage, from the youth subculture which originated among the black and Hispanic communities of New York City. The subversive reversal of meaning recalls the use of *bad* for 'good' in Black English, although it is probably simply short for *shit-hot*, a term of approval.

shoot *verb* **– shoot oneself in the foot** to act inadvertently to one's own detriment; bring about one's own downfall

Just when the Greater London Council appears to be persuading people that it is a Good Thing and should be spared Mr Jenkin's axe, it proceeds to shoot itself in the foot.

Guardian 28 May 1984

The manner of Johnson's dismissal, bat tangled up in his pads, by Walker only emphasised the fact that Notts have rather shot themselves in the foot in this game.

Daily Telegraph 7 Sept 1987

▶ The keynote of this recently voguish phrase is ineptness. It conjures up the new recruit so gormless that he discharges his rifle when it is pointing at himself. Compare OWN GOAL.

short *verb, American* (on the Stock Exchange) to sell (shares which one does not own)

Selling short is common among large investors, and increasingly so among little guys. To short a stock, an investor borrows a block of shares, then sells them at the prevailing price. After the price drops, the investor buys shares outright to make good. ... The difference between the proceeds from the sale of the original block and the cost of buying the devalued stock later is profit. ... Scandals date back to the great stock market crash of 1929, when the chairman of the Chase National Bank personally shorted more than 40,000 shares of his bank's stock – using his bank's funds.

Newsweek 4 Apr 1988

▶ The expression 'selling short' (in its literal sense) dates back to the middle of the 19th century, but this conversion of the adverb to the verb is a comparatively new development.

short tennis *noun* a version of tennis for young children, played on a short court with small rackets and a low net

Looking over the shoulder of every short tennis organiser are the moralists who believe that competition is bad for children.... Mr Blincoe sees a critic round every corner, but no one has been able to fault his extremely sensitive handling of the short tennis game.

Observer Magazine 19 June 1988

▶ Short tennis was introduced into Britain in 1980, and by 1988 had caught on to the extent of being taught in over 1000 schools. Its aim is to instil the essentials of tennis technique at an early age, and ultimately foster higher standards in the adult game. Matches are of short duration, and are won by the first player to win 11 points or more with a two-point lead. See also KWIK CRICKET.

show-cause *adjective* offering (legally) satisfactory reasons for not carrying out a particular step

> MIC vice-presidents M. G. Pandithan and S. S. Subramaniam were handed show-cause letters yesterday asking them why they should not be expelled from the party.
>
> *The Star* (Malaysia) 3 June 1988

▶ In English law, to 'show cause' signifies to offer arguments against the confirmation of a judgment previously passed.

shutout *noun, American* a person who is excluded or prevented from succeeding

> Michael Jackson performed live. He didn't get a trophy – but neither did eternal Grammy shutout Little Richard, who nonetheless announced, as he gave the best-new-artist award to Jody Watley, 'The winner is ... me!'
>
> *Newsweek* 14 Mar 1988

▶ *Shutout* is well established in American English in the sense of 'a defeat in which the losing side scores no points,' but here there is a slight shift of focus to the one who is defeated.

Sichuan flu *noun* a virulent strain of flu originating in China

> A new and unusually disabling variant of the influenza virus – known to doctors as 'Sichuan flu' – has broken out in 41 American states so far this winter and is arriving in Europe.
>
> *Daily Telegraph* 4 Mar 1988

> Sichuan flu first surfaced when more than 100 American passengers cruising between China and South Korea went down with flu.
>
> *Daily Telegraph* 13 Sept 1988

▶ Sichuan (formerly known as Szechwan) is a south-western province of China. This new variant of the flu virus was first discovered there in 1987. The symptoms (fever, muscle aches, sore throat, etc) are similar to those of standard flu, but are noticeably more intense.

Sid *noun* side-impact dummy: a human-like dummy used for testing the effect of side-on collisions on car passengers

US government officials, not surprisingly, want Sid to be adopted. Sid is the product of extensive research, including testing on bodies of human donors.

Sunday Times 8 May 1988

SIDS *noun* SUDDEN INFANT DEATH SYNDROME

silicone *verb* to implant silicone into a woman's breasts as a cosmetic surgery procedure, to alter their shape

Painted, dyed, shorn, siliconed, she seemed not quite real, like a magnificent transvestite, or an android.

Options Mar 1988

silly money *noun* money in amounts beyond most people's experience, making possible the indiscriminate purchase of very expensive items; funny money

Superstar Michael Jackson now has an incredible £7 million contract with soft drinks giant Pepsi – silly money even to him.

Daily Mirror 30 Mar 1988

simian immunodeficiency virus *noun* (*abbreviation* **SIV**) a retrovirus similar to the human AIDS virus, which attacks the immune system of monkeys

The lack of such an 'animal model' may make it difficult to do certain kinds of research. One way round the problem may be to study similar viruses in other species. The simian immuno-deficiency virus (SIV), for example, can infect rhesus monkeys. Treatments or vaccines that are successful in combatting SIV in monkeys may provide clues to how to treat the human virus.

New Scientist 10 Dec 1987

single-union agreement *or* **single-union deal** *noun* an agreement between a company and a trade union that the employees of that company in a given factory or plant shall belong to no union other than the one that is party to the agreement

Trade union membership at Nissan, the Japanese-owned car manufacturer in the north-east, is as low as 7 per cent, according to local figures from the AEU engineering union, which has a single-union agreement with the company.

Financial Times 26 Apr 1988

▶ Single-union agreements as a contentious issue came to the fore in Britain in early 1988 with the Ford/TGWU affair. Ford proposed to build a new factory in Dundee, Scotland, but only on condition that they could conclude (with the AEU) a single-union deal for it. The TGWU resolutely opposed this, and in due course Ford scrapped their plans for the factory. Such agreements are commonplace in many other European countries, and many large firms are keen on implementing them in Britain, to simplify management-union negotiations and cut down on interunion disputes. Some unions, though, have argued against them and declined to enter into them, on the grounds that they tie unions' hands and allow managements to impose exploitively low wage rates.

Singlish *noun* a simplified and regularized form of English spoken by inhabitants of Singapore

And Singaporeans came to speak a hybrid language known as Singlish, an English patois full of Malay and Chinese expressions translated literally: I bring you where you stay is it? (Shall I take you home?) Modern playwrights like to use Singlish as an assertion of identity. Even when they have been trained in London and speak perfectly good English.

New York Times Magazine 12 June 1988

▶ Singlish has been studied by John Platt, who coined the term *creoloid* to characterize the nature of its development from the base language English.

sit-tragedy *noun* a radio or television drama series featuring the same basic cast of characters in stories of misfortune or conflict

Central TV started a new sit-com last night, A Kind of Living. ... The script shows remarkable observation – Carol and Trevor bicker despairingly in an appalling neurotic symbiosis which carries all too much conviction; a great deal of talent and perception have gone into 'A Kind of Living' and I cannot think of anything to criticise, except the idea that it is comedy. It is more sit-tragedy than sitcom.

Daily Telegraph 20 Feb 1988

SIV *noun* SIMIAN IMMUNODEFICIENCY VIRUS

skin tag *noun* a small nonmalignant epidermal excrescence

Skin tags – superficial tags of skin which look like warts and occur on the neck, under the breasts and in the armpits of plump women – may cause confusion too. They can easily be snipped off and cauterised by a doctor.

Good Housekeeping Mar 1988

skip park *noun* an area with skips for the deposit of various sorts of refuse

In Belgium, the town of Leuven has the world's largest 'skip park' where people separate and deposit all re-usable waste into different banks.

Cosmopolitan July 1988

skippering *noun, slang* the practice of taking over a deserted dwelling to live in it without permission or payment; squatting

Most of the advisory services try to persuade young people to get out of central London. But many get a thrill out of street life and are loth to give up. They sleep on friends' floors, or resort to 'skippering.'

Economist 27 Dec 1987

slamdancing *noun* dancing engaged in by fans of heavy metal and similar forms of rock music, in which dancers jump up and down frenziedly and collide violently with each other

The trouble began when the party goers started slamdancing to the Beasties' hit 'Fight For Your Right To Party.'
New Musical Express 23 July 1987

A spectator among the 90,000 crowd at an open-air heavy metal concert at Donnington Park race circuit in Leicestershire in which two fans were crushed to death described yesterday how he saw one of the dead being trampled on by other fans 'slam dancing.'
Daily Telegraph 22 Aug 1988

▶ Compare MOSHING.

slam dunk *noun* (in sailing) an act of changing direction extremely close to another boat

Murray answered with the now conventional 'slam dunk' tack, but the slight lack of boat speed with which he went into the tack was his undoing. Conner sailed through his lee and forced Murray to tack away again.
Guardian 3 Feb 1987

Did the 1988 committee make the right decision? Was the 1972 decision correct? Is the slam dunk a legitimate tactic? Can you only do it if the boat on top of which you are tacking is not affected in any direct way?
Yachts and Yachting Mid Aug 1988

▶ This term is American in origin, deriving from the *slam dunk* in basketball, in which the player leaps into the air and deposits the ball into the basket from above.

slap *verb, informal* to impose a fine on

The FAA announced a 30-day inspection to determine whether all the Texas Air units are fit to fly. The agency slapped Eastern with an $823,000 fine for safety violations.
Newsweek 25 Apr 1988

▶ This usage derives from the already well-established 'slap a fine on someone.' It is a fairly common phenomenon among verbs of this type, in which the thing with which an action is done is the object of the verb, and the person to whom it is done is indicated by the preposition *on*, for these two elements to be reversed, with *on* being replaced by *with*: for example *spray paint on the wall* becomes *spray the wall with paint*.

SLD *noun* SOCIAL AND LIBERAL DEMOCRATS

sleeperette *noun* a large reclinable passenger seat on a train, aircraft, etc designed to allow the occupant to sleep

Now jet your way, cosy and comfortable, in one of our new stretched first-class seats – the sleeperettes of Kuwait Airways on Boeing 747s will get you fresh to your destinations.

Economist 13 Apr 1985

sleep strike *noun* a form of industrial action in which employees continue to work without sleep, becoming progressively less able to work properly

Air-traffic controllers in Greece began a hunger and sleep strike yesterday which is expected seriously to disrupt flights to and from the country. Though they are at work, it means that, by today, they will be too weak to guarantee the safe arrival and departure of flights.

Daily Telegraph 7 July 1988

slipmat *noun* a circular piece of thin rubber placed on a turntable to prevent records from slipping

Don't forget a pair of good slipmats – these aren't provided with the turntables and are absolutely essential.

City Limits 24 Mar 1988

slo-mo *or* **slowmo** *noun, informal* slowed-down action on film or videotape; slow motion

Frank Cvitanovich, who has directed some fine documentaries about football and racing, here adds little to the faded-tackles-in-slowmo tradition.
Listener 21 Apr 1988

A diligent run-down of variety and life-cycle is juiced up with ... slo-mo for a cobra *v* monitor lizard battle ... that suggests a Ray Harryhausen model sequence in a dawn-of-time movie.
Independent 27 May 1988

smart card *noun* a credit or debit card with an inbuilt memory chip which keeps a record of transactions conducted with the card

Smart cards are going to be particularly useful to replace cheques in shops, so that the buyer's account can be debited automatically from the till.
Economist 30 Apr 1988

▶ The advantage of smart cards (a French invention) is that they do away with the need to refer back to the bank's central computer to check every instance of use (for example when making a withdrawal from a cash point). The card can remember how much you have in your account, and so transactions are considerably speeded up. See also SUPER-SMART CARD.

smoke and mirrors *noun* something illusory or deliberately misleading

The disinvestment campaign appears largely to be what one senior diplomat in Johannesburg called 'all smoke and mirrors.'
Daily Telegraph 7 Mar 1987

President [Reagan] was asked whether the timing of the INF accord with Mr Gorbachev, at 1.30pm, had been decreed by astrology, as some aides have claimed. He replied: 'No it wasn't. Nothing of that kind was going on. This was all once again smoke and mirrors. We made no decisions on it and we're not binding our lives to this.'
Daily Telegraph 18 May 1988

▶ An allusion to the stage or film illusionist's art (as in 'it's all done with mirrors') appropriately favoured by the grand old showman and president, Ronald Reagan.

snack pellet *noun* a convenience food in the form of an extruded and shaped mass of edible matter

The value of the snack-pellet market alone is estimated to be $25 million and one cannot help thinking that more money is currently being spent on pushing back the frontiers of snackdom than on cancer research.

Listener 31 Mar 1988

snail park *noun* an establishment where edible snails are commercially reared

Mr Aubrée's chemical-free acres are run on traditional 'snail park' lines, with 1.5 million snails fattening on naturally grown plants.

Guardian 27 June 1988

▶ See also HELICULTURE.

snake hips *noun plural* attractively slim hips, especially in a man

It's no end of a laugh to spot the Speaker in full drag for the first time ..., and the snake hips of the Serjeant-at-Arms, who has to wear another sort of fancy dress, are worth a few moments of your time.

Punch Feb 1988

s'n'f *noun* a type of pulp fiction featuring rich glamorous high-spending, highly sexed women

Women, on the other hand, go for fat, glossy books where the heroine inherits a struggling company from her father or husband, and turns it into a mighty multinational, in spite of the fact that she appears to be horizontal for almost all her waking hours and pays far more attention to her couturier than her accountant. These Sidney Sheldon, Judith Krantz, Jackie Collins, Shirley Conran books have the generic title of s'n'f.

Guardian 6 Feb 1986

▶ The *s* in *s'n'f* stands for 'shopping,' the *f* for 'fucking.'

snort and tell *adjective* revealing secret drug taking among former associates

Later, the American press, having discovered the post-Watergate
delights of 'snort and tell' journalism tried repeatedly to pin drug
raps on Mr Hamilton Jordan, the White House chief of staff.

Financial Times 26 Apr 1988

▶ *Snort* is a slang term for inhaling cocaine or similar drugs
through the nose. The model for this formation is KISS-AND-
TELL.

snuff *verb, slang* to kill

Worse, his [Sherlock Holmes's] client got snuffed by the bad guys
and Holmes was even cheated of his tit-for-tat by the intervention
of the equinoctial gales.

Listener 17 Sept 1987

▶ *Snuff out* was used as early as the 19th century to mean 'to
die' ('The old man was very feeble, and looked like snuffing
out before he had completed his story': A C Bicknell, *Travels
in Northern Queensland* 1895), and the related *snuff it* is still
very much with us. The transitive use, however, meaning
'kill,' is a more recent development, which is now showing
signs of crossing the Atlantic from American to British
English.

Soanly Ranger *noun, British* a member of a supposed
social group, similar to but slightly downmarket from
the Sloane Rangers, who typically live in inner South
London boroughs

She [the Duchess of York] was, and is, not so much a Sloane Ranger
... as that slightly lesser breed known as 'Soanly Rangers' – these
are Sloanes who find it cheaper to live in places like Clapham and
Stockwell.

Observer 6 Mar 1988

▶ The name, based of course on *Sloane Ranger*, derives
from the fact that the Soanlies explain their location (in a
hitherto démodé but rapidly gentrifying part of London) by
saying that 'it's only ten minutes from Sloane Square.'

soap opera *noun* a continuing set of events marked by melodrama, reminiscent of a television soap opera

Some of the viewers who were eager to watch Westminster's soap opera may well have been alarmed, last week, by television detector-vans on the rampage.

Punch Feb 1988

Social and Liberal Democrats *noun plural* (*abbreviation* **SLD**) a British political party formed in 1988 from the Liberal party and sections of the Social Democratic party

The Social Democratic party ... has itself been shattered. ... The bigger piece, within the new Social and Liberal Democrats (SLD) is encumbered with an eminently forgettable name.

Economist 6 Feb 1988

▶ The Social and Liberal Democrats were the outcome of the political saga of the Alliance, a loosely-knit union of the Liberals and the SDP formed in autumn 1981. Its failure to make any headway in the 1987 general election, following a similar lack of success in 1983, led to increased calls for a complete merger, the ambiguous nature of the two parties' relationship with each other having been viewed as a major reason for its inability to make a political breakthrough. Negotiations for such a merger got under way at the end of September 1987, but only in the face of fierce opposition from certain sections of both parties who wished to remain independent; indeed, so severe was the rift within the SDP that the antimergerites, under the party leader David Owen, refused to join any new party, and split off to retain their own independent SDP. After a lengthy incubation, the birth of the new party was announced in the first week of March 1988. Much agonizing had gone on over its policies and organization, but not the least of the difficulties had been the choice of a name, a major stumbling block being that the Liberals insisted that *Liberal* had to be in it and the SDP insisted that *Social Democratic* had to be in it. A wide variety of candidates was thrown into the ring, including the *Liberal Democrats*, which was thought to be too reminiscent of right-wing groupings in certain European parliaments; the *Radical Party*, which was found to be too Thatcherite; the *Progessive Party*, which was too foreign-sounding; and the *Liberals and Social Democrats*, whose simplicity recommended it until someone pointed out the triple entendre of its abbreviation. Early in Decemeber 1987 it was announced that the name would be the *United Liberal and Social Democratic Party*, to be known commonly as the *Democrats*. However, it emerged that Liberal leader David Steel was opposed to 'the Democrats', and on 10 December it was finally officially promulgated that the new party would be known as the *New Liberal and Social Democratic Party*, to be called commonly the *Alliance*. But the saga was not yet over: from further consultation it emerged that the new name was too long, and the *Alliance* was associated with failure, so it was back again to the drawing board. And at last, in mid-January 1988, the *Social and Liberal Democrats* was agreed on – and stuck to. It has not averted all difficulties, since the abbreviation *SLD* has led to members being rather derisively nicknamed *Salads*; and a further twist was added at the party's conference in autumn 1988, when it was decided to use the term *The Democrats* as the shorthand version of their name.

See also MERGERITE.

social fund *noun* (in Britain) an amount of money set aside by the government for loans and grants to those in need

> In future the government will run a loans scheme for poor people who have special needs, such as a cooker or clothing. These will come from the social fund.
>
> *Sunday Times* 10 Apr 1988

▶ The social fund was introduced on 11 Apr 1988 under the terms of the Social Security Act 1988, to replace the previous single-payments grant scheme. Over two thirds of the cash available under its terms will be given as loans rather than grants, repayable over a period of up to 18 months. See also FAMILY CREDIT, INCOME SUPPORT.

sociobabble *noun*, *informal derogatory* sociological jargon

He [Peter Imbert, Metropolitan Police Commissioner] has a very different style from the cerebral intellectualism of his predecessor, Sir Kenneth Newman, whose preoccupations seemed to be with managerial reforms and who was considered too remote by many of his officers. Mr Imbert does not spout sociobabble, like Newman.
Guardian 18 Mar 1988

▶ This formation is based on *psychobabble,* a disparaging term for the impenetrable jargon of American psychoanalysts coined by R D Rosen in 1975 and used by him as the title of a book.

solar pond *noun* an artificially constructed pool of salty water designed to collect the sun's heat for conversion to electricity

Scientists at the University of Mexico in Albuquerque have boiled eggs in solar ponds which have reached 109°C.
New Scientist 3 July 1986

▶ The idea of solar ponds has been around since 1902, but it is only recently that energy technologists have begun to take an interest in them again. They consist of a layer of very salt water, covered by a layer of fresh water. The sun's rays heat up the salt water, but the heat does not escape through the fresh water, which is a poor conductor. Ponds three to four feet deep can reach temperatures of 50–60°C, but as the above extract suggests, far higher temperatures are possible. The hot water is used to drive a turbine for generating electricity. Israel is a world leader in solar pond technology.

sonoluminescence *noun* the glow emitted by a fluid when irradiated by a powerful ultrasound beam

[Dr Kenneth S] Suslick and Dr Edward B Flint reported that they had induced sonoluminescence, a 'cold, blue flame,' in a hydrocarbon liquid called dodecane. This was the first time sonoluminescence had been triggered by ultrasound in a liquid other than water.
Sunday Times 8 May 1988

▶ Research by Drs Suslick and Flint, of the University of Illinois, suggests that the phenomenon of sonoluminescence may be caused by the heat produced by the sudden collapse of microscopic bubbles.

source *verb* **1** to obtain (materials) from a particular producer, country, or other source

GM reckons that 10% of the components it now makes would be better bought elsewhere. It has the highest level of in-house sourcing of components of any large car company worldwide.

Economist 19 Dec 1987

This brings to 807 the total number of manuscripts obtained locally by the Malay Manuscript Centre of the National Library. ... Many of these manuscripts were already overseas and had to be sourced from even Sotheby's.

Business Times (Malaysia) 3 June 1988

2 to locate (a productive activity)

British manufacturing is at last sharing some of the spending spoils. The car industry is a notable example, with not only the multinational car-makers announcing plans to source more production in Britain, but even BL regaining market share.

Listener 12 Mar 1987

sourced *adjective* attributed to a source

There have been other sweeping but vaguely sourced stories by the political writers of The Guardian, Times, Standard, Mail, Telegraph, Scotsman, Yorkshire Post.

Guardian 11 Mar 1986

The gossip mills were already spinning with the well-sourced word that Mrs Reagan is unhappy about the presidential retirement home, a mansion in Bel Air, Calif, that was bought for $2.5 million by a group of the Reagans' friends to be leased to them after they leave Washington.

Newsweek 25 Apr 1988

space-nap *noun* the abduction of a human being by creatures from outer space, who take him or her into their spaceship

Streiber, a highly successful American author of horror fiction, claimed his own close encounter in 1987 in Communication, his book about his alleged 'space-nap' by ugly little creatures, published in paperback this month.

Guardian 17 Feb 1988

spaghetti *noun,* *informal* a confused multiplicity of wires, pieces of string, etc, often inextricably intertwined

You can't use a heavy desktop computer, with its main plug and its spaghetti of cables, in a railway carriage or on a beach.

Daily Telegraph 15 Jan 1988

Today's hypertexts allow any piece of data to be linked to any other piece for any reason. Too often, this creates a sort of logical spaghetti, hard for the user to untangle.

Economist 30 July 1988

▶ The best-known application of *spaghetti* to bewildering complexity is Spaghetti Junction, the familiar name given to the mazelike road interchange at Gravelly Hill, to the north of Birmingham. This no doubt gave impetus to the wider use of the metaphor.

spearchucker *noun,* *taboo* a black person

Corporal Louis Taylor, aged 28, who was also accused of using abusive terms like 'nigger,' 'coon,' and 'spearchucker,' told the army's Special Investigation Branch that he 'only wished to encourage competition.'

Caribbean Times 27 May 1988

spectator catch *noun* (in cricket) a catch which to spectators appears to be a legitimate dismissal of the batsman but is not (for example, when the ball has hit the pad rather than the bat, or bounces up after being hit into the ground)

I think it was a spectator catch, and well taken too.

Test Match Special, BBC Radio 3, 23 July 1988

speed-metal *noun* a style of powerfully amplified rock music with a very fast heavy beat – called also *thrash, thrashcore, thrash metal*

351

Richard Grabel reports from New York City, crossing point of hardcore and metal – birth place of speed-metal. ... Speed-metal is the largest, most vital cult in American rock. Metallica are the reigning gods, easily selling out large arenas, and on the next rung down, the speed-metal/thrashcore shows promoted at New York's Ritz by the Rock Hotel organisation are also regular sell-outs. ... The rising popularity of this punk-metal hybrid has brought together two very distinct groups that until recently were completely mutually exclusive. These groups are commonly defined through a series of cliches, but several visits to the Rock Hotel speed-metal extravaganzas confirm that those cliches are born out of practice. The metal kids have long hair, wear denim and leather and T-shirts extolling Iron Maiden, Motorhead or Metallica. They headbang. The hardcore kids have short hair, wear denim and leather and T-shirts in praise of Suicidal Tendencies, Millions Of Dead Cops and the Cro-Mags.

New Musical Express 21 Mar 1987

▶ Essentially speed-metal is a development of heavy metal, a style of loud rhythmic rock music, speeded up through the influence of hardcore, a variety of punk rock. See also MOSHING.

spend *noun* an amount (to be) spent

With all this added up you get a total spend of somewhere around £80 million, and that is really quite a formidable sum of money.

Environment Now Jan 1988

It is also believed the winning agency could benefit from an increased spend on the account of up to £1.5 million.

Campaign 1 July 1988

spendolas *noun plural, informal* money

Stephanie Mills is one of soul's new generation women singers, the Daughters of Diana; women who insist on producing, writing, arranging and raking in the lion's share of the spendolas.

New Musical Express 15 Aug 1987

▶ Perhaps a blend of *spend* and *payola*, with subliminal memories of *spondulicks* (a superannuated slang term for 'money').

spiderous *adjective* spider-like

> Bette Davis, clad in spiderous black, the gaunt conqueror of cancer and the stroke that followed her 1983 mastectomy elegantly chain-smokes through our conversation in a Central Park South hotel, too, and mocks the idea of anti-nicotine laws.
>
> *Time Out* 25 May 1988

▶ A derivative of *spider* not recorded by the OED after 1648, and noted as 'obs[olete],' *spiderous* was presumably re-coined by the writer of this extract to circumvent the connotations of *spidery*, which in current English now usually suggests 'thin and sharply angular.'

spin *noun, chiefly American* a particular interpretation or slant given to a proposal, policy, piece of information, etc

> Since a small majority in the House of Representatives disagrees with this thesis, ... the administration has been twisting and turning this week to give the message a more acceptable spin.
>
> *Economist* 30 Jan 1988

> With so much positive 'spin' in the Moscow spring air, it seems almost churlish to point out that much more had been hoped for at this summit: a Strategic Arms Reduction Treaty ..., topping the INF deal signed in Washington in December.
>
> *Daily Telegraph* 27 May 1988

▶ From the spin imparted to the ball by the cue in pool, which controls its direction. Donald Regan, former White House chief of staff, was informally known as the Director of Spin Control.

spin-meister *or* **spin doctor** *noun,* *American* a person who provides SPIN

> Much of the input comes indirectly from the spin-meisters – these are senior campaign strategists who give the most flattering read-out for their candidates of the latest vote or debate to accompanying journalists.
>
> *The Times* 17 Mar 1988

> The theme of the two men having talked bluntly yet courteously ... is likely to be stressed further by Reagan Administration 'spin doctors' who will try to present the summit in a favourable light in the days to come.
>
> *Daily Telegraph* 11 Dec 1987

News coverage of the campaign can be influenced to a candidate's advantage by 'spin doctors' – professionals whose job it is to persuade political journalists to put the right spin on the story.

Economist 26 Dec 1987

spree *noun* a bout of violent activity

Local artist went on a shooting spree 13 years ago and then put a bullet through his own head.

Newsweek 19 Oct 1987

Gun-spree youth kills himself [headline]

Daily Telegraph 12 Sept 1988

▶ Hitherto the word *spree* has been used for activities which, while they are engaged in with a certain lack of restraint, are essentially harmless to anyone else (e g a 'spending spree'). The application to shooting, killing, etc is a comparatively recent development.

spunk *noun, Australian informal* a devastatingly handsome young man

Sydney also has an unfair share of fantastically handsome men, 'spunks' in Oz parlance: beach boys, surfers, Californian blonds, Robert Redfords on an epic scale. The bad news for hunk-hunters is that after San Francisco, Sydney is the next major gay metropolis.

Cosmopolitan June 1987

squaerial *noun* a flat diamond-shaped aerial for receiving satellite television broadcasts

The company has exclusive rights to the 'squaerial' when it starts transmitting three national networks at the end of next year.

Daily Telegraph 3 Aug 1988

The squaerial ... is much smaller, likely to be easier to install, less obtrusive and more attractive than Astra's two-footer.

Listener 18 Aug 1988

▶ It is envisaged that this new form of aerial (its name is a blend of *square* and *aerial*) may replace the conventional dish-shaped reflector. Compact in size and containing an array of small antennae set on a flat surface, it can be fixed to the wall of a house.

squiffing *noun,* *British slang* the practice of postal workers reposting mail that is ready for delivery

> Other common practices range from 'squiffing' ... to 'doubling,' in which mail is deliberately delayed for 24 hours to give the postman a day off. The wonder is not that a quarter of all letters fail to arrive in time, but that the overwhelming majority do eventually get delivered at all.
>
> *Observer* 11 Sept 1988

▶ Squiffing is a handy way for postmen to cut short an onerous round. If you still have a sackful of letters when the time comes to knock off, simply put them in the nearest pillar box to go through the same process all over again.

stabilizer *or* **stabiliser** *noun* (in the EC) a mechanism for cutting the guaranteed price paid to farmers for a particular product when its output exceeds a specified limit

> West Germany and France still refuse to accept the automatic application of agricultural 'stabilisers'.
>
> *Economist* 12 Dec 1987

> The unexpected decision to agree to more 'stabilisers' on prices paves the way for Common Market foreign ministers to give formal approval to the deal on EEC financing reached at the Community summit 10 days ago.
>
> *Daily Telegraph* 23 Feb 1988

staff doctor *noun* (in Britain) a grade of hospital doctor between senior house officer and consultant

> The new staff doctors' jobs will be created at the rate of 200 a year for the next five years and will be open to qualified hospital doctors with at least three years' experience as a senior house officer.
>
> *Daily Telegraph* 10 Feb 1988

▶ This new grade of doctor was announced in 1988. The intention is to provide enhanced career opportunities for hospital doctors, whose chances of advancement have hitherto been limited by the relatively small number of consultancy posts.

355

stand-alone *adjective* operating independently; self-contained

Stanley Kalms wants to turn Woolworths into a chain of accessory stores for his highly-successful Dixons and Currys outlets. ... That is the secret behind his plan ... to put Dixons and Currys outlets under the same roof as Woolworths stores. They will be stand-alone sites, physically distinct from Woolworths with their own entrances.

Sunday Times 1 June 1986

▶ The metaphor derives from computing, in which *stand-alone* has been used since the mid 1960s for a system or part of a system that can operate on its own, as opposed to being, for example, part of a network.

standfirst *verb* to provide (a newspaper article) with a standfirst, an introductory paragraph summarizing its contents

What you have been looking at in a proper paper such as *The Times* consists of as many words as are in three novels of average length, written, subbed, designed, cut to fit exactly into the jigsaw, stand-firsted, headlined, printed and delivered on to your breakfast table in 12 hours flat.

The Times 15 Feb 1988

stand-off *noun, informal* a withdrawal of friendship or close association; cooling-off

Though Princess Diana was originally helped by Anna Harvey, a fashion editor at Vogue, she is now a free-wheeling and independent shopper amongst Britain's designers. ... There was a distinct stand-off with the Emanuels after the wedding-dress designers signed up with showbiz PR Mark McCormack and began lending their name to commercial lines of tights, sunglasses and scent.

Guardian 22 July 1986

▶ The noun is probably a back-formation from the adjective *stand-offish*, itself derived from the now rather dated phrasal verb *stand off*, meaning 'remain aloof.'

standstill agreement *noun* an agreement by which one company undertakes not to attempt to take over another or buy shares in it in return for confidential information about its operations

Companies in America have found a way to block potential take-overs without informing their shareholders. They sign confidential 'standstill agreements' with a list of the most obvious bidders.
Economist 30 Apr 1988

▶ Like *poison pills* (see *Longman Guardian New Words*), a *standstill agreement* is a ploy to ward off unwelcome take-over bids. The reason a potential bidder might be willing to enter into such a deal is that the inside information they receive as a quid pro quo would put them in an advantageous position to make an offer should the target company ever actually be willing to put itself up for sale.

star-warrior *noun* an advocate of 'Star Wars,' the USA's Strategic Defense Initiative which envisages the deployment of satellite-mounted devices to destroy enemy missiles in flight

The Japanese know-how that would most interest American star-warriors is thought to be in the field of optoelectronics.
Economist 15 Mar 1986

Stealthie *noun, American informal* a person who is obsessively interested in and tries to find out more about the US 'stealth' secret military aircraft

Something more tangible materialized before Sam Jones, a veteran Stealthie and writer for Metalworking News. He was driving when he stopped to allow a freight train to pass. He noticed that 'on one of the flat-bed cars was a triangular object ... wrapped in blue plastic.' It bore a striking resemblance to an aircraft wing, but one outside his experience.
Guardian 3 May 1988

▶ 'Stealth' is a code name for a new generation of highly secret US military aircraft, said by Stealthies who claim to be in the know to include a fighter being built by Lockheed and a bomber produced by Northrop (see ATB). It refers to, in the jargon of military technology, the aircraft's 'low radar, infra-red and optical signatures' which enable them to creep up unobtrusively on their enemies; that is to say, their shape, the materials they are made of, and the reduction of heat emissions make them hard to spot visually, on radar, or using infra-red detectors. In 1988 the US announced plans to develop warships using the same design concept.

The veil of secrecy which surrounds stealth aircraft was embarrassingly rent when model designer John Andrews marketed what he claimed was a precise replica of the RF19 stealth fighter in plastic kit form – 700,000 were sold. An official artist's impression of the plane, released by the US Air Force in September 1988, did resemble the model in several ways.

The suffix *-ie*, meaning an enthusiast for something, is becoming a linguistic growth area. It seems likely that the usage may have originated in *groupie* (which first appeared in the late 1960s).

steam *verb* to engage in STEAMING

> Four teenagers who were part of a 30–40 strong gang that 'steamed' the top deck of a bus last November were sentenced to four years youth custody each this week.
>
> *South London Press* 12 June 1987

> The jury heard how a 12-strong gang ... 'steamed' through the carriages, pulling necklaces, rings, bracelets and cameras from passengers, and punched a pregnant woman.
>
> *Daily Telegraph* 8 July 1988

steamer *noun* a person who engages in STEAMING

Detective Chief Inspector Jeff Rees ... explained 'Traditionally buses have been a police-free zone. The steamers have picked on the old open-backed routemaster vehicles which offer ease of access and escape not available on the newer buses with automatic doors controlled by the driver.'

Sunday Times 21 Feb 1988

London Transport claimed big successes yesterday in curbing gangs of robbers, known as 'steamers', who took to the Underground earlier this year.

Daily Telegraph 16 July 1988

steaming *noun* multiple mugging in which a gang of youths raids a bus, railway carriage, shop, etc, rapidly robs its victims, and makes a quick escape before the police can be summoned

Hackney's street thieves have adopted a frightening new method of robbery and are working in huge mobs. Gangs of as many as 50 youths are roaming the streets and mugging as many passers-by as they can. They have also invaded stores and off-licences to stage shoplifting blitzes. The mobs call their method of robbery 'steaming,' a term first coined in America's crime-ridden inner-city ghettos.

Hackney Gazette 24 Apr 1987

The police justify their hostility to the [Notting Hill] carnival by reference to the death on Sunday last year, and the 'steaming' on Monday.

Caribbean Times 27 May 1988

▶ The practice of carrying out such mass robbery originated in the US in the early 1980s, particularly in run-down areas of the big cities, but it was soon imported into British cities.

steering *noun, American* the practice of trying to ensure that non-white prospective tenants or house-purchasers do not move into all-white areas

MacRae said the study would spot blatant discrimination, but also would try to measure practices such as 'steering' in which a rental agency or Realtor steers minority clients away from all-white neighborhoods or into racially segregated neighborhoods.

Roanoke Times and World-News 11 Apr 1988

stick *noun*   an instance of a bank or other financial institution being left with an unsold portion of a share issue which it had underwritten, and therefore having to buy the shares itself

> Mr Brian Quinn, executive director in charge of the Bank of England's supervision department, says that for the large-exposure rule – though not the other capital requirements – the Bank would accept parental guarantees rather than paid-in capital. But he denies that the Bank is over-cautious on large exposures. 'Underwritings are getting larger, and the incidence of stick is rising,' he said.
>
> *Economist* 25 June 1988

stiff *verb, slang*   to be a commercial failure; flop

> I've had singles that stiffed.
>
> Sheena Easton, *Esther Interviews* ..., BBC1, 21 July 1988

▶ The verb derives from the noun *stiff*, the macabre colloquialism for a corpse; appropriate enough for a record, theatrical production, etc that dies.

store card *noun*   a charge card issued by a particular shop, and usable only to buy goods from that shop

> As for the store-card charges, which in the case of some shops (including Selfridges, Habitat, Richard Shops, British Home Stores, Mothercare, Heal's, Next and Boots) are well over 30 per cent.
>
> *Daily Telegraph* 13 Apr 1988

streaker *noun*   a fast, highly manoeuvrable ferry operating on the River Clyde

> The 20-minute crossing was made by the MV Juno, one of the three sister ships operated by Caledonian MacBrayne on the Clyde services. The vessels are dubbed 'streakers,' not because they lack a coat of paint, but because of their amazing manoeuvrability.
>
> *Cambridge Pride* Mar 1988

street *adjective*   of the culture of young working-class people, without an overlay of sophistication

Despite rumours to the contrary, they will not be working with Michael Jackson on his new LP as they feel he isn't 'street enough.'
Melody Maker 10 Jan 1987

But is Hurby selling out? Can he be accused of deserting 'the street'? 'I never was "street",' he replies. 'Even when me and my boys were a rap group, the Super Lovers, we weren't street but ladies' rap.'
City Limits 18 Feb 1988

▶ The concept of the 'street' as the place where the tougher aspects of city life are played out has been productive of several 80s expressions defining it as a cultural gestalt, notably *street-credibility* and *streetwise*, culminating recently in its installation as an adjective in its own right.

street-fighter *noun, informal* a tough combative person

In New York, a veteran feminist street-fighter, Mrs Bella Abzug has the chance to return to Congress, this time from suburban Westchester.
Economist 13 Sept 1986

Gerry Austin, Jesse Jackson's new campaign manager ... is only half the streetfighter he once was.
Daily Telegraph 14 Apr 1988

stun gun *noun* a weapon which discharges high-voltage electricity

Stun guns ... were 'reluctantly' freed from British firearms laws in the High Court yesterday. The devices, which can emit a 40,000-volt charge, were in the same category as machine-guns in the firearms laws.
Daily Telegraph 7 Nov 1987

▶ The term *stun gun* was originally applied to guns which fire ammunition intended to stun rather than wound its targets, used for example in riot control or for subduing wild animals. This new and rather sinister weapon started life in America, where its users have included policemen with awkward suspects to deal with and criminals with sadistic inclinations. Its precise legal status in Britain remained in doubt until five law lords unanimously declared it illegal in February 1988.

style counsellor *noun* an arbiter of or adviser on what is currently fashionable

The Style Counsellors who dictate what is and is not fashionable seem to be succeeding in killing off the cocktail revival. For a year or two you could hardly move in any bar for Pina Coladas, Tequila Sunrises and Margaritas, but once cocktails became essential drinking in the suburbs in such style outposts as Milton Keynes discos, it was doomed.

Daily Mail 30 Jan 1986

▶ Compare TASTEMAKER.

submerger *noun* a merger resulting in loss of separate identity for one or both of the parties involved

The first indication that opposition to the submerger of Queens Park Rangers and Fulham football club might not be that passive came fully 90 minutes before kick-off on Saturday.

Guardian 2 May 1987

sudden infant death syndrome *noun* (*abbreviation* **SIDS**) the sudden unexplained death of a baby

Mike Bolger began fundraising for cot death research about two years ago when a friend, Fred Cook, lost a child to the mysterious sudden infant death syndrome.

Eastern Daily Press 7 Mar 1986

▶ In common with most others, the medical profession craves respectability and gravitas in its terminology; hence the coining of the rather ponderous *sudden infant death syndrome* to challenge the demotic *cot death*.

The defining characteristic of such deaths is that the baby had no previous symptoms of illness, and no certain cause of death can be found post mortem. The victims, who simply stop breathing, are typically between two and five months old. It is still far from clear what lies behind the syndrome, but among factors that have been implicated are having a mother younger than average, having a low birthweight, involvement in a multiple birth, and membership of a large family. Instances had been falling over the past 20 years, but an increase in 1986 (to 1536, possibly caused by the cold winter) gave rise to concern.

suicide gene *noun* a gene possessed by certain bacteria which terminates their life

> The new technique is based on a discovery that many bacteria have 'suicide genes' regulating their life cycle.
>
> *South China Morning Post* 21 Apr 1988

▶ The reason for the sudden celebrity of suicide genes is the prospect of their use artificially for the purpose of destroying toxic wastes. Certain species of bacteria that possess suicide genes can be used to degrade such wastes, but it is undesirable that they should go on living and reproducing after they have done their work. Dr Stephen Cusky, of the US Government Environmental Protection Agency laboratory, is developing a method of regulating the effect of a counterbalancing, protective gene, using a trigger such as benzoic acid, so that as soon as the acid has been consumed the protector gene is 'switched off,' and the suicide gene can do its work, killing the bacterium.

summilexic *noun* a person whose surname begins with any of the letters A-M

> Not only am I a statistic; I am a ranked statistic. The world, I now understand, is divided into summilexics, whose names begin with A-M, and fundilexics, whose names begin with N-Z.
>
> *New Scientist* 22 Oct 1987

▶ See ALPHABETISM.

summitry *noun* the practice of holding or manner of conducting summit conferences

> Kemp ... argued that the White House's leap into summitry at Reykjavik 'was not the proper way to engage in summitry.'
>
> *Guardian* 27 Oct 1986

> The problems of summitry linguistics get murkier still.
>
> *Independent* 23 Feb 1988

> When Ronald Reagan became president, summitry was out of fashion.
>
> *Economist* 28 May 1988

supercollider *noun* an extremely large powerful particle accelerator

> Another casualty of the House's budget proposal is likely to be the super-conducting supercollider, a giant new particle accelerator for research in subatomic physics. It will produce particles 20 times as energetic as any other machine.
>
> *New Scientist* 31 Mar 1988

▶ Although one of the chief functions of a particle accelerator is to cause highly energized particles to collide with other particles (to provide evidence about how the fundamental forces of nature work), there does not appear to be any actual precedent for the term *collider* before the coming of this new compound.

superdelegate *noun* (in the USA) a delegate to a Democratic party convention other than one of those selected by party members in primary elections

> Their hope must be that they could pick up enough delegates from the dropout candidates and superdelegates to win the nomination without having to cut a deal with Jackson.
>
> *Newsweek* 18 Apr 1988

> Mr Michael ... said Mr Dukakis should now begin to pull in support from the 646 power-brokers known as 'super-delegates'.
>
> *South China Morning Post* 21 Apr 1988

> The Democratic party does not like Mr Carter these days. It has made him a 'superdelegate' to the convention, but this was the least that it could decently do for its only living ex-president.
>
> *Financial Times* 26 April 1988

▶ The extent to which Democratic party delegates to the convention which chooses their presidential candidate have been appointed rather than elected has varied over the years. The notorious wheeling and dealing by party bosses at the 1968 convention in Chicago prompted a change to a totally elected body, but subsequently it was felt that the will of the members needed stiffening with some solid political experience, and the concept of superdelegates was introduced in 1980. The precise proportions of elected and nonelected delegates has since been refined, and for the 1988 convention superdelegates represented 15% of the total, consisting of 250 members of Congress, the 363 members of the Democratic National Committee, 26 governors and five elder statesmen.

super G *noun* super giant slalom: a skiing event intermediate between downhill racing and giant slalom, skied over a shorter course than downhill and with gates spaced at greater intervals than giant slalom

> Pirmin Zurbriggen, after losing both World Ski Championships he had held, the Downhill and Combined, finally gave his bellclanging fans the victory they were waiting for in the Super G at Crans-Montana, Switzerland.
>
> *Daily Telegraph* 3 Feb 1987

▶ This new discipline was admitted to World Cup skiing in 1982/3. The course is essentially a slalom one – the skier has to negotiate a zigzag series of gates – but it is much longer and wider than that for the giant slalom, with higher speeds and larger swing radiuses, and to make downhillers feel even more at home there are standardly two jumps. There has been an element of controversy about its introduction (as favouring the spectacular downhill over the more skill-intensive slalom), particularly since it has on occasion replaced the giant slalom.

supergravity *noun* a hypothetical natural force which includes comparatively weak antigravity as well as gravity

> In supergravity theory, there can be a component which acts like electrical forces, but much more feebly; indeed the theory suggests that it is about one per cent of what we call gravity.
>
> *Guardian* 14 Mar 1986

▶ The theoretical antigravity component of supergravity repels ordinary matter, so it is perhaps fortunate that unlike 'normal' gravity, which exerts its pull over infinite distances, it only acts over a few hundred metres.

supermembrane *noun* a postulated fundamental constituent of matter that is two-dimensional, like a membrane, moving in a third dimension of time

It appeared that the three-dimensional supermembrane (with two spatial dimensions and one time dimension) would form the boundary of the four-dimensional space-time of the real world, rather as the two-dimensional surface of a soap bubble encloses a three-dimensional volume – the membrane at the end of the Universe. ... The supermembrane may cast light on why we live in a four-dimensional space-time. Whatever happens, however, supermembranes, superstrings, or both, will have to confront experiment with testable predictions before the accolade of 'theory of everything' can be finally awarded. And that may prove the most difficult hurdle of all.

New Scientist 30 June 1988

superminicomputer *noun* an advanced powerful minicomputer

The Data General user group has accepted the company's statement which means users who have not taken the latest revision 7.5 can continue to use the older version on their MV superminicomputers.

Computer Weekly 10 Mar 1988

▶ Confusingly, the world of computers currently boasts both *superminicomputers* and MINISUPERCOMPUTERS. The former are simply relatively sophisticated versions of ordinary minicomputers, whereas minisupercomputers are compact versions of the newer breed of supercomputer.

super second *noun* a claret from the Médoc or Graves region which is officially in the second category of excellence, but is generally recognized as being superior to this

Jean-Eugène Borie and his team at Ducru[-Beaucaillou] make a wine fully worthy of the term 'super second.' Indeed, the wine was of super second quality before the expression was even invented.

The Vine May 1987

Despite the fame [Château] Léoville-Poyferré was to enjoy in the inter-war years – it was the leading 'super-second' of its day – the wine of [Château] Camensac [then under the same ownership] never seems to have caused much of a stir.

Decanter Mar 1988

▶ The wines of the Médoc were officially classified in 1855, and four chateaux – Lafite, Latour, and Margaux, plus one interloper from the Graves, Haut-Brion – were categorized as 'first growths.' Naturally, many of those which failed to make the grade felt they had been hard done-by, and indeed Baron Philippe de Rothschild of the second growth Mouton Rothschild campaigned so vigorously on behalf of his wine that in 1973 it was promoted to first-growth status. Over the past decade or so a discernible group of about half a dozen second growths has broken away from the pack (there are 14 in all), being generally recognized as consistently superior in quality to the rest and fetching higher prices than them (though not yet as stratospherically high as those for first growths). Membership of the group is not entirely cut and dried, but most would agree that the following belong: Châteaux Ducru-Beaucaillou, Gruaud-Larose, Léoville-Las Cases, La Mission-Haut-Brion, Palmer, Pichon-Longueville Lalande, and probably Cos d'Estournel.

supersmart card *noun* a SMART CARD with a keyboard and display panel

> The big drawback of smart cards is that, although they know how much is in the holder's acount, they cannot tell the holder. This is where so-called 'supersmart' cards, like those to be tested in Japan by Visa and Toshiba, come in.
>
> *Economist* 30 Apr 1988

▶ The supersmart card's keyboard and display panel enable its owner to interrogate it, to find out, for example, how much money there is in his or her account.

superstring *noun* a postulated fundamental constituent of matter that is one-dimensional like a very thin string

> Hypothetical particles that are the result of efforts to advance the theoretical understanding of matter have also been put forward as the embodiments of missing mass. ... A third possibility is suggested by superstring theory, which ascribes as many as 11 dimensions to spacetime and postulates particles more than 10^{19} times as massive as the proton.
>
> *Scientific American* May 1985

It's been called the theory of everything, a way of describing the very nature of matter. But will superstring theory really tie up all the loose ends?

Radio Times 16 Apr 1988

▶ See SUPERMEMBRANE.

Super Tuesday *noun* the Tuesday, typically in March, on which primary elections and caucuses take place in a large number of US states, often giving a reliable indication of who will eventually be chosen as the parties' presidential candidates

Democratic political consultants are not unmindful of polls showing that most Americans support barriers against imports. In the final days before this week's Super Tuesday voting, Albert Gore tried to slip into Gephart's suit, proclaiming his defense of 'workingmen and -women' and boasting, in North Carolina, of his support for the textile-limit bill.

Newsweek 14 Mar 1988

▶ Super Tuesday sees primary elections or caucuses in Alabama, American Samoa, Arkansas, Florida, Georgia, Hawaii, Idaho, Kentucky, Louisiana, Maryland, Massachusetts, Mississippi, Missouri, Nevada, North Carolina, Oklahoma, Rhode Island, Tennessee, Texas, Virginia, and Washington, in which party members choose the candidate they would like to go forward to the presidential election in November. The other states hold their primaries on other days in the early part of the year, but Super Tuesday accounts for 50.9% of all delegates. In the 1988 campaign it fell on March 8.

survivable *adjective* not liable to be destroyed or damaged

Based on a high capacity network of radio relays, computer switches and trunk 'nodal points,' Ptarmigan provides an area communications system which is survivable, mobile, encrypted and resilient to enemy interference.

Daily Telegraph 26 Apr 1985

For reasons of nuclear strategy and geography, the US has traditionally relied on survivable second-strike weapons such as submarine-launched ballistic missiles.

Christian Science Monitor 24 May 1986

Mr Paul Nitze, the arms-control adviser to the president, has coined a popular set of criteria for judging the suitability of a star-wars weapon. He says that before its deployment can be considered, it must be cost-effective ...; 'survivable' ...; and likely to work.

Economist 26 Mar 1988

▶ The suffix *-able* is standardly passive, not active. Hence one might reasonably expect *survivable* to mean 'able to be survived,' as in 'a survivable crash' (as it usually does), not 'able to survive,' However, at an earlier period in the history of the language this active use was more common (it lies behind *comfortable* and *suitable*) and in fact *survivable* started out this way. The *OED* (1918), which calls it 'rare,' gives examples from the late 19th century, and it is not until as late as the 1960s that the now familiar 'able to be survived' came into use. 'Able to survive' seems to have gone to ground meanwhile, and began to emerge again in the 1970s in military contexts, with reference to weapons systems that can withstand counterattack and go on to deliver their own strike.

survivalist *adjective*   concerned with the hobby of collecting hand weapons (guns, knives, etc) and various other sorts of military equipment, and using them in quasi-military exercises

Worried about the growth of dangerous weapons such as military-style survival knives, cross-bows and garottes, Scotland Yard has ordered a study into the spread of 'survivalist' shops in London.

Daily Telegraph 8 Oct 1987

▶ The phenomenon of survivalism was brought forcibly to public attention in Britain by the so-called 'Hungerford massacre' of 19 August 1987, when in a bizarre series of crazed shootings Michael Ryan killed 16 people and then shot himself. Ryan was a survivalist; in pursuit of this 'hobby,' which appeals to perverted notions of self-reliance and the frontier spirit, he collected and practised with a considerable armoury of guns. But perhaps an even more alarming aspect of survivalism is the associated proliferation of a wide array of lethal knives (e g flick knives and butterfly knives) and similar weapons (e g DEATH STARS) on the streets of inner cities.

suspenser *noun, informal* a suspense film

> *Panic on the 5.22.* Three incompetent hoodlums hold up wealthy train passengers but are frustrated by finding only plastic money in their wallets. Original idea and smarter moments can't sustain unusual suspenser which goes on a bit too long.
> *Time Out* 4 May 1988

▶ *-er* has become quite a popular suffix amongst movie buffs for designating various types of film (for example *oater*, a western and *actioner*, an all-action film).

swaption *noun* an option to take part in an interest swap

> Some of Britain's most left-wing ... councils ... have had their rates ... 'capped' by the central government, and are therefore topping up their resources in other ways. They have discovered that there is money to be made in writing swaptions.
> *Economist* 28 May 1988

▶ In return for making a loan, a bank receives the right, under the terms of a swaption, to force the borrower to pay interest at a floating rate pegged to the current money market once that rate goes above a pre-agreed figure. Swaps, the booming financial business of the mid-1980s, are transactions in which two parties exchange the payments of the interest or principal of debts in such a way that each has debts in a more convenient form (e g long-term rather than short-term, or in dollars rather than sterling).

Swissification *noun* political deradicalization, so that a society or community formerly polarized by political debate agrees on a consensus

Behind this, however, lies the continuing process of the 'Swissification' of Finnish politics. Ideological debate has almost ceased; the
dominant questions are practical ones, export-competitiveness being one main item on the national agenda.

Economist 23 Jan 1988

▶ Switzerland is famous, even notorious, for the blandness
of its political life, all the nation's energy being unanimously directed towards commercial success, not dissipated in
factional arguments.

swivel-wing *adjective* (of an aircraft) having wings that can
be slanted backwards and forwards for optimal performance at different speeds; swing-wing

The swivel-wing Tornado, a rare visitor to Wales, is the product of
trinational co-operation between Britain, Germany and Italy.

Western Mail 27 Jan 1988

synergy *noun* (in business) the potentiality of two individual organizations to be more successful, efficient,
productive, etc when joined together than either of
them had been on its own

The property industry is in an acquisitive mood and ... mergers and
takeovers have become ... commonplace. ... Usually the firms join
forces because a potential synergy is evident. Each bring [sic]
benefits to an enlarged practice which would not exist without the
inter-action of two hitherto unrelated elements.

Daily Telegraph 15 Sept 1987

Daimler puts the customary case for its acquisitive drive, making
much of the 'synergy' all conglomerateurs promise to foster between different parts of their empires.

Economist 12 Dec 1987

▶ *Synergy* in this sense has been around since the 1950s, but
as the second extract suggests, it has suddenly become the
buzzword of the late 1980s in the world of takeover bids. As
ever more (apparently) unlikely partners propose getting
into bed together, shareholders need to be persuaded of the
viability of the merged company. And usually the magic
formula turns out to be synergy, the promise that each

partner has some asset or assets which in isolation are not fully exploited, but when combined produce an exponential growth in effectiveness. Sometimes the claimed synergy is hard to detect. When the merger of British Aerospace and Austin-Rover was proposed in early 1988, for example, various synergetic characteristics were claimed for a partnership which on the face of it seemed ill-matched: it was said, for instance, that Rover's strong links with Honda would provide British Aerospace with improved access to the lucrative Far East market. Critics remained unimpressed, but Austin-Rover chief Graham Day was quoted as saying 'To spot the synergy, you must focus on the manufacturing process, not the product!'

Compare DYSERGY.

tabloid television *noun*   populist television programming designed to appeal to a mass audience by featuring pop music and videos, news and gossip about celebrities, etc

Night Network is in the front of ITV's battle to capture the attention of Britain's viewers, especially young ones, using the latest technique in the broadcasting world: tabloid television.
Sunday Times 28 Feb 1988

Tabloid television in the US is plumbing new depths. ... American television producers have been hurtling downmarket in a search for something extra. Sex and sensation sell. Re-enactments of violent crimes are popular, especially when the real victims play themselves. Love triangles are big on the new tabloid talk shows at the moment.
Listener 25 Aug 1988

▶ The main impetus for the introduction of the typical subject matter and presentation techniques of tabloid newspapers into television has come from the advertisers, who see the young employed as a group whose large spending potential is currently being massively underexploited by television. The idea is that a diet of non-stop popular culture fronted in a relatively unstructured way by unstuffy street-credible presenters will attract this audience as never before and help to syphon off some of its surplus spending power.

tack *noun*   squalid, dirty, untidy conditions; tackiness

'I dedicate my life,' Goldsmith claims solemnly, 'to fighting tackiness. Tack is everywhere. Go into the Underground. Go into the tunnel under the Thames from the Isle of Dogs to Greenwich. Built by Brunel, it could be spectacular, but it stinks like a toilet.'
Sunday Times 3 July 1988

▶ This back formation recalls the longer established *sleaze*, coined from *sleazy*.

tag¹ *noun, slang* a personal symbol, typically a name or other word, sprayed in paint on a wall or other surface in a public place

Two or three friends aged from 12 to 15 are thought to have been on the platform delaying trains by tampering with the doors to give John more time to spray his stylised 'tag' – the single word 'evil' – on the sides of the carriages.

Daily Telegraph 11 Nov 1987

▶ A tag was originally simply a signature to identify the author of a larger piece of graffiti, but it quickly became an object in its own right, used in the practice of tagging (see TAG²).

tag² *verb, slang* to spray one's tag (on)

Danny's friends had talked of how they hated this man ... and would love to tag his house.

Guardian 14 Oct 1987

▶ The craze of tagging, imported from the USA, quickly caught on among young teenagers, and soon spawned its own subculture, with its own vocabulary (see BITING). Armed with spraycans, the youngsters roam around leaving their mark wherever they can: tube trains are a favourite target (one boy, arrested by the police for his pains, admitted to leaving his tag in more than 2000 locations). To those in the know the graffiti-devices, usually bizarre nicknames (Dime, Riz, Rut, Scrime, Sheen, etc) and often very stylishly drawn, are instantly identifiable with their owners. And 'own' is very much the appropriate word: the tags are highly personal but also marketable possessions, which can be sold to the highest bidder when the owner decides to move on to a new one.

tagger *noun, slang* a person who tags

Now, though, there are more taggers than artists, and all they do is 'tag everything in sight' in the street, in buildings, and in particular on the tube.

Times Educational Supplement 21 Aug 1987

tag sale *noun, American* a sale of low-value household items held at the vendor's own home

Rather than sell lowticket items in a tag sale, as Sotheby's has sometimes done in estate auctions, the house is auctioning even the cheapest lots, banking on hoards of fans to bid up prices in their lust for Warhol memorabilia.

Newsweek 18 Apr 1988

▶ The tag sale is in many respects the equivalent of the British car-boot sale (see BOOT SALE), in that it is a means of disposing of old and unwanted clothes, tools, etc, but it takes place in the owner's house, often in the garage (hence the alternative name *garage sale*), rather than in a car park or similar venue. The name refers to the price tags put on the items for sale.

targetry *noun* the setting of aims to be achieved

Industrial countries have as much recent experience that real-growth targetry is worthless as they have that inflation is harmful. Yet politicians retain the language of that targetry, using it most recently at the Tokyo summit.

Economist 31 May 1986

▶ The suffix *-ry*, meaning 'the art or practice of,' is enjoying a minor boom, particularly in the area of international relations. SUMMITRY appears to have set the trend, and *targetry* is almost certainly based on this model.

target tuner *noun* a small radio preset to receive only one frequency

The first people to pass the taste test ... will be given a smart new gadget: a radio the same size as a packet of Swan Vestas, locked into one frequency – that of the local commercial radio station. More than 30,000 of these nifty 'target tuners' will be given away.

Sunday Times 22 May 1988

tarmac *verb, American slang* to go by air in short hops from location to location when electioneering

This year's buzzword is *tarmac* and it is already reaching verb status, as in: 'He spent the day tarmacking across the South.' Linguistic purists in *The New York Times* and the *Chicago Tribune* complained this week, depicting the word as an unwanted immigrant from British English. Americans talk about runways and asphalt.

The Times 17 Mar 1988

tastemaker *noun* an arbiter of what is currently acceptable or fashionable

Whilst import shops here feed the DJs and tastemakers, imports are too expensive and few in number to play a part in the national spread of a scene, so what's available on UK release is crucial.

New Musical Express 15 Aug 1987

Twenty years ago, the idiosyncratic American guitarist John Fahey was the sort of chap who could find himelf being written up in awed tones in publications like *International Times* and the *East Village Other*, his records to be found in hippie tastemakers' pads alongside those of the Velvet Underground, Tim Buckley and the Incredible String Band.

The Times 9 Oct 1987

Behind the scenes of the food business lurk the tastemakers ... an even more shadowy crew of strategists, promoters and pundits, who can mould our very attitudes.

Independent 23 July 1988

▶ This word seems to be used mainly in the context of popular music – it is the pop world's equivalent of the more upmarket *opinion-former*. Compare STYLE COUNSELLOR.

tasting *noun* **– on tasting** (especially of wine) available to be tasted to assess quality

We have no fewer than 14 wines from Penfolds and Tullochs, on FREE tasting. Why not sample them for yourself at any time throughout the weekend of 21 and 22 May. [advertisement]

London Evening Standard 17 May 1988

▶ The basic model for this slightly anomalous phrase seems to be *on show, on view, on sale,* and the like, but the use of the *-ing* form in preference to *on taste* (influenced no doubt by the frequency of *(wine) tasting* as a noun) is a new departure.

tasty *adjective,* *slang* highly attractive or desirable; excellent

It includes the single *Motortown* – a perfect piece of pop if ever I heard one, all jangly guitars and tasty voices – and a brilliant cover version of the old Dennis Edwards song, *Don't Look Any Further.*
Cosmopolitan Sept 1987

Now with two dancefloors that should satisfy both the hot Latin/ Afro-Cuban rhythm-merchants and any Zouk and African fans at this tasty, two floor venue with pub prices at the bar.
Time Out 4 May 1988

▶ It seems quite likely that this broadly approbatory meaning of the adjective developed from the more restricted sense of 'sexually attractive'; its frequent use in the television series *Minder* may partly account for its rise (see HER INDOORS).

tax break *noun* an opportunity for financial gain or for reducing one's tax liability provided by the taxation system (e g the receipt of perks, such as company cars, which are not taxed as heavily as their equivalent in money income would be)

For safety's sake, Lawson should have abjured an overall tax injection and financed tax reform by an aggressive attack on unwarranted tax breaks.
Sunday Times 20 Mar 1988

For a limited time we'll pay all the closing costs we require to open your account. And that could save you hundreds, even without the tax break you'll be getting.
Roanoke Times and World-News 11 Apr 1988

tax therapist *noun,* *American* a tax expert who advises clients on filling in income-tax forms

American nerves are becoming increasingly frayed as the April 15 deadline for tax returns approaches. Confusion and paranoia is at an all-time high, particularly since tax penalties tripled from $3.5 billion in 1986 to $9.9 billion in 1987 following complicated new tax laws. Los Angeles tax lawyer Joyce Rebhum has now placed a notice outside her office offering her services as a 'tax therapist.'
Daily Telegraph 6 Apr 1988

▶ The formidable US income-tax forms, like mini telephone directories beside which British tax returns look distinctly undernourished, take an inordinate amount of time to fill in, and are a major undertaking of the year.

teabagging *noun,* *informal* the partial submersion of helmsman and crew when hanging over the side of a boat while attached to a wire

The wings [seatlike arrangements attached to the side of the boat] meant that teabagging, when twin-wiring helmsperson and crew settle in the water, is not that likely a pastime.

Yachts and Yachting 8 July 1988

techno-babble *noun,* *derogatory* jargon used by technologists, full of high-sounding technical terms incomprehensible to the lay person

[The magazine *Nam*, about the Vietnam War] is written, too, in that pacy, knowledgeable language of warfare, studded with acronym and techno-babble.

Daily Telegraph 11 Sept 1987

The English language is being murdered by people in the computer industry, according to a computer expert. Their 'techno-babble' includes words and phrases such as 'analysation' instead of analysis.

Daily Telegraph 22 Sept 1987

▶ On the use of *babble* as a combining form, see SOCIO-BABBLE.

technology transfer *noun* the making available of technological expertise and hardware by those who possess it to those who do not

And Chancellor Helmut Kohl told Hu that 'West German industry is ready for comprehensive industrial cooperation with your country and for an extensive technology transfer.'

Newsweek 30 June 1986

teen *noun* a teenager

A neighbourhood teen burst in. Darden shot him in the face, too, but the 16-year-old escaped.

Newsweek 8 Feb 1988

Sixties pop produced the Supremes: three teens from a housing project who re-sculpted radio fodder as sophisticated showbiz.

City Limits 18 Feb 1988

telebook *noun* a book published to accompany, and give further background detail relating to, a television series

'Roosevelt's Children' belongs to the new hybrid genus, the tele-book. It is a record and analysis of interviews carried out for the current series of Channel 4 programmes and aims at painting a collective portrait of a generation of future world leaders.

Daily Telegraph 12 June 1987

telecomms *noun, informal* telecommunications

Its work will cover proposals on high technology, telecomms and public procurement.

Computer Weekly 10 Mar 1988

▶ Compare COMMS.

teledish *noun* a dish-shaped aerial for receiving satellite television transmissions

There was not a building, antenna, teledish, electric sign or billboard to be seen.

Blitz Apr 1988

▶ Compare SQUAERIAL.

telenovela *noun* (especially in South and Central America) a romantic television soap opera

Continuing his study of a continent and its societies, Jack Pizzey probes the South American psyche, seeking to establish what it is that fires the South American souls by investigating shared passions – for bullfighting, for boxing, and for the telenovelas..., which can draw 56 million viewers every night.

Guardian 6 June 1986

tele-operated *adjective* remote-controlled

It is difficult to predict exactly when remotely controlled feller-bunchers will be available on the market, but Lawrence is hopeful that the world's largest tele-operated robots will be at work felling in Canadian forests 'within a couple of years.'

New Scientist 17 Mar 1988

televangelism *noun*   the activities of a televangelist

Since his father dropped televangelism to pursue the Republican nomination for president, Tim Robertson has tried to assume his father's role as cohost, primary prayer leader and chief fund raiser of The Christian Broadcasting Network.

Newsweek 8 Feb 1988

televangelist *noun*   (especially in the USA) a Christian minister, typically of a Pentecostal church, who hosts television shows in which the church's message is preached with great fervour and donations are sought

Robertson, the aging doyen of the breed now generally ... known as 'televangelists' announced some time ago that unless the faithful stumped up to the tune of $8 million by March 31, he was going to be 'called home'.

Daily Telegraph 10 Apr 1987

Mr Robertson's religious-right supporters ... are likely to be un-affected by the come-uppance of a fire-and-brimstone televangelist.

Economist 27 Feb 1988

▶ Religious broadcasting in the USA is an altogether different matter from the rather staid British version. The Christian message is sugared with (indeed some would say lost among) a shower of Hollywood-style glitz. The born-again zeal with which the televangelists preach their fundamentalist gospel has gained enormous popularity, and has no doubt contributed to the rise of the MORAL MAJORITY (many have seen this 'electronic religion' as contributing to the electoral success of the Baptist Jimmy Carter and of Ronald Reagan). Those, on the other hand, who view these egregious performers as whited sepulchres have had their suspicions confirmed with recent revelations that two leading televangelists, Jim Bakker and Jimmy Swaggart, are not the blameless citizens they would have their congregations-cum-audiences believe: Bakker, head of the PTL club (it stands for People That Love and Praise The Lord, but has been alternatively interpreted as Pass The Loot), confessed in 1987 to having had an affair with a church secretary; and in 1988 the Louisiana ranter Swaggart (the televangelist with the largest audience) was unfrocked by the Assemblies of God for having committed 'lewd acts' with a prostitute. These scandals, and also the departure of Pat Robertson (who founded the Christian Broadcasting Network in 1965) to fight for the Republican presidential nomination, led to a big slump in audience figures and in donations in 1987.

terrain *noun* PISTE

> As American football and Australian rules are entering English sporting consciousness through TV, pétanque may well follow via pub car parks and purpose built 'terrains,' like those in Hampshire.
>
> *Daily Telegraph* 26 Feb 1986

terrestrial *adjective* (of television transmissions) carried out from conventional ground stations rather than by satellite

> A radical plan to make BBC2 and Channel Four available only to viewers with satellite TV dishes is being examined by the Government. ... 'BBC2 and Channel Four would continue to be transmitted terrestrially for a number of years,' the Home Office said yesterday. 'If and when terrestrial transmission ceased....'
>
> *Daily Telegraph* 11 June 1988

> The Government's proposal ... will open up terrestrial competition by freeing capacity, and will act as a loaded gun at Murdoch, who will be faced with the prospect of competition from three or four terrestrial channels.
>
> *Campaign* 1 July 1988

tetrahydroamino-acridine *noun* (*abbreviation* **THA**) a drug being tested for use in the treatment of Alzheimer's disease

> Treatment: there is currently a lot of interest in a drug called Tetrahydroamino-acridine (THA). This prolongs the life of acetyl choline (ACH), a neurotransmitter, or chemical messenger, in the brain which is important for memory and which breaks down in Alzheimer sufferers. Studies on the drug are now underway in America and Britain.
>
> *Observer* 22 May 1988

theatrically *adverb*   in cinemas

> Never released theatrically in this country, this [*I'm Dancing As Fast As I Can*, 1982 film] sounds like it might be worth a look, if only for the acting.
>
> *Time Out* 16 Mar 1988

▶ The usage is of US origin: in American English 'theater,' or 'movie theater,' is a standard term for 'cinema.'

theme *noun*   a topic or subject which forms the basis of an activity or presentation

> Crest is to launch a new style of theme restaurant at its Cardiff hotel this summer. ... The theme revolves around the fictional Cornelius Cook setting off from Cardiff on a trip to North Africa.
>
> *London Evening Standard* 10 May 1988

> Connoisseurs of bad taste will love the whole page colour illustrations of 'theme' cakes. The 'cherub and mandolin' is a 'romantic engagement cake' prepared, appropriately enough, for 'Ryan and Sonja.'
>
> *Decanter* May 1988

▶ The word *theme* conventionally refers to the topic of a work of art or of a discourse, and this extended sense probably started life with the *theme park*, an amusement park in which the structures and settings are all based on a specific theme, such as space travel.

themed *adjective*   provided with a particular THEME

> A real theme park consists of discrete 'themed' environments, like film sets where not only facades but entire buildings have been constructed to create the illusion of another time, another place. ... Disneyland and its offspring ... incorporate several themed areas.
>
> *Economist* 11 Jan 1986

> Cashier/receptionist reqd. for fashionable themed restaurant in the City.
>
> *London Evening Standard* 1 Apr 1986

> Food is themed too, where the Bum Steer Trading Post vies with Ma Eat's chicken 'n' ribs.
>
> *Sunday Times* 3 July 1988

thermal pulse *noun* a spreading wave of heat generated by a nuclear explosion

Put simply, the thermal pulse from a nuclear explosion ignites materials over a wide area, starting both city fires and forest fires.
New Scientist 2 Jan 1986

thigmorphogenesis *noun* the response of plants to mechanical stimuli, including tactile stimuli

Greenhouse plants should be given a quick daily stroke to toughen them up, according to Professor Mordecai Jaffe. ... His group investigates the stroking of plants ... thigmorphogenesis.
Daily Telegraph 24 Nov 1986

▶ The effect of mechanical stimulation on plant growth was first studied by Professor Mordecai Jaffe of Wake Forest University, N Carolina, USA, and indeed it was he who coined the term (from Greek *thigma* 'touch'). In practice, for plants in their natural environment it is a mechanism for adaptation to wind: trees in windy places, for example, respond to being blown about by growing more cells around their circumference, making them thicker and stiffer. But to some extent the effect can be reproduced for houseplants; according to Professor Jaffe, stroking plants makes them squatter, tougher, and more resistant to disease and drought than plants which have been ignored.

thin cat *noun, informal* a person without wealth, privilege, or influence

The Bar's concern that solicitors in the big City firms ... are attracting most of the new entrants to the legal profession is shared by solicitors outside the City. If the High Street solicitors who act for individuals rather than corporations cannot attract articled clerks and junior solicitors, then what is going to happen in, say, five years from now? Who will help these individuals with their problems? Who will undertake the 'thin-cat' legal aid work?
Daily Telegraph 9 June 1988

▶ The *fat cat* on whom this coinage is based was originally a provider of funds to political parties in the USA in the 1920s, but has since come to mean simply an unduly rich person who uses his wealth to control affairs.

thrash *noun* SPEED-METAL

All thrash albums are not created equal, that much even a nonce like myself understands. Not everyone who learns to pussy-whip a guitar to within an inch of its electrical existence can necessarily generate Metallica style credentials.

Kerrang 11 June 1987

thrashcore *noun* SPEED-METAL

Richard Grabel reports from New York City, crossing point of hardcore and metal – birth place of speed-metal. ... Speed-metal is the largest, most vital cult in American rock. Metallica are the reigning gods, easily selling out large arenas, and on the next rung down, the speed-metal/thrashcore shows promoted at New York's Ritz by the Rock Hotel organisation are also regular sell-outs.

New Musical Express 21 Mar 1987

thrash metal *noun* SPEED-METAL

In a form of music which has never encouraged innovation, a new strain has emerged called thrash metal, which seeks to invest classical HM [heavy metal] with the dynamics of punk.

Daily Telegraph 4 Apr 1987

Thrash metal, like [the band] Slayer, originated in California, where heavy metal fans ... were prepared to acknowledge the similarities between punk and metal, and that the new form had something to offer the old: an extra violence, lyrics that were easier to write than all that fanciful stuff about men with big swords riding around on horses.

Daily Telegraph 24 Apr 1987

Anthrax are a thrash metal band named after a sheep disease; with all respect to the sheep, the disease is almost certainly preferable to the band. Thrash metal is a form of music – if one is being broad-minded – designed for those who found punk too melodious or subtle.

Daily Telegraph 4 May 1987

throat ball *noun* (in cricket) a fast short-pitched ball aimed at the batsman's throat, with intimidatory intent

In the [West Indies] there were the likes of Marshall, Garner, Holding, Courtney Walsh and ... Patrick Patterson, constantly assailing the England batsmen with 'throat balls.'

Frances Edmonds, *Cricket XXXX Cricket* 1987

ticket broker *noun, euphemistic* a ticket tout

> The inner-sanctum top brass pop their collar studs over the hospitality pirates, but they rage even more purple over the ticket touts who – let's not shilly-shally – make the whole corporate circus at Wimbledon possible. This year one arrested tout announced himself as a 'ticket broker,' another as a 'turnstile executive.'
>
> *Byline*, BBC1, 22 Aug 1988

tilt-rotor *noun* an aircraft having rotors mounted on the end of short wings, allowing it to take off vertically and hover like a helicopter and to fly like a fixed-wing aeroplane

> Even if tilt-rotors are not flying in and out of Docklands in the 1990s, the US's armed forces will be transporting troops or military provisions between bases in tilt-rotors.
>
> *New Scientist* 1 Oct 1987

> A unique tilt-rotor aircraft, due to make its first flight on Aug 15, will roll out for its public debut at Fort Worth, Texas, this morning.
>
> *Daily Telegraph* 23 May 1988

▶ The V-22 Osprey tilt-rotor aircraft, developed in the USA by Bell Helicopters and Boeing Helicopters, is the realization of a design that dates back to the 1950s but was never feasible until new lightweight materials became available.

time-graft *noun* a person or thing removed artificially from one time period and imposed on another

> Harry Perkins [in *A Very British Coup*] couldn't happen because he is a time-graft, an authentic worker from the days of mass unionism, heavy boots and proletarian solidarity. He is a Lech Walesa or an Ernie Bevin without the distressing encumbrance of their opinions.
>
> *Sunday Times* 3 July 1988

tin parachute *noun* a contractual guarantee of financial compensation to all the employees of a company if it is taken over

> The big furniture manufacturer, Herman Miller Inc, in Zeeland, Michigan, disclosed yesterday how a tin-parachute ploy had a remarkably reassuring effect on its workforce of 3,300.
>
> *Daily Telegraph* 20 Mar 1987

▶ Golden parachutes have existed since 1982 (see *Longman Guardian New Words*), but the tin parachute is a new development along the same lines. As its name suggests, it is a rather less grand affair; for whereas golden parachutes guarantee large payments to the top executives of a company, the tin version distributes the benefits over the whole workforce. They are both forms of 'poison pill,' intended to scare off potential takeover predators by facing them with a huge compensation bill should they be successful.

tizzy *adjective, informal* (of sound) tinny and buzzing

> Since Sony invented the Walkman, the Japanese electronics industry has flooded the world with millions of similar gadgets. Although they envelop the user in a cocoon of personal music, the headphones let enough tizzy sound leak out to infuriate anyone sitting or standing close by.
>
> *New Scientist* 31 Mar 1988

toss *verb, Australian slang* to defeat

> Everyone realises Canberra [Rugby team] is very hard to toss at home, but the confidence is very high that we can beat them.
>
> *Daily Telegraph* (Sydney) 15 Apr 1988

totting *noun, British dialect* a method of catching eels by baiting a thin line with a worm which the eel bites, so entangling its teeth in the line

> Few young people take part in totting, which is largely practised as a sport, although eels still have a place on the national menu.
>
> *Guardian* 3 May 1988

▶ The word is not recorded in the *English Dialect Dictionary*.

touch dancing *noun, chiefly American* DIRTY DANCING

> Touch Dancing is the closest you can get to making love with a stranger without actually taking your clothes off.
>
> *London Evening Standard* 20 Oct 1987

touchy-feely *adjective, informal derogatory* characteristic of the sort of group therapy which stresses the importance of mutual touching

> He shrugs off the stigma attached to group therapy such as that undergone by the New Zealand Government. 'I think Lange is doing something terrific. It is not 'touchy-feely' or trendy. It is a good team-building session like any good football team.'
> *Sydney Morning Herald* 13 Apr 1988

▶ *Touchy-feely* is essentially a term of ridicule coined by those who find the sort of tactile awareness promoted by certain psychotherapists – emphasizing the need for people to touch each other in order to get in touch with their own feelings – risible, or perhaps threatening. The particular formation of the compound may owe something to the infatuated old lady's repeated appeals to Zero Mostel to 'Hold me, touch me!' in Mel Brooks's film *The Producers.*

towie *noun, Australian* the driver of a breakdown lorry

> Len, who doubles as secretary of the Auto Recovery Association, has been a towie for 30 years and 'on-call' continuously for the last nine.
> *Sydney Morning Herald* 13 Apr 1988

▶ The word is based on *tow truck*, Australian English for *breakdown lorry*. Australians are fond of making familiar forms with often abbreviatory suffixes: *-ie* is perhaps the commonest, as in *cosie* (for 'costume'), *tinnie* (for 'tin'), although *-o* is not far behind.

toy-boy *noun* a young man who is the lover of (and often kept by) an older woman

> Their romance has survived 'savage' toyboy snipes. 'I know what people think,' he said. 'But we have a great relationship that will last. I'm not bothered by the "older woman syndrome".'
> *Sunday Mirror* 11 Aug 1985

> Rumour has it that she prefers the company of older men. ... No toy boys for her.
> *Cosmopolitan* June 1987

Walton was relatively new to the business after years of being
something of a toy-boy to the Mitford clan.

Punch Feb 1988

▶ A word which manages to combine derogation with envy;
it has been around since the early 1980s, but the slight metaphoricization of the third extract above suggests that it is
now well established.

toytoon *noun* an animated cartoon for children featuring
characters of which models can be bought as toys

Toys with ties to television shows 'reached saturation point' –
about 40 – last year, says Rick Anguilla, editor of *Toy and Hobby
World* magazine. Expect fewer toytoons in 1988.

USA Today 8 Feb 1988

▶ Children's traditional importuning of their parents for
toys has been given a new twist in the 1980s with the deliberate tying in of a television series with toys. In many cases
the two come as a prepared package, and as soon as a particular character or set of characters has received television exposure, a version of it is available in toy shops. The
dividing line between programming and advertising becomes ever thinner.

TPA *noun* tissue plasmogen activator: a drug used for
dissolving blood clots

The latest drug to be approved by the Food and Drug Administration (FDA), Genetech's TPA ..., looks like being biotechnology's
first moneyspinner. ... Several companies are already developing
second-generation TPAs.

Economist 30 Apr 1988

▶ The biotechnological intervention alluded to in the above
extract is the alteration of TPA's genetic structure by a
technique known as PROTEIN ENGINEERING in order to
prolong its effective life in the bloodstream.

tracker *noun* someone officially appointed to accompany
or check on the movements of a convicted person, to
ensure that he or she stays out of trouble

When the tracker makes appointments, Charlie has to turn up....
The tracker turns up in the most unexpected places, to make sure
Charlie keeps his word.

6 O'Clock News, BBC1, 14 July 1988

▶ Tracking is one of various methods of community supervision for convicted criminals being explored as alternatives to long prison sentences.

trail *verb* **1** to advertise in advance in or by means of a
trailer

Written by Carla Lane ... the series promised to be a treat. But it
failed to rise to the occasion: the laughs, spread very thin and
sandwiched between wodges of waffle, had all been trailed for days.

News of the World 4 May 1986

2 to give advance notice or indication of

Last Friday's 135 dismissals from Woodmac and County Nat-
West were well trailed and given market conditions, inevitable.

Daily Telegraph 25 Jan 1988

train surfer *noun* a person who engages in TRAIN SURFING

Standing on top of fast commuter trains with their arms tucked in,
train surfers show their skills by dodging 3,300-volt electrical
cables, while keeping their balance to avoid falling down on to the
gravel.

Daily Telegraph 15 July 1988

train surfing *noun* the practice of riding on the outside of a
moving train as a 'sport' or for a dare

Train surfing ... has already claimed its first victim here. An 18-
year-old 'surfer' was critically injured when he fell from a train on
the London Underground.

Star 28 July 1988

▶ The craze of train surfing began in the USA, apparently
as a development of so-called 'urban surfing,' the practice of
hitching rides on the roof of moving cars, inspired by the
cult film *Teenwolf*. It has been responsible for killing or
seriously injuring scores of American teenagers, and has
also become a dangerous cult in Rio de Janeiro.

tranche *noun*   any of a number of groups or sections into which a whole is divided

The intention is to call them [women due for cervical smears] in tranches over a period of five years.

Edwina Currie, 28 Mar 1988

The six contributors [to *The Oxford Illustrated History of Medieval Europe*] operate in two sub-teams of three, and break down the history of their respective segments into three temporal *tranches* (400-900, 900-1200, 1200-1500).

Sunday Times 3 Apr 1988

▶ The word *tranche* (literally, in French, a 'slice') has a fairly long pedigree in the world of stocks and shares, where it means 'a block of shares, usually supplementary to an already existing issue.' The signs are, though, that it is now acquiring a much more general meaning. Its rise may be helped to some extent by a growing awareness of another specialized (French) meaning of the word, 'a portion of the annual production of a wine which is issued at one time':

Each new tranche will normally be sold at a higher ... price than the last. In other words the first tranche is the cheapest.

Decanter Apr 1988

transdermal *adjective*   acting through the skin

The best-known new method on the market is the transdermal patch, which adheres to the skin like a bandage and secretes the drug in a constant dosage through the skin into the blood stream.

Turkish Daily News 23 May 1988

transgenic *adjective*   (of an animal or plant) produced by the artificial insertion of genetic material from one species into another

Other teams around the world have produced transgenic mice and American researchers had inserted human growth hormone last year into pigs.

New Scientist 10 July 1986

ABC ... has already produced two generations of transgenic pigs which contain a growth hormone gene.

Daily Telegraph 24 June 1987

trash *noun, American slang* a lap-top computer

> For a crash course in the campaign lexicon, the novice may always turn to the hotline. This indispensable tool is a computerized compilation of inside dope, press gossip and comment prepared before dawn by an enterprising group of campaign junkies in Washington. Downloading the hotline into your trash... is an essential ritual before hitting the daily trail anywhere in America.
> *The Times* 17 Mar 1988

treebank *noun* a store in which a range of tree seeds and related material is held in reserve

> Since the late 1970s there have been no treebanks to provide local authorities and private individuals with young trees. The Greater London Council, which has a statutory requirement to provide treebanks, quietly closed them down.
> *Environment Now* Dec 1987

▶ The need for the capacity to regenerate a large proportion of an area's tree stocks was highlighted in Britain by the great gale of October 1987, which cut great swathes through the woods and parklands of Southern England.

tree bending *noun* a phenomenon which affects trees when their natural bending frequency coincides with gusts of wind, which accentuate the bending and may break or uproot them

> Scientists from the Institute of Terrestrial Ecology are investigating the mechanics of tree bending, which fells hundreds and thousands of trees every year.
> *New Scientist* 10 Dec 1987

▶ The various effects of high winds on trees were highlighted in Britain by the great gale of October 1987. The colloquial expression used in the forestry industry for *tree bending* is *wind waggle*.

tregnum *noun* a wine bottle holding three times the amount of a standard bottle, or approximately 2.25 litres

Believed to be of Scottish origin, a tappit-hen can vary, according
to which definition one follows, from 1½ bottles to a tregnum or
3-bottle bottle.
Catalogue, Christie's Finest and Rarest Wines 23 June 1988

▶ A coinage formed from *tre-* (an alternation of *tri-*) and
magnum (a two-bottle bottle).

trick roll *noun, slang* a prostitute who lures a customer
into a situation where he can be attacked or robbed

Wendy's profession as a prostitute with a reputation as a 'trick roll'
... made her just another specially vulnerable statistic in a very
common story.
Observer Magazine 10 Jan 1988

trim trail *noun* a prepared cross-country track for jogging,
with additional facilities for other sorts of exercise

The 340-acre site will include dry ski and toboggan runs down the
slag heap, a motel and what the developers call 'trim trails,' leisure
jargon for jogging tracks with 'exercise stations.'
Daily Telegraph 24 Aug 1987

Trojan horse *noun* a computer program deliberately intended to damage the computer it is used with, sold
maliciously under the guise of ordinary computer software

Trojan horses are the creations of a particularly warped mind.
Their purpose is intentionally to damage the computer system that
they are run on. Usually they will aim to destroy other equipment
too.
New Scientist 28 Jan 1988

▶ The legendary Trojan horse was the massive wooden
horse constructed by the Greeks besieging Troy. Having
filled the horse with soldiers, they tricked the Trojans into
taking it into their city and thus were able to conquer Troy
from within. There have been previous metaphorical uses
of *Trojan horse* – *Webster's Third New International Dictionary* (1961) defines it as 'a person, organization, or factor
that is intended or likely to undermine an established institution' – but its latest application seems particularly apt.
See also BOGUSWARE.

trunk show *noun, chiefly American* a private viewing of new dress fashions for wealthy prospective customers

The spend spend spend set who change outfits at least three times a day as they shop, lunch and socialise at charity events, does exist this side of the Atlantic, and its members expect a personal service when spending up to £3,000 on an evening dress. An invitation to a favourite designer's trunk show makes them feel they are getting just that.

Sunday Times 3 July 1988

tweak *verb, American slang* (of a drug addict) to exhibit withdrawal symptoms such as twitching, when unable to get a fix

Up the block in the men's room in a gay pickup bar, a more typical scene is played out. 'You want to go all night?' a well dressed man is asking a fat blond teenager. 'No. man, I can't do that again. I'm whipped and I'm tweaking.'

Newsweek 25 Apr 1988

twin-track *adjective* (especially of a proposal for nuclear arms reduction) reciprocal

At the outset in 1979 ... Nato proposed that all LRINF (longer range) missiles should be withdrawn from Europe. The motive was to prevent Soviet deployment of its versatile and menacing SS-20, against which Nato emplaced cruise and Pershing II, stating that it would reverse deployment when the Soviet Union did likewise. This 'twin-track' offer evoked no response until the Reykjavik meeting last October when Mr Gorbachev offered not only to meet it but to go further.

Daily Telegraph 21 May 1987

▶ See ZERO OPTION.

tycoonography *noun* a biography of a business tycoon

The big bang in the City seems to be having its reverberations in publishing and hardly a week passes without the appearance of yet another example of that new and highly popular literary genre, the tycoonography.

Observer 10 May 1987

▶ In characteristic style Mr Robert Maxwell, proprietor of the *Daily Mirror*, contrived to lead in this as in other fields, having three tycoonographies of himself in print simultaneously in 1988: *Maxwell*, by Joe Haines; *Maxwell – The Outsider*, by Tom Bower; and *Maxwell – A Portrait of Power*, by Peter Thompson and Anthony Delano (which, following representations by Mr Maxwell, was banned by the High Court and ordered to be pulped). Compare AUTO-HAGIOGRAPHY.

uncap *verb* to remove an upper limit on

> He [Nigel Lawson] also converted to the faith of exchange-rate
> stability, especially of the pound against the D-mark; last week he
> had to uncap sterling, and what he said this week about exchange-
> rate policy was neither clear nor compelling.
>> *Economist* 19 Mar 1988

> Sir Alan [Walters] is understood to have been influential in the
> Prime Minister's decision earlier this year to 'uncap' the pound,
> which resulted in a public clash between Mrs Thatcher and the
> Chancellor.
>> *Daily Telegraph* 16 July 1988

▶ The notion of 'capping' came into prominence in Britain
in the early 1980s, with the Conservative government's rate-
capping policy – imposing an upper limit on the rates local
authorities were allowed to levy.

unijambist *adjective* one-legged

> The visual style is Renoir on a compost heap: the mournful
> syphilitic young man is trailed by death, debauchery, disease, and
> a unijambist beggar through landscapes of luxury and pleasure.
>> *Listener* 31 Mar 1988

▶ The word is a borrowing of French *unijambiste*.

unimpress *verb* to leave (someone) unimpressed; fail to
impress

> Sir Ian's credentials were impeccable, he asserted, and his record
> spoke for itself. But his plea unimpressed the vast majority of
> shareholders present.
>> *Daily Telegraph* 28 Aug 1987

▶ This formation represents an interesting blend of what
are in fact two etymologically distinct *un-* prefixes. The
word *unimpressed* uses the standard adjectival prefix *un-*,

meaning simply 'not,' but the prefix *un-* used with verbs generally carries the sense of reversal or removal (as in *undress, unfold, untie*) rather than a bare negative. *Unimpress* therefore appears to suggest that someone was at first impressed, but became less so – was 'disimpressed,' in fact – but that does not seem to be what the coiner had in mind in the above passage.

untie *verb* to allow private sector companies to compete for (government business)

> The PSA's civil business has already been 'untied' ... from 1 April, and civil service union leaders fear the removal of guaranteed military work will lead to the collapse of the massive organisation.
> *Independent* 25 May 1988

up and running *adjective* currently viable; having got under way

> Lori Miles ... has been appointed editor of the *London Evening News*. ... 'They've convinced me it's an up and running entity, a goer,' she said of the paper that was launched in February.
> *UK Press Gazette* 18 May 1987

> There's no up-and-running alternative that either works or can be administered.
> Nicholas Ridley, *Breakfast Time*, BBC1, 19 Apr 1988

▶ The metaphor probably derives from computers, which when they are in working order are said to be *up* (as opposed to their apparently more usual condition of being *down*, or out of order).

upchuck *verb, informal* to vomit

> The quickest way to upchuck at present is to watch Patsy Kensit miming her new record on Top of the Pops.
> *Sunday Times* 24 Apr 1988

▶ According to Wentworth and Flexner's *Dictionary of American Slang*, this was in the USA 'considered a smart and sophisticated term around 1935, especially when applied to sickness that had been induced by overdrinking.' Its move into British English, however, seems comparatively recent.

The placing of the adverbial particle in front of the verb for emphatic effect is a fairly familiar device in English, but comparatively few of these prefixed forms gain a permanent place in the language; indeed, some coinages rather similar to *upchuck* have been tried in the past and faltered:

Theire steed hath upvomited from gorge a surfet of armd men.
Richard Stanyhurst, *Aeneis* 1582

Til from their inly Maw their Loads they did upspew.
Samuel Croxall, *An original canto of Spenser* 1714

up-front *adjective, informal* positive; outgoing; extrovert

Vaughan Richards, of the AMMA union, held up a newspaper cutting accusing Labour of being 'lacklustre' in opposing the Bill. Party member John Rogers criticised Labour's education spokesman Jack Straw – 'He has not been up-front enough.'
Western Mail 27 Jan 1988

Everybody who's involved in kind of upfront stuff needs to have an ego and I don't think there's anything wrong with that.
Blitz Mar 1988

▶ *Up-front* is undergoing an interesting progression of metaphorical meaning. The literal notion of being in front of or before others produced more or less simultaneously in the late 1960s and early 1970s the 'up-front' payment (payment in advance) and the more figurative sense 'frank and honest, not concealing anything.' It appears that approval may be now being transferred from 'lack of concealment' to 'lack of reserve.'

up-frontness *noun, informal* the quality of being UP-FRONT

When Degsy was young he wanted to be an actor for a while, loving the 'upfrontness' of it. 'Upfrontness' is a word he uses a lot, covering everything from hype to hyperbole. He loves to be looked at, to act.
Blitz Mar 1988

upscale *adjective*   high in status or prestige; upmarket

Conde Nast Publications Inc. is launching a revamped version of its House and Garden magazine today in a bid to regain some ground in the increasingly crowded field of upscale magazines about the home.

Wall Street Journal 8 Feb 1988

Mrs Reagan is unhappy about the presidential retirement home. ... 'She'd rather be a little more upscale,' says a friend. ... The house is the least fancy dwelling in the neighborhood.

Newsweek 25 Apr 1988

Cosmetics companies are ... courting the upscale cradle set with fragrances, soaps, shampoos and even a scent for those born yesterday.

The Gazette (Montreal) 17 May 1988

ursaphobic *adjective*   frightened of or anxious about bears

Iceland was in the throes of an ursaphobic fit on Monday after hunters near the northern hamlet of Haganesvik said they had shot and killed a dog-sized polar bear cub. A nationwide alert was issued for fear the cub's mother and other vicious bears could be approaching on fleets of ice floes.

Daily Telegraph 16 Feb 1988

▶ *Ursus* is Latin for 'bear'. Purists who deprecate linguistic miscegenation of the *television* type, in which a compound is formed from a Latin element and a Greek element, would no doubt prefer *arctophobic*, *arktos* being the Greek for 'bear.'

V

vaccine *noun* a piece of software designed to counteract ELECTRONIC VIRUSES

Electronic 'vaccines' have been invented to combat viruses. One such product is Safeguard, being sold by the London firm Prosoft ... for £175. 'Prosoft will check a legitimate program to make sure that no alterations have been made to it since it was last run,' says the firm's manager Robert Mathias.

Daily Telegraph 13 June 1988

vad *noun* value-added and data: a communications network with additional data services

This joint government and industry initiative aims to promote the use of value added and data services (vads).

Computer Weekly 10 Mar 1988

▶ Value-added networks or Vans (see *Longman Guardian New Words*) are communications services which as well as transmitting data via a common carrier offer some sort of extra (added-value) facility, such as a particular sort of software. In the case of *vads* this is specifically a data service. A notable example is British Telecom's Prestel.

value-added *noun* the amount by which the value of an article is increased at each stage of its manufacturing process

It is a mistake to make rigid distinctions between high tech and low tech in industry. What really matters is the value added. Dutch agriculture shows examples of slick marketing and the application of advanced information technology to increase value-added.

Economist 12 Sept 1987

The Q Guild [of butchers] insists on rigorous inspection for quality of meat, hanging, cutting and so on, for decent premises and service, for charcuterie (in the trade jargon, value-added products).

Observer 11 Sept 1988

▶ An economist's term which has come increasingly out of the textbook and the lecture hall into the public domain in the 1980s – a sign of the ever-intensifying quest for cost-effectiveness.

Technically, value-added tax is a tax on this 'value-added,' although in practice it operates as a form of purchase tax.

vapourware *noun* newly-developed computer software or hardware whose introduction has been announced but which is not yet actually available for purchase

Last week saw the third running of the annual European Unix User Show. This year the show was at Olympia. It saw some 130 exhibitors offering mostly real and buyable products rather than the vapourware promises of past years.
Daily Telegraph 9 June 1986

In an industry noted for producing almost as much 'vapourware' as hardware and software, the past six months have seen some of the most vaporous of desktop hyperbole.
Economist 24 Jan 1987

Even people who make no use of computers are probably familiar with some of the jargon, for instance 'hardware' and 'software' which denote, respectively, the physical equipment used and the programs people happily run on their computers. In a more humorous vein computer folk also speak of ... 'vapourware,' products announced at exhibitions but not yet ready for sale.
New Scientist 28 Jan 1988

varroasis *noun* a serious disease of bees caused by a parasitic mite, *Varroa jacobsonii*

Another more pervasive hazard [in bee-keeping] is on the horizon. It is an epidemic, called varroasis, that has swept every continent except Australasia and Antarctica but has apparently not reached Britain yet.
New Scientist 12 Nov 1987

▶ The microscopic mite which causes this disease is native to the Far East, but the species of bee living in that area can tolerate its presence. However, when colonies of western bees were introduced there, an epidemic of infestation was sparked off which is now causing great alarm to bee-keepers throughout the world. The mites feed on the blood of larvae, giving rise to deformed adults, and as the number of mites rapidly multiplies they can wipe out entire colonies.

The mite was named in 1904, by A C Oudemans, after the Roman author Marcus Terentius Varro, who wrote on bee-keeping.

veg out *verb,   Australian slang*   to live a passive monotonous existence; vegetate

'The Government gives us $50 a fortnight to live on and they wonder why there is trouble,' said Daphne Bates, 16. 'We can't afford to go out, we can't even afford to buy clothes to go to job interviews. What do you do? You tend to just veg out.'
Daily Telegraph (Sydney) 13 Apr 1988

veinprint *noun*   a pattern of veins on the back of the hand, which is distinctive for each individual

Because a veinprint is very unlikely to be used as police evidence, people will be less worried about having it on file.
Tomorrow's World, BBC1, 21 Apr 1988

▶ The veins on the back of the hand form a pattern rather like a bar code, which can be read with an infrared sensor (blood absorbs the infrared, other tissues reflect it). It is envisaged that the unique nature of everyone's pattern will enable veinprints to be used as a foolproof personal identification on 'smart' cash cards and the like: pass the sensor-equipped card over the back of one's hand, and it will allow one to withdraw money from one's account via a dispenser.

Velcro *verb*   to be fastened by means of Velcro

Duvets have become increasingly sophisticated and you can now buy one which consists of two different weight duvets which Velcro together to give extra warmth in winter.
Ideal Home Nov 1987

▶ Velcro joins the long list of proprietary names, from the now defunct *to Kodak* ('photograph with a Kodak') to the commonplace *to hoover* ('clean with a hoover'), that have been turned into verbs.

velocious *adjective,* *formal* fast

> Cycling clubs fought for better roads, for improved eating and lodging facilities, for road-signs. But dominion over the roadway would go to more velocious vehicles.
>
> *Times Literary Supplement* 26 Feb 1988

▶ Not a new word, but distinctly a revival. As a pedantic Latinism it enjoyed a certain vogue in the 17th and 18th centuries, but then it seems to have fallen out of favour. There is a report, however, in Sir George Dasent's *Three to One* 1872, of bombastic Americans using it to refer to 'fast' women. In the above context the writer was no doubt influenced by the etymological proximity of *velocipede*.

vicar *noun* a variant species that has developed in isolation from other species that share a common ancestor

> The 'hyper-robust' hominid *Australopithecus boisei* is well known from several East African Plio-Pleistocene deposits dated between 2.2 and 1.2 Myr. ... It has been thought of variously as: the northern vicar of the equally well-known *A. robustus*; the extremely specialized end-member of the robust clade, an already developed species which immigrated from another, unknown area; and as representing individuals at the large end of a single *Australopithecus* species that also encompasses *A. robustus* and *A. africanus*.
>
> *Nature* 7 Aug 1986

▶ This term is a derivative of the adjective and noun *vicariant* (of similar meaning), which was introduced into English in the early 1950s. Its immediate origin is German: the term *vikarirend spezies* (literally 'substituting species') was used by German evolutionists of the 19th century. It comes ultimately from the same source (Latin *vicarius*) as that of the religious *vicar*.

vice-presidentitis *noun* (in the USA) the political disadvantages inherent in being vice-president

> But Bush suffers from vice-presidentitis. He's associated with all the weaknesses, not strengths, of the Reagan presidency.
>
> *The World This Week*, Channel 4, 12 June 1988

► The catch-22 of the deputy's position – powerless at the centre of power, being tarred with the brush of failure but getting no credit for success – has traditionally been the kiss of death for the political ambitions of US vice-presidents.

vid *noun, informal* a short video film

> In amongst the aquatints and pastel washes, where even the dead can dance, two vids stand out: the one, *Fish* by Throwing Muses, edgily superior to anything else; the other, *Hot Doggie* by Colour Box, just gloriously incongruous.
>
> *New Musical Express* 22 Aug 1987

> Was making the film a way of escaping the conventions of normal promo vids?
>
> *Underground* Jan 1988

video jockey *noun* a person who presents a continuous programme of short video films and similar material on television

> A new TV service has just opened up to cater for the hopelessly addicted. It's called Movietime, it's available 24 hours a day on cable TV, and it's anchored by video jockeys who present a constant mix of film previews, location reports, star interviews, and general news.
>
> *Film 88*, BBC1, 9 May 1988

videolog *noun* a videocassette featuring advertisements for items (e g clothes) that can be bought via mail order

> Two new words have entered the fast-expanding vocabulary of mail-order fashion. We can thank Kit, the cheap and cheerful fashion division of Great Universal Stores, for 'magalog' and 'videolog,' natural offspring of the now superseded catalogue. ... The magalog includes an offer to buy its stylish sister, the videolog, a two-cassette package for £4.99, with a watch-and-wipe fashion show, filmed on location in France.
>
> *Daily Telegraph* 19 May 1988

► See MAGALOG.

vidkid *noun, American* a child who is a compulsive watcher of television or video

'We are appealing to the viewer who switches off or over the moment what they're watching becomes the slightest bit boring,' he says. That means, in America, the vidkid – who watches TV out of the corner of one eye while thumbing a magazine and phoning for a takeaway pizza.

Guardian 22 June 1987

viral infection *noun* the degradation of a computer system by means of an ELECTRONIC VIRUS

Robert Woodhead ... has developed a program called Interferon to stop the recent spate of viruses which have hit Macintoshes across Europe and the USA. The Interferon program is already available and is being continually updated as Woodhead is sent fresh copies of viral infections.

Datalink 25 Mar 1988

visagiste *noun* a cosmetician; beautician

If your skin is oily/combination, combat the shiny centre panel with a 'blotting' lotion. ... Advises their visagiste Peter Campbell, 'Choose a foundation with a higher water content and less oil for hot weather wear.'

Cosmopolitan May 1987

▶ A direct loan from the French word *visagiste*.

VJ *noun* VIDEO JOCKEY

And in a more literal attempt at putting on a new face, MTV has divested itself of the last of its five original VJs, replacing them with an altogether less smarmy bunch.

New Musical Express 23 July 1987

Boyish, confident Brian Diamond is the director of studio productions for MTV Europe and one of the original MTV team in America. He's sure the channel will be a success. ... We're 24 hours, we're fresh every day, all the VJ links are new.

News on Sunday 26 July 1987

volunteerism *noun* the practice of engaging in voluntary social work

BMW's and the Almighty Buck are out. The new Yuppie rallying cry is volunteerism. Increasingly, young professionals are penciling compassion into their appointment books. They see social programs as a way to salve consciences and meet new friends.

Newsweek 8 Feb 1988

Vuzak *noun* a system for displaying an ever-changing electronic pattern of kaleidoscopic images on screens in public places

Soon any symptoms of airport tension could be soothed away by a new invention: Vuzak. The visual equivalent of Muzak, that bland rendition of classical favourites played in supermarkets, Vuzak is still in its initial stages. It will be beamed via satellite to airport lounges, cruise-ships and even aeroplanes.

Daily Telegraph 18 June 1987

walk-in *adjective* (of buildings, accommodation, etc) vacant and available for immediate occupation

> But Richard Ellis' City expert ... stresses: 'Rents in the City are driven by availability – or the lack of it in terms of walk-in space. There is a very low vacancy rate in the City.'
> *Observer* 12 June 1988

walk-up *noun, American* preparatory hype

> Now that summits are media extravaganzas ... manipulating expectations is part of the walk-up.
> *Time* 25 Nov 1985

▶ The expression derives from the US term for the walking of race horses to the starting tape.

wallyball *noun* a court game similar to volleyball but permitting the ball to be played off the side or back walls or the ceiling

> Here's an idea: Why not play volleyball on a racquetball court? That way you can bounce the ball off the walls and call it wallyball. ... This off-the-wall idea for a sport is a big hit where it began in southern California in 1976. Now, more and more clubs are beginning their own wallyball programs.
> *Chicago Tribune* 11 Mar 1988

▶ Not, as its name might at first suggest to British eyes, a game played by wallies, but simply a version of indoor volleyball adapted to make it more exciting by allowing the ball to bounce off the walls. It was invented by a Californian named Joe Garcia, and uses a ball (called a wallyball) of similar size to a volleyball but rather harder, to improve its bounce.

wan *noun* wide area network: a communications network which links up LANS situated over a wide area

Spidergate X100 from Spider Systems is an Ethernet to X.25 Gateway which provides a link from lan to wans. ... Logic Replacement Technology ... has developed a direct-connect Megastream wide area network (WAN) bridge of communications between remote Ethernet lans.

Mini-Micro News Jan 1988

wannabee *noun, informal, chiefly American* a person who wishes to be (like) someone or something else

Madonna wannabees look pretty much the same in Tokyo as their counterparts in London and New York.

Sunday Express Magazine Oct 1987

Brass Tacks (BBC2) ... 'addressed' the topic of Wannabees, an American term for children who wanna be grownup.

Sunday Telegraph 20 Dec 1987

want *noun* desire; ambition

Bill Rogers, who won the 1981 Open, once described Strange as having 'more determination, more fire, more *want* than any player I have ever seen.'

Daily Telegraph 16 July 1988

waribashi *noun* a pair of chopsticks formed from a single piece of wood which can be split in two by the user at table

Renewable plastic chopsticks had become an ecological problem in Japan. And renewable wooden chopsticks were suspected of carrying disease. Despite the shortage of wood, disposable, splittable wooden chopsticks, or waribashi, seemed the wave of the future. 'The Japanese like to know no one has used a chopstick before,' Ward said. 'They like to split their own wooden stick in half. That's hard to emulate with plastic.'

San Francisco Sunday Examiner and Chronicle 12 June 1988

wash-trade *verb* (of a small group of speculators) to buy and sell (a particular stock) amongst themselves in order to push its price up and so encourage investors' interest in it

'It's difficult to wash-trade IBM shares,' Milliken says, 'because few people have the money.'

Business Mar 1988

wasm *noun,* *informal* an obsolete or outdated doctrine or theory

All the evidence suggests that it is Mr Reagan the voters like, not his policies. ... It raises the questions of whether Reaganism will outlive Mr Reagan, or whether, like other isms of today, it will join the wasms of tomorrow.

Economist 3 Jan 1987

water sports *noun plural,* *informal* sexual gratification involving urination; urolagnia

I have lost count of the times I have mentioned what I considered perfectly acceptable parts of the modern sexual repertoire such as sodomy, sadomasochism and water sports to otherwise sophisticated, often promiscuous girls, only to have them blanch with horror and gasp 'I couldn't do that!'

Cosmopolitan July 1988

wave-sailing *noun* sailing a sailboard on waves

He can be ranked among the top all-rounders, being adept in the three disciplines of wave-sailing, slalom, and racing.

Guardian 23 July 1985

▶ In competitive sailboarding, racing is won by speed, slalom by speed and agility, but wave-sailing is the discipline whose outcome depends on the judges' opinions. Plunging across the wavetops at high speed, the boardsailors perform a programme of tight acrobatic turns and gravity-defying leaps into the air.

weaponize *or* **weaponise** *verb* to adapt (something) so that it can be used as a weapon

Dr Immele described America's progress since successfully testing the first laser of this kind in 1980 as 'spectacular,' although he bemoaned lack of funding for the programme and added that 'weaponising it is a lot harder.'

Daily Telegraph 23 May 1988

weathervane *adjective* (in politics) being a reliable indicator of current voting trends, from which election results can be predicted

Labour is in a very strong position ... according to a poll carried out for BBC Newsnight last week in three 'weathervane' constituencies.

Guardian 11 June 1986

In Lancaster, a so-called weathervane town, which has accurately predicted the presidential winner every time since 1952, the official Republican tally gave Mr Bush 39 per cent and Mr Dole 22 per cent.

Daily Telegraph 17 Feb 1988

well *adverb, British slang* very

Dancewise brings us to MC Shan's 'Down By Law' (*Cold Chillin'*), an intense, hard-hitting mix of bass-heavy drums and well tough vocals along the usual lines.

New Musical Express 2 May 1987

▶ This usage seems to have originated in London street slang of the 1970s, in which *well* was employed as an emphatic qualifier in passive constructions, meaning 'completely' or 'conclusively' (as in 'I was well stitched up by the police'). From this, it was a fairly short step to using it with past-participial-style adjectives ('He was well pissed'), and now its application has spread to virtually any adjective.

well-wedged *adjective, British slang* rich

Prior to his current and sometimes controversial popularity as Stavros, the kebab shop *raconteur*, and Loadsamoney, the well-wedged plasterer, as seen on *Friday Night Live*, Enfield has appeared in or on *The Lenny Henry Show* ..., *Girls on Top, Filthy, Rich and Catflap, French And Saunders, The Tube* and *Frocks On the Box*.

Blitz May 1988

▶ Someone's *wedge*, in recent British slang, is their personal money supply, in reminiscence of the wedgelike shape of a thick wad of banknotes folded in half.

Whanny *noun, British* a person who employs a nanny to look after his or her children

Now, hard on the decline of padded shoulders and the return of busts we have the Whannies. ... A status symbol if ever there was one!

Daily Telegraph 26 Jan 1987

▶ This semi-acronym is yet another in the apparently inexhaustible stream of life-style coinages with which newspaper editors and the like seek to out-Yuppie *Yuppie*. This one stands for 'We have a nanny.'

white-knuckle *adjective* full of tension and anxiety

> The collapse of the EUA issue shows just how quickly white-knuckle time can arrive in the junk-bond market.
> *Wall Street Journal* 8 Feb 1988

▶ The metaphor derives, of course, from the ashen knuckles of one whose grip on any handy support tightens as his apprehension becomes more acute.

Margate has a White Knuckle Theme Park, featuring hair-raising, nail-biting and presumably fist-clenching rides on roller-coasters and the like.

white label *noun* a label designating a pre-release issue of a record, e g for promotional purposes

> A sturdy House track with reggae overtones and cut ups from gangster movies, sci-fi, and the kitchen sink. Released on white label before Christmas but now available for all.
> *The Face* Feb 1988

white squire *noun* any of a number of people who buy shares in a company to help to save it from being taken over by another company

> Standard Chartered lent a total of £73.6 million last year to the three 'white squires' who bought shares in the company to help fight off the £1.3 billion bid from Lloyds Bank.
> *Daily Telegraph* 17 Apr 1987

▶ The source of this new coinage is *white knight*, a term for the saviour of a threatened company which first entered the language around 1981. The distinction is that whereas the knight actually makes a bid for the whole company to prevent someone else from taking it over, the more humble squire simply acquires a large shareholding in it to help forestall the unwanted suitor.

who he? (used facetiously for referring to an obscure or insignificant person)

This month, for instance, has been the time for remembering the 110th anniversary of the birth of Grigori Petrovsky. Who he? He was a Bolshevik worker elected to the Tsarist parliament in 1912.
New Statesman 26 Feb 1988

▶ This usage probably originated in, or at least was popularized by, the satirical journal *Private Eye*, whose pages have long been peppered with the editorial aside '[Who he? Ed.].'

wholesale politics *noun, chiefly American* electoral campaigning via the media, especially television, rather than by the politician's traditional methods of addressing meetings, canvassing, etc

Iowa is in the middle of the Middle West, and 25th among the 50 states in population. It is not too large to preclude 'retail politics,' making an impact by shaking scores of thousands of hands at hundreds of meetings in coffee shops and living rooms. But it is large enough that 'wholesale politics,' selling candidates like cookies in 30-second television commercials, matters, too.
Daily Telegraph 5 Feb 1988

▶ Compare RETAIL POLITICS.

wide *verb* (of a cricket umpire) to call (a bowler) for bowling a wide ball

If he bowls too far outside the leg stump he'll be wided.
Jack Bannister, *Sunday Grandstand*, BBC2, 14 Aug 1988

▶ This coinage was no doubt formed on analogy with 'to no-ball,' a verb first recorded in the 1860s. That 'to wide' has only put in an appearance so recently is probably due to the upsurge in the number of deliveries penalized as 'wides' to discourage defensive bowling in limited-over cricket.

wimp out *verb, informal* to withdraw or refuse to participate because of lack of nerve; chicken out

411

Similarly, a once-invincible national cricket team which now wimps out of facing up to the mighty West Indians in their own ... back yard, would appear to be sadly indicative of a country whose once boundless self-confidence seems to have taken a temporary downturn.

Frances Edmonds, Cricket XXXX Cricket 1987

wind park *noun* an array of wind turbines for generating electric power

Plans for the construction in Britain of three 'wind parks,' together with the world's first offshore wind turbine, were announced yesterday as part of a £30 million investigation into the prospects of wind power being used for large-scale electricity production.

Daily Telegraph 24 Mar 1988

▶ The term seems to be synonymous with the previously coined (1980) *wind farm* (see *Longman Guardian New Words*).

wind waggle *noun, informal* TREE BENDING

If gusts of wind coincide with the natural swaying frequency of trees, they can begin to move violently, subjecting them to forces strong enough to break or uproot them. Foresters call this 'wind waggle.'

New Scientist 10 Dec 1987

winie *noun* a person with an obsessive interest in wine, especially the evaluation and comparison of fine wines

Christian Delteil prepared three different puddings – milk chocolate and praline mousse, a dark chocolate cake, and a marquise – for sundry foodies, winies, and chocoholics to sample with each of 11 wines and one armagnac.

Sunday Times 10 July 1988

winkler *noun, British slang* a person employed to persuade tenants to vacate property

A winkler may see if a tenant can be bought out, or he may use other methods. 'Everything from taking the roof off,' says Hoogstraten, 'to making sure they meet with a nasty accident along the road.'

Guardian 28 June 1988

wipe *verb* to pass (a credit or debit card) through a machine which decodes the information contained on its magnetic strip

> This concept [eft/pos], it is hoped, will give birth to the true cashless citizen, with cards being wiped through terminals at shop check-outs, directly debiting the customer's bank account.
> *Observer* 10 Apr 1988

▶ See also CARD SWIPE.

wobbly *noun, British informal* a fit of uncontrollable rage

> If everything – even dressing in the morning – throws you, if every little setback makes you throw a wobbly then you don't have style.
> *Cosmopolitan* June 1986

> I screamed 'Get them out of here' but they stayed and had a good view of what was going on. I was in a bit of a state. When they'd gone I threw a wobbly, kicking and screaming.
> *Time Out* 25 May 1988

▶ *Wobbly*, often, as here, in the phrase 'throw a wobbly,' seems to have emerged into the general language in the last four or five years, probably from a London subculture argot. It may derive from the violent shaking of someone who cannot control his or her anger.

A less common variant is *wobbler*:

> When the Dutch bosses in Eindhoven heard the ads they threw a wobbler and cancelled them.
> *New Scientist* 4 Aug 1988

wobbly Thursday *noun* 4 June 1987, the day on which during the British general election campaign, the Conservative party leadership, having been confident of victory, was disconcerted by indications that it might not win

> On 'wobbly Thursday,' just seven days before polling, Mrs Thatcher received two polls ... both narrowing the Tory lead, plus a related stock market collapse. She apparently 'panicked' and turned to anyone who might offer consolation.
> *Sunday Times* 24 Apr 1988

▶ In sharp contrast to the stereotypical pattern, the Labour party's general election campaign in 1987 was slick and well run, whereas the Conservatives were in some disarray. Their party machinery was ill-coordinated, and internal wrangling over which advertising agency should have their account fuelled rumours of a leadership divided over election strategy. It was against this background that Mrs Thatcher received the adverse reports on 4 June which reportedly sent her into a flat spin; pre-campaign euphoria, in which victory had seemed a pure formality, evaporated in a panic of recrimination and course-changing. She need not have worried; the unsettling opinion polls turned out to have been mistaken, and the Conservatives won at a canter.

wok *verb* to cook using a wok

> His [Ken Hom's] BBC cookery series has been repeated so often, and the book of the series has sold so many copies (over *half a million* when I last counted), that he has been responsible for more people learning to wok than anyone else in history.
>
> *Observer* 11 Sept 1988

woman *verb* to supply with female operatives or crew

> Later this month the stretch of river alongside the Palace of Westminster will witness a unique event: a charity regatta in which dozens of boats manned (and womanned) by various Parliamentary groups will compete.
>
> *Guardian* 4 July 1986

wonder *verb* to ask, enquire

> 'As a means of reducing the level of crime,' Mr Marlow wondered of the Home Secretary, 'will you consider the reinvention of a modern system of stocks.'
>
> *Guardian* 22 Apr 1988

▶ *Wonder* is standardly used as an implied interrogative – 'I wonder if he'll come' is a slightly indirect way of asking the question 'Will he come?' – but its use with direct speech usually implies a sort of rhetorical self-examination ('Should I wait any longer?' she wondered). In the above extract, though, the move over to overt (though still polite, unaggressive) interrogation is signalled by the preposition *of*.

woopie *noun, British informal* a well-off older person

> The 'Woopies' ... live up to their nickname, looking for activity rather than rest and relaxation.
>
> *Guardian* 25 June 1988

> Junior health minister Edwina Currie seems to be credited with inventing the term 'Woopies' for well-off older people, and others in the government seem to have fallen for the sound of it.
>
> *Ideal Home* Sept 1988

▶ Compare GLAM.

workaholicism *noun* a compulsive need to work hard; condition of a workaholic

> When asked to describe what makes one employee more likely to succeed than another, 93 percent of bosses plump for high commitment to work. And, in the finance houses, 63 percent go even further and say 'workaholicism.'
>
> *Today* 24 Oct 1986

▶ This irregular formation (used in preference to *workaholism*) no doubt reflects the non-existence of a word 'workahol'; *workaholism* (the more usual form) is based directly on an analogy with *alcoholism*, whereas *workaholicism* appears to be a new coinage, formed from *workaholic* + *-ism*. See also -AHOLIC.

workalike *noun* a machine or implement that works in a similar way to another

> Amstrad plans to conquer the less expensive end of the European market with a range of cut-price PC workalikes.
>
> *Economist* 6 Sept 1986

▶ This formation is based on *lookalike*, which has also spawned *soundalike*.

wrinkly *noun, slang* an older person; CRINKLY, CRUMBLY

> Although birthrates are also declining in most developing countries, their factories will be manned by hearty young men and women when those of West Germany and Japan are filling with wrinklies. By 2025, nearly 41% of West Germany's adult population of working age will be 50 or over, compared with 27% today.
>
> *Economist* 17 Jan 1987

writing *noun* – **at (this) writing** at the time when this is being written; currently

At writing the West Indies are engaged in a gripping Test match against a Pakistan side who are running Viv Richards's men very close to a series defeat on home soil.

Time Out 4 May 1988

▶ A usage of American origin, which still seems rather incongruous in the un-American context of a cricket report.

x-rated *adjective* of excessive brutality or horrificness

Billy Gilbert was lucky to stay on the pitch after two x-rated tackles in the first eight minutes.

Daily Mirror 30 Mar 1988

▶ The metaphorical application of the cinema's X, denoting a film unsuitable for children, to the repulsive or shocking in the world at large is no new phenomenon, but in British English until recently *X-certificate* was the preferred form. *X-rated* is of American origin. Meanwhile, back in the cinema, X was replaced by the ratings *15* and *18* in 1983.

XST *noun* experimental stealth technology: an experimental aircraft built to test out newly developed systems for countering enemy radar and heat-seeking missiles

Between five and seven XSTs are believed to have been built, and two at least are thought to have crashed.

Jane's All The World's Aircraft 1987-88

▶ See also ATB, STEALTHIE.

yah *adverb, British slang* yes

> Good luck, Mark. Hope the presentation went well in Leeds, and
> that you were finally able to get in touch with Crispin. Right on.
> Yah.
>
> *Punch* Feb 1988

▶ This spelling is by no means new (it has been used in the
past to represent the pronunciation of *yes* or *yeah* in several
varieties of English, from American to South African), but
its current specific application in Britain is to the nasal bray
of the Sloane Ranger, perhaps with a side-glance at the
homographic exclamation of derision, and even at *yahoo*.

Yardie *noun* a member of a West Indian drug-trafficking
syndicate

> Chief Superintendent Peter Twist of Dalston police said: 'A man
> commonly regarded as one of the Yardies who could be billed as a
> godfather was among those arrested. He is a major figure and is
> possibly not only the top Yardie in Britain but in the world.'
>
> *Guardian* 15 Apr 1988

> Detectives have discounted theories that 'Yardies', criminal gangs
> that originated in Jamaica, are involved.
>
> *Independent* 4 June 1988

> Last February, Scotland Yard set up a squad to combat the Yardies,
> who ... are a relatively new phenomenon in Britain and first came
> to the notice of the police about two years ago.
>
> *Daily Telegraph* 12 Sept 1988

▶ The Yardies operate worldwide in the propagation of
drugs, including cocaine, and of the concomitant violent
crime, but they originated in the Caribbean. *Yard* is a term
used for their home country by Jamaicans living abroad.

yarg *noun* a mild white moist cheese made in Cornwall

> Cornish yarg ... sold well enough in the towns and villages around
> their home near Liskeard.
> > *Daily Telegraph* 27 Feb 1988

> On to cheese; for me a good Cornish Yarg and for my husband a
> generous helping from the range of English and French cheeses.
> > *Daily Telegraph* 2 July 1988

▶ Convincingly bucolic as its name sounds, this cheese is in
fact quite a recent introduction, and *yarg* is simply a backwards spelling of the name of its makers, Allan and Jennifer
Gray.

yeepie *noun, informal* an active older person

> 'Yeepies' is a new term for the 'Youthful Energetic Elderly People
> Involved in Everything' or parents of 'Yuppies!'
> > *Weekly World News* 21 June 1988

yips *noun plural* (in sport) acute nervousness or trembling
when about to play a stroke or perform some other
action

> [Stefan Edberg's] serve has been vulnerable under pressure in the
> past. Boris Becker, mindful of these yips and not averse to games-
> manship, deliberately stalled play during the crucial third set of
> their Queen's final last month. Edberg double faulted.
> > *Sunday Times* 3 July 1988

▶ Originally this was a golfing term, referring to the disabling tension which grabs a player faced with a difficult
putt (it first appeared in the early 1960s, although it is not
clear where it came from), but it was a natural progression
to apply it to other sports where a motionless build-up of
concentration is followed by a sudden but highly controlled
burst of activity, such as snooker, darts, or (as in the above
extract) tennis – where this sort of seized-up serve is usually
known in the trade as 'getting the elbow.'

yottie *noun, derogatory* a brash wealthy person whose
hobby is yachting

In this non-Admiral's Cup year, rich international yotties are at the Kenwood Cup in Hawaii and quarter-ton boats are away racing in West Germany.

Guardian 5 Aug 1988

▶ A term coined by ordinary boating enthusiasts for rich Sunday and August sailors who descend on Cowes Week and similar events with large gleaming yachts and throw their weight around.

young fogey *noun, British* a person, typically a middle-class male, of less than middle age who adopts or affects the dress, habits, and right-wing views of an earlier generation

Conservative Philosophy group. Mostly right-wing young fogeys meeting at Mr Jonathan Aitken's house, with strong admixture of extra-parliamentary academics and journalists.

Economist 12 Jan 1985

▶ The young fogey in his most extreme form can easily be identified by sight: typical garb is a bristling tweed suit or jacket (often with leather patches), a waistcoat, brown brogues, a Viyella shirt, a tie that looks vaguely regimental, and a short back and sides, usually topped off with a trilby hat; watch-chains are a common accessory, and a florid complexion helps to complete the picture. In other words, a sort of embalmed Evelyn Waugh. As a social phenomenon, the young fogey represents the renewed access of the reactionary to respectability; but his rightish views are usually based more on nostalgia than political fervour. Although the image he wishes to put across is that of the sort of upper-middle-class English gent who died out with the 1950s he himself may well hail from the lower band of that class. He often interests himself in literature of a belletristic sort.

youth cottage *noun, Australian* a hostel for homeless young people

We would like to see Mr Greiner fund more grants for youth cottages. They would be homes for the homeless young people and the young people who would otherwise find their way on to the streets of Kings Cross.

Daily Telegraph (Sydney) 15 Apr 1988

youthocracy *noun* a socially influential coterie of young people

Remarking that the cuttings are all about Nick Bright-Sparkly and that every one of the photographs on his wall shows this vibrant young man in the company of Paula Yates, Nicholas Coleridge, Ben Elton and other members of the youthocracy, I dive in with the question that has been troubling traditionalists within the trade.
Publishing News 11 Mar 1988

yuppie flu *noun, British informal* MYALGIC ENCEPHALO-MYELITIS

Is this 'yuppie flu' simply a fashionable malaise or should we be treating sufferers with more sympathy – and urgency?
Observer 26 June 1988

yuppiefy *verb, derogatory* to transform into something appropriate to yuppies; introduce elements of middle-class trendiness into

Mr Gould, who has been accused of 'yuppiefying' Labour, strongly defended its proposals for employee shareownership schemes.
Daily Telegraph 1 Oct 1987

Z

zaitech *or* **zaiteku** *noun* large-scale financial speculation engaged in by a company

A lot of industrial companies that played the zaitech ... game may be sitting on nasty paper losses on shares.

Economist 7 Nov 1987

Like any buzzword, zaitech carries with it a bundle of hyped connotations. Foreigners especially tend to associate it with free-wheeling financial dealing of the sort that disrupts money markets and whipsaws global exchanges.

Newsweek 23 Nov 1987

The Euromarkets have already drawn Japan's banks and securities houses to London. Now the country's companies are arriving – for the zaiteku.

Economist 28 June 1986

Playing the financial markets – zaiteku operations – is fashionable for Japanese industrial companies, who have used it to sustain their flagging profits.

Daily Telegraph 19 Oct 1987

▶ The concept of zaitech originated in Japan (*zai* is Japanese for 'wealth'), and has fuelled the major expansion of Japanese financial institutions into European and American markets in the 1980s. Japanese firms trade heavily in Eurobonds; Mitsubishi, for example, has a London office which earns an average of $25 million a year by issuing low-interest Eurobonds and investing its profits from them in higher yielding securities.

zero option *noun* a proposal for the reduction of nuclear weapons which envisages all NATO and Soviet longer-range intermediate nuclear missiles being withdrawn from Europe

Mr Younger, Defence Secretary, made it clear, however, that strict conditions attached to Nato acceptance of the zero option.

Daily Telegraph 15 Apr 1987

▶ The zero option (the implication is that each side ends up with no nuclear missiles in the given category) was first put on the table in 1979. Largely at the instigation of West Germany, NATO proposed that all missiles in Europe with ranges longer than 1000 kilometres should be removed. The main motivation behind this was to stop the Soviet Union deploying its SS 20s. The proposal failed, and NATO deployed cruise and Pershing II missiles in retaliation.

zero-zero *noun*   a proposal for the reduction of nuclear weapons which envisages all NATO and Soviet longer- and shorter-range intermediate nuclear missiles being withdrawn from Europe – called also *double zero*

At least four important shifts were signalled by Gorbachov during the summit. ... His opening bid had been to offer zero-zero in Europe, combined with a freeze at existing levels in Asia.

Observer 19 Oct 1986

West Germany's Chancellor, Herr Kohl, yesterday effectively vetoed Allied acceptance of Moscow's zero-zero offer on missiles as it stands.

Daily Telegraph 16 May 1987

▶ While the zero option proposes withdrawing only longer-range nuclear weapons from Europe, zero-zero envisages also the removal of shorter-range missiles (such as NATO's Pershing Ia's and Scuds), which can reach targets at a distance of between 1000 and 500 kilometres. It was sprung on the surprised Americans by Mr Gorbachev at the Reykjavik summit in October 1986, and was formally offered when the Secretary of State, George Schultz, visited Moscow in March 1987. The main resistance to such a deal came from the West Germans, who wished to see a third category of weapon – the battlefield nuclear weapons with ranges of less than 500 kilometres – included (this refinement is known as *triple zero*). Nevertheless, the proposal remained on the table, and before long agreement was reached; on 8 December 1987 an INF treaty was signed in Washington by President Reagan and Mr Gorbachev which essentially embodies zero-zero. Under its terms 2800 missiles, with 3800 nuclear warheads, are to be destroyed.

zidovudine *noun* an antiviral drug used in the treatment of AIDS

A course of treatment for AIDS with the drug zidovudine can cost around $12,000. In developed countries, the cost of zidovudine will soon sorely tax those whose task it is to allocate resources for health services – if it is not already.

New Scientist 17 Mar 1988

▶ Zidovudine is the official name for a drug previously known as Azidothymidine or AZT. It impedes the replication of the AIDS virus (HIV), but does not actually effect a cure.

Zift *noun* zygote intra-fallopian transfer: a method of artificial insemination in which a fertilized egg is implanted in one of a woman's fallopian tubes

Mrs Forrester's pregnancy was unique because the embryo storing was combined with implanting the fertilised egg in the fallopian tube, rather than in the womb. The process is known as Zift.

Daily Telegraph 25 Feb 1988

ZIFT ... is a new treatment which could help women who can't conceive because they are unable to produce eggs of their own.

Family Circle July 1988

▶ Zift is a variant of Gift (gamete intra-fallopian transfer; see *Longman Guardian New Words*), in which the egg and sperm are injected independently into the fallopian tube for fertilization to take place there; in Zift, fertilization happens outside the body, and the resulting zygote is then inserted.

zootique *noun* a pleasantly landscaped zoo featuring animals in natural-style habitats, and comfortable facilities for those in a spectating situation

The Central Park Zoo was re-opened in New York this week after a five-year renovation. ... This is a New Zoo, a state-of-the-art zoo, an elegant landscape of eco-system display units, a pleasant blend of humane comfort for exhibits and human comfort for spectators. It is, said New York Parks' Commissioner Henry Stern, a 'zootique.'

Daily Telegraph 11 Aug 1988

▶ A blend of *zoo* and *boutique*, a favourite marketing word of the 1980s denoting specialization and high quality (see BOUTIQUE).